RAND McNALLY

World Facts & Maps

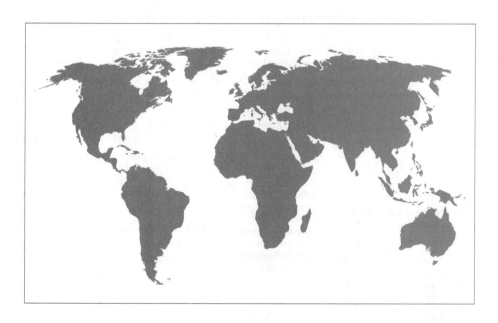

Contents

Hot Spots: Current Events in Focus

World Facts & Maps

Copyright © 1999 by Rand McNally & Company. All rights reserved.
ISSN 1057-9834
ISBN 0-528-83994-2

www.randmcnally.com

Published and printed in the United States of America

Photograph credits:
© Reuters/Erik de Castro/Archive Photos, p. 5
© Andrea Booner/Tony Stone Images, p. 69

World Gazetteer: Profiles of Countries and Places

Hot Spots:
Current Events in Focus

Traders at the Stock Exchange in Manila, Philippines

The World

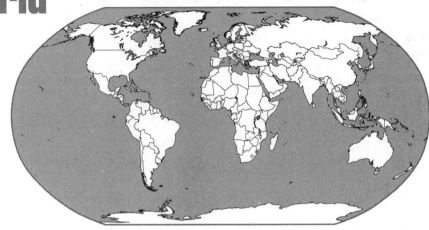

As improved transportation and communication systems work to shrink distances on Earth, people and countries are now capable of causing harm to the entire world, rather than just the parts they immediately occupy. Three of the most alarming crises are the population explosion, income disparity for both countries and individual people, and the dramatic effects of El Niño on the global ecosystem.

Once human life appeared on Earth, it took four million years for the population to reach one billion persons in 1825. It has taken only 175 years since then for the population to approach nearly six billion people. Some experts argue that we have already exceeded the maximum number of humans that the world can reasonably support. The world's population has grown to the point that there is extreme competition between different groups for resources in certain areas. This is especially true in Africa, where entire ethnic groups have been targeted for genocide by other ethnic groups through politically orchestrated famines, such as in Sudan, or violence, such as in Rwanda. Overpopulation is mainly to blame for the continent's suffering and instability.

The United Nations projects that the world's population will exceed nine billion before 2050 and stabilize at 11 billion in 2200. This estimate assumes that the current trend of decreasing birthrates worldwide would continue. If present birthrates remain constant, however, the UN projects the world's population could be nearly 300 billion by 2150.

Feeding a growing population is becoming increasingly difficult. Already millions of people worldwide die from hunger each year. Hundreds of millions do not get enough food to support

normal daily activity. Politics and economics play a role, but it may be a signal that Earth is reaching the limit of its food production capacity.

The growing population also contributes greatly to the destruction of natural habitats, the depletion of resources, global warming, and pollution. As human population increases, more of the environment is plowed under for agriculture, especially in developing countries.

Because developing countries have the largest populations and the highest population growth rates, these problems have a particularly strong impact there. These countries are especially vulnerable to natural disasters and disease epidemics because of their lack of medical resources and public services, which limits their ability to respond to large-scale crises. If their populations continue to increase, living conditions in developing countries will worsen.

On average, population growth in industrialized countries is negative, with the largest population decreases occurring in Europe. The birthrate that the UN has calculated for Europe is 1.6, the lowest of any continent. Europe's population is projected to decrease from its present 730 million to 638 million in 2050 and then to 579 million in 2100. In developing countries with high birthrates, many international organizations and national governments are working to reduce birthrates and stabilize the world population growth before overpopulation becomes critical. Since 1979, China has had the most restrictive population growth control policy in the world: Women in urban areas are only allowed to give birth to one child, and in rural areas, two children. The Chinese government has enforced the policy by enacting mandatory sterilization for couples who have reached their limit and strongly pressuring women who are illegally pregnant to have an abortion. In most other developing countries, family practice policies are less extreme and include education and the distribution of birth control devices.

Just as the population boom is worsening globally in developing countries, so is the economic plight of the Third World. Per capita incomes of the industrialized countries have been increasing, while those of developing countries have been decreasing. This disparity between rich countries and poor countries has been widening since the early 1980s.

Economic disparity has also been heightened within most countries. The earnings of the wealthiest families have been increasing, and the incomes of the poorest families have been decreasing, with middle class family incomes decreasing slightly. Among the top industrialized countries, the United States has the largest income disparity. Between the late 1970s and the mid-1990s, the average income of the poorest 20 percent of American families fell by $2,500, from $11,760 to $9,250. During the same period, the average income of the richest 20 percent of families increased by almost $27,000, from $90,730 to $117,500.

No one has yet identified a reason for the increases in family income disparity. One theory is that the demand for workers with high technology skills has been increasing, resulting in higher incomes for those who possess or have the means to acquire these skills. Conversely, the demand for workers who lack these specialized skills has decreased, thus driving their wages down. Another possible reason is that companies are reinvesting more of their revenue in equipment, leaving less for wage increases for lower-level workers.

If these disparities continue to grow, friction between social classes and between poor countries and wealthy countries will increase. The polarization of rich and poor in large cities already contributes to high crime rates, and many poor countries have relatively unstable governments. As the global economy completes its transformation toward higher technology and fewer trade restrictions, economic conditions must become more equitable.

Human activity may also be contributing to a global weather disruption. El Niño, an abnormal warming of the Pacific Ocean that occurs every two to seven years and wreaks havoc around the world, may be occurring more frequently due to global warming.

Two or three times per decade, when the westward air and ocean currents of the Pacific are disrupted, the warmest part of the ocean spreads eastward, causing unusually warm water temperatures across the entire ocean and shutting off the upwelling of cool water in the east. This causes a marked decrease in marine life off South America's western coast, reducing the fish supply.

The air flow also changes direction, moving toward the east. Because the warm air and warm water are not flowing toward the western Pacific, the southeast Asian monsoons are weak or do not occur at all.

The effects of the 1997-1998 El Niño were first recorded in September 1997, and were felt most strongly in and around the Pacific Ocean. A serious drought in Papua New Guinea, Indonesia, and the Philippines resulted in hundreds of deaths due to famine and smoke inhalation from forest fires. El Niño also caused heavy rainfall and flooding in western South America, drought in eastern South America, and fires in the Amazon rain forest. In Central America rainfall diminished to the point that the Panama Canal operated at an unusually shallow depth, disrupting shipping operations. Hawaii experienced severe droughts, while Mexico saw increased rainfall on the west coast, with drought and forest fires inland. Mexico also suffered from Hurricane Pauline, which caused hundreds of deaths. There was much higher rainfall in the western U.S., and an early tornado season in the southeastern U.S. Central Europe experienced floods while Russia had record cold temperatures. In eastern Africa there was increased rainfall and widespread flooding. In southern Africa drought caused wildfires.

The effects of an El Niño are not just confined to the weather. Increased rainfall in the American Southwest produced a much denser growth of scrub plants and a better habitat for mice, causing their population to explode. In March 1998 the National Centers for Disease Control canvassed a section of desert in New Mexico and found a tenfold increase in the number of mice carrying the hanta virus, a potentially fatal disease that humans contract through dust particles contaminated by mouse droppings.

Many scientists debate whether El Niño episodes are occurring more frequently or becoming more severe. The general consensus is that if global warming continues, normal weather patterns may begin to resemble El Niño conditions.

With rising world population growth and increased income disparity, this El Niño has had the most detrimental effect on developing countries, causing social unrest, hundreds of deaths, and the displacement of hundreds of thousands of people due to smoke inhalation, hunger, and severe storms. Great advances have been made recently in El Niño prediction, however, and this information has been useful in protecting lives and property. As the quality of predictions improves, early warnings may help people prepare for El Niño and avert disaster.

East Asia and the Pacific

The next century is expected to be the Age of the Pacific, the natural consequence of 20 years of economic growth and prosperity in East Asia. Both China and Japan, with their long histories and rich cultures, have recently become world leaders. Japan has risen to become the world's second-largest economic power and is under mounting pressure to accept a greater leadership role in world affairs. Although China's economic policy was stilted under Communism, the country has experienced impressive growth over the last few years as its leaders attempt to implement economic reforms without creating political instability.

While China and Japan have enjoyed relative economic stability, other smaller East Asian countries have been less fortunate. This was especially true in 1997 when a currency crisis in Thailand devastated the economies of South Korea and Indonesia, while people in Japan and China felt little negative impact.

Politically, regional peace is close at hand, despite the fact that conflicts resulting from the Cold War between the United States and the Soviet Union plagued the area for decades. Korea was split into two parts after Communists failed to take over the country in 1950. Vietnamese Communists were more successful, and after a devastating war with the U.S. they managed to gain control of South Vietnam. Cambodia was unwillingly drawn into the Vietnam War and was later invaded by Vietnam. Taiwan and the People's Republic of China have maintained an uneasy standoff since China's Communist revolution.

Today these conflicts have less international significance. Relations between the two Koreas and the two Chinas have thawed considerably,

and both are discussing reunification. Vietnam has begun to recover economically and politically from the war.

Despite improved relations among the countries in the region, there are still threats to long-term stability. The Spratly Islands, a group of reefs in the South China Sea, are the site of frequent skirmishes involving China, Taiwan, Vietnam, Malaysia, and the Philippines—all of which claim to own all or part of the island chain. North Korea's clandestine nuclear program is also a matter of regional concern, although development has supposedly been halted.

In the Pacific, competing ethnic groups struggle to create a common vision for the future. Tensions between ethnic Fijians and Indians sparked a military takeover in Fiji. The people of East Timor have long protested the illegal occupation of their territory by the Indonesians. In Papua New Guinea, the inhabitants of Bougainville have declared their independence from the central government; they continue to struggle for control of their land. Native Kanaks in New Caledonia have been battling for independence from France, despite objections from islanders of European descent.

The Pacific islands also suffer from the effects of ongoing nuclear testing by western countries. Several of the Marshall Islands were devastated by nuclear tests performed by the U.S. in the 1940s and 1950s; today the islanders receive compensation from the U.S. government for their exposure to deadly radiation and the loss of their land. Although the U.S. stopped underwater testing in the 1960s, France continued to detonate nuclear devices in its Pacific colonies in the 1990s.

Economic Crisis: SOUTH KOREA

Perspective

1945	*Korea is partitioned after World War II.*
1950-1953	*Korean War is fought.*
1961	*Park Chung Hee leads a military takeover.*
1979	*Park assassinated. Martial law imposed.*
1980	**May 18.** *Government brutally represses Kwangju student uprising.*
1993	**December 18.** *Korea elects Kim Young Sam, its first civilian president.*
1997	**January 23.** *Bankruptcy proceedings begin against Hanbo chaebol.* **July.** *Thailand economic crisis reverberates across eastern Asia.* **November 21.** *Korea requests economic assistance from the International Monetary Fund (IMF).* **December 3.** *IMF agrees to record-setting $57 billion rescue package.* **December 18.** *Reform candidate Kim Dae Jung wins presidential elections.*
1998	**February 14.** *Government passes economic restructuring plan.*

South Korea's economic development was a phenomenal success story. After decades of war and foreign occupation, South Koreans set out to transform themselves from a poor, rural agricultural society to a modern, industrialized country. By 1997 South Korea had succeeded in becoming the world's eleventh-largest economy, and was on the verge of entering the ranks of the world's most industrialized countries. But economic calamity struck with the collapse of important corporations and the devaluation of local currency, forcing South Korea to seek financial aid. This dramatic turn of events forced South Koreans to reexamine their political system as well as their economy.

Issues and Events

Much of South Korea's economic success after the Korean War can be attributed to the development of the *chaebol*. Originally, the *chaebol* were family-owned businesses that grew rapidly with the help of government tax breaks. They received financing for expansion through low-interest loans rather than through the issuing of stocks and bonds. With these incentives, *chaebol* such as Samsung and Hyundai grew into huge conglomerates that led the country's economic development.

Trouble started in early 1997 when the Hanbo *chaebol* applied for bankruptcy protection, becoming the largest corporation to collapse in more than a decade. An investigation resulted in the prosecution of Hanbo's founder, as well as several high-ranking bankers and politicians, for fraud, bribery, and embezzlement. South Korean President Kim Young Sam, who made a major campaign promise to end government corruption, was humiliated when the investigation revealed that his son was involved in the Hanbo scandal. In the wake of the Hanbo collapse, several other *chaebol* announced that they, too, were on the verge of bankruptcy.

Thailand's 1997 currency crisis put all of Southeast Asia on edge, and its effects soon spread to other countries. The value of South Korea's currency declined dramatically in October, and a November stock market plunge forced the country to turn to the International Monetary Fund (IMF) for emergency aid to stabilize its financial markets and prevent economic catastrophe. The Washington-based IMF, a United Nations agency created to promote world monetary stability and economic development, awarded South Korea a record-setting $57 billion in loans and aid; in exchange, South Korea agreed to restructure its economy. Although the economy soon stabilized, it became increasingly apparent that the higher prices and unemployment—results of economic reform—would bring hardship to the Korean people.

Koreans expressed their discontent by electing reform candidate Kim Dae Jung as president and supporting his economic program. In Southeast Asia, the prevailing wisdom is that economic stability requires strong leadership and that democracy and prosperity cannot coexist. Kim argued that only strong democracy can break the corrupt ties between government and business that were encouraged by the *chaebol* system.

Background

Throughout most of its history, the Korean Peninsula has been controlled by foreign powers, including China, Mongolia, and Japan. After Japan was defeated in World War II, Korea was split into two sectors by the victorious Allies. The United States administered South Korea, and the Soviet Union was given control of North Korea. A North Korean invasion of South Korea in 1950 started the Korean War, which lasted until 1963.

Although the end of the war marked a period of rapid economic growth, South Korea was plagued by political instability and corruption. Military leaders ruled until 1993 when a civilian president was elected. Student riots are now commonplace; the worst of which occurred in 1980 in Kwangju where 200 people were killed. Newly elected President Kim Dae Jung was sentenced to death for inciting the Kwangju riot, but he was later released at the urging of the U.S. He was imprisoned, tortured, and exiled by South Korea's military government.

East Asian Time Bomb: INDONESIA

Perspective

1943	**March.** *Japan invades Indonesia during World War II.*
1945	**August 15.** *Japan surrenders.* **August 17.** *Indonesia declares its independence from the Netherlands, initiating a war for independence.*
1949	**December 27.** *Dutch relinquish Indonesia to Sukarno's government.*
1963	*Irian Jaya obtained from the Dutch.*
1965	**September 30.** *Abortive coup sparks widespread violence; 500,000 killed.*
1966	**March 11.** *Suharto takes over.*
1969	*Irian Jaya rebellion begins.*
1975	**December 7.** *Indonesia invades Portuguese East Timor.*
1989	*Aceh rebellion flares.*
1991	**November 12.** *Indonesian troops open fire on East Timorese protesters.*
1996	**July 27.** *Anti-government rioting erupts in Jakarta.* **December 31.** *Transmigration policies incite ethnic unrest in Kalimantan.*
1997	**July.** *Thailand economic crisis spreads throughout the region.* **August.** *Drought causes forest fires and crop failure.* **October.** *Indonesia requests financial assistance from the International Monetary Fund (IMF).* **December 24.** *Muslims destroy a Christian church.*
1998	**January 8.** *Currency collapse triggers financial and social panic.* **January 15.** *IMF agrees to give Indonesia $43 billion in aid.* **May 13.** *Riots break out after police open fire on student demonstrators.* **May 21.** *Suharto resigns.*

Rich in both natural and human resources, Indonesia is one of the Pacific Rim's most powerful and influential countries. Home to more than 200 million people, it is the fourth-most populous country in the world. It is a land of intricate diversity, where both world-class business tycoons and primitive tribesmen live. More than 300 different ethnic groups inhabit Indonesia's 13,500 islands, and most of the world's major religions are well represented. Two things have held Indonesia together: strong leadership and economic prosperity. In 1997 Indonesia's economy began to collapse, its leadership faltered, and by 1998 its people panicked.

Issues and Events

Like many other east Asian countries, Indonesia has experienced explosive development since the 1960s. Under the leadership of President Suharto, its economic growth rate was an enviable six percent per year . Over the last decade, the number of people living in dire poverty dropped dramatically, and per capita income doubled.

Indonesia's prosperity resulted largely from its considerable oil, mineral, and forest reserves. Over the years, revenues from these export products were wisely invested in economic development and antipoverty programs. Indonesia also has a huge labor force, and the country opened its doors to substantial amounts of foreign investment. It was also aided by the strong, effective leadership of Suharto, who made virtually all of Indonesia's economic decisions.

The country's economic problems began in 1997 after a currency collapse in Thailand triggered a regional financial crisis. The value of Indonesia's currency soon fell, leaving many companies and banks technically bankrupt and driving up the prices on imported goods and foreign debt. In October Suharto turned to the International Monetary Fund (IMF) for help. The IMF awarded Indonesia $10 billion in exchange for closing 16 insolvent banks and making some changes to the economy. The value of Indonesian currency continued to fall, however, and by January 1998 Suharto was desperate. He was forced to sign another agreement with the IMF for a huge rescue package of $43 billion, contingent on Indonesia's implementation of drastic economic changes. These changes included the elimination of government fuel and food subsidies, the disbanding of monopolies owned by Suharto's family, the reduction of trade barriers, and the creation of stringent banking regulations.

By the end of January protests had erupted throughout the country. Many of these riots, like the one in Pamanukan on February 13, were directed against ethnic Chinese who own most of the businesses in Indonesia and had been forced to raise the prices of goods in their stores. Food shortages and rising prices also escalated tensions among other ethnic groups. In December 1997 Muslims destroyed a Christian church near the capital of Jakarta. This kind of violence is common under Indonesia's "transmigration" policy, by which people are moved from densely populated areas to uncrowded rural areas. In 1996 more than 300 people were killed in Kalimantan (the Indonesian portion of the island of Borneo) in fighting between the indigenous people and transmigrants. There is increasing likelihood that as economic and political conditions deteriorate, various ethnic groups will grow to resent the people of Javanese descent who control the government yet account for less than one-half of the population.

In the wake of Indonesia's steady economic decline, tensions continued to rise, and when the government announced that it was ending fuel subsidies in accordance with the IMF agreement, the price of gasoline rose more than 70 percent in one day. Rioting ensued, and several people were killed. A few days later, police were accused of firing indiscriminately at peaceful student demonstrators. Full-scale pandemonium broke out in Jakarta and quickly spread throughout the country. Within days the death toll had reached 500, and Suharto reluctantly submitted his resignation on May 21 in an effort to end the bloodshed. Suharto's Vice President, B.J. Habibie, was sworn in quickly, but many assume that Suharto will continue to rule through him.

Without Suharto's firm leadership Indonesia's future looks even more uncertain. One future option is military rule, which could ultimately increase popular discontent. Another option is democracy, but this could easily result in the kind of political and ethnic-based violence that destroyed the Soviet Union and Yugoslavia.

Indonesia's political problems extend beyond its economic woes. When Indonesia declared its independence, many of the islands—including the Moluccas, Celebes, and Sumatra—resisted central authority. The Aceh people of western Sumatra have been engaged in a long-standing conflict with the Indonesian government, and more than 2,000 people have died as a result. As Indonesia consolidated its rule throughout the region, other disputes arose. Irian Jaya, the western portion of the island of New Guinea, has experienced violent demonstrations since it was ceded to Indonesia in 1963 despite the fact that the Dutch had promised the island independence. East Timor gained international recognition in 1991 after Indonesian troops opened fire on unarmed civilians, killing as many as 200. The Indonesian army has been condemned for routinely torturing and executing those suspected of complying in the Timor separatist movement.

Even if the political situation improves, some economists predict that it may be years before Indonesia's economy returns to its previous growth levels—if it ever does. Although previous economic growth was impressive, it was insufficient to absorb an additional 2.3 million workers annually that entered the labor force. As in Russia, government subsidies kept prices for basic goods artificially low and impaired healthy economic development.

A collapse of the Indonesian economy would seriously imperil the economies of Japan, China, Singapore, South Korea, and other Asian countries. If additional violence breaks out, millions of Indonesian refugees would flood these neighboring countries, creating further economic problems as well as political instability. Indonesia's ethnic Chinese are often the targets of violence, so civil unrest could also provoke Chinese intervention and provide an excuse for Chinese territorial expansion.

Background

In the 1400s, when Europe was emerging from the Middle Ages, the Indonesian islands of Java and Sumatra were enjoying the fruits of advanced civilizations already in place for more than 1,000 years.

In the early 1600s the Dutch established sovereignty over the islands of Indonesia. During the next 300 years they turned the Netherlands East Indies into one of the world's most profitable colonies. The rich, fertile soil of Java was perfect for the cultivation of coffee, sugar, indigo, and other cash crops. During the 1840s and 1850s famine occurred when land needed for food was devoted instead to these valuable export commodities. Also during the period of Dutch rule a large colony of Chinese, mostly traders and craftsmen, settled in Indonesia.

The Indonesians began to clamor for independence in the early 1900s. Many of the early leaders, including Indonesia's first president, were imprisoned by the Dutch for their political activities. Japan invaded Indonesia during World War II and occupied it for three years, during which the Japanese allowed Indonesian independence activists to participate in local government. Three days after the Japanese surrendered in 1945, the Indonesians declared their independence, hoping to establish their leadership before transfer back to Dutch rule could be accomplished. Under the leadership of President Sukarno, they quickly set up an effective military organization that successfully repelled British and Dutch troops. United Nations-sponsored negotiations led to true independence in 1949.

At first, Sukarno tried to establish a democratic government, but increasing regional rebellions and economic malaise led him to set up an authoritarian government in 1957, eventually declaring himself president for life. Sukarno supported a growing Communism movement in Indonesia, and by 1965 the Communist Party sought to set up its own army there, which angered the regular Indonesian army. The country was plunged into violence after Communist sympathizers murdered six generals in the regular army as part of a successful takeover plot.

After the violence subsided, Indonesians were ready for a change in leadership, and Sukarno was unable to restore his authority. In 1966 he transferred much of his power to Suharto, who was named President the following year. Suharto made prosperity a high priority, and he is credited with raising million of Indonesians out of poverty. A masterful politician, Suharto ushered in a period of more than 30 years of economic growth and relative social harmony.

Ethnic Unrest: CHINA

Perspective

1949-1950	*Chinese Communists conquer Xinjiang and Tibet.*
1959	*Dalai Lama flees to India during a popular uprising in Tibet.*
1966	*Chinese ban religion during the Cultural Revolution.*
1988	**December.** *Chinese police kill 18 people during Tibetan rioting.*
1989	**March.** *Hundreds of people killed when police open fire on Tibetan rioters.*
1990	**April.** *Rioting erupts in Xinjiang when the Chinese close a mosque.*
1995	**December 8.** *Chinese reject Dalai Lama's choice for Panchan Lama.*
1997	**February 5.** *Anti-government protests in Xinjiang turn violent.* **February 25.** *Three bus bombs explode in Xinjiang's capital of Ürümqi.* **December 22.** *China ignores international pressure to conduct a referendum on Tibet's future.*

L ocated more than 1,000 miles from Beijing, the Chinese regions of Tibet and Xinjiang are among the most remote areas of the world. For many decades after the Communist takeover, they were shrouded in mystery. Today they are featured in news headlines as simmering hotbeds of discontent.

Issues and Events

The Chinese have made many serious errors in managing their far-flung territories. One major problem is that they have often been insensitive to minority cultural issues. Although the people of Tibet and Xinjiang have vastly different cultures from the Chinese, the Communists encouraged the Chinese to settle in these regions. The Chinese soon controlled the local governments and economies, arousing the anger of the indigenous people.

Another huge problem with China's territorial administration has been the government's ongoing interference in religious affairs; for a short period during the 1960s Cultural Revolution the government banned all religious activity. Since then the Chinese have continued their attempts to regulate religion, and have repeatedly chosen to close or destroy places of worship and persecute religious authorities. In a blatant instance of interference in 1995, the Chinese tried to control the selection of the Panchan Lama, the Tibetan Buddhists' second-highest religious figure.

The Chinese Communists have also failed to provide the people of Tibet and Xinjiang with autonomy. For centuries the Tibetans and peoples of Xinjiang accepted Chinese rule because they were allowed to govern themselves. As the Chinese tried to increase their influence, the people rebelled. The Chinese would have been wiser to provide the peoples of Tibet and Xinjiang with resources and training; the tools for economic dependency.

Finally, law enforcement presents problems. The Chinese government often uses excessive force to punish relatively minor offenses. When the Tibetans revolted against Chinese rule in 1959, more than 100,000 Tibetans were killed. Responding to anti-government protests in Xinjiang in 1997, the government arrested more than 1,700 people; of which dozens were executed. This kind of strong response to political unrest has ignited nationalist passions and unrest.

Ethnic tension has increased during the last decade. One factor is the publicity received by the Dalai Lama as he travels around the world campaigning for Tibetan autonomy. Another is the breakup of the former Soviet Union and the resulting independence of neighboring central Asian republics made up mainly of Turkish-speaking Muslims. Also, China is being pressured by the United States and other countries to improve its human rights record. Finally, the Xinjiang independence movement is of interest to Islamic fundamentalists around the world.

While the people of Tibet and Xinjiang are unlikely to succeed in forming independent countries, it is also unlikely that they will stop trying to do so. Unrest will continue until the Chinese leadership grants them some level of political autonomy and economic justice.

Background

Xinjiang and Tibet are among the world's most exotic lands, rich in history and culture. It was through Xinjiang (Sinkiang) that the Romans established the Silk Road. The Mongolian Genghis Khan conquered Xinjiang in the 1200s, and it became a Chinese province in 1884. The region was the independent country of East Turkestan from 1944 to 1949. Tibet was also conquered by the Mongols in the 1200s, but the Mongols adopted Buddhism as their state religion and allowed the monks to rule Tibet for almost 700 years. The country was independent between 1911 and 1951. Both Tibet and Xinjiang were conquered by China shortly after the Communist Revolution.

While the people of Tibet are somewhat homogeneous, the inhabitants of Xinjiang are extremely diverse. Most are Muslims who were traditionally nomadic herdsmen. The largest group, the Uygurs, are China's third-largest minority group.

The Tibetans and people of Xinjiang routinely demonstrate against Chinese rule, but in recent years the bombings have become more frequent. The Xinjiang independence movement is believed to be fueled by an influx of weapons from Pakistan and Afghanistan.

Desperate Times: NORTH KOREA

Perspective

1910	**August 22.** *Japan annexes Korea.*
1945	*Following World War II, the Allies divide Korea into Soviet and United States zones.*
1948	*North and South Korea establish separate governments.*
1950	**June 25.** *North Korea invades South Korea; U.S. sends troops to repel invasion.*
1953	**July 27.** *Armistice signed between North and South Korea.*
1968	*North Koreans attempt to assassinate South Korea's president.*
1990	**September.** *Peace talks begin.*
1993	**March 12.** *North Korea withdraws from Nuclear Non-Proliferation Treaty.*
1994	**July 8.** *President Kim Il Sung dies.* **October 21.** *North Korea agrees to curtail its nuclear program.*
1995	**July.** *Flooding destroys rice crops.*
1996	**May 13.** *World Food Program warns of a food emergency in North Korea.* **July.** *More flooding jeopardizes food production.*
1997	**January.** *Severe food rationing imposed.* **August.** *Drought causes crop failure.* **December 9.** *Two Koreas, China, and U.S. begin peace talks.*

For almost five decades, Kim Il Sung ruled North Korea with an iron hand. He led the country into the Korean War, sponsored terrorism against South Korea, and served as the leader of one of the world's most closed and repressive political regimes. After his death in 1994, natural disaster and economic collapse combined to bring this once-proud country to its knees.

Issues and Events

The collapse of Communism in the Soviet Union and around the world initiated a rapid downhill slide for North Korea. Its leaders quickly realized that North Korea must enter the world economy in order to survive. In 1990 relations thawed between North Korea and capitalist South Korea, and for the first time the two countries began negotiating terms for reunification. Growing speculation about North Korea's clandestine

nuclear weapons program undermined the peace process, however, and returned the two countries to the brink of war.

The nuclear inspections stalemate lasted until Kim Il Sung's death in 1994. With the economy deteriorating, North Korea's new leadership decided to use the country's nuclear capabilities to extract concessions from its enemies. It received two nuclear reactors and a precious five-year supply of oil from the U.S. and its allies in exchange for agreeing to dismantle its nuclear weapons program and submit to unlimited inspections.

Conditions in North Korea continued to decline, and after a flood in 1995 destroyed the rice crop the country was forced to ask for emergency food aid from the United States, Japan, and South Korea. Flooding continued throughout 1996, followed by a severe drought in 1997. By early 1998 the situation had reached the crisis point. Thousands of North Koreans migrated to China in search of food, and there were reports that one million or more may have perished from starvation.

The political situation remains extremely volatile despite ongoing peace talks. U.S. analysts predict that within the next few years one of three things could happen. It is possible that North Korea will adopt a new, more democratic form of government and reenter the international community. Another scenario is that North and South Korea will continue toward a peaceful reunification. Finally, the country could plunge into economic and political chaos and set off another war on the beleaguered Korean peninsula. With more than one million troops and a huge arsenal of chemical and conventional weapons, North Korea could inflict enormous damage upon itself and its neighbors.

Background

Neighboring Japan, China, and Russia have long fought over Korea. Japan gained control of Korea in 1910 and held the peninsula until the Soviets and Americans divided it following World War II. In 1949 rival governments were established in North and South Korea. Two years later, North Korea, supported by the Soviet Union and China, invaded the South but was repelled by the U.S. The war lasted three years and killed three million people. Because they never signed an official peace treaty, North and South Korea remain technically in a state of war.

North Korea has committed numerous acts of terrorism against the South Koreans, including an assassination attempt against South Korea's president in 1968 and the bombing of a South Korean airliner in 1987. In stark contrast to North Korea, South Korea has had a thriving economy and enviable productivity, despite recent economic setbacks and recurrent protests against government repression.

Power Struggle Continues: CAMBODIA

Perspective

1941	*Norodom Sihanouk crowned king of Cambodia.*
1953	*Cambodia gains independence.*
1969	*United States bombs Cambodia.*
1970	*Lon Nol unseats Sihanouk.*
1975	*U.S. withdraws from Vietnam; Cambodia falls to the Khmer Rouge under Pol Pot.*
1978	*Vietnam invades Cambodia.*
1979	*Vietnam overthrows Pol Pot. Hun Sen assumes power.*
1989	**September 26.** *Vietnamese troops leave Cambodia.*
1991	**October 23.** *Peace treaty signed between various warring factions.*
1992	**March 11.** *United Nations peacekeepers arrive in Cambodia.*
1993	**May 23-28.** *Sihanouk's royalist party wins elections.* **June 16.** *Hun Sen and Prince Norodom Ranariddh named co-Prime Ministers.* **September 24.** *Sihanouk becomes king for second time in 50 years.*
1994	*Fighting with Khmer Rouge continues.*
1997	**July 5.** *Hun Sen ousts Ranariddh.* **July 25.** *Pol Pot captured.*
1998	**April 15.** *Pol Pot dies.*

One of the worst cases of genocide in the twentieth century occurred in Cambodia during the regime of the Khmer Rouge, a Communist organization that ruled the country from 1975 to 1978. Led by Pol Pot, the Khmer Rouge implemented a reform program resulting in the death of almost one-sixth of the population and the total collapse of the country's economic and social structures. Despite Pol Pot's death in 1998, his Khmer Rouge followers carry on his terrorist legacy against Cambodia's people.

Issues and Events

In 1991, after decades of civil war, various Cambodian factions, including the Khmer Rouge, signed a cease-fire agreement. The treaty called for disarmament of warring groups and UN-supervised elections in May 1993. The Khmer Rouge failed to honor the agreement when it refused to surrender its weapons and recognize the elected government.

The winner of the elections was one of the world's most enduring politicians, Norodom Sihanouk. As king of Cambodia, Sihanouk had already ruled the country from 1941 until he was forced from office by Lon Nol in 1970. Sihanouk was returned as a figurehead when the Khmer Rouge took over in 1975. In 1993 Sihanouk was reinstated as King. His son, Prince Rinariddh, was named co-Prime Minister along with Hun Sen, who had ruled the country during the Vietnamese occupation.

Sihanouk's government failed to bring peace. By early 1994 fierce fighting had erupted between government forces and Khmer Rouge guerrillas in northern Cambodia. In 1996 the Khmer Rouge split, and war broke out between two of its factions. During the next year the legendary Pol Pot was captured by an opposing faction and was sentenced to life imprisonment for the murder of a rival Khmer Rouge leader, Son Sen. He died in 1998, apparently without remorse, never having been punished for his crimes.

The government has also been plagued by division. The alliance between Hun Sen and Rinariddh was an uneasy one, and in 1997 serious fighting broke out between forces loyal to each of the Prime Ministers. Rinariddh was soon defeated, and even King Sihanouk was unable to negotiate a reconciliation between the two sides.

Many of those involved in the peace process fear that time and money invested in Cambodia by the international community has been wasted. Cambodia's UN seat remains vacant, and the fighting has driven away foreign businesses. The economy is on a downhill slide, unlikely to improve until political stability is achieved.

Background

Cambodia, under the leadership of King Norodom Sihanouk, broke away from French rule in 1953. Sihanouk's attempts to maintain neutrality in the Vietnam War failed, and in 1969 the U.S. began bombing North Vietnamese bases and supply routes within Cambodia. A U.S.-backed general, Lon Nol, came to power by overthrowing Sihanouk. Continued bombing by the U.S. military fostered a hatred of Lon Nol's regime that led to a bloody civil war and the rise of the Khmer Rouge. In 1975, as the Vietnam War was drawing to a close, the Khmer Rouge became strong enough to overthrow Lon Nol.

The Khmer Rouge sought to establish peasant rule, an idea that still appeals to many of the rural poor in northern Cambodia. Under the leadership of Pol Pot, the Khmer Rouge began a genocidal reign of terror. Urban residents of all ages were placed in work camps in an attempt to create farmland out of the jungle, and anyone with an education was murdered. Political exterminations, famine, and rigors of the work camps killed at least one million of Cambodia's six million people. The Khmer Rouge was forced into exile by the Vietnamese, who ruled the country from 1979 to 1989.

Bougainville Uprising:
PAPUA NEW GUINEA

Perspective

1905	*Bougainville becomes part of the Territory of Papua.*
1972	*Panguna mine begins production.*
1975	**September 16.** *Papua New Guinea gains independence; North Solomon Islands, including Bougainville, try to secede.*
1988	**April.** *Bougainville landowners demand compensation from mine owners.* **November.** *Acts of sabotage against the Panguna mine begin.*
1989	**May 15.** *Panguna mine closes.*
1990	**March 1.** *Cease-fire goes into effect.* **March 16.** *Government security forces withdraw from Bougainville; rebels take over.* **May 17.** *Rebels declare their independence; government imposes embargo.*
1991	**January 22.** *Peace accord signed; government eases embargo; fighting continues.*
1995	**November 10.** *Peace talks abandoned.*
1996	**October 12.** *Bougainville Premier Theodore Miriung assassinated.*
1998	**January.** *Another peace agreement reached.*

The South Pacific country of Papua New Guinea has long been a favorite of anthropologists. With thousands of tribal groups and hundreds of languages, its cultural diversity is unrivaled. The tribes of Bougainville, one of the largest of the country's myriad islands, place a special social, almost religious, significance on their land.

Bougainville also contains fabulous mineral reserves, including copper, gold, and silver. Foreign interests have controlled these resources in a way that has conflicted with the values of the people of Bougainville. In 1988, smoldering resentments erupted when Bougainville residents took up arms against those they believed were exploiting them.

Issues and Events

When the isolated Bougainville natives agreed in 1967 to allow their land to be mined, they were led to believe that mining would make them rich. They were unaware that mining operations would devastate their land. Today much of the land surrounding the enormous Panguna mining complex lies in ruins. The river is severely polluted, and traditional hunting grounds have been destroyed. Only five percent of the profits went to the island government, and one percent was allotted to the landowners.

In 1988 the landowners demanded almost $10 billion in compensation, a claim that the mining company did not take seriously. A terrorist campaign, led by landowner Francis Ona, targeted first the mine, then government offices and installations, and finally plantations. Using stolen dynamite from the mine, the Bougainville Revolutionary Army (BRA) increased their demands as they achieved greater military success. Ultimately they forced the mine to close indefinitely, an event that has profoundly affected the country's economy.

In early 1990 a cease-fire was negotiated, but as soon as government forces were withdrawn the BRA took over the entire island and issued a declaration of independence. The government retaliated by imposing a complete embargo against Bougainville, which resulted in thousands of deaths, mainly from lack of medicine. In 1991 another peace accord was signed, but sporadic fighting continued. The government was unable to regain control of the island despite a major 1996 military offensive. In 1995 Theodore Miriung, a former rebel committed to finding a negotiated solution to Bougainville's problems, became the island's Premier. Neither the Papua New Guinea armed forces nor the rebels took responsibility for his assassination in 1996. A third peace agreement was reached in early 1998, but the island's future has not yet been resolved. Ona and others still dream of an independent Bougainvillea.

Twenty thousand people have died in the Bougainville uprising, the only armed conflict in the South Pacific. The outcome is of enormous importance to indigenous people around the world who are trying to reclaim their traditional lands, and to mining companies that have invested heavily in these lands.

Background

Britain claimed Bougainville in 1884 and placed it under Australian administration in 1902. The island became part of the Territory of Papua in 1905. The territories of Papua and New Guinea were united after the Japanese invasion during World War II, and in 1975 Papua New Guinea gained independence. At that time the people of Bougainville tried to secede, either to join the neighboring Solomon Islands or to form their own independent state. The government granted the Bougainvilleans limited autonomy and promised them benefits from the mining profits.

The people of Bougainville are diverse and speak about 20 languages. Theirs is a subsistence economy, and many people still live in primitive isolation.

The Middle East and North Africa

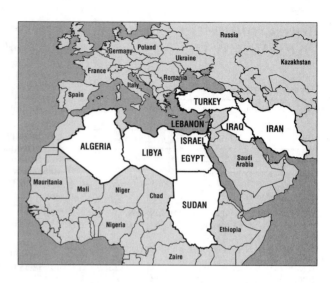

Since the 19th century, the Middle East has been described as a "powder keg"—a cliché that has never lost its accuracy. Wars have occurred sporadically between Israel and its Arab neighbors ever since Israel declared its independence in 1948. Factional fighting between rival political groups in Lebanon began in 1975 and rendered the country practically uninhabitable. In the 1980s, as many as one million people were killed when Iran and Iraq engaged in one of the bloodiest wars in the region's history. In the early 1990s, Iraq's unsuccessful attempt to incorporate neighboring Kuwait left both Iraq and Kuwait in ruins. The struggle between secular governments and Islamic fundamentalists has left hundreds dead in Algeria and Egypt, and continues to threaten peace and stability throughout the region.

The area known as the Middle East generally includes the countries of the Arabian peninsula and Iraq, Iran, Israel, Jordan, Lebanon, and Syria, as well as the Arabic-speaking countries of Northern Africa. Islam is the majority religion of the area, with the exception of Israel, where most people practice Judaism. Arabic language and culture are dominant in all countries except Israel and Iran.

It is often difficult to separate religion from politics in the Middle East. In many countries there is little or no separation of church and state. The region is the birthplace of three of the world's great religions: Judaism, Christianity, and Islam, all of which are intertwined with the political or cultural problems of the region. Islam, the religion of the overwhelming majority, is composed mainly of two sects: the majority Sunnis and the rapidly growing Shiite minority. In recent years the differences between these two sects were sharply defined when Shiite fundamental-

ists in Iran overthrew the government in 1979 and threatened the economic and political stability of the entire region. The Shiites claimed that the Sunni-controlled governments of the region were too closely allied with Western countries and that outside contacts were corrupting Islam. The Sunnis regarded the Iranian Shiites as radicals who would destroy the economy and social order of the region if their brand of religion were allowed to spread. A third Muslim group, especially prominent in Syria and Lebanon, is the Druze. Although the Druze regard their religion as a branch of Islam, other Muslim sects view them as heretics. There is also considerable tension in Israel between Orthodox Jews and members of other branches of Judaism. In Lebanon, where Christians, Muslims, and others make their home, political and military groups have formed along religious lines and have seriously fragmented the country.

The site of some of the world's most ancient civilizations, the Middle East has always hosted people of many different cultures. The great civilization of ancient Egypt developed on the banks of the Nile, and the area between the Tigris and Euphrates Rivers saw the society of Mesopotamia flourish. Invaders and immigrants were diverse—the many peoples coming to the region included Assyrians, Hebrews, Phoenicians, Chaldeans, Medes, and Persians. Islam was founded in the seventh century A.D. and had a profound influence on the culture and politics of the people. As the Arabs expanded their empire, their religion and culture spread throughout the Middle East.

The Arab Empire came to an end around the tenth century and was followed some centuries later by the empire of the Ottoman Turks, who were also Muslim. The Ottoman Empire dominated the region until Turkey was defeated in

World War I and control of many Middle Eastern lands passed to France and Britain. The British and French established political boundaries with little regard for the natural boundaries established by ethnicity or tribal allegiances.

Countries of the Middle East thus came to be demarcated by artificial borders created by treaties and agreements among the colonial powers. The geography of the region had fostered a nomadic lifestyle, and the new foreign-imposed boundaries prevented the people from following their traditional way of life. Hardship often ensued.

When independence was finally achieved, the artificial boundaries remained, sometimes uniting diverse peoples into a single country, as exemplified in Iraq, Lebanon, and Syria. Dissension was often the result, and many borders remain in dispute. Long-standing border disagreements led to both the Iran-Iraq War and the Iraqi invasion of Kuwait.

Attempts by the colonial powers to establish political systems capable of diffusing cultural differences were ineffective. Nowhere was this more apparent than in the effort to establish both Arab and Jewish states in the former British mandate of Palestine. Palestine, corresponding roughly to present-day Israel, was mandated to the British in 1920. Arab outcry about Jewish immigration into Palestine resulted in the division of Palestine into separate Arab and Jewish states. When Israel declared its independence, the surrounding Arab states declared war on Israel; in effect, they rejected the United Nations' vote for partition. The Arab state envisioned by the UN never materialized, and Palestinian Arabs became refugees. Major conflicts between Israel and the surrounding Arab states included a 1956 war focused on the Suez Canal, the Six-Day War of 1967, and a war in October 1973. Arab resentment about the establishment of Israel and the unresolved status of the stateless Palestinians has been a major source of continuing tension in the Middle East. Lebanon was nearly destroyed when thousands of immigrating Palestinians upset the delicate political and religious balance and vaulted the country into war and chaos.

A major step toward regional peace and stability was taken when the Arabs and Israelis joined together for peace talks that began in 1991 and continue today. In 1993 the discussions bore fruit in the form of an agreement resulting in limited autonomy for Palestinians living in Israeli-occupied territories. The peace process has been repeatedly jeopardized by frequent terrorist attacks masterminded by Israelis and Palestinians who oppose any form of compromise. These attacks led to the 1996 election of a conservative government in Israel, which has dramatically slowed the progress of the negotiations.

The Palestinian independence movement is not the only one in the region. Like the Palestinians, the Kurds are also a people without a country; most of the region of Kurdistan is divided between Iraq, Iran, and Turkey. In 1991 the UN established a "no-fly" zone in northern Iraq to protect rebellious Kurds who had hoped to defeat Saddam Hussein during the Gulf War. Kurds in Turkey continue to wage a violent terrorist campaign against the Turkish government.

In most Arab countries, the response to years of foreign intervention has been fervent nationalism. A distaste for Western institutions, combined with a passionate appreciation for tradition, have hindered the spread of democracy in the Middle East. Some countries, such as Saudi Arabia, Bahrain, and Qatar, are ruled by traditional hereditary monarchies. Others are governed by authoritarian leaders, as is the case with Hussein in Iraq, Assad in Syria, and Qadhafi in Libya. In 1996, resentment about a continuing U.S. military presence in Saudi Arabia resulted in the terrorist bombing of an American military base there.

The majority of the countries in the region boast enormous oil resources, while others, such as Jordan, have very little or none. Some countries, like Iran, Iraq, and Libya, have squandered their assets through military adventurism or economic isolation. Political stability in Saudi Arabia, the United Arab Emirates, and many other oil-rich states of the Persian Gulf has resulted in a remarkable level of affluence for the citizens of these countries, although falling oil prices have led to economic decline throughout the region. The income disparities between countries contribute to growing instability, and the prosperous sheikdoms of the Gulf have become tempting military targets for their poorer neighbors. Iraq's invasion of Kuwait was motivated by economics.

Poverty and governmental corruption fueled Iran's Islamic revolution in 1979, an event which had a profound effect on politics throughout the entire region. Empowered by the Iranian example, Islamic fundamentalist movements began to gain strength in almost every corner of the Middle East and Northern Africa, and are now considered the greatest threat to regional stability.

A return to traditional Islamic values has provided an outlet for the desperate poor and powerless. However, it has also spawned violence and chaos. Most of these traditional movements are supported by Iran and Sudan, the two countries where fundamentalists are in control of the national governments. In Algeria, however, the government refused to honor the results of an election that would have brought fundamentalists to power. In southern Lebanon, peace is threatened by Islamic fundamentalists bent on the destruction of Israel. In Egypt, fundamentalists have declared war against both tourists and the Egyptian government. The Saudi Arabian government is also being challenged by Islamic radicals who seek to depose the monarchy.

Battling Militant Islam: ALGERIA

Perspective

1830	*French colonial rule in Algeria begins.*
1954	**November.** *National Liberation Front (NLF) formed. War against France ensues.*
1962	**July 3.** *Algeria achieves independence under NLF leadership.*
1989	**February.** *A new constitution allows for multiparty elections.*
1990	**June 13.** *Islamic Salvation Front (ISF) wins local elections.*
1991	**December 26.** *ISF wins first round of national elections.*
1992	**January 11.** *Military seizes power.* **February.** *Riots break out.* **June 29.** *President Mohammed Boudiaf assassinated.*
1994	**December 24.** *Islamic terrorists hijack a French airliner.*
1995	**January 30.** *Car bomb kills 42 people.* **July 26.** *Paris subway bombing linked to Algerian terrorists.*
1996	**March 27.** *Seven French monks kidnapped and later killed.*
1997	**June 5.** *Elections ignite unprecedented violence.*
1998	**January.** *Terrorists massacre 400 villagers.*

The 1970s were a time of peace and prosperity in oil-rich Algeria. Its secular, one-party socialist government served as a model for many other African countries. In 1990, though, the government was swept away by democracy and civil war broke out.

Issues and Events

When a deteriorating economy forced the ruling National Liberation Front (NLF) to implement a more democratic constitution in 1989, the group was sure that it could win in the country's first free elections. Shock waves rippled through the Arab world when the newly formed Islamic Salvation Front (ISF), a fundamentalist religious group, won the local elections instead.

In 1991 the ISF scored a major victory in national elections, but the military took over and set up a military council. Violence flared, and the council declared a state of emergency. Public outrage ensued, and Algeria's elected president was assassinated in June 1992.

Also in 1992 the Islamic Salvation Army, the military wing of the ISF, organized a terrorist campaign that included bombings, airline hijackings, and kidnappings. The government responded by jailing, torturing, and executing ISF leaders.

As the relatively moderate, well-educated ISF leaders were killed or jailed, ruthless new organizations emerged to take their place. One of these groups, the Armed Islamic Group (GIA), is blamed for the deaths of thousands of innocent civilians during 1997 and 1998. Mainly composed of young men, the GIA has brought a new level of violence to the war. In the war's worst single incident, GIA members killed 400 villagers with axes and knives during one night. Attacks of this nature now occur frequently.

The government has been accused of doing little to prevent these ongoing massacres; in fact, at least some of the killings may be attributed to army "death squads." Because civilian casualties are increasing so rapidly, the international community will likely exert strong pressure on the government to end the war and return to a true democracy.

So far 80,000 people have been killed, making this the most deadly conflict at the moment in the Middle East region. Public outrage was renewed in 1998 when military-backed candidates won national elections amidst claims of fraud and vote-rigging. Many people saw the election as a weak attempt to legitimize the increasingly repressive military regime. Ironically, the ISF was a moderate Islamic group before the war; political repression sparked the kind of militant Islamic fervor that the Algerian military was trying to avoid when it cancelled the 1991 elections. Today the government refuses to negotiate with the ISF, the GIA, or any other terrorist group.

Background

Arabs brought Islam to Algeria in the eighth century, and the people have remained devoutly Muslim. In 1830 the French began to establish colonies and exert control over the area. But in 1954 the Algerians formed the National Liberation Front and waged war against the French. More than 500,000 people were killed before Algeria became independent in 1962 and the NLF established itself as the sole political party. Under its leadership, Algeria flourished in the 1970s when vast oil resources commanded high prices on the world market. By the 1980s, oil prices fell, severely affecting the Algerian economy. Food shortages prompted riots, and one-quarter of the people were unemployed. Inefficient centralized planning for agriculture also took its toll on the Algerian economy. Once self-sufficient in food production, Algeria now must import most of its food.

Fundamentalist Terrorism: EGYPT

Perspective

1922	*Britain abolishes protectorate and recognizes Egyptian independence.*
1923	*Constitutional monarchy established.*
1952	**July 23.** *King Farouk overthrown by military junta.*
1953	**June 18.** *Egypt declared a republic.*
1967	**June.** *Israel wins Six-Day War, occupies Gaza Strip and Sinai.*
1970	*President Gamal Abdel Nasser dies; succeeded by Anwar el-Sadat.*
1973	*Egypt and Syria attack Israel.*
1976	*Sadat cancels friendship treaty with Soviet Union.*
1979	**March 26.** *Camp David peace accords signed between Egypt and Israel.*
1981	**October 6.** *Sadat assassinated by Muslim extremists; succeeded by Hosni Mubarak.*
1992	*Upsurge in militant violence begins.*
1993	**February 26.** *Egyptian radicals bomb the World Trade Center in New York.*
1995	**June 26.** *Islamic Group attempts to assassinate President Mubarak.*
1996	**April 18.** *Terrorists kill 18 Greek tourists.*
1997	**November.** *Islamic Group kills 58 tourists at Luxor.*

Seeking to overthrow the secular government of Hosni Mubarak, Islamic militants have targeted both government officials and Egypt's three-billion-dollar-per-year tourism industry for their terrorism campaign. They have killed foreign visitors; reports of bullet-riddled tour buses, boats, and trains have received extensive coverage worldwide. Their terrorism has devastated both tourism and foreign investment. In response, the government has executed dozens of suspected terrorists and jailed thousands more. Such harsh measures have sparked protests over human rights abuses and have further inflamed fundamentalist passions.

Issues and Events

Since 1992 almost 900 government officials, police, informants, Christians, and innocent bystanders have been killed in attacks across the country, from Cairo to the impoverished south where some villages have become armed camps.

Militancy is rooted in Egypt's vast slums, where, despite economic reforms, the gap between the country's rich and poor continues to grow. Egypt's population, currently at 60 million, is expected to reach 80 million by the year 2010. Half of the people are illiterate, unemployment is a serious problem, and government corruption is widespread. Under these conditions, the militants have found many sympathizers.

The Islamic Group, which has claimed responsibility for much of the violence, is linked to most of the people convicted for the 1993 bombing of New York's World Trade Center. During 1995, it claimed responsibility for a failed assassination attempt against Egypt's President Mubarak, as well as the shooting of 18 Greek tourists in 1996.

In late 1997 the Islamic Group ambushed two busloads of foreign visitors at Luxor, one of the country's most popular tourist sites. Fifty-eight foreigners and ten others were killed in the massacre. The Islamic Group claimed that its original intent was to take the tourists hostage to secure the release of those convicted of the World Trade Center bombing. All of the Islamic Group's leaders are believed to have been arrested, but the few militants who have eluded capture are believed to be increasingly violent. They have achieved their goal of disrupting the tourist economy: Hotel occupancy rates plummeted in the week following the massacre, and have yet to return to normal levels.

The rebels want to replace Egypt's secular government with an Islamic state. Most Egyptians oppose the kind of strict Islamic society that the rebels advocate.

Background

With its diverse religions, democratic traditions, rich cultural arts, and close Western ties, Egypt has been among the most liberal of Arab states. After engineering a 1952 coup, Gamal Abdel Nasser boosted nationalist pride by thumbing his nose at Egypt's colonial past. He began grand projects, such as the Aswan Dam, and played the superpowers against each other by courting the Soviet Union. After disastrous losses from the 1973 war with Israel, President Anwar el-Sadat gradually shifted Egypt's allegiance to the West and signed the historic peace treaty with Israel in 1979. During the 1980s, Egypt received extensive U.S. aid. However, neither Sadat's policies nor those of his successor Mubarak could cope with a rapidly expanding population no longer self-sufficient in food production.

After Iran's Islamic revolution, radical Islam spread throughout the Arab world. Based on strict religious interpretations, the movement decries liberal Western influences and has found willing believers among the poor who have not been helped much by foreign aid.

Sanctions Continue: IRAQ

Perspective

1968	July 17. *Members of the Arab Baath Socialist Party (Baathists) overthrow the Arab nationalist government.*
1979	July 16. *Saddam Hussein takes over.*
1980	September 22. *Iraq invades Iran.*
1983	February. *Iraq begins using chemical weapons against Iran.*
1987	January. *Iran attacks Basra; 70,000 people killed.*
1988	July 18. *War with Iran ends.*
1990	August 2. *Iraq invades Kuwait.* August 6. *United Nations organizes economic embargo against Iraq.*
1991	January 16. *"Operation Desert Storm" begins as allied forces bomb Iraq targets.* February 27. *Iraq surrenders.*
1992	*UN establishes "no fly" zones in northern and southern Iraq.*
1993	January 15. *Allies bomb Iraq.* June 27. *United States missiles target Baghdad.*
1996	December 10. *Iraq resumes limited oil exports.*
1998	January 13. *Iraq temporarily blocks UN weapons inspection team.*

Iraq under the rule of Saddam Hussein is a country isolated from the rest of the world. After years of UN sanctions, its economy is failing and its people are impoverished. Holding more than ten percent of the world's oil resources, Iraq could have led the Arab world economically without all of the violence and bloodshed of recent years.

Issues and Events

Saddam Hussein had held the reins of power for little more than a year when he launched an attack against Iran and began the region's bloodiest war in modern times. By the war's end in 1988, more than one million people had been killed, one-tenth of whom were civilians.

During the war, Iraq received support from both Arab and Western countries eager to suppress Iran's fundamentalist Islamic revolution, led by the Ayatollah Khomeini. Consequently, Iraq acquired the latest weapons from around the world, including technology for chemical, biological, and nuclear weapons.

In 1990 Iraq invaded Kuwait to secure more oil resources and improve its access to the sea. Its occupation of Kuwait continued until early 1991 when the U.S. defeated Iraq in Operation Desert Storm. The war brought profound hardship to the Iraqis. More than 100,000 people were killed and 72,000 were left homeless due to the fighting.

After its surrender, Iraq was required to destroy its biological and chemical weapons, allow UN inspections of its nuclear program, compensate Kuwait for financial losses incurred during the invasion, renounce terrorism, and cede its territorial claims to Kuwait. Iraq's failure to comply resulted in severe economic sanctions, including an oil embargo.

The crippling embargo and sporadic U.S. military actions have coaxed Iraq into complying with most of the UN's demands, but there are still concerns that Iraq might possess enough chemical and biological weapons to destroy several major cities. Its lack of cooperation with UN arms inspectors has been an ongoing source of friction between Iraq and the rest of the world. Iraq claims that inspection teams include U.S. spies, while the U.S. claims that Iraq routinely stalls the inspectors so that weapons can be transported away from targeted sites.

International enthusiasm for the embargo waned when the UN warned that embargo-related food and medicine shortages were contributing to the deaths of 4,500 Iraqi children each month. Although the embargo remains in place, Iraq received permission in 1996 to begin exporting limited amounts of oil under strict UN supervision to purchase food and medicine.

Background

Iraq lies within Mesopotamia, the birthplace of civilization. The ancient Sumerians who inhabited the region were the first people to develop written language, agriculture, and irrigation techniques.

Following World War I, the League of Nations took Iraq from Turkey and placed it under British rule. Oil was discovered in 1923, and the country gained its independence in 1932. Political stability has eluded Iraq, which began experiencing military coups just four years later. Most of its governments were pro-Western until 1958, when General Abdul Karim Qasim created an Arab nationalist state. In 1963, members of the Arab Baath Socialist Party killed Qasim. The Baathists were ousted later in the year, but regained control in 1968, and Saddam Hussein took over the government in 1979.

Saddam quickly established a ruthless regime, and reportedly used napalm and other weapons of war against dissidents: Kurds in the north and Shiite Muslims in the south. Despite his renowned brutality, however, Saddam Hussein enjoys the support of many Iraqis for promoting education, health care, and housing. He is also credited with eradicating financial corruption in government.

Kurdish Uprising:
IRAQ AND TURKEY

Perspective

1826	*Kurds revolt against the Turks.*
1932	*Independence of Iraq leads to Kurdish uprising.*
1945	*Independent Kurdish state created in Iran but lasts only six months.*
1961	*Kurds begin armed revolt against Iraqi government.*
1974	*Kurdistan Workers' Party (PKK) formed in Turkey.*
1979	*Iran's Islamic revolution fails to bring autonomy to the Kurds.*
1989	**June.** *Iraq forcibly relocates 100,000 Kurds.*
1991	**February 28.** *Iraqi Kurds launch violent revolt in aftermath of Gulf War.*
1992	**May 19.** *Iraqi Kurds hold elections in United Nations' supervised "safe zone."*
1994	**May.** *Fighting breaks out between rival Kurdish factions in Iraq.*
1995	**March 20.** *Turkey invades Kurdish territory in Iraq.*
1996	**August 31.** *Kurdish fighting prompts Iraq to invade the "safe zone"; United States retaliates.*
1997	**September 23.** *Turkey launches another offensive into Iraq.*

For thousands of years, the Kurds have been waiting and fighting to establish their own homeland. Numbering 20 million, they are one of the largest ethnic groups without a homeland. Spread out in a region called Kurdistan that comprises parts of Iraq, Iran, Turkey, Syria, Armenia, and Azerbaijan, the once-nomadic Kurds have long been pawns in a region that has seldom known peace.

Issues and Events

To quell Kurdish rebels, governments of the region have indiscriminately killed hundreds of thousands of civilians and repeatedly relocated, tortured, and executed suspected insurgents. In Iraq, the government allegedly used poison gas against entire Kurdish villages.

International attention focused on the Kurds in 1991 after the Gulf War. Encouraged by the U.S. to rebel against Saddam Hussein, Iraqi Kurds launched a major rebellion. When Iraq's army defeated their forces, more than 1.5 million Kurds fled to squalid refugee camps in the mountains.

To lure the Kurds away from the camps and back to their settlements, the U.S. established a "no-fly zone" in northern Iraq and forbade any Iraqi flights over the region. The UN later took responsibility for monitoring the safe zone, and the Kurds seized the opportunity to elect their own government in 1992. Sheltered from Iraqi reprisals, the Kurds could have established a strong government and lobbied for international recognition. Instead, two years after the elections a power struggle within the Kurdish leadership erupted into factional fighting between the Kurdistan Democratic Party and the Patriotic Union of Kurdistan. Since then, thousands of people have been killed, the territory has been divided into sectors, and any hopes for autonomy or independence have been postponed indefinitely.

Although Iraq's Kurds have received more publicity, Turkey's Kurds have waged the fiercest war for independence in recent times. Living in the country's southeast provinces, Turkey's ten million Kurds are divided into multiple factions. The most notorious is the Kurdistan Workers' Party (PKK), which has been at war with the Turkish government for more than a decade. The PKK is linked to numerous bombings and assassinations.

Turkey has waged a brutal war against the PKK. In the 1980s Turkey began a campaign to destroy more than 3,000 Kurdish villages and force the Kurds to abandon their culture. During 1994 and 1995, Turkish troops drove thousands of Kurdish civilians into northern Iraqi refugee camps, culminating in a full-scale invasion of the Kurdish area of Iraq. Fighting in the border region continues as Turkey attempts to establish a nine-mile-wide buffer zone. More than 37,000 people have already died in Turkey's war against the Kurds.

Background

The Kurds are descendants of semi-nomadic Aryan people who have inhabited the mountainous region of Kurdistan for thousands of years. Situated between the Persians and the Turks, the Kurds have never had a homeland. Rebellions were common throughout the 1800s as the Kurds began to agitate for independence. They have frequently reached autonomy agreements with various governments, but promises made to them have never been met. The British and their allies promised the Kurds their own state in 1920, but never enforced its creation.

Although known for intertribal warfare, the Kurds' shared culture, territory, lifestyle and blood ties have united them through the centuries. All Kurds speak Kurdish, but there are many different dialects. Most Kurds adhere to moderate forms of Islam, though women are not secluded or veiled. Most rely on farming and shepherding for their livelihood.

Year of Jubilee:
ISRAEL

Perspective

1897	*World Zionist Organization founded.*
1920	*British mandate for Palestine established.*
1947	**November 29.** *United Nations divides Palestine into Jewish and Arab territories.*
1948	**May 14.** *Israel declares independence.* **May 15.** *Arab armies invade Israel; Arabs flee Israel.*
1949	**January.** *Arab-Israeli War ends; Israel expands its territory.*
1964	**June.** *Palestine Liberation Organization (PLO) founded.*
1967	**June.** *Israel captures all of Palestine during the Six-Day War.*
1970	*PLO moves its base to Lebanon after being expelled by Jordan.*
1973	**November 9.** *Egypt, Syria, and Jordan start third Arab-Israeli war.*
1985	**June 6.** *Israel establishes "security zone" in southern Lebanon.*
1987	**December.** *Palestinian uprising, or* intifadah, *begins.*
1988	**November.** *PLO declares Palestinian independence from Israel.*
1993	**September 13.** *Israel and PLO sign peace agreement in Washington, D.C.*
1994	**February 25.** *Israeli radical kills 48 Palestinians in Hebron mosque.* **May 4.** *Palestinians get limited autonomy in Gaza Strip and Jericho.* **October 19.** *Hamas bomb kills 23 people in Israel.*
1995	**January 22.** *Islamic Jihad bomb kills 19 Israelis.* **November 4.** *Prime Minister Yitzhak Rabin assassinated.*
1996	**January 20.** *Palestinians hold first elections.* **February.** *Hamas suicide bomber kills 25 people on a Jerusalem bus.* **March.** *Hamas bombs kill 32 more.* **April 18.** *Israeli assault in Lebanon kills 91 Palestinian civilians.* **May 31.** *Israeli conservatives win elections.*
1998	**May 14.** *Israel commemorates 50 years of independence.*

Ancient Hebrew law called every 50 years for a jubilee, a time in which slaves were freed, captive lands were returned to their owners, and debts were forgiven. In 1998 Israel marked the anniversary of 50 years of independence, and this year of jubilee was a time for both celebration and introspection. While some people enjoyed cookouts and fireworks, others used the time to remember the 20,000 Israeli soldiers killed in defense of their country, and still others contemplated Israel's future and that of the Palestinian people whose land remains under Israeli occupation.

Issues and Events

The founding of Israel was a remarkable achievement. After thousands of years, the Jews were finally given the opportunity to re-enter the Promised Land and establish a homeland. Israel flourished economically and politically despite three wars instigated by three neighboring Arab countries, even as lands captured during these wars have fueled international controversy. Palestinian tensions in the occupied territories erupted in December 1987. Scores of Palestinians were killed, and many thousands wounded and arrested in the *intifadah*, or uprising. Increasingly regarded as the oppressor rather than the oppressed, Israelis found themselves under growing pressure from the international community to allow for the development of a Palestinian homeland, just as they were once supported in their quest for a land of their own.

In 1993 Israeli Prime Minister Yitzhak Rabin and Palestinian Liberation Organization (PLO) leader Yasser Arafat signed an historic peace agreement signalling the beginning of a new era in Middle East politics. As a result of ongoing negotiations, the Palestinians were granted limited self-rule in the Gaza Strip and parts of the West Bank in 1994. Autonomy was expanded in 1995, and the first Palestinian elections were held in 1996. Yasser Arafat was elected President, and his supporters achieved a majority in the legislature.

Ironically, the peace agreement, which was designed to stabilize the region, resulted in an increase in violence as radical Palestinian and Israeli factions maneuvered to derail the peace process. The Hamas and other groups, like the Islamic Jihad, have launched violent terrorist attacks against Israeli and Palestinian targets. Another group that does not welcome the peace talks is the Hizbullah, or Party of God. The Hizbullah sporadically launch rockets from their base in southern Lebanon into sparsely inhabited areas of northern Israel. Israeli retaliatory attacks often have tragic consequences, as in 1996 when Israelis killed 91 civilians in a Lebanese UN peacekeeping camp.

Many Israelis also oppose the peace process, and the West Bank has become a breeding ground for violently anti-Arab Jewish radicals. One Israeli radical massacred 48 Arabs at a Hebron mosque in February 1994. Another stunned the country when he assassinated Prime Minister Yitzhak Rabin in November 1995.

During 1996 both the Palestinians and the Israelis held elections, and while the Palestinians expressed their approval of the peace process by voting for Arafat, the Israelis voiced their dissatisfaction by electing conservative candidate Benjamin Netanyahu as Prime Minister. While the Netanyahu government has promised to continue to negotiate with its Arab neighbors, it is unwilling to offer any meaningful concessions, despite the fact that there are still many serious issues to be resolved.

The status of the city of Jerusalem is an unresolved issue because it is claimed by both the Israelis and the Palestinians. Israel claims the entire city, but the Arabs want East Jerusalem to serve as the capital of their new state.

To stop the fighting, a permanent border between Israel and the Palestinian territory needs to be established. The Palestinians hope to control all of the West Bank, but the Israelis want to carve out blocks of Israeli settlements for annexation. This issue is of critical importance to 130,000 Israeli settlers currently living in Palestinian territory.

Another formidable problem is that of the three million Palestinian refugees who currently reside in other countries. These people, many of whom either fled or were forced to leave when Israel became a state, are demanding the right to reclaim their homes and property. The Palestinians insist that these people are entitled to compensation, but Israel refuses to acknowledge any responsibility for the refugees.

There is also the larger issue of Palestinian statehood and what shape it will take. Although most Palestinians would be satisfied with nothing less than complete independence, Israel has never accepted this concept.

Perhaps most disturbing to the Arab world is Netanyahu's decision to resume Israeli housing construction in the occupied territories. Rioting broke out in 1997 after the government began to build 6,500 apartment units in East Jerusalem, despite stern reprimands from both the UN and Israel's Arab neighbors.

Now that peace seems attainable after 50 years of struggle, Israel is acutely aware of its deep divisions. When the country was founded, it was conceived as a Jewish state, but its religious extremists and secular Jews disagree profoundly about the role of religion in determining government policy. Secondly, while the country has achieved ethnic diversity and harmony within its Jewish population, Arab Muslims and Christians—who live within Israel's borders and account for more than ten percent of Israel's population—are treated like unwanted guests. Finally, the country remains divided between those who want to make peace with the Arabs, and those who believe that peace can only come through the use of force.

Background

Conflict between Jews and Arabs has erupted sporadically since the British received a League of Nations mandate for Palestine in 1920. The mandate, which included a provision for the creation of a Jewish homeland, marked the beginning of massive Jewish migration to the area. When Jewish settlers first began to arrive in Palestine in 1920, they lived in peace with their Arab neighbors. However, as their numbers began to swell after World War II and the Holocaust (in which six million Jews were exterminated), they were greeted with increasing hostility from the Arabs, who had lived in the area for centuries and feared that they would be overrun by the newcomers.

In November 1947 the UN approved a plan that partitioned Palestine into roughly equal Jewish and Arab states. When the British mandate over Palestine ended in 1948, the Israelis declared their independence, but the Arab state envisioned by the UN never came into being. Egypt, Lebanon, Syria, Jordan, and Iraq declared war on the new Jewish state of Israel, but Israel defeated the invaders. Thousands of Palestinian Arabs, fearing for their lives, left their homes only to find that they were not welcome to return. Arab countries boycotted all Israeli goods and refused to recognize Israel's right to exist.

Fighting broke out again in 1956, and again Israel made substantial territorial gains. Israel later traded this territory back to Egypt. The Six-Day War of 1967 was by far Israel's most convincing victory against the Arabs. By the time the war ended, almost 20,000 Arabs had been killed and Israel occupied the former Egyptian Sinai Peninsula, the Gaza Strip, all of Jerusalem, Syria's Golan Heights, and the Jordanian-controlled West Bank of the Jordan River. In 1973 Egypt, Syria, and Jordan attacked Israel but were driven back by 1974. The Camp David accords of 1979 (in which Israel and Egypt agreed to a peace treaty) provided for the return of the Sinai Peninsula to Egypt in 1982, but all of the other occupied territories remained under Israeli rule.

The Palestine Liberation Organization (PLO) was founded in 1964 to represent and unite the Palestinians, but it became notorious for its terrorist acts. Until 1988, when the Palestinians declared their independence from Israel, the PLO denied Israel's right to exist and refused to try to arrive at any negotiated settlement. First based in Jordan, the PLO was driven into Lebanon in 1970. As a result of PLO attacks against Israel, Lebanon has experienced several Israeli invasions in the last 20 years. Israel and Lebanon are separated by a UN-supervised security zone.

Middle East Battleground: LEBANON

Perspective

1943	**November 22.** *Lebanon gains independence from France.*
1975	**April.** *Fighting erupts between Christians and Palestinian guerrillas.*
1976	**April.** *Syria invades Lebanon.*
1978	**March 15.** *Israel invades Lebanon; United Nations deploys peacekeeping forces.*
1982	**June 6.** *Israel invades Lebanon.*
1985	**June 6.** *Israel withdraws, establishes a "security zone" in southern Lebanon.*
1986	**April 7.** *Israelis bomb Palestinian refugee camps.*
1989	**October 22.** *Taif Accord reached.*
1990	**December 3.** *Private militia withdraw from Beirut.*
1991	**April 29.** *Most militia surrender arms to the Lebanese army.* **July.** *Palestine Liberation Organization (PLO) defeated by government troops.*
1993	**July 25.** *Israelis launch "Operation Accountability" to drive civilians from southern Lebanon.*
1996	**April 11.** *Israel attacks Beirut suburbs.* **April 18.** *Israeli artillery strikes UN peacekeeping camp, killing 91 civilians.*

After serving for years as the central battle-ground in Lebanon's civil war, the city of Beirut has begun the long process of rebuilding, both physically and economically. With the advent of relative tranquility in northern Lebanon and continuing progress in peace talks between Israel and its Arab neighbors, it is perhaps true that the worst is over for Lebanon. However, an ongoing conflict in southern Lebanon involving Israel, Lebanon, Syria, and Iran reached Beirut in 1996 and reminded everyone that peace is still an elusive commodity in this war-torn land.

Issues and Events

Civil war ended in northern Lebanon with the implementation of the Taif Peace Accord, a result of negotiations sponsored by Saudi Arabia. After Lebanese Christians were defeated in an all-out attempt to drive Syria from Lebanon, the accord went into effect and all private militia evacuated Beirut for the first time in the war's history. By mid-1991 most of the militia had surrendered their arms, and in July the PLO was forced to surrender its 20-year reign over southern Lebanon.

Not all of the militia were disarmed, however. The Iranian-backed Hizbullah has continued to fight against Israel's occupation of a six-mile-wide "security zone" along the southern Lebanese border. The Hizbullah have the implicit approval of both the Syrians and the Lebanese government, who hope that the Hizbullah's on-going presence will drive the Israelis out of Lebanon. Another group that has not surrendered, the Southern Lebanon Army, is allied with Israel and opposes the Syrian occupation of Lebanon.

Israeli efforts to defeat the Hizbullah have been disastrous. Usually the Hizbullah attack Israeli military targets in the security zone, then Israel's retaliatory strikes kill civilians. The Hizbullah then shoot rockets into sparsely inhabited northern Israel, and Israel responds with massive force. This was the pattern in 1993 when Israel's "Operation Accountability" against 70 impoverished villages resulted in 130 civilian deaths, 500 injuries, and massive property destruction. It was also the pattern in 1996 when an Israeli attack on the suburban Beirut headquarters of the Hizbullah destroyed a UN peacekeeping camp and killed more than 150 civilians. In contrast, the Hizbullah have killed only 12 Israeli civilians since Israel's 1982 invasion of Lebanon.

Although both sides agreed in 1996 to end their attacks on civilian targets, there is growing Israeli concern about continuing military casualties. During 1997, 39 Israeli soldiers were killed in battle and another 73 were killed in a plane crash. The Israeli government has offered to withdraw from Lebanon if the Lebanese government will guarantee the security of Israel's northern border. Lebanon has rejected the offer, stating that Israel's withdrawal must be unconditional.

Background

Established by the French in 1943, the Lebanese government provided fixed representation for various religious groups according to the 1932 census. The Christian community, which then comprised 51 percent of the population, was given a dominant role in government. The situation was soon complicated by a huge influx of Palestinian refugees, who were Muslim. By the 1970s, the Palestinians had established their headquarters in Beirut and the Muslim population outnumbered the Christians. When Muslims were unable to gain a more dominant government role commensurate with their numbers, sectarian tensions erupted into civil war in 1975.

By the 1980s Lebanon had fractured into various groups, each with its own small army. More than 150,000 people were killed during 15 years of fighting, and much of Beirut was destroyed.

The Syrians, who entered the war in 1976, control most of the country and are allied by treaty with the Lebanese government. About 1,500 Israeli troops and 4,500 UN peacekeepers have been stationed in the security zone, which was established in 1985.

The Revolution Continues: IRAN

Perspective

650	*Arab armies introduce Islam to Iran.*
1908	*Oil discovered in Khūzestān province.*
1941	*Mohammad Reza Pahlavi becomes shah.*
1979	**January 6.** *Shah flees Iran.* **February 1.** *Ruhollah Khomeini takes charge of the government.* **November 4.** *Iranian students seize United States embassy and 66 hostages.*
1980	**September 22.** *War with Iraq begins.*
1988	**August 20.** *War with Iraq ends.*
1989	**June 3.** *Khomeini dies.* **July 28.** *Hashemi Rafsanjani elected president.*
1992	**May 30.** *Rioting breaks out in Mashhad.*
1994	**February 1.** *Assassination attempt made on Rafsanjani in Tehran.* **June 20.** *Bomb kills 25 in Mashhad.*
1995	**April 4.** *Riots in Imamshahr.* **May 8.** *U.S. imposes trade embargo.*
1996	**July 24.** *U.S. imposes more sanctions.*
1997	**May 23.** *Mohammed Khatami, a moderate, is elected president.*

The Islamic fundamentalist revolution that swept through Iran has been likened to a tidal wave that could engulf the Middle East and plunge the region into a new Dark Age. The death of the Ayatollah Khomeini in 1989 led to a more moderate regime in Iran, but growing economic and political unrest continues to destabilize the government.

Issues and Events

In 1979 the Ayatollah Khomeini changed the course of international politics when he established a new theocratic republic based on the tenets of Islam. An important goal of Khomeini's regime was to spread the new Islamic revolution throughout the world.

When war broke out between Iran and Iraq in 1980, moderate Arab countries feared an Iranian victory could strengthen the appeal of the fundamentalist movement. Consequently, Iraq enjoyed the support of the U.S., the Soviet Union, and the oil-rich Arab countries, while Iran drifted deeper into economic and diplomatic isolation. Ending in 1988, the war was one of the worst in history; approximately one million people were killed.

Since Khomeni's death in 1989, Iran has struggled to end its diplomatic isolation and restore its battered economy. In 1992, poverty ignited the worst rioting in Iran since the 1979 revolution. Squatters who were forced from their land destroyed more than 80 government buildings in the city of Mashhad. In February 1994 riots broke out in Zahedan and an attempt was made on President Rafsanjani's life at a rally in Tehran. In June, a bomb killed 25 people and injured many more in Mashhad. Unrest continued in 1995 with rioting in Imamshahr over price increases. In 1997 rioting stemmed from a power struggle among Iran's religious leaders.

More than one-half of Iranians are under 20 years old and are more concerned about jobs and consumer goods than they are with religious ideals. Others have become disillusioned by the Islamic revolution, which has failed to improve living conditions for the poor. They displayed the depth of their discontent by electing moderate presidential candidate Mohammed Khatami in a 1997 landslide victory. Supported by women, young people, and the middle class, Khatami promised to improve the economy, initiate dialogue with the U.S., and allow more freedom of speech. While Khatami and those who elected him desire a more moderate government, real power remains with the country's ultra-conservative religious leaders. Thus Iran's economic recovery and reintegration into the international community will be a slow, painful process.

Despite Iran's problems, millions of Shiite Muslims throughout the world are fighting to establish similar regimes in their own countries, often with the support of the Iranian government. For a growing number of poor people in Asia and Africa, Islamic fundamentalism provides an alternative to Western social systems that have left them with little hope of improving their condition.

Background

The ancient Persian Empire came to an end in A.D. 650 when it was defeated by the Arab armies of Islam. Until the late twentieth century, various foreign powers or dynasties ruled Iran. Iranian rulers, who were called shahs, wielded absolute power in 1906 when the country adopted its first constitution. In 1908 the country discovered oil in the Persian Gulf area. The Pahlavi dynasty began in 1925 when Reza Khan, an army officer, seized the throne. In 1941 he was forced to abdicate, and his son, Mohammad Reza Pahlavi, became the last shah of Iran.

The shah initiated a massive modernization program in 1961, but development brought an influx of foreign workers with new, Western ideas. A nationalist uprising began to develop in 1977, and by January 1979 the situation was so serious that the shah fled the country, opening the door for the Ayatollah Ruhollah Khomeini, a radical religious leader, to seize power.

The Enigmatic Qadhafi: LIBYA

Perspective

1951	*Libya gains independence from Italy.*
1959	*Oil is discovered.*
1969	*Qadhafi leads a coup that overthrows King Idris.*
1973	*Libya confiscates United States' oil interests.*
1979	*Qadhafi gives up public office.*
1981	**August.** *U.S. and Libyan air forces clash over Gulf of Sidra.*
1986	**January.** *U.S. freezes Libyan assets.* **April 5.** *West Berlin discotheque bombing linked to Libya.* **April 15.** *U.S. bombs Libya.*
1989	**January 4.** *U.S. shoots down two Libyan military aircraft.*
1992	**January 21.** *United Nations demands that Libya extradite two suspected terrorists.* **March 31.** *UN imposes sanctions against Libya.*
1995	**September 7.** *Islamic militants riot against Qadhafi.*
1996	**August.** *Libyan troops allegedly bomb rebel military bases.*
1997	**October 22.** *Nelson Mandela calls for an end to UN sanctions.*

Colonel Mu'ammar al-Qadhafi, the charismatic and eccentric leader of Libya, is a favorite villain in the Western press. Qadhafi's power results from petroleum revenues that have been at his disposal since the mid-1970s, when the Arab oil boycotts caused world oil prices to escalate dramatically. Since then, relations between Libya and the West, notably the U.S., have been especially bitter. The U.S. and most of the other Western powers have objected in particular to Qadhafi's support, financial and otherwise, of international terrorist organizations. He has also angered fellow African leaders with his territorial ambitions, notably in Chad and Sudan, which have disrupted African political affairs.

Issues and Events

Relations between the U.S. and Libya reached an all-time low on April 15, 1986, when the U.S. Air Force hit five military targets in Libya to retaliate for the bombing of a West Berlin discotheque frequented by American military personnel. It is believed that more than 100 Libyans, including Qadhafi's adopted infant daughter, died during the bombings.

Relations between the two countries were strained again in late 1991 when the U.S. accused two Libyans of the 1988 bombing of Pan Am Flight 103 over Lockerbie, Scotland, which killed 270 people. The French also demanded justice for presumed Libyan involvement in the 1989 downing of a French airliner. In early 1992 the UN passed a resolution calling for extradition of those suspected in the bombings. Libya refused, and the UN imposed limited sanctions against Libya.

Libya claims that the alleged bombers cannot receive a fair trial in either the United Kingdom or the U.S., and has appealed to the International Court of Justice to set the trials in a neutral country. Qadhafi gained a powerful ally in 1997 when South African president Nelson Mandela defied the international community by visiting Qadhafi, calling for an end to the sanctions, and admonishing the West for refusing to negotiate with Qadhafi.

Qadhafi's reign is tenuous, demonstrated by persistent reports of clashes between his government and a growing number of militant Islamic protesters. The U.S. has not succeeded in its attempts to dethrone him by organizing an international oil embargo against Libya.

Oil-rich Libya undoubtedly will remain influential in the Arab world. Many Western countries see in Libya vast economic opportunities. Many poor African countries have received large sums of aid and see Libya as a great benefactor, while others fear Qadhafi's territorial goals. Most Arab leaders regard Qadhafi with suspicion, despite his diplomatic overtures and professed dedication to all Arab people.

Background

Following Libya's independence in 1951 from Italian colonial rule after World War II, the country was ruled by King Idris. King Idris was overthrown 14 years later by an army force led by 27-year-old Lt. Mu'ammar al-Qadhafi, who instituted massive economic reforms. Qadhafi also launched a cultural revolution to free Libya from foreign influences. Although he resigned from public office in 1979, Qadhafi has continued to rule the country despite his lack of a formal title.

Diplomatic ties between the U.S. and Libya were severed in 1981 after Libya was linked to international terrorist attacks. Qadhafi has unfailingly denied any involvement but he has been an outspoken advocate of Palestinian rights. He has been accused of helping train and shelter radical terrorists such as Abu Nidal's group, although he denounces acts of violence against innocent civilians. The U.S. has stated that Libya must end its support for terrorism before normal diplomatic ties can be reestablished.

A Clash of Cultures: SUDAN

Perspective

1898	*British and Egyptian forces conquer Sudan, administer it as two territories.*
1946	*Northern and southern territories are united.*
1955	*Fighting begins between north and south.*
1956	*Sudan gains independence.*
1962	*Fighting escalates to civil war.*
1969	*Military coup places Gaafar Nimeiry in power.*
1972	*Government and rebels sign peace accord in Addis Ababa.*
1983	Sharia *(Islamic law) imposed, causing renewed fighting.*
1985	**April 6.** *Military coup overthrows Nimeiry.*
1986	**April 11.** *Sadiq Mahdi becomes prime minister.*
1988	*About 250,000 die from famine.*
1989	**April 1.** *Operation Lifeline-Sudan prevents mass starvation.* **June 30.** *Military coup ousts Mahdi.*
1994	**March.** *Peace talks begin.*
1996	**January 31.** *UN condemns Sudan for sheltering terrorists.* **March 12.** *UN Human Rights Commission denounces Sudan.*

Sudan is the largest country in Africa—so large, in fact, that its people are irreconcilably diverse. Differences in their religions, languages, and cultures have polarized Sudan's two major ethnic groups and threaten to tear the country apart. Nine years after the two halves of the country were united in 1946, fighting erupted between the northern Islamic Arabs and the southern Christian and Animist blacks. The most recent round of violence began in 1983 when the Muslim-controlled government attempted to impose traditional Islamic law in the south, where most people do not practice Islam.

Issues and Events

The coup that overthrew the government of Sadiq Mahdi in 1989 sparked hopes that the ongoing conflict might end, but Sudan's new rulers proved equally ineffective at achieving a military victory and imposing Islamic law. Fighting between the government and the rebels continues, complicated by the splintering of the rebel forces into many factions. Both the government and its opponents routinely attack civilians. An estimated one million Sudanese have died from war or famine. Journalists have been evicted from the war zone, so very little world media attention has been focused on Sudan. Three million people have been displaced by the fighting, and the capital of Khartoum has been overwhelmed with an influx of poverty-stricken refugees from the south.

In early 1996, the UN condemned Sudan for sheltering terrorists accused of the attempted assassination of Egypt's president Hosni Mubarak in 1995, and mild diplomatic sanctions were passed three months later. In March 1996 the UN alleged that the Sudanese government engaged in torture, executions, rape, slave trading, and other human rights abuses. Aid workers also accuse the Sudanese government of trying to orchestrate a major famine in southern Sudan by destroying crops, stealing livestock, and blocking emergency food deliveries from international relief agencies.

Sudan's rulers want to ignite Iranian-style religious fervor among the people, but they have been unsuccessful. Increasingly isolated because of its support for Islamic terrorists, Sudan has been experiencing steady economic and political decline. Most people are tired of the war and weary of the current government's abuses, but there is no alternative leadership.

Several rounds of government-initiated peace talks, which began in 1994, have been unproductive. The government continues to insist that Islamic law must prevail in the south, while the rebels demand the right to determine their own future and practice their own religions.

Background

In 1898 British and Egyptian forces conquered Sudan. They governed the region as two territories until 1946, and in 1952 preparations began for Sudanese independence. The southern Sudanese feared domination by the northern Muslims and started a revolt that continues today, but Sudan became independent in 1956.

In 1957 Christian mission schools in the south were forced to close, and all foreign missionaries were expelled in 1964. The southern Sudanese responded with military resistance.

Col. Gaafar Nimeiry seized control of the government in a military coup in 1969. In 1972 he signed the Addis Ababa accord with the southern Sudanese, granting them some autonomy and temporarily halting the civil war. Renewed fighting resulted in 1983 when Nimeiry imposed the *sharia*—a controversial Islamic legal code that prescribes punishments such as flogging, amputation, and stoning.

Widespread famine, economic instability, and the ongoing war led to Nimeiry's downfall in a 1985 military coup. In 1986 Sudan held its first democratic election in 18 years, but the south protested the *sharia* by refusing to participate.

Sub-Saharan Africa

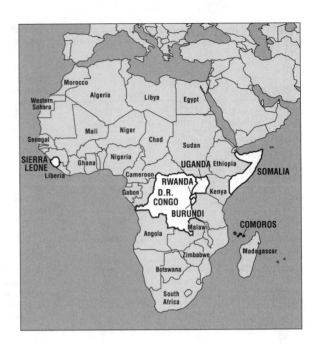

Home to more than ten percent of Earth's inhabitants, Africa is second in land area only to Asia. It is the most ethnically diverse continent; its people speak more than 1,000 different languages. This enormous variety creates unique challenges. Today's Africa south of the Sahara Desert is at a crossroads as it struggles to achieve political stability and economic prosperity.

Many of the problems that plague Africa today are the direct result of colonial occupation by European countries during the 19th and 20th centuries. Before the European occupation, the history of Africa—like that of all of the other continents—is marked by the growth and decline of various empires, such as those of the Aksum, Nubia, Ghana, Mali, and Kongo peoples. European intervention in African affairs began when the Portuguese started exploring the coastline in the 1400s. Soon thereafter a host of European explorers and missionaries began to try to penetrate the continent.

Unlike the Americas, where Europeans settled and decimated the indigenous people, Africa was not a favored destination for European colonists. The notable exceptions were the Dutch Boers, who settled large areas of South Africa that they claimed were uninhabited at the time of their arrival in the 1650s. The Europeans sought to establish trade and treaty relationships with Africa, to siphon off its resources without supplanting its people. Today, Africa remains 90 percent black, and most of those who are not black are Arab.

In the 1500s a lucrative slave trade began to supply laborers to Spanish and Portuguese colonists in the New World. By the 1700s, the slave trade exploded, and at least ten million Africans were forcibly deported to the Americas. The Spanish and Portuguese slave traders were joined by others from Britain, France, the Netherlands, Sweden, Denmark, and Germany.

Although the European countries and the United States eliminated slavery in the 1800s, commercial trade with Africa continued. As trade increased, territorial disputes among the Europeans arose. This led to the Berlin-West Africa Conference of 1884-85, where the countries of Europe devised preposterous boundaries that bore no relationship to African ethnic and tribal realities. By 1914 Belgium, France, Germany, Italy, Portugal, Spain, and the United Kingdom had colonized all of Africa except Liberia and Ethiopia. The Berlin Conference boundaries were rigorously imposed and enforced, regardless of local sentiments.

After World War II, most African countries began to seek independence from their colonial rulers, beginning in northern Africa with Libya in 1951 and spreading throughout the rest of the continent over the next 20 years.

The European-imposed boundaries of the newly independent countries sometimes enclosed enemy tribes within the same political unit, and in other cases divided a single ethnic group into several countries. This dangerous legacy of colonial rule became apparent in 1967 when the Ibo, one of three major ethnic groups enclosed within the boundaries of Nigeria, failed in their attempt to establish their own independent country called Biafra. More than two million people died as a result of fighting and ensuing famine. This horrific experience served as a warning to other African countries that any resistance to the European boundaries would be met with force. Further, the territorial integrity of the new states could be maintained only if the European concept of national identity could somehow replace traditional tribal loyalties. To this end, most African countries evolved into either single-party socialist states or one-man dictatorships. Often these governments were corrupt and oppressive, characterized by extravagance, censorship, and human rights abuses.

During the 1980s, most African countries began to shift to more democratic forms of government as a result of popular demand. In 1985 there were 36 states that had either no political party or only one legal party; by the end of 1995 that number had been reduced to four. The shift to democracy has not been easy. Most new political parties are based on ethnicity or tribal affiliations, causing ethnic tensions to rise. Many feared that when true democracy came to South Africa it would result in a race war between the whites and the blacks, or that the whites would be subjugated by the blacks. Although relations between South Africa's blacks and whites have been cooperative, tribal political violence among the blacks has increased significantly.

Similarly, struggles in Somalia, Liberia, and Sierra Leone started as political conflicts and degenerated into tribal or clan warfare. In all of these countries the conflict has been so devastating that it has resulted in the virtual collapse of the authority of the central government. Politics and ethnic hatred are also inextricably tied in Rwanda, where more than half a million people were killed in 1994, victims of an ancient rivalry between the Hutu and Tutsi people.

One stabilizing force in African politics has been the Organization of African States (OAU), founded in 1963 to mediate disputes between member countries. As a result of the OAU's efforts there have been few international wars in Africa, despite the problems inherent in the boundary situation. Although the OAU endorses the maintenance of existing political boundaries, it made an exception when it recognized Eritrea after it won independence from Ethiopia in 1993. The northern part of Somalia, which calls itself the Republic of Somaliland, hopes to follow in Eritrea's footsteps. It is inevitable that more new countries will try to seek independence, and that ethnic groups like the Tuareg, who are divided between Niger and Mali, will try to carve out their own countries.

Africa's unstable political situation has hindered its economic growth. With untold mineral riches and other natural resources, there is enormous potential for economic development. However, the standard of living in most African countries has declined steadily since independence. In some countries the infrastructure is deteriorating, and cities are strained from massive rural-to-urban migration. Many African countries are going through the same economic problems as the countries of Eastern Europe as they struggle to shift from centrally planned to market economies. Unfortunately, economic and political problems compound each other. For example, Nigeria's economy declined in 1994 despite its massive oil resources. This, in turn, has increased political unrest, which ultimately ignites tribal antagonisms, creates instability, and reduces much-needed foreign investment. Lack of economic opportunity also contributes to the duration of many African conflicts because soldiers can make a better living looting villages than working regular jobs.

Agriculture is another problem in Africa, where only about six percent of the land is arable, compared to 12 percent in North America and 16 percent in Asia. The continent is also subject to devastating droughts, such as the one that struck in the early 1980s and prompted worldwide relief efforts in Ethiopia and other areas. In many countries agriculture is accomplished at the subsistence level, and when war creates refugee situations agricultural production grinds to a halt. More than five million Africans have been forced to flee across international boundaries in recent years. The result is often malnutrition and starvation.

Other problems that beset Africa have already been solved in the rest of the world. Today, many African people suffer from tuberculosis, hepatitis, malaria, and other infectious diseases for which there are known cures and vaccinations. Africa is also plagued with other diseases for which there are no cures. Acquired Immune Deficiency Syndrome (AIDS), which has spread throughout the world, is believed to have originated in Africa. Estimates suggest that 70 percent of the people with AIDS live in Africa, and that they number more than nine million. Long ago the disease would not have spread beyond the continent, but with today's improved transportation and increasing urbanization it is now possible for tropical diseases to spread farther and faster than ever before.

The world was alarmed in 1995 by an outbreak of the mysterious Ebola virus, which had previously occurred in parts of Sudan and Democratic Republic of the Congo in 1976 and 1979. Scientists fear that other virulent tropical diseases may emerge and infect people throughout the world before a cure can be found. Conversely, it is also possible that Africa's vast rain forests and rich biological diversity may harbor cures for some of the incurable diseases that plague the Western countries.

Although Africa has many problems, it is a land of promise and opportunity. The rich diversity of its people and the abundance of its landscape will inevitably enable the continent to realize its economic potential. As the era of European domination ends, Africans will gain the experience and confidence that they need to seek their own unique solutions to the problems at hand.

Rift Valley Crisis: RWANDA

Perspective

1400s	Tutsi establish a monarchy in the Rwandan area.
1916	Belgium gains control of Rwanda.
1959	Rwandan war for independence ends with Hutu in power.
1962	160,000 Tutsi refugees flee Rwanda.
1973	July 5. Military coup launched by General Juvenal Habyarimana.
1990	Tutsi soldiers known as the Rwandan Patriotic Front (RPF) attempt to take over Rwanda.
1994	April 6. Habyarimana killed in suspicious plane crash. Hutu militia begin slaughtering Tutsi. July 18. RPF invades and declares victory over the Hutu government. One million Hutu flee to Zaire.
1996	December. Hutu refugees return.
1997	June. Hutu rebels launch a major insurgency, resulting in thousands of civilian casualties. December. UN accuses Rwandan army of killing 8,000 unarmed Hutu.

For centuries the cattle-rearing Tutsi and the agrarian Hutu lived together relatively peacefully along Africa's Rift Valley in the area now known as Rwanda. First Germany, then Belgium, set up regimes that insidiously played the two tribes against each other. The minority Tutsi were given preferential treatment, which raised the ire of the majority Hutu.

Ethnic and political tensions exploded in 1994 and the world witnessed one of history's most tragic cases of genocide. Hutu military units began a systematic killing spree in which at least 500,000 people—mainly Tutsi—were murdered. The massacre ended when Tutsi defeated the Hutu, but the hatred unleashed by these events remains strong.

Issues and Events

The violence began when the President of the Hutu-dominated government, Gen. Juvenal Habyarimana, was killed in a mysterious plane crash. Because the nationwide massacre of Tutsi began only hours after the crash, many suspect that the crash was engineered by radical Hutu who opposed the increasingly liberal government of the late President. Besides killing Tutsi, Hutu militia and government troops also execut-ed moderate Hutu who had favored political empowerment for the Tutsi.

Horrific reports filtered out to the rest of the world. Tutsi hiding in churches were locked inside while the buildings were set on fire. People were buried alive. Refugees were bombed. Entire villages were wiped out. Red Cross workers and the orphans they were guarding were killed.

The massacre ended in July 1994 when the Tutsi-dominated Rwandan Patriotic Front defeated the Hutu government. The RPF had been at war with the government since 1973 and, despite being outnumbered, were able to defeat the Hutu with their superior military skills and rigid discipline. Most of the RPF members had been refugees since the war for independence in the late 1950s and had served in the Ugandan army.

After the Tutsi gained control of the country, between one million and two million Hutu refugees fled Rwanda and ended up in refugee camps in neighboring countries, where starvation, exhaustion, cholera, and dysentery claimed thousands of lives. While many of the refugees were destitute, others brought considerable money with them. With this wealth, the Hutu were able to rearm themselves; reports claimed that some of the camps resembled training grounds. The refugees were forced to return to Rwanda by the end of 1996, although most did so reluctantly. By mid-1997 news began to surface that serious fighting had broken out between government troops and Hutu rebels, and that innocent civilians were being targeted routinely by both sides. Since then, thousands of people have been killed in ongoing violence.

In December the UN issued a statement accusing the Tutsi government of human rights violations, including the shelling of a cave where 8,000 unarmed Hutu were believed to have been hiding. It also criticized the government for arbitrary arrests and serious prison overcrowding. The government denies the accusations and asserts that it is doing everything possible to stop the Hutu attacks, establish justice by trying those accused of war crimes, and gain the confidence of the people. It is unlikely, however, that the Hutu will soon abandon their fight to regain control of the country.

Background

Tutsi kings ruled Rwanda for hundreds of years before the arrival of Europeans. Germany colonized Rwanda for a short time, but Belgium soon gained control. The first mass slaughter of Tutsi in Rwanda occurred in 1959, when 20,000 to 100,000 died, and the Hutu took power. Rwanda gained independence in 1962, and a 1973 military coup created a Hutu-dominated government.

Rwanda is a poor country that suffers from severe overpopulation. Observers fear that violence there could spark the first of many "population wars" caused by a scarcity of land and other resources.

Rift Valley Crisis: BURUNDI

Perspective

1400s	*Tutsi invade and dominate Hutu territory.*
1916	*Belgium seizes control of Burundi.*
1962	*Burundi gains independence with Tutsi in power.*
1972	*Hutu uprising kills 100,000 people.*
1987	**September 3.** *Pierre Buyoya leads a coup, establishes himself as President.*
1993	**June 1.** *Melchior Ndadaye, a Hutu, elected President of Burundi.* **October 21.** *Ndadaye killed, sparking countrywide violence.*
1994	**April 6.** *Presidents of Burundi and Rwanda killed in a suspicious plane crash.*
1995	**March 11.** *Violence escalates after a Hutu official is assassinated.*
1996	**July 25.** *Military coup places Pierre Buyoya back in power.* **July 31.** *Embargo imposed.*
1998	**January 1.** *Rebels attack Burundi's main airport, killing 300 people.*

Since gaining independence in 1962, the small mountainous country of Burundi has been a tribal battleground for the Hutu and the Tutsi. Although the Hutu form the majority, the Tutsi have long held the reins of power in the region. When European countries invaded the region in the 1900s and tried to establish Western-style governments, the results were devastating. Since then, Burundi has been plagued with repeated conflicts resulting in unimaginable suffering and hundreds of thousands of deaths.

Issues and Events

Melchior Ndadye won a surprise landslide victory in the presidential election in 1993 and ignited the latest round of violence because he was Burundi's first Hutu president following centuries of Tutsi domination. After less than five months in office, however, Ndadaye was killed in a coup attempt. The violence that erupted immediately following his assassination killed more than 100,000 people in the first year and produced more than 500,000 refugees.

By 1994, fighting had subsided somewhat so that Burundi remained relatively calm when Burundi's new president and the president of Rwanda were killed. In 1995 violence in Burundi flared again, however, and in 1996 the UN began to investigate rumors of genocide. The leaders of

Tanzania, Kenya, Uganda, Ethiopia, Rwanda, and Burundi began to discuss the feasibility of installing a regional peacekeeping force.

The Tutsi military were angered by the idea of foreign troops, and in mid-1996 they led a coup and reinstated former president Pierre Buyoya. Neighboring African countries retaliated quickly by imposing a total economic embargo against Burundi, but the embargo was so devastating to the poor that shipments of food, medicine, and essential items were allowed to resume. Attacks by Hutu rebels, especially the national Council for the Defense of Democracy (CNDD), escalated sharply after the Buyoya coup and continue today. Hutu guerrillas invade villages and force the people to join them, and then the army sweeps through and punishes the villagers for complying with the enemy. There are persistent rumors that entire villages are routinely destroyed and all inhabitants massacred by either the Hutu or the Tutsi. In one substantiated 1998 report, the rebels attacked Burundi's main airport and killed 300 unarmed people.

The CNDD says that it will fight until Buyoya relinquishes power and allows free elections, which would almost certainly be won by a Hutu. However, regardless of which tribe holds the presidency, real power is actually wielded by the Tutsi military, which will not tolerate a Hutu president. The Tutsi government calls the CNDD "genocidal maniacs" and believes their intention is to kill all of the Tutsi in Burundi.

The refugee camps that have been set up in Burundi, supposedly to protect villagers from Hutu rebels, are another serious problem. In reality, the camps are squalid death traps where hunger and disease are taking a serious toll.

At this time a negotiated settlement seems almost impossible. It is more likely that the hatred will eventually burn itself out after a few years, only to flare up again after a decade or so. Until the people of Burundi can learn to live together, a violent future is almost certain and regional stability will be imperiled.

Background

The Tutsi invaded the Great Rift Valley area in the 1500s and established a feudal monarchy with the Hutu as the peasants. In 1885, Germany gained control of the region, which was transferred to Belgium after World War I. Since independence, Tutsi have been in control both politically and economically. The country experienced major Hutu uprisings in 1965, 1969, 1972, and 1988. The 1972 fighting was among the worst, resulting in 100,000 deaths.

Surprisingly, there are few differences between the Hutu and the Tutsi: Both groups share the same language and culture. But the Hutu are poor and powerless, while the ruling Tutsi control the money and the power. In today's society, if a Tutsi experiences financial ruin, he is automatically downgraded to Hutu status.

Rift Valley Crisis: DEMOCRATIC REPUBLIC OF THE CONGO

Perspective

1960	**June 30.** *Republic of the Congo gains its independence from Belgium.*
1961	**January.** *Laurent Kabila leads rebellion after Lumumba is assassinated.*
1964	*Country name changed to Democratic Republic of the Congo.*
1965	**November 24.** *Col. Joseph Mobutu gains power following a coup.*
1971	**October.** *Mobutu changes the country name to Zaire.*
1990	**May 11.** *International condemnation follows student massacre.*
1991	**September 30.** *Parliament appoints Tshisekedi as Prime Minister.* **October 21.** *Mobutu dismisses Tshisekedi.*
1994	**April.** *One million Hutu refugees from Rwanda flock to Zaire.*
1996	**October 8.** *Kabila leads a rebellion.*
1997	**May 17.** *Kabila declares himself president and renames the country Democratic Republic of the Congo.* **May 23.** *Tshisekedi supporters launch protests.* **June 20.** *UN investigation begins.*

Soon after Col. Joseph Mobutu seized control of the newly independent Democratic Republic of the Congo in 1965, he sought to erase all evidence of colonial rule. Mobutu renamed himself Mobutu Sese Seko and changed the name of the country to Zaire. He shaped a new kind of socialist government that served as a model for other African countries before it degenerated into a corrupt dictatorship.

After 31 years of rule, Mobutu was defeated by longtime rival Laurent Kabila. In a symbolic act, Kabila changed the country name back to Democratic Republic of the Congo (D.R.C.). Unfortunately, the country has changed in name only. Kabila's new government seems to be as corrupt, repressive, and ineffective as Mobutu's.

Issues and Events

Mobutu was one of Africa's most powerful and resilient dictators: He hung onto power despite ongoing secessionist and pro-democracy movements. Ultimately, the uprising that led to his downfall was sparked, like so many other African disputes, by ethnic conflict.

Tribal warfare in neighboring Rwanda brought an influx of more than one million Hutu refugees into D.R.C., straining its scarce resources beyond their limits. Fighting on the D.R.C. side of the border erupted in 1996, and thousands of Hutu refugees were reportedly massacred.

The fighting gained momentum, and at first the composition of the rebel forces was unclear. By 1997 Laurent Kabila, one of Mobutu's long-time rivals, had emerged as the leader of the growing insurrection. In May the fighters reached the capital city, and Mobutu was forced to flee. Kabila quickly assumed the presidency, but demonstrations against him erupted almost immediately when he denied other long-time Mobutu political opponents, like Etienne Tshisekedi, a role in the new government.

Kabila had hoped that D.R.C. would receive development aid from the international community, but assistance was withheld after D.R.C. refused to allow UN investigators access to 100 mass grave sites where Hutu refugees were allegedly slaughtered by rebel troops. Western countries were also suspicious of Kabila's dictatorial style. Reports of corruption and human rights abuses continue to surface.

To further complicate the situation, fighting continues in eastern D.R.C. where Hutu, Tutsi, and other tribes battle for territorial control. Rwanda, Burundi, and Uganda claim that Kabila is not doing enough to control Hutu rebels from Rwanda who continue to use D.R.C. as their base, a situation that imperils regional stability. It is believed that several thousand people were killed during the second half of 1997.

Background

Europeans began to penetrate the African interior in the mid-1800s, and Belgium claimed the D.R.C. region. Anti-colonial demonstrations led to independence for the Belgian Congo in 1960. Upon independence, the country changed its name first to the Republic of the Congo, and then to Democratic Republic of the Congo. The country soon experienced turmoil in the wake of the mysterious assassination of Prime Minister Patrice Lumumba. Laurent Kabila emerged as one of many leaders of the rebellions that killed thousands.

In the 1960s, D.R.C. was of particular strategic importance to the United States because of its vast mineral resources and proximity to the Marxist uprising in Angola. The U.S. ultimately backed Mobutu in a successful 1965 coup.

Nationalization of foreign economic interests in 1973 was a disastrous mistake for D.R.C., and most of the enterprises became Mobutu's personal property. While Mobutu's personal wealth was estimated to be at least $5 billion, the country remains one of the poorest in the world despite its many resources. Today, the people of D.R.C. have a lower standard of living than they had during colonial rule.

Rift Valley Crisis: UGANDA

Perspective

1962	**October 9.** *Uganda gains internal self-government from Britain.*
1966	**February.** *Milton Obote assumes dictatorial powers.*
1971	**January 25.** *Idi Amin Dada seizes power in a military coup.*
1979	**April 11.** *Idi Amin ousted with the help of the Tanzanian military.*
1980	**December.** *Obote wins presidential elections. Yoweri Museveni forms the National Resistance Movement.*
1986	**January.** *Museveni's troops defeat government. Holy Spirit Movement begins.*
1987	**November.** *Holy Spirit Movement crushed. Joseph Kony recruits the Lord's Resistance Army (LRA).*
1994	*LRA receives support form Sudan.*
1996	**May 9.** *Museveni wins elections.*
1997	**June.** *Allied Democratic Forces emerge during rebellion in Democratic Republic of the Congo.*

While conflicts in Rwanda, Democratic Republic of the Congo (D.R.C.), and other countries along the Rift Valley have captured news headlines, Uganda has been quietly engaged in a violent conflict since 1986; tens of thousands have been killed. Despite the country's rich promise, Uganda's modern history has been one of dictatorship, bloodshed, and wasted opportunity.

Issues and Events

Like most of Uganda's modern leaders, Yoweri Museveni gained power after a violent takeover in 1986. Unlike the others, he has brought a measure of stability to this troubled country. Under his leadership prosperity has grown, the economy has expanded significantly, and corruption has been noticeably absent. In remote areas of Uganda far from the capital city of Kampala, however, seething resentment about the takeover erupted into a strange rebel movement. As Museveni assumed power, Alice Lakwena founded a Holy Spirit Movement based on Old Testament law and traditional animism. She convinced her followers that they could defeat Museveni's army without weapons because they had been anointed with the spirit of God.

Within two years the uprising had been defeated and Lakwena was forced to flee the country, but her followers joined a new group, under the leadership of Joseph Kony, called the Lord's Resistance Army. Unlike the Holy Spirit Movement, the LRA is a violent organization that has been accused of routinely massacring and mutilating civilians. It is estimated that as many as 8,000 children have been kidnapped and forced to join the LRA, and that tens of thousands of people have been killed in the fighting.

Museveni's interference in African politics has also threatened Uganda's stability. One of Museveni's ambitions is to increase economic cooperation among African countries so that they can end their dependence on foreign aid. In 1994 the LRA began to benefit from Museveni's foreign policy agenda when it started receiving military aid from neighboring Sudan in retaliation for Uganda's support of Sudanese rebels. Similarly, Uganda aided Tutsi rebels in D.R.C. during their insurrection in 1997, which led to the formation of another rebel group called the Allied Democratic Force. ADF seeks to overthrow Museveni because of his involvement in D.R.C. politics.

For many years these and other rural conflicts drew little attention from the outside world. During the last year, however, international aid donors have become increasingly alarmed about Uganda's growing military expenditures and the negative effect of ongoing guerrilla wars on continued economic growth. They are also concerned about Museveni's apparent unwillingness to establish democratic institutions (he claims that Western-style political parties don't work in Africa because they are invariably used as vehicles for promoting tribal domination and divisions), and Museveni has been increasingly criticized for his unwillingness to negotiate a settlement with any of Uganda's rebel groups. He has yet to demonstrate that he is capable of implementing a military solution to the problem.

Background

When Uganda gained self-government from Britain in 1962 its future looked bright. Unlike other African countries, it did not inherit a legacy of ethnic violence. Its transition to independence was peaceful, and because very few Europeans had settled in Uganda the country was uniquely untouched by societal schisms based on race, class, or economic status. It also possessed a wealth of natural resources and a well-established middle class capable of developing a competent, effective government and a prosperous economy.

Hopes for a promising future were dashed when Milton Obote seized control of the young government in 1966, followed five years later by Uganda's most famous dictator, Idi Amin Dada. Idi Amin ushered in an era of economic decline and massive human rights violations, during which as many as 100,000 Ugandans were murdered. Idi Amin was defeated in 1979 by Ugandan rebels backed by the Tanzanian army, but the military government that succeeded him brought more misery and conflict.

Corruption and Chaos: SIERRA LEONE

Perspective

1878	*Freetown established as a refuge for freed slaves.*
1961	**April 27.** *Sierra Leone achieves independence from Britain.*
1967	**March 17.** *Contested election causes the first of a series of military coups.*
1989	**December.** *War breaks out in Liberia.*
1990	**August 25.** *Sierra Leone participates in a Liberian peacekeeping force.*
1991	**March.** *Revolutionary United Front (RUF) launches rural guerrilla war along the Liberian border.*
1992	**December 30.** *Western countries protest the official execution of 26 people.*
1995	**January.** *Government launches major military offensive against the RUF.*
1996	**February 26.** *RUF boycotts elections.* **November 30.** *Government and RUF sign peace accord.*
1997	**May 25.** *Military coup brings return to chaos.*

As a British colony, Sierra Leone served as an important trade and education center in western Africa. Thirty years after gaining its independence, the country remained one of the world's poorest. Even before war broke out in 1991, the capital of Sierra Leone was already without phone, electrical, or television service. Neglect had transformed Freetown, once considered a charming city, into ruins. The country's currency was worthless, and the economy had shifted to a barter system. During the war, most of the remaining infrastructure was destroyed, and in the end the same officials who were responsible for Sierra Leone's economic and social demise were restored to power.

Issues and Events

With its ample mineral resources, Sierra Leone should be a wealthy country. Since its independence, however, government corruption has caused a steady economic decline. Government officials routinely sold out to foreign mining companies and accepted bribes from smugglers, who then plundered the country's mineral resources with impunity.

When war erupted in neighboring Liberia in 1989, Sierra Leone, along with other African countries, sent troops in an effort to end the war

and stabilize the region. Fighting broke out on the Sierra Leone side of the border, however, and quickly spread throughout most of the countryside. The Sierra Leone government stepped up its war against the rebels in 1995 by enlisting the aid of mercenaries, as well as soldiers from other African countries. It has been estimated that during 1995 the government spent at least three-quarters of its meager revenue on the war.

Little was known about the rebels, who called themselves the Revolutionary United Front (RUF). One theory was that the RUF was founded by Liberian rebels to punish Sierra Leone for its participation in the Liberian peacekeeping force. In addition to the RUF, there were also other rebel groups composed of renegade soldiers who roamed the countryside killing civilians and looting villages.

The civil war, which caused so much suffering, went largely unnoticed by the outside world. There were the same massacres of innocent civilians, the same refugee problems, the same starvation and disease, and the same tales of horror that in other places prompted international outrage. Estimates of the number of people who were killed vary widely, but if those who died of starvation are included, it is certain that tens of thousands perished.

By 1996 the war was winding down, and the military government agreed to hold elections. The elections restored the same former government officials who had been responsible for massive corruption in the past. The military staged a coup in 1997, and fighting resumed when Nigerian troops moved in to try to restore the elected government.

Months of chaos followed, with both the rebels and the new government fighting against the Nigerians. Food and fuel were unavailable, and civilians feared both the war and the repressive military leadership.

In early 1998 Nigerian forces broke through and defeated the military junta, paving the way for the return of the elected president one month later. Although the people of Sierra Leone were jubilant about the return of democracy, the prospects for peace and stability are dim, and the outlook for economic prosperity is even worse.

Background

Freetown, the capital of modern-day Sierra Leone, was founded in 1878 by the British as a haven for freed slaves. Today there are at least 20 different ethnic groups, and the Creoles who descended from the slaves are a sizable minority. The other main ethnic groups are the Mende and the Temne.

Sierra Leone became independent in 1961. Six years later, ethnic and political tensions erupted and the country experienced decades of military and civilian dictatorships. Sierra Leone also suffers from rapid population growth that has severely depleted forest, fish, and soil resources.

Clan Warfare in the Horn of Africa: SOMALIA

Perspective

1960	**July 1.** *Somalia receives independence from Italy and Britain.*
1969	**October 1.** *General Mohammed Siad Barre stages a coup.*
1977	**June.** *War with Ethiopia begins.*
1988	**April.** *War with Ethiopia ends.* **May.** *Civil war expands.*
1990	**December 28.** *Rebel forces attack Mogadishu.*
1991	**January 26.** *Siad Barre overthrown.* **January 28.** *Ali Mahdi Mohammed named President.* **May 18.** *Northeast Somalia secedes and forms the Somaliland Republic.*
1992	**September 14.** *UN troops arrive.* **December 9.** *United States sends 24,000 troops to Somalia.*
1993	**May 4.** *UN takes over relief effort.*
1994	**March 25.** *Most U.S. forces leave.*
1995	**March 3.** *UN soldiers withdraw.* **June 15.** *Aidid declares himself president of Somalia.*
1996	**August 1.** *Aidid dies in battle and is succeeded by his son.*
1997	**October.** *Anarchy contributes to flood disaster.* **December 22.** *New peace treaty signed.*

They were nightmarish pictures to startle a world seemingly immune to any more horrors: hundreds of thousands of Somalis dead from hunger—with thousands more mere walking skeletons, awaiting a tragic fate. The world collectively acted to stop the famine, a consequence of anarchy and clan fighting, which had destroyed the small African country's economic and social fabric. In 1992 international military forces led by the U.S. landed in Somalia with one goal: to restore order so that food aid could reach the starving people. After these foreign troops failed to restore peace, the world lost interest in Somalia. It is now up to the Somalis to devise their own solutions to their many problems.

Issues and Events

Somalia has been at war since 1977, when conflict with Ethiopia broke out over territorial control of the Ogaden region. When this war ended 11 years later, rural rebel groups that had been allied with the Ethiopians continued to fight against the Somali government.

In 1991, rebel troops ousted Siad Barre after 22 years of autocratic rule and set off a chain of events that plunged the country into an ever steeper downward spiral. Although Ali Mahdi Mohammed was appointed President days after Siad Barre's resignation, his government never gained control of the country. Clan warfare terrorized Somalia and created so many refugees that commerce, agriculture, and transportation were virtually halted. The result was famine.

In the fall of 1992, the UN and U.S. agreed to send 24,000 U.S. troops to Somalia to restore order. Although successful in providing immediate relief to the starving, the UN mission failed to bring about a permanent solution to Somalia's food crisis by helping the Somalis create a stable government. The U.S. withdrew most of its troops in 1994, and the UN followed in 1995.

During the UN mission one warlord, General Mohammed Farah Aidid, proved especially troublesome and was targeted by UN troops. Aidid eluded capture and declared himself president of Somalia in 1995, but he never gained real control of the country before his death in 1996. Aidid was succeeded by his son, a former U.S. Marine and resident of Los Angeles. The younger Aidid has shown greater interest than his father in negotiating a settlement with his rivals, and in 1997 26 of Somalia's 29 factions signed a peace treaty. One hopeful sign is that the new agreement was endorsed by the leader of the breakaway republic of Somaliland, which declared its independence from Somalia soon after the war began. If this agreement succeeds, it will create the first centralized government for all of Somalia since 1991.

Lack of central authority contributed to a major flood disaster in 1997 in which at least 1,400 people were killed. Famine, disease, and disaster will continue to plague Somalia until national unity is restored.

Background

Modern Somalia was formed when British and former Italian lands were merged to form an independent country in 1960. For the next nine years, the country enjoyed a thriving democracy, which ended with the assassination of the president by the army. General Mohammed Siad Barre was installed as president, and he established a socialist state.

During the next two decades, reports of human rights abuses increased. Siad Barre attempted to defuse the growing unrest by allowing limited democracy, but most felt that he was offering too little, too late. The coup that unseated Siad Barre took place only two months later.

Even before the war, Somalia was one of the world's poorest countries. It is largely undeveloped, and nomadic herding is the principal occupation. Clan rivalries abound despite the fact that almost all Somalis share the same culture, language, and religion.

Colonial Envy: COMOROS

Perspective

1841	*France gains control of Mayotte.*
1912	*The four Comoros islands become a French colony.*
1975	**July 6.** *Three Comoros islands declare their independence from France.* **August 3.** *President Ahmed Abdallah overthrown in a coup. A socialist government is installed.*
1978	**May 12.** *A second coup returns Abdallah to power. He establishes a one-party state.*
1989	**November 26.** *Abdallah assassinated.* **December 15.** *French troops restore order.*
1990	**March.** *First free elections held.*
1995	**September 28.** *Bob Denard launches an unsuccessful coup.* **October 4.** *French troops invade.*
1996	**February 4.** *Mohéli declares its independence from Comoros.*
1997	**August 3.** *Anjouan declares its independence from Comoros.* **September 3.** *Comoran invasion of Anjouan is repelled.* **October 26.** *Anjouan voters overwhelmingly support independence.* **December 13.** *Anjouan government rejects compromise at negotiations.*

L ocated between Malawi and Madagascar off Africa's southeast coast, the tiny country of the Comoros has had more than its share of trouble since it attained independence in 1975. Plagued by poverty, political instability, and physical disasters, the country now faces secessionist movements on two of its islands.

Issues and Events

The islands of the Comoros archipelago have been divided ever since the country gained independence from France in 1975. At that time three of the islands—Grand Comore (Njazidja), Anjouan (Nzwani), and Mohéli (Mwali)—opted for independence while the fourth island, Mayotte, voted to remain a French territory.

Since that time the Comoros has been in continual political upheaval. The country's first president was overthrown less than one month after taking power, and there have been more than a dozen coups or coup attempts. Much of the turmoil can be attributed to the presence of French mercenary Bob Denard, who made the Comoros

his home and was believed to have been involved in many of the coups. Some claim that he virtually ruled the country between 1978 and 1989. In 1995 he led a final attempt to overtake the government, but was thwarted when French troops invaded and arrested him.

Meanwhile, the island of Mayotte remained peaceful under French rule. With guaranteed minimum wages, free education, and better health benefits, the people of Mayotte enjoyed a much higher quality of life than the Comorans. By the mid-1990s many Comorans were risking their lives, swimming through shark-infested waters to find a better life in Mayotte.

Popular unrest continued to swell as the residents of Mohéli and Anjouan charged that most of the government's money went to projects on Grand Comore, the main island, at the expense of the other islands. Mohéli was the first to declare its independence in 1996, followed by Anjouan in 1997. Both islands have expressed interest in becoming French territories like Mayotte. While the separatist movement in Mohéli has been relatively quiet, Anjouan has been the site of serious rioting and demonstrations. One month after Anjouan declared its sovereignty, the Comoros military invaded the island with 300 underfed, ill-equipped troops who were quickly repelled or captured. The island has since elected a president and is trying to gain international recognition.

While France has stated that it is not interested in acquiring Anjouan and Mohéli, it has also done nothing to help the Comoros reestablish its authority on the islands. The Organization of African Unity (OAU) and the Arab League have denounced the separatist movements and are trying to facilitate a negotiated settlement. So far there has been little progress, and the discontented islanders have rejected the government's offer of more resources and regional autonomy.

Background

French influence in the Comoros began in 1841 when it gained possession of Mayotte. The islands were ruled as part of Madagascar from 1908 until 1912, when they became a separate colony. The French established plantations that grew vanilla, perfume oil, cloves, cocoa, copra, and other tropical crops. Most of the cash from these operations went back to France, however, and the Comoros remained impoverished.

The country is one of the world's poorest and least developed. It has a high population growth rate and few natural resources. Most of its people exist on subsistence agriculture, fishing, and French foreign aid.

Democracy has come slowly to the Comoros. Until its first free presidential elections in 1990, Comoros had been under authoritarian rule.

In addition to political instability, Comoros also contends with natural disasters. At least twice each decade cyclones and volcanic activity cause extensive damage.

South Asia

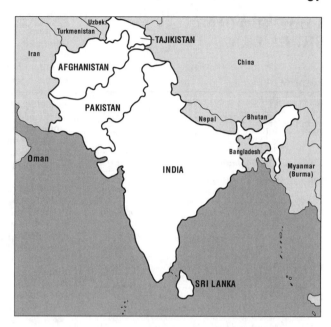

For modern manifestations of ancient problems, look to the major sources of conflict in South Asia. In India, the Sikhs have been fighting for their own country since Sikhism was founded in the fifteenth century. In Sri Lanka, the tribal wars between the majority Sinhalese and the minority Tamils can be traced as far back as the early centuries A.D., when the ancestors of the modern Tamils began migrating south from India. Afghanistan, strategically located between such great powers as Russia, Iran, and India, has historically been viewed as a buffer state by its powerful neighbors, who fought over it. The invasion of Afghanistan by the Soviet Union in 1979 is only the modern manifestation of Russia's traditional desire to extend its power to the south and gain Russian access to the Indian Ocean.

On top of the cessation of aid from the United States and Russia, Afghanistan faces a continuing civil war among various tribes and religious groups. In 1996 the *Taliban*, an Islamic fundamentalist group, captured the capital and began imposing elements of Islamic law.

Religious and tribal antagonisms and rivalries continue to abound throughout South Asia. The seemingly irreconcilable differences between the Hindus and Muslims in India have cost the lives of millions of Indians in the twentieth century. Hindu-Muslim violence has also sporadically erupted into wars between India and Pakistan. Though brief, these fierce battles have claimed the lives of tens of thousands of people since the Hindu Indians and the Muslim Pakistanis gained independence in 1947.

Many minority ethnic groups in India have been agitating for independence since the country was founded in 1947. The Muslim people of Jammu and Kashmir held out for independence rather than union with Pakistan, but eventually found themselves under Indian occupation. Sikhs have long sought their own homeland in the Punjab region and thousands have been killed in their struggle for independence. Violence has also flared in Assam, where Bodo tribesmen demand their own land, and in Nagaland, where the Naga people have rebelled against Indian rule.

Neighboring Pakistan is also wracked with violence as a result of the partition of India in 1947. Many Indian Muslims moved to Pakistan at the time of India's independence, and this upset the ethnic balance in urban centers such as Karachi. Today Karachi is plagued by ethnic and religious strife that has made it one of the most dangerous cities in the world. The country is also being torn by various radical factions of Islam.

To the south, Sri Lanka has been in the grip of an ethnic war between the country's Tamil and Sinhalese populations. The conflict has also enraged Tamils living in India.

Political violence is common throughout the region, and many of India's leaders have met violent ends. Mahatma Gandhi, architect of Indian independence from Britain, was killed by a Hindu radical. Prime Minister Indira Gandhi was killed by Sikh separatists, and her son Rajiv was also assassinated, allegedly by Tamil terrorists.

Tamil Terrorism:
SRI LANKA

Perspective

1948	**February 4.** *Sri Lanka (Ceylon) gains independence.*
1983	**July.** *Rioting sparks civil war between Sinhalese and Tamils.*
1987	**July 29.** *Indian troops sent to Sri Lanka.*
1989	**June.** *Tamil Tigers and government agree to a cease-fire.*
1990	**March 24.** *India withdraws troops.* **June.** *Renewed fighting breaks out; government declares war against Tamils.*
1991	**May 21.** *Rajiv Gandhi, India's prime minister, is assassinated.*
1992	**May 20.** *India formally charges the Tamil Tigers with Gandhi's death.*
1993	**May 1.** *Sri Lanka's president assassinated.*
1994	**November 9.** *New president elected.*
1995	**January 8.** *Cease-fire takes effect.* **April 18.** *Tamils break cease-fire.* **December 6.** *Rebels ousted from their headquarters at Jaffna.*
1996	**January 31.** *Tamil truck bomb in the Sri Lankan capital of Colombo kills 80 people.* **July 18.** *Rebels attacks army base.* **July 24.** *Commuter train bombing kills 78 people.*
1997	**May 13.** *Government launches a major offensive.*
1998	**January 25.** *Truck bomb damages Sri Lanka's most holy Buddhist temple.* **March 5.** *Bus bomb kills 32 people in Colombo.*

Sri Lanka, formerly Ceylon, a teardrop-shaped island off the southern tip of India, has long been plagued by violence between factions of the majority Sinhalese and the minority Tamils. The Sinhalese, who compose three-quarters of the population, are primarily Buddhist, while the Tamils are primarily Hindu and speak the language of the 50 million Tamils in India. The Tamils live mainly in northern and eastern Sri Lanka, which is less prosperous than the south and west.

Issues and Events

Traditional rivalries exploded into violence in 1983 when the Tamil Tigers, a radical separatist guerrilla group, killed 13 Sinhalese soldiers. In response to what they claim is centuries of discrimination and mistreatment by the ruling Sinhalese, the Tamil Tigers aspire to establish an independent Tamil nation called Ealan in northern Sri Lanka.

Since the fighting began, the sporadic war has escalated; more than 50,000 Sri Lankans have been killed. The Tamils have been accused of ethnic cleansing in areas under their control, and the government has repeatedly been criticized for torture and other abuses against the Tamils. Neighboring India, which also has a large Tamil population, became involved in 1987 when it sent troops to monitor a negotiated settlement and enforce a cease-fire agreement.

The Tamil Tigers, as well as other Sri Lankans, resented the presence of the Indian troops. The level of violence quickly escalated. The withdrawal of Indian troops in March 1990 did not improve the situation. Fighting intensified three months later as the Tamils and Sinhalese abandoned their negotiations and resumed their struggle for a decisive victory.

The violence spilled over into India when an organizer of the Tamil Tigers was accused of masterminding the 1991 assassination of India's former prime minister, Rajiv Gandhi. The Tamil rebels denied involvement in the crime, but it was a Tamil woman who carried the suicide bomb that killed Gandhi. Sri Lanka's own president was assassinated in 1993.

By 1994 most Sri Lankans were anxious for a return to peace, but negotiations during 1995 were fruitless and the conflict quickly escalated. In 1997 the government launched a major offensive, intent on winning the war. Months of heavy fighting ensued in the northern part of the country, and the Tamil Tigers began a new wave of suicide bombings in the capital and other major cities. Animosity reached unprecedented heights in early 1998 when the rebels exploded a truck bomb at the site of Sri Lanka's most holy Buddhist shrine.

The Tamils vow that they will continue to fight until they are recognized as an independent country. Although the government is capable of inflicting serious casualties, it has been unable to win the war. Even if the army were to regain control of areas that are currently under the Tamil control, it is unlikely that the bombings and terrorist attacks would cease.

Background

The Sinhalese have lived on the island of Ceylon since the sixth century B.C., but the Tamils did not appear in substantial numbers until the tenth century. Controlled first by India, then by the Portuguese, the Dutch, and finally, the British, Ceylon achieved independence on February 4, 1948. The country adopted a new constitution on May 22, 1972, which changed the island's name from Ceylon to the Republic of Sri Lanka.

Cold War on the Subcontinent: INDIA AND PAKISTAN

Perspective

1947	**August 15.** *India and Pakistan gain independence from Britain.* **October.** *War between India and Pakistan begins.*
1949	**January 1.** *War ends. United Nations mandates plebiscite.*
1965	**August.** *Armed Azad Kashmir troops invade India from Pakistan.*
1971	**December 3.** *War breaks out in Kashmir over India's support for Bangladesh.*
1988	*Kashmiri dissidents begin an armed insurrection.*
1991	**May.** *Indian troops kill 66 militants during one week of fighting.*
1992	**February 12.** *Pakistani troops shoot Azad Kashmiri dissidents.*
1995	**May 11.** *A disastrous fire erupts during a standoff between Indian troops and Kashmiri rebels.*
1997	**August 23.** *India and Pakistan exchange artillery fire.*
1998	**May.** *India detonates a series of underground nuclear bombs; Pakistan responds with its own nuclear tests.*

Nestled high in the remote Himalayas, the Vale of Kashmir is renowned for its legendary beauty. Part of the region known as Jammu and Kashmir, this picturesque and densely populated valley is the setting for a decades-old stand-off between Pakistan and India that has produced three wars and could spark a nuclear showdown between the two regional powers.

Issues and Events

Relations between India and Pakistan were already strained when Kashmiri separatists in India began to wage a major terrorism campaign in 1988. Ongoing bombings, kidnappings, and strikes prompted the Indian government to send troops to the area in December 1989. Massive demonstrations ensued, and Pakistan accused Indian troops of indiscriminate burnings, shootings, abductions, and torture of innocent Muslim Kashmiris. India accused Pakistan of arming and training Kashmiri rebels in camps on the Pakistani side of the border, known as Azad Kashmir. Pakistan denied training the rebels, but continued to champion their cause and provide them with arms.

Kashmiris are divided on the future of the region: Some favor union with Pakistan, while others want independence. The Pakistani government wants India to allow the Kashmiris to decide their own future. India maintains that Jammu and Kashmir are integral parts of India.

Tensions remain high, and thousands are killed each year. In 1992 war was narrowly averted when Pakistani radicals tried to march into India. They were stopped only after Pakistani troops opened fire on the group. In 1995 violence escalated after Indian police beseiged an Islamic shrine occupied by Kashmiri rebels. More than 600 homes and businesses were engulfed by an ensuing fire. Both the Indian army and Pakistani militants were accused of setting the blaze.

Although these and many other incidents have been resolved without disaster, more than 150,000 Indian and Pakistani troops are stationed in the region and there is a constant threat of all-out war. Sporadic artillery battles continued throughout 1997.

The threat of a nuclear confrontation continues to increase. India first tested nuclear weapons in 1974, and in 1998 it became a nuclear weapons state after successfully completing a series of underground tests. Pakistan was outraged by the testing and responded with its own underground tests. Both countries are poor and cannot afford to divert their scarce resources to a nuclear arms race. However, India claims that it needs nuclear weapons to defend itself against China, and Pakistan asserts that it must provide a clear nuclear deterrent to India.

Background

Home to both Hindus and Muslims, Jammu and Kashmir has long served as a battleground. Trouble began when Britain created two independent countries in the region. Pakistan was envisioned as a Muslim homeland, and India, although predominately Hindu, was established as a secular nation. Jammu and Kashmir was given the opportunity to join either India or Pakistan, but it held out for independence.

In October 1947 Pakistani-backed Kashmiri militants demanding independence led an armed revolt. The Kashmiri government enlisted the aid of India to stop the violence, leading to the first war between India and Pakistan. According to the terms of a truce in 1949, the Kashmiri people were to be allowed to determine their future by means of a plebiscite, or referendum.

War broke out again in 1965 when armed Azad Kashmir troops from Pakistan once again invaded India. More than 20,000 people were killed in the month of fighting that ensued. The next crisis began in 1971, when Pakistan accused India of aiding East Pakistan (now Bangladesh) in its quest for independence. In retaliation Pakistan invaded Jammu and Kashmir, but was defeated. The fighting lasted only two weeks but left 11,000 people dead.

Sectarian Politics in a Secular State: INDIA

Perspective

1528	*Babri mosque built on the site of a Hindu temple.*
1850s	*British gain control over most of India.*
1855	*Indians try to destroy Babri mosque.*
1947	**August 15.** *India gains its independence but is partitioned to form a Muslim homeland called Pakistan. Unprecedented violence erupts between Hindus and Muslims.*
1948	**January 30.** *Indian leader Mahatma Gandhi killed by a Hindu radical.*
1949	*Babri mosque is ordered closed.*
1980	*Bharatiya Janata Party (BJP) formed.*
1984	*Hindu fundamentalists launch a campaign to destroy the Babri mosque.*
1989	**November.** *BJP gains support in national elections by supporting Hindu fundamentalists.*
1990	**September.** *BJP stirs up violence when it sponsors a march to protest the Babri mosque.*
1991	**June.** *BJP becomes the major opposition party in national elections.*
1992	**January 26.** *BJP marches to protest separatist movements in Kashmir and the Punjab. Thirty people are killed.* **December 6.** *Babri mosque razed during a BJP rally. Rioting breaks out throughout the country.* **December 15.** *Federal government ousts all BJP-controlled state governments.*
1993	**January 6.** *Serious rioting erupts in Bombay when Hindus attack Muslims.* **March 12.** *Thirteen bombs detonated in Bombay kill 260 people.*
1995	**March.** *BJP gains strength in state elections.*
1996	**May.** *BJP wins national elections but fails to form a government.*
1998	**February 14.** *Fifty people are killed in bombings by Muslim extremists.* **March.** *BJP wins parliamentary elections and forms coalition government.*

When India gained its independence in 1947, tensions between Hindus and Muslims exploded and threatened India's survival. One million people were left dead in the wake of the fighting. Although the government eventually established order, the resentment between Hindus and Muslims continues to smolder. In the early 1990s, a Hindu nationalist movement threatened to again plunge the country of almost 900 million into religious violence.

Issues and Events

At the center of the most recent conflict between the Hindus and the Muslims is the sixteenth century Babri mosque in the city of Ayodhya. For Hindu fundamentalists seeking to establish Hinduism as India's state religion, the Babri mosque has long been a symbol of Hindu subjugation to foreign rule. The mosque is believed to have replaced a Hindu temple to the god Rama in 1528. It was locked up in 1949 to prevent any further quarreling about the site.

Trouble began again in 1984 when Hindus launched a campaign to destroy the Babri mosque and rebuild a Hindu temple on the site. In 1986 the government tried to placate the Hindus by permitting them to worship on the grounds of the Muslim shrine. This action only encouraged the fundamentalists in their drive to take over the land, and in 1989 they began collecting holy bricks for their new temple. This action sparked rioting by Muslims throughout India.

The Babri mosque issue took on political overtones when the cause was embraced by the Bharatiya Janata Party, one of India's many minor political parties. Backing from the Hindu fundamentalists gave the BJP a new base of support, and it did well in elections held in 1989. The BJP then began to campaign actively for the destruction of the mosque, and in September 1990 they sponsored a march that once again stirred up communal violence between Hindus and Muslims. The following month thousands of militants gathered at the site and tried to destroy the mosque. Once again rioting broke out and 1,000 people were killed in clashes across India. This incident ultimately led to the downfall of India's Prime Minister V.P. Singh and served notice that the BJP's power was increasing dramatically.

In 1991 the BJP's success in stirring up Hindu nationalist sentiments was reflected in Indian elections. The BJP became the leading opposition party in India, second only to the Congress party that has ruled India since its independence. Several months later the BJP-controlled government of the state in which the mosque is located took possession of the land, but the Indian Supreme Court ordered the state not to alter the site.

Despite ongoing negotiations between the Indian government and the BJP, the situation exploded in December 1992 when a BJP demonstration turned ugly and Hindu radicals reduced the mosque to rubble. Muslims throughout India and neighboring countries were infuriated by the act, and well over 1,000 people were killed in the ensuing riots that gripped the country for days.

The Indian government responded by outlawing all four BJP-controlled state governments, arguing that because they had supported radical Hindu groups banned by the Indian government they had failed to maintain the separation of church and state.

In January 1993 an international incident was avoided when Bangladeshi police turned back 150,000 Muslims who were threatening to invade India and rebuild the mosque. Two days later severe rioting broke out in Bombay, India's commercial and financial capital, when Hindu radicals began targeting Muslim homes and businesses. Hundreds of Muslims were killed, many of them burned alive. Almost 100,000 Muslims evacuated the city. The government was accused of inaction, and the police were charged with complicity in the massacre.

In February the government tried to prevent any further violence by barring the BJP from staging in the capital of New Delhi a massive demonstration to demand fresh elections. The BJP hoped to be catapulted to power by the momentum of the growing Hindu nationalist movement. Although the government contained the BJP by arresting tens of thousands and assaulting demonstrators with tear gas, water cannons, and rubber bullets, the BJP became known as a force to be reckoned with.

In March, just as Bombay was recovering from the January riots, the city was terrorized by a series of bombings that left several buildings in ruins and killed more than 250 people. It is widely believed that the bombings, which were carried out by organized crime figures, were in retaliation for the January riots.

In 1996 legislative elections the BJP claimed more seats than any other single party, but was unable to find enough allies to form a coalition government. As a result, the government collapsed in a mere 13 days. Two years later they won again, and this time a successful coalition was formed. In exchange for the support of other parties, the BJP was forced to temporarily abandon some of its more extremist policies.

Some fear that factional violence will rise as a result of the BJP victory. The elections were marred by violence between Hindus and Muslims, and in the city of Coimbatore more than 50 people were killed in multiple bombings attributed to one of many new Muslim extremist groups.

The BJP claims that factional violence has not increased in the states where it has gained control, and that Muslims have not been driven out or overtly discriminated against. Supporters of the party applaud the BJP's efficiency and honesty in government, but detractors warn that the party is closely allied with the National Self-Service Organization (RSS), a paramilitary group that models itself after Germany's Nazis. It was an RSS member who assassinated Mahatma Gandhi in 1948. The BJP is also supported by the Shiv Sena, another Hindu radical group that also promotes German-style fascism and is allegedly responsible for the 1993 riots in Bombay.

Background

Civilization in India began around 2500 B.C. in the Indus River valley, and Hinduism is the traditional religion that developed with the Indian culture. Islam is a relative newcomer to the region, having arrived in India with Turkish and Afghan invaders in the tenth and eleventh centuries.

In 1525 India was conquered by Babur, a descendant of Genghis Khan, who established the Mogul Dynasty in India. Three years later the Muslim invaders reputedly tore down a Hindu temple in Ayodhya and built in its place the Babri mosque in Babur's honor.

The British gained their first foothold in India in 1619, and by 1850 they were in control of almost all of India. As the increasingly restive Indian population began to protest against British rule, the mosque at Ayodhya became one of the targets of their frustration. The first demonstration at Ayodhya took place in 1855.

In 1920 Mahatma Gandhi initiated a popular movement against the British colonialists that eventually led to Indian independence in 1947. On the eve of independence, the British tried to solve the problem of rising tensions between Indians and Muslims by partitioning India into Hindu and Muslim homelands. The Hindu part became the secular republic of India, which stressed tolerance and respect for all religions. The predominately Muslim areas east and west of India were called Pakistan, but the eastern part ultimately broke away from Pakistan and named itself Bangladesh.

The partition of India created disaster when violence between Hindus and Muslims erupted and as many as one million people were killed. More than ten million people fled to their new homelands to avoid being targeted by mobs who sought to wipe out any minorities in their midst. The violence subsided only after Mahatma Gandhi was assassinated by a Hindu radical.

Since that time, the specter of Hindu-Muslim violence has loomed large in India, where Muslims still constitute more than ten percent of the population. The Indian government has continually sought to placate the Muslims and other minorities, but their efforts have not always been fruitful. Muslims in Jammu and Kashmir began an armed insurrection against the Indian government in 1988, and Sikh militants in the Punjab region of India were responsible for the assassination of Prime Minister Indira Gandhi in 1984. The Indians have a reputation for ruthlessness in these conflicts, and thousands have been killed in recent years.

Taliban Takes Over: AFGHANISTAN

Perspective

1919	**August 19.** *Afghanistan gains independence from Britain.*
1978	**April 28.** *Violent coup establishes Marxist government.*
1979	**December.** *Soviets invade Afghanistan, sparking a prolonged war against the* mujahidin.
1986	**May 4.** *Najibullah rises to power.*
1989	**February 15.** *Soviets complete troop withdrawal.*
1992	**January 1.** *United States and Russia agree to halt arms shipments.* **April 25.** Mujahidin *invade Kabul and depose Najibullah.* **May 5.** *War among various tribal groups begins. Kabul is devastated.*
1996	**September 27.** Taliban *conquers Kabul and establishes a strict Islamic regime.*
1997	**May.** Taliban *suffers major defeat in northern Afghanistan.*

Afghanistan has been at war since 1979. First, it was the target of Russian expansionism and rural tribesmen fought to expel the Soviet invaders. After the Soviets were repelled, the tribes continue to fight among themselves and the war continued unabated. By 1996 most of Afghanistan had been conquered by the *Taliban*, a religious group that established an Islamic government so repressive that it made Iran's theocracy seem liberal by comparison.

Issues and Events

The *Taliban* made its first appearance in 1994, just two years before it captured Kabul, the capital of Afghanistan. Because the group promoted traditional religious and tribal values, it encountered very little military resistance and was often greeted as a liberating force as it swept across the rural countryside. It denounced rival *mujahidin* leaders for their corruption, ambition, and disregard for civilian lives. Fearing the wrath of both God and the people, regional warlords usually surrendered their territories to the *Taliban* without a battle.

After taking control of Kabul, the *Taliban* instituted a strict Islamic regime. Women were forced to give up their jobs and stay indoors, and girls were forbidden to go to school. Men were forced to pray five times a day. A general ban was placed on all movies, televisions, cassette recorders, and VCRs. A strict dress code was put into effect, and religious police were established to enforce the new laws. As in Iran and Sudan, a controversial legal system called the *sharia* was adopted to impose harsh punishments (flogging, amputation, and stoning) for crimes such as stealing and adultery.

Surprisingly, Iran is strongly opposed to the *Taliban*. Although Iran and Afghanistan are both run by Islamic fundamentalists, it is there that the similarities end. Iranian leaders are from the Shiite sect of Islam, while the *Taliban* is made up of Sunni Muslims. Iran is committed to spreading its religion beyond its own borders, while the *Taliban* has little interest in the outside world.

Meanwhile the war continues unabated in the northern Afghanistan, home to most of the country's minority ethnic groups. Under the leadership of Gen. Abdul Rashid Doestam, an anti-*Taliban* alliance has successfully blocked the advance of the *Taliban* into this part of the country. Thousands of *Taliban* soldiers are believed to have been killed, many of them as prisoners of war. This kind of brutality was also demonstrated by the *Taliban*, which is believed to have massacred hundreds of villagers in early 1998. The *Taliban* has also been accused of blocking humanitarian aid, poisoning wells, and destroying crops.

Although there have been no reports of mass executions or arrests, people are routinely beaten for violating the strict Islamic laws. The *Taliban* claims that it has the support of the people and that it will eventually unify the country under one government and one religion.

Background

Turbulence has been the only constant in the region now called Afghanistan, located in the path of major trade and invasion routes from central Asia into the Middle East and India. All of the invasions created great ethnic diversity among the people of the region, and society developed as a complex network of tribal interrelationships.

The arrival of Islam in A.D. 642 provided a common bond among the various tribes, which united to form a country in 1747. After resisting a British takeover in the 1800s, Afghanistan gained full international recognition in 1919. Political stability was elusive, however, and real power was still vested in tribal leaders.

After an internal Marxist coup in 1978, Afghanistan was invaded by the Soviet Union during the following year. Despite the fact that Afghanistan suffered more than two million deaths during this period, the Soviets were unable to win the war and they finally gave up in 1989. Tribal warfare broke out in 1992 after the Soviets stopped sending aid to Afghanistan's government, which was under the leadership of the Soviet-appointed Najibullah. The ensuing conflict killed at least 25,000 people and virtually destroyed the capital.

Communism Prevails:
TAJIKISTAN

Perspective

1825	*Russians invade Central Asia.*
1929	*Tajik Soviet Socialist Republic formed.*
1991	**September 9.** *Tajikistan declares its independence.* **November.** *Rakhmon Nabiyev elected president.*
1992	**March.** *Violent demonstrations begin.* **May 11.** *Coalition government installed.* **June.** *Fighting erupts between supporters and opponents of the new government.* **September 7.** *Opposition forces seize the capital, force Nabiyev to resign.* **December 10.** *Communists regain power.*
1993	**March 3.** *Russian peacekeeping forces arrive in Tajikistan.*
1996	**June 27.** *Peace agreement is signed.* **August 9.** *Fighting erupts in Dushanbe.* **November 22.** *Rebel group abducts French aid workers.*
1997	**January 15.** *Peace talks break down.*

The demise of the Soviet Union caused many of its former republics to implement democratic reforms. The pattern has been different in most of Central Asia, where Communists have remained in command. Throughout Central Asia people fear that democracy will pave the way for radical Islamic rule, and the Communists play on these fears by asserting that only they can guarantee peace and stability. In Tajikistan the Communists were briefly usurped by reformers, but they managed to regain power by launching a bitter civil war in which tens of thousands were killed. Communist rule was strengthened by the introduction of Russian peacekeeping forces to keep the rebels at bay.

Issues and Events

The first serious threat to Communist leadership took place in March 1992 when a series of violent demonstrations was launched by a coalition of opposition forces. One of the main groups, known as the Democratic Party of Tajikistan, was founded by intellectuals who promoted market reforms and increased political freedom. The other group, called the Islamic Renaissance Party, emphasized traditional religious values. Despite the fact that Tajikistan's Muslims are of the moderate Sunni sect and have expressed no desire to establish an Iranian-style autocracy, the Islamic Party was labeled as a radical Islamic fundamentalist group by the Communists.

Continuing pressure forced the government, under the leadership of former Communist party boss Rakhmon Nabiyev, to allow these groups a limited role in the government, but this failed to appease opponents of the Communists. Fighting broke out, fueled by arms that began pouring into Tajikistan from neighboring Afghanistan. In September Nabiyev was forced to resign, and in October the Communists were ousted from the capital city of Dushanbe.

The reformers failed to consolidate their rule, and two months later the Communists managed to retake the capital. The Communists immediately implemented a Stalin-like purge, and hundreds of thousands of villagers were forced to negotiate Tajikistan's rugged landscape and seek shelter in neighboring Afghanistan.

Despite the signing of a major peace agreement in 1997, the situation remains highly volatile because most of the country remains under the control of minor rebel groups that have not been incorporated into the peace process. In August fighting broke out in the capital city between troops allied to rival government officials. In September there were terrorist bombings, and in October there was an assault on a government military base. The international community expressed outrage in November when a French aid worker was abducted and killed, and by early 1998 the peace process seemed to have broken down. The opposition claims that the government is not moving quickly enough to share power. The government responds that the opposition has violated the accord by perpetuating violence throughout the country.

Background.

Iranian people settled in the region around the first century B.C., and the area was subsequently invaded by many different groups through the centuries. From marauding Persians the Tajiks inherited their language, and from the Arabs Tajikistan received its Islamic heritage. In 1895 Russia conquered Tajikistan along with the rest of Central Asia. Most Tajiks were opposed to Russian rule and fought against the Bolsheviks for several years before they were finally subdued in 1925. Violence continued as the Soviets seized all farmland and tried to force the people to abandon Islam.

The Russians remained suspicious of the Tajiks, and thus the Tajiks were ignored when the Soviets initially carved the region into republics. Tajikistan was not recognized as a separate state until 1929. The Soviets did little to establish industry in Tajikistan; economic activity was mainly confined to growing cotton. Despite an unrelenting campaign against religion throughout the Soviet period, Islam remained an important part of Tajik culture.

Europe

The end of the twentieth century will be remembered as a time when change came to Europe at a dizzying pace. In the east, new political and economic structures replaced the totalitarian Communist governments that were legacies of the two World Wars in the first half of the 1900s. In the west, countries buried old resentments and worked to forge a Europe unified both politically and economically.

The World Wars devastated much of the continent and ultimately divided Europe into East and West. While the Soviet Union controlled the countries of the East, the countries of Western Europe were allied with the United States, and Germany was partitioned between the two. The "Cold War," an ideological and military standoff that saw a massive military buildup and severe restrictions on communications, trade, and travel between the two sides, characterized European politics during this era. The nations of Eastern Europe evolved into Soviet-style, centralized Communist governments dominated by policies set by Moscow, while Western Europe maintained its capitalist systems; each bloc jealously guarded its sovereignty against outside influences.

By the late 1980s it became apparent that the Cold War was coming to an end as the countries of Europe shifted their priorities to the revitalization of their economies. Both the decentralized capitalist countries and the centralized socialist countries were suffering from low growth rates, a decreasing standard of living, and an aging industrial base. While inflation, recession, and unemployment plagued the capitalist countries, the socialist countries suffered more from morale problems within the work force, which resulted in declining productivity and severe distribution problems. Trade deficits became a major issue as light, high-technology industries were developed in the United States, Japan, and other Asian countries. The world market was subsequently flooded with ingenious products that Europeans wanted to own but were not prepared to produce.

Ironically, each of the two opposing sides in the Cold War looked to the other for a new direction in an attempt to dispel its economic woes. The West moved toward centralization while the East has been decentralized; the West experimented with socialism while the East opened the door to capitalism and democracy. These transitions have not been easy, but they are signs of a Europe that will continue to transform itself in the coming decades.

Western European centralization has been taking shape as the European Union attempts to bridge centuries of national and economic rivalries to create a common prosperity. In 1993, the nations of the European Union took a dramatic step toward unity when they removed many trade, enterprise, and mobility barriers themselves. They are also working toward full monetary union using a single currency. But these moves have not been easy, and the question of full political union has been hotly debated. The United Kingdom, for one, has been very reluctant to relinquish any sovereignty to a supranational European state.

The desire to create more equitable societies has led individual European countries such as Sweden, France, and Greece to experiment with socialist programs that have had varying degrees of success. None of the countries of Western Europe used the Soviet model for development—a monolithic, centralized, single-party Communist state. Instead, socialists rose within the existing multi-party political framework and exerted their influence to enact socialist legislation.

Overshadowing the affairs of Western Europe have been the astonishing changes that have ripped through the former Soviet Union and the nations it once dominated. Following World War II, policies set by Moscow firmly governed Eastern Europe, which had learned the lessons of the Soviet military invasions of Hungary in 1956 and Czechoslovakia in 1968 following protests for reform and increased personal freedom. The Soviet Union, with its vast natural resources, supplied raw materials to the countries in its sphere of influence, which automatically returned manufactured goods to the Soviet Union. This closed economic system, along with declining productivity, resulted in ever-increasing shortages in the entire Soviet bloc.

Mikhail Gorbachev's rise to power in the Soviet Union marked the dawn of a new age. His program of restructuring, or "perestroika," decentralized some of the decision-making in the Soviet economy to encourage the development of privately owned enterprise that will stimulate growth and alleviate shortages. Gorbachev also implemented a policy of "glasnost," or openness, the purpose of which was to speed the reform process, stimulate creativity and personal initiative, and prepare the way for more decentralized decision-making. Glasnost resulted in greater personal freedom, artistic expression, and access to information.

In the Soviet Union, glasnost had a profound effect, especially on the country's 100 ethnic minorities who, for the first time, were allowed to express their grievances about Soviet rule. New political parties founded along ethnic lines sprang up across the country as various nationalities began to press for more autonomy and even independence. Glasnost also fueled rising nationalism, which led to renewed animosity between various ethnic groups. Fighting soon erupted between the Armenians and their Turkish rivals in neighboring Azerbaijan.

Another significant change in Soviet policy was the renunciation of the so-called "Brezhnev Doctrine," which asserted the Soviets' right to interfere in the affairs of other Communist countries. Accordingly, the Soviets began to withdraw their troops from many foreign countries, including the countries of Eastern Europe.

Cautiously at first, the countries of Eastern Europe began to test the limits of the new Soviet tolerance. When it became clear that the Soviet military was no longer a threat, reform movements and revolution began to spread across Eastern Europe like wildfire. In 1988 the Communists were firmly in control; by the end of 1989 all of the Communist governments had been either replaced or radically altered. Even the Soviet Union's powerful Communist Party relinquished its stranglehold on the Soviet people by giving up its monopoly on power and establishing political pluralism.

The event that best symbolized the incredible changes was the demolition of the Berlin Wall in 1989 and the subsequent absorption of East Germany into West Germany. By early 1990, all of the countries had restored basic personal freedoms and were moving toward establishing market economies and relations with the West. In 1999 it is expected that three countries—Poland, Hungary, and the Czech Republic—will be admitted to NATO, based on their strong success with political and economic reforms.

Events in the East reached a climax in 1991 with the breakup of the Soviet Union and the rise of Russian President Boris Yeltsin. Yeltsin has shown remarkable resilience in resisting efforts by the Communists to regain power. At times he has resorted to brute force, such as in 1993 when he violently evicted opposition politicians from the Russian parliament. As Russia's economy has been wrenched by change, many citizens have become impoverished and are out of work. This has given rise to ultra-nationalists who clamor for a return of the Soviet Union and its repressionist policies. It is a measure of the disillusionment of the Russian people that Yeltsin was almost defeated by a Communist in 1996 presidential elections.

Change has also been difficult for other republics of the former Soviet Union. Georgia, Tajikistan, Azerbaijan, Uzbekistan, Kazakhstan, and Kyrgyzstan have all experienced violent clashes between rival ethnic and political groups. Along the Baltic Sea, Latvia, Estonia, and Lithuania have all found independence complicated by the large numbers of Russians who settled in those nations after World War II. Relations with Moscow have been strained by accusations that these and other former Soviet republics are discriminating against their sizable Russian minorities.

Elsewhere in Eastern Europe, former Communists have gained renewed strength as people become disillusioned with economic reforms. In most cases, the transition to a market economy has resulted in inflation and unemployment. Many people look back fondly to the days when Communist governments tried to provide all of their citizens with food, housing, and employment. In search of greater prosperity, the people of Bulgaria, Hungary, and other countries have voted reformers out of office in favor of traditional socialists.

While the breakups of both the Soviet Union and Czechoslovakia were relatively peaceful events, thousands have died since the fall of the Yugoslavian federation in 1991. As each of the constituent republics declared its independence, the Serbian-dominated federal government fought to maintain control of Serbian-inhabited areas within the new nations. Fighting abated in 1995 following arduous negotiations and the deployment of tens of thousands of troops by the North Atlantic Treaty Organization (NATO). All of the region's ethnic groups remain deeply divided, however, and the prospects for long-term peace are highly uncertain.

War in the Balkans: YUGOSLAVIA

Perspective

1918	*South Slavic countries unite to create the Kingdom of Serbs, Croats, and Slovenes.*
1929	*Conflict between Serbs and Croats results in the failure of democracy.*
1945	*Communist government established under the leadership of Josip Tito.*
1980	*Tito's death renews fears of ethnic strife.*
1987	*Slobodan Milosevic attacks Kosovo autonomy.*
1989	**February 27.** *Troops invade Kosovo to restore order.*
1990	**September 9.** *Police break up riots in Bosnia and Herzegovina.* **September 28.** *Kosovo loses its autonomy.* **October 1.** *Serbs in Croatia declare autonomy following weeks of escalating violence.*
1991	**June.** *Croatia and Slovenia declare their independence; fighting breaks out.* **December 19.** *Macedonia declares independence.*
1992	**February 21.** *United Nations approves peacekeeping force for Croatia.* **February 29.** *Bosnia and Herzegovina declares independence, sparking fighting between Serbs and Bosnian Muslims.* **April 26.** *Yugoslavia proclaims a new federation consisting of Serbia and Montenegro only.*
1993	**May 6.** *UN places six "safe areas" under its protection.*
1994	**March 1.** *Bosnian Croats and Muslims agree to unite their forces.* **April 10.** *North Atlantic Treaty Organization (NATO) launches first of many air strikes against Bosnian Serbs.*
1995	**August.** *Serb mortar attack against civilians prompts NATO offensive.* **December 14.** *Dayton Peace Accord signed.*
1996	**September.** *Bosnia and Herzegovina elections result in victories for nationalist candidates.*
1998	**September 14.** *Local elections increase ethnic tensions.*

The fragile union of republics known as Yugoslavia seemed hopelessly destroyed by World War II. Croatian fascists and Serbian terrorists killed thousands of their own countrymen and created a legacy of hostility that might have prevented the reemergence of the federation. After the war, however, Yugoslavia was reunited by force under the dictatorship of Josip Tito. Although the country prospered under his rule, the postwar bitterness among the people was not forgotten. Reaching far into the next generation, this hatred resurfaced when economic problems and political changes in Eastern Europe created a climate for resurgent nationalism that ultimately ignited Europe's bloodiest war since World War II.

The war that erupted in the Balkans was a war against civilians. First, 10,000 people were killed in a conflict between Serbs and Croats, but this was merely a prelude to the disaster that left 200,000 people dead or missing in Bosnia and Herzegovina. A shaky truce was established in 1995, but a lasting peace is by no means assured.

Issues and Events

In 1987, Serbian leader Slobodan Milosevic rose to national prominence by championing the cause of Serbs living in Kosovo, an Albanian enclave within Yugoslavia. Despite protests, Kosovo lost its autonomy in 1990. Milosevic's inflammatory rhetoric aroused nationalist passions in Serbs throughout the country and alarmed Yugoslavia's other ethnic groups.

While the Albanians continued their fight in Kosovo, rioting broke out between Muslims and Serbs in the republic of Bosnia and Herzegovina. Serbs living in Croatia declared their allegiance to Serbia, and Croats and Slovenes became increasingly restless.

In 1991, Serbia was the first to declare the supremacy of its laws over those of the federal government. Three months later, the republics of Croatia and Slovenia declared their independence from the central government, and the Serbian army moved in to support rebel Serbs in those areas. The fighting quickly subsided in Slovenia, but the conflict exploded in Croatia. In the next few months more than 10,000 people—many of them civilians—were killed. The fighting escalated until early 1992, when the warring parties bowed to international pressure and allowed the UN to send in a peacekeeping force to monitor a cease-fire between the two groups.

The clash between the Serbs and Croats did not prevent tiny Macedonia from declaring its independence in December 1991, nor did it thwart the aspirations of the ethnically mixed republic of Bosnia and Herzegovina. After Bosnia and Herzegovina's declaration of independence in February 1992, Serbs from Yugoslavia moved in to protect areas inhabited by Bosnian Serbs. Fighting soon erupted among Muslims, Croats, and Serbs in the new country. Although the UN tried to quell the rapidly escalating conflict by imposing an arms embargo, the Bosnian Serbs continued to receive arms and supplies from Serbs in Yugoslavia. Without similar outside support the Muslims were unable to defend themselves, and the Serbs began driving Muslims out of Serb-held areas, a tactic that came to be known as "ethnic cleansing."

In May 1993, in an attempt to protect besieged Muslim civilians, the UN declared six Bosnian cities to be "safe areas." The measure was largely ineffective and Bosnian Serbs continued to launch attacks against these cities. In 1994 the powerful North Atlantic Treaty Organization (NATO) launched an offensive against Serbs who were attacking the safe areas. At first, Russia bitterly protested the attacks on the Serbs. After a series of Russian-negotiated cease-fires were violated by the Serbs, Russia changed its policy and began supporting air strikes.

During 1995 the war heated up on another front when Croatia began to grow impatient about Serbian occupation of about 30 percent of its territory. Despite the presence of UN peacekeepers, the Croats launched a successful attack and recaptured all of the Serb-held territory. The Serbian Croats fought back by shelling the Croatian capital of Zagreb in a desperate attack against civilians there, but they were ultimately defeated in November and forced to renounce their claims to Croatian territory.

After dozens of failed cease-fire agreements, an October 1995 truce led to a U.S.-sponsored accord the following month and provided war-weary Bosnians with hope that peace might be restored. Under the terms of the agreement, Bosnia and Herzegovina is divided into two areas united under a weak federal government. The Serbs were given 49 percent of the territory, while 51 percent was placed under the control of a Muslim-Croat federation. Each side was required to relinquish some of its territory to the other. The peace accord is being enforced by 60,000 NATO troops, the largest NATO troop deployment since World War II.

Many problems remain. Conditions in Kosovo have not improved. The new Bosnia and Herzegovina is as unstable and hate-filled as was Tito's Yugoslavian federation. Elections held in 1996 produced victories for hard-line nationalist candidates, many of whom remain committed to the concept of permanent partition of Bosnia and Herzegovina. Throughout the former Yugoslavia, violence erupted when refugees attempted to cross ethnic boundaries to return to their former homes. Local elections increased tensions when refugees gained political control of towns in which they are not yet allowed to live. Tensions are particularly high in the Serb sector, where a power struggle continues between the former president Radovan Karadzic, who has been indicted for war crimes, and Biljana Plavsic, the new president. Karadzic has refused to surrender to NATO troops and is accused of corruption by Plavsic. The people in this area are suffering from extreme poverty, and the unemployment rate has reached 90 percent.

Background

Serbia was established as an independent kingdom in the thirteenth century, and in the next century it gained control of Montenegro. The Ottoman Turks conquered the Serbs in 1389, but the Serbs never ceased to rebel against Turkish oppression. In 1828 Turkey recognized Serbia as a self-governing country, and conferred independence in 1878. In the mid-1800s a movement arose to advocate the creation of a new state uniting Serbs, Croats, Slovenes, and other Slavic people, despite vast cultural differences between the groups. The Croats and Slovenes were predominately Roman Catholic, while the Serbs were Orthodox. Many of the Bosnians were Muslims as a result of years of Turkish rule. Each group had its own Slavic language and culture.

Still, the movement gained strength, and when a terrorist advocating a Slavic homeland assassinated an heir to the throne of the Austro-Hungarian empire, it served as the spark that led to World War I. After the war, the Kingdom of Serbs, Croats, and Slovenes became a reality, but relations between the Serbs and Croats deteriorated. The Serbs dominated the union and advocated a strong central government, while the Croats and Slovenes favored a looser confederation. Unable to find a peaceful solution to the conflict, the Yugoslavian king abolished the constitution, changed the country's name to Yugoslavia, and assumed dictatorial powers in 1929. Angry Croats responded by forming the Ustashe, a Fascist separatist movement.

After Germany invaded Yugoslavia in 1941, the country was divided among Germany and its allies, except for Croatia, where the fascist Ustashe were rewarded with control over an independent Croatia. During the war, the Serbs, Jews, and Gypsies were viciously persecuted by both the Croats and the Germans. Meanwhile, two different resistance groups—the Chetniks and the Partisans—engaged in a power struggle. More than 1.5 million Yugoslavians died during the war, but perhaps the worst legacy was the ethnic hatred engendered among the various Yugoslav peoples.

After the war, a new Communist government was established under the firm leadership of Josip Tito. The new Yugoslavia consisted of six republics: Serbia, Croatia, Slovenia, Bosnia and Herzegovina, Macedonia, and Montenegro. Over the years, the Yugoslavians resisted Soviet domination by practicing their own brand of Communism and maintaining contacts with the West. Tito attempted to moderate Serbian dominance by giving each of the republics greater autonomy and establishing Kosovo and Vojvodina as self-governing provinces within Serbia. However, prosperous Croatia and Slovenia continued to protest that they were being exploited by the Serbs.

War in the Balkans: KOSOVO

Perspective

1389	*Ottoman Turks defeat Serbia at Kosovo.*
1912	*Serbia regains control of Kosovo.*
1974	**February 21.** *Kosovo receives autonomous status within Serbia.*
1980	**May 4.** *Josip Tito dies.*
1987	*Rising Serbian nationalism threatens Kosovo's autonomy.*
1989	**February 27.** *Serbian army dispatched to Kosovo.*
1990	**June.** *Kosovo government dissolved. Serbian government imposes police state.* **July 2.** *Kosovo secedes from Serbia.* **September 28.** *Kosovo officially loses its autonomous status.*
1991	**June.** *Wars accompanying the breakup of Yugoslavia begin.* **September.** *Kosovo declares its independence from Yugoslavia.*
1995	**December 14.** *Dayton Peace Accord fails to address the Kosovo issue.*
1996	**February.** *Kosovo Liberation Army (KLA) formed.*
1998	**February 28.** *Police crackdown in Drenica kills 80 people.*

In the southernmost part of Yugoslavia lies the region of Kosovo, an Albanian enclave within Serbia and the lynchpin of Yugoslavia's extended conflicts. The Serbs' harsh treatment of Kosovo ignited the devastating wars that led to the breakup of Yugoslavia. Although the Dayton Peace Accord restored an uneasy peace to the rest of the region, it left the Kosovo issue unresolved. Sporadic warfare in Kosovo continues to smolder within what's left of Yugoslavia.

Issues and Events

With a population that is more than 90 percent Albanian, Kosovo has always resisted Serbian rule. After World War II, Yugoslavia remained stable under the leadership of dictator Josip Tito, but demonstrations broke out a year after his death in 1980. In 1987 Slobodan Milosevic began his Serbian nationalism campaign, targeting Kosovo as an area where the Serb population was being threatened.

In early 1989 a state of emergency was declared in Kosovo, and troops were dispatched to restore order. In June 1990 the Kosovo government was dissolved. One month later, Kosovo unilaterally seceded from Serbia, and three months later Serbia officially revoked Kosovo's autonomous status. Other republics within the Yugoslavian federation felt threatened by Serbia's treatment of Kosovo, and war broke out when Croatia and Slovenia each declared their independence. Shortly thereafter Kosovo declared its independence and elected its own government.

The war ended in 1995, but the problems continued in Kosovo. In 1996 Kosovo Albanians turned to violence to achieve either total independence or integration into neighboring Albania. After the Kosovo Liberation Army (KLA) emerged, the struggle quickly escalated and at least 150 people were killed during a three-month period in 1997. As KLA attacks have increased, so have Serb police attacks against civilian women and children.

The people of Kosovo are well-organized and the shadow government they established in 1991 is running the territory effectively. Taxes are paid and used for schools, clinics, and other public services. Although the KLA has only about 500 members, they are well-armed with weapons smuggled across the Albanian border. The people of Kosovo directly support the KLA by providing them with shelter, food, and information.

By contrast, the Serbian army and police are poorly trained, badly equipped, and demoralized about the breakup of Yugoslavia. The Serbian people are tired of war, and polls show that although they want to retain control over Kosovo, they are unwilling to die for the cause. The loss of Kosovo would be a humiliating political defeat for Milosevic, and he is not likely to relinquish Serbian control.

The international community shares an intense interest in Kosovo and has declared its full support for a unified Serbia. It has also demanded that Serbia restore Kosovo's autonomy, a solution that appeals to neither the Serbs nor the Albanians. Albania has vowed that it will fully support Kosovo if war breaks out. Until the situation is resolved, Kosovo will remain a European hot spot that could erupt into a wider regional conflict at any time.

Background

Serbs consider Kosovo to be their spiritual homeland despite the fact that most of its residents are Albanians. It was in Kosovo that Serbian knights were defeated by Ottoman Turks in 1389, a battle which came to symbolize the Serbian struggle for independence and freedom.

Serbia regained control of Kosovo after World War I, but almost lost it after World War II when the region was contested by Albania. Following the war, the Kosovo Albanians were severely persecuted and thousands were deported to Turkey. By 1966 conditions had begun to improve, but the area remained very poor. Demonstrations and riots in 1968 led to increased political autonomy in 1974, but Kosovo continued to agitate for political status equal to that of Serbia.

Turmoil in Transcaucasia: ARMENIA AND AZERBAIJAN

Perspective

Throughout history the Armenian people have endured hardship and foreign rule. During the early 1900s more than one million Armenians were the victims of a genocidal campaign by Turkey. Today 3.5 million Armenians, out of a total population of 5.5 million, reside in the independent republic of Armenia. Another half million reside in the Nagorno-Karabakh region of neighboring Azerbaijan. Conflict over this region has resulted in a bitter conflict between the Armenians and the Turkish Azerbaijanis.

Issues and Events

In October 1987, an Azerbaijani ruling banning Armenian history in the schools of Nagorno-Karabakh touched off massive demonstrations by Soviet Armenians. In February, the territory requested an administrative transfer to Armenia, but the Soviet government quickly vetoed the move. Tensions between the two groups finally erupted into war in February 1988 after Azerbaijanis killed 32 Armenians in the city of Sumgait.

Soviet efforts to end the violence were unsuccessful. In January 1989 the Soviet government placed Nagorno-Karabakh under direct rule, a move which angered both the Armenians and

Azerbaijanis. The enclave was returned to Azerbaijan later that year, and Armenia showed its outrage by unilaterally annexing the territory a few days later. Enraged Azerbaijanis responded with renewed attacks. A Soviet invasion did little to end the violence, and the Soviet troops withdrew shortly after Armenia and Azerbaijan gained their independence in 1991.

In 1992 the Armenians defeated the Azerbaijanis and gained control over all of Nagorno-Karabakh. They proceeded to open a corridor between the enclave and Armenia through undisputed Azerbaijani territory. By the end of 1993 ethnic Armenians from Nagorno-Karabakh occupied 20 percent of Azerbaijan.

A cease-fire agreement between Azerbaijan and the Armenians was signed in May 1994 but prospects for a peaceful settlement remain dim. Early 1997 was marred by serious cease-fire violations, and later in the year Nagorno-Karabakh asserted its independence by holding its first presidential elections. This is a war with bitter roots, and ongoing negotiations have failed to provide any solutions.

Azerbaijan is outraged by the continuing Armenian occupation, and insists upon the return of all of its lands, including Nagorno-Karabakh. Armenia has renounced its claim to Nagorno-Karabakh, but thousands of Armenian soldiers occupy the territory. The Armenians of Nagorno-Karabakh continue to assert their right to determine their own future by declaring either independence or unification with Armenia.

Background

The region which now encompasses Armenia and Azerbaijan emerged as a separate country in the first millennium B.C. It reached its greatest extent in the first century B.C. when it included parts of present-day Turkey, Syria, Iraq, Iran, and the Caucasus region. In A.D. 301 Armenia became the first country to declare Christianity as its official state religion. In the late 300s the region was successively conquered and divided by the Romans, Persians, Arabs, Mongols, and Turks.

In 1828 the Russian Empire conquered the northern part of Armenia, leaving the southern part in Turkish possession. At the same time, the region known as Azerbaijan was formally divided between Russia and Persia (now Iran). In 1915 the Turks began a systematic slaughter of Armenians in Turkish territory that resulted in one million deaths and mass emigration to Russian Armenia. After the Russian Revolution Armenia, along with the Turkish republic of Azerbaijan, became part of the Soviet Union.

The Armenian-dominated oblast of Nagorno-Karabakh was awarded to Azerbaijan in 1921 because transportation and other economic factors linked the territory to Azerbaijan rather than Armenia. Although the Soviets believed that nationalism would eventually disappear under Communist rule, the enmity between the Armenians, Turks, and Azerbaijanis continues.

Turmoil in Transcaucasia: CHECHNYA

Perspective

1817–1864	*Russians consolidate control of Chechnya during the Caucasian Wars.*
1922	*Chechen Autonomous Oblast formed.*
1944	*Chechens deported by Stalin.*
1956	*Chechens allowed to return to their homeland.*
1991	**August.** *Dzhakhar Dudayev overthrows Chechnya's Communist government and declares its independence.* **November 10.** *Russian troops sent to Chechnya are forced to withdraw.*
1993	**April 17.** *Dudayev imposes presidential rule.*
1994	**September 1.** *Fighting breaks out between Chechen factions.* **December 11.** *Russians invade Chechnya.*
1995	**February 8.** *Russians capture Chechen capital of Groznyy.*
1996	**April.** *Dudayev killed.* **August 6.** *Rebels launch major assault against Russia.* **August 22.** *Peace agreement reached.*
1997	**January 5.** *Russian troops leave Chechnya.*

For almost 300 years, the Chechens have longed for independence from their powerful Russian neighbors. In the aftermath of a 1991 abortive coup by hard-line Communists against Soviet president Mikhail Gorbachev, the Chechen Communist government was overthrown by Dzhakhar Dudayev. Dudayev promptly declared the independence of the Chechen republic. War ensued, and it is a testament to the determination of the Chechens that powerful Russia was ultimately unable to defeat this tiny country, which is about the size of Connecticut.

Issues and Events
Russia dispatched troops to Chechnya soon after the republic declared its independence in 1991, but they were immediately surrounded by armed Chechens and forced to retreat the following day. Russia, preoccupied with the breakup of the Soviet Union and the outbreak of ethnic conflicts throughout the region, made no further attempts to enforce its rule on Chechnya. Russia imposed an embargo against Chechnya in 1991, and civil unrest ensued two years later. This turbulence quickly escalated to full-scale warfare, with both sides employing tanks, aircraft, and heavy artillery.

In 1994 Russia invaded Chechnya to restore Russian control of the area, an act which was condemned by more than three-quarters of the Russian population. After four months of heavy fighting, which included massive aerial bombardment of the Chechen capital, the Russians had captured all of Chechya's major cities. The Russians believed they had delivered a fatal blow to Chechen independence in April 1996 when a rocket attack killed Dudayev, but fighting continued until August when a massive rebel offensive forced the Russians to the negotiating table. The two sides soon signed an agreement, and by the beginning of 1997 the defeated Russian troops completed their withdrawal from Chechnya.

Although the peace accord defers a decision on Chechen independence until the end of 2001, the tiny republic is functioning as though it were already autonomous. The Chechens have elected their own President, and they fly the Chechnyan flag throughout the country. The country has renamed itself as the Republic of Ichkeriya, and it has also adopted Islamic law.

To avert more violence, complex negotiations are ahead. Most of Chechnya's cities lie in ruins, and Chechnya is demanding help from Russia to pay for rebuilding. Guns are everywhere and lawlessness is a serious problem. Russia claims that the situation is out of control and that the Chechen government is powerless to stop a steady stream of kidnappings and bombings throughout the region. For Russia, however, the most serious threat is that Chechen independence could spark similar aspirations among Transcaucasian people in the adjacent Russian territories of Dagestan, Ingushetia, and North Ossetia.

Background
Tensions have run high between the Russians and the Chechens ever since the bloody Caucasian Wars of the 1800s. Although the Russians were victorious, the Chechens never accepted Russian rule. Their hatred of the Russians was reinforced after Stalin deported the Chechens from their homeland in 1944, resulting in the deaths of more than one-third of the population. The Chechens were not allowed to return until 1956.

The Chechens' language, culture, and religion are all distinct from those of Russia, and most Chechens are fiercely nationalistic. Although the region has large oil reserves, most of the country's 1.2 million people are relatively poor and live quiet lives in rural areas. Many Russians are fearful of the Chechens because they have a reputation for ruthlessness, and also because some Chechens are involved in organized criminal activities throughout Russia.

Turmoil in Transcaucasia: GEORGIA

Perspective

1989	**July 14.** *Fighting between Georgians and Abkhazians prompts a state of emergency.*
1990	**September 20.** *South Ossetia announces its intent to secede from Georgia.* **December 10.** *Georgia abolishes South Ossetia.*
1991	**April 9.** *Georgia declares its independence from the Soviet Union.*
1992	**January 6.** *President Zviad Gamsakhurdia ousted by military coup.* **February 6.** *Tensions in Abkhazia escalate under military rule.* **October 11.** *Eduard Shevardnadze elected President.*
1993	**September.** *Abkhazian rebels overrun most of Abkhazia.*
1994	**February 3.** *Georgia and Russia sign the first of several accords.* **June 24.** *Russian military forces arrive in Abkhazia.*
1997	**July 7.** *Fighting flares between the Abkhazian army and Georgian guerrillas.*

Georgia's independence from the former Soviet Union has proved short-lived. Political instability and a series of ethnic rebellions ultimately forced Georgia to sign several accords with Russia that limit Georgian sovereignty. In return, Russia has agreed to back the Georgian government with its military might and end the ethnic fighting that has claimed tens of thousands of lives.

Issues and Events

Georgia's recent troubles began in the southern territory of South Ossetia. In late 1990 the Ossetians announced their intention to secede from Georgia and join with the Russian territory of North Ossetia. Ongoing strikes and demonstrations prompted the Georgian government to abolish the territory in 1990. When the Soviet government tried to intervene in 1991, Georgia imposed a blockade against South Ossetia and ultimately declared its independence from the Soviet Union.

Amidst the chaos following the breakup of the Soviet Union and subsequent military coup, the war between South Ossetia and Georgia quickly escalated. Talks between Georgia, Russia, and the Ossetians in 1992 ended the mounting violence and resulted in the establishment of a joint Russian-Georgian peacekeeping force operating under United Nations auspices.

Meanwhile, the Abkhazians were among the first to clamor for independence from the Soviet Union after Mikhail Gorbachev came to power and instituted glasnost. Abkhazia, a popular Black Sea tourist destination, was a site of repeated nationalist demonstrations that gradually escalated to violence. Fighting broke out between Georgia and Abkhazia in 1989, and the rebels succeeded in driving Georgian forces from the territory in 1993. More than 250,000 ethnic Georgians had to flee their homes in Abkhazia.

After the United States and the UN failed to provide military support to the Georgians, President Shevardnadze was forced to turn to Russia for help. Georgia was required to join the Commonwealth of Independent States (CIS) and agree to give Moscow significant influence over Georgian affairs. In June 1994 Russia stopped the bloodshed by ordering thousands of troops into Abkhazia and establishing military bases throughout Georgia.

Although most of the fighting has abated, peace talks have been unproductive and the situation remains unstable. Both Abkhazia and South Ossetia are in reality independent, each with its own government and army over which Georgia has no control. One of the most contentious issues facing negotiators is the fate of 15,000 Georgian refugees who were forced to flee from Abkhazia during the fighting and have not been allowed to return to their homes. It is estimated that more than 1,000 people have been killed in the Abkhazia conflict since the official cease-fire in 1994, and the Abkhazian government asserts that it will renew the war if the Russians pull out. Georgia's dependency on Russia continues to grow, much to the disdain of many Georgians whose hopes for a truly independent country have been shattered.

Background

Georgia was incorporated into the Soviet Union in 1921, but only after several years of violent resistance. The Georgians argue that Abkhazia and South Ossetia are an integral part of Georgia and that the territories were created by the Soviet Union to divide Georgia and diminish its importance. Both South Ossetia and Abkhazia are run by conservative governments and remain committed to Communism despite the breakup of the Soviet Union. Georgians gained independence in 1991 and were fiercely determined to preserve their territorial integrity; Georgia was one of the last former Soviet republics to join the CIS.

Russia's interest in Georgia dates back centuries. By exerting influence over Georgia, Russia maintains its links and controls in the region. Georgia also buffers Russia from the potentially destabilizing influence of Iran.

Struggling with Democracy: RUSSIA

Perspective

800s	*Russian empire begins with emergence of the state of Kiev.*
1800s	*Pre-Communist military expansionism ends.*
1917	*Bolshevik Revolution brings Communists to power.*
1922	*Union of Soviet Socialist Republics formed.*
1985	**March 11.** *Mikhail Gorbachev appointed general secretary of the Communist party.*
1988	**February 28.** *Armenians and Azerbaijanis clash, causing 32 deaths.* **November 16.** *Estonians enact "Home Rule" legislation.*
1990	**March 11.** *Lithuania votes to secede from the Soviet Union.*
1991	**June 13.** *Boris Yeltsin elected president of Russia.* **August 19.** *Communist hard-liners launch coup against Gorbachev.* **December 8.** *Russia, Belarus, and Ukraine initiate the Commonwealth of Independent States.* **December 25.** *Gorbachev resigns.* **December 26.** *Soviet congress acknowledges the dissolution of the Soviet Union.*
1992	**February 23.** *Anti-Yeltsin protesters clash with police.* **March 31.** *Russian Federation Treaty signed by most of Russia's republics.*
1993	**April 25.** *Referendum gives Yeltsin a mandate for continued rule.* **October 2.** *Hard-line parliamentary deputies stage an unsuccessful armed revolt against Yeltsin.* **December 12.** *Russian voters approve new constitution backed by Yeltsin; they also elect many hard-liners to parliament.*
1994	**December 11.** *Russia invades Chechnya.*
1995	**December 18.** *Communists win parliamentary elections.*
1996	**July 3.** *Yeltsin reelected president.*
1998	**March 23.** *Yeltsin fires all of his advisors.*

While a nervous world looks on, Russia has begun to emerge from the tumultuous post-Soviet years and lay the foundations of permanent democracy. President Boris Yeltsin continues to face serious challenges from hard-line former Communists who want to return to the past, disenchanted economic reformers who think that things aren't changing quickly enough, and newly rich tycoons who want to use their money to control the government. Yeltsin has defied the odds by remaining in power despite periods of ill health, political ineffectiveness, and waning popular support. He continues to shepherd the country through the pitfalls of economic reform and help the country redefine itself in the aftermath of the collapse of the Soviet empire.

Issues and Events

As president of Russia, Boris Yeltsin replaced Mikhail Gorbachev as the leader of the largest portion of the former Soviet Union. Yeltsin wasted no time in implementing a rapid economic reform program to transform the country from a centralized, Communist economy to a free market, capitalist one. Hardship ensued in the forms of massive inflation, poverty, crime, corruption, and political instability.

A dangerous power struggle between Yeltsin and the conservative Russian parliament escalated quickly. In March 1993 the legislature voted to curtail Yeltsin's powers, and he retaliated by invoking presidential rule and calling for a special referendum. Weeks later the Russian people voted in support of Yeltsin and his economic reform program, and also indicated that fresh parliamentary elections should be held. However, the parliament, dominated by Communists appointed in the waning days of the Soviet Union, continued to block Yeltsin at every move.

The situation reached a breaking point in October 1993 when Vice President Aleksandr Rutskoi and Parliamentary Speaker Ruslan Khasbulatov led an armed rebellion from their headquarters in the Parliament building in Moscow. Yeltsin responded harshly, ordering loyal army troops to storm the building. The ensuing battles were broadcast around the world.

December elections resulted in the approval of a Yeltsin-backed constitution that restructured the Parliament with a new upper house called the Federal Assembly. However, the voters also elected many independents and extremists who promised to oppose the President at every turn. The most notorious of the new deputies was Vladimir Zhirinovsky, whose open racism and calls for a restoration of the Soviet Empire were viewed with alarm in the West. In January 1994 Yeltsin announced changes to his cabinet that included the departure of many economic reformers, such as Yegor Gaidar, in what was seen as an effort to mollify those hard hit by the economy's fitful shifts to capitalism.

Communists continued to gain political ground in 1995 when they won a majority of the seats in parliamentary elections, soundly defeating Yeltsin's "Our Home" party. Although the legislature's power is limited by Russia's strongly presidential system of government, the parliament defied Yeltsin by calling for an end to economic reform and denouncing the breakup of the Soviet Union. Loss of confidence in Yeltsin increased even more when it was reported that he was seriously ill.

The outcome of the 1996 presidential elections was uncertain when Yeltsin faced a serious challenge from Communist Party leader Gennady Zyuganov, an admirer of former Russian dictator Joseph Stalin. The two faced off in a runoff election and Yeltsin scored a clear victory, but his health remains a serious concern.

In 1998 Yeltsin surprised everyone when, after recovering from another major illness, he returned to work, fired all of his chief advisors, and brought in a new team of young economic reformers. This event followed his earlier announcement that the economy was expected to grow for the first time since the country abandoned Communism; the change should accelerate the pace of reform. This shake-up rebuffed both the Communists and the tycoons, infused the government with a fresh approach and a new sense of purpose, and proved once again that Yeltsin still maintains firm control over the Russian government.

In his continuing battle with rival politicians, Yeltsin has enlisted the support of Russia's ethnic-based republics by granting them greater autonomy. This new, looser relationship was defined in the Russian Federation Treaty, which was approved by 18 of Russia's 20 republics in March 1992. Tatarstan and Chechnya, the two republics that refused to sign the treaty, are both Islamic republics that possess rich oil resources. Tatarstan and Russia settled their differences and approved a treaty in 1994, but war broke out in the republic of Chechnya in the Caucasus region. With its myriad ethnic groups, Russia is particularly fearful of any further collapse of its empire to independence movements. Nevertheless, Yeltsin was accused of mishandling the Chechnya rebellion when Russian troops sent to the republic inflicted devastating damage.

Although the threat of ethnic tensions in Russia should not be underestimated, the shaky economy presents even more peril. So far, the economic reforms have brought mostly hardship to the Russian people. Huge and inefficient former state-owned industries continue to fire tens of thousands of people as they try to address the realities of the emerging free market economy.

Although there are signs that the economy has begun to stabilize, most people have seen their standard of living decline and as many as 25 percent live below the official poverty level. Unemployment is high, and many workers are paid infrequently. The once-proud Russian military is in a shambles, plagued by malnutrition and alcoholism. Some fear that if economic conditions do not improve, a military coup or Communist takeover is inevitable. Such actions would receive the support of many who would gladly relinquish their new freedom in exchange for food, jobs, and housing.

Background

The steady expansion of the Russian Empire began in earnest under Ivan the Terrible in the late 1500s. By 1700, the empire stretched to the Arctic Ocean in the north and the Pacific Ocean in the east. During the end of the eighteenth century, Peter the Great sought to end Russia's isolation by opening up relations with Russia's western European neighbors. Catherine the Great further expanded Russia's boundaries to include Crimea, Ukraine, and Belarus. By the mid-1800s, Russia's expansion was essentially complete.

Due to the vast distances involved and the lack of modern communications, the Russians' influence in much of their empire was minimal until the Bolshevik Revolution in 1917 brought the Communists to power. Under the leadership of Vladimir Lenin, the state seized all private property, which resulted in a bitter civil war that lasted until 1922, when the Union of Soviet Socialist Republics was formed.

Lenin advocated self-determination for all of the peoples of the old empire. After Lenin's death in 1924, Joseph Stalin put an end to this policy and extended the Soviet Union to its present size. Stalin's purges in the 1930s and 1940s resulted in the deaths or forced relocation of those whose loyalty was questioned. The Stalinist system did not tolerate dissent, and successive Soviet leaders ruled their regime with an iron fist until Gorbachev came to power in 1985.

Gorbachev inherited a stagnating society. When he implemented reforms to revitalize the economy, he also loosened the bonds that held the Soviet Union together. Fighting erupted between neighboring republics of Armenia and Azerbaijan in 1988, resulting in hundreds of deaths, and the Soviet government was unable to help the two groups reach a negotiated settlement. Military force was ineffective in stopping recurrent violence in Uzbekistan, Azerbaijan, Georgia, Kyrgyzstan, Moldova, Lithuania, and Latvia.

When Communist hard-liners launched a coup against Gorbachev in August 1991, they were soon defeated by a people's movement led by Russian president Boris Yeltsin. However, the country was transformed by the chaos, and 11 of the 15 Soviet republics quickly declared their independence from the Soviet Union. The Commonwealth of Independent States was formed in December, and Gorbachev was ultimately forced to accept the inevitable collapse of the Russian empire. As changes swept the country at a dizzying pace, Gorbachev was swept aside as well, replaced by Yeltsin.

Building Peace:
NORTHERN IRELAND

Perspective

1607	*British occupation of Ireland begins.*
1801	*Irish unite with Great Britain.*
1846	*Potato famine prompts unrest.*
1858	*Irish Republican Brotherhood formed.*
1919	*Irish Republican Army (IRA) formed; war of independence begins.*
1920	*Ireland is partitioned.*
1921	*Southern Ireland gains independence.*
1968	*IRA begins bombing British targets in Northern Ireland.*
1972	*Direct British rule imposed on Northern Ireland.*
1993	*United Kingdom and Ireland sign the Downing Street Declaration.*
1994	*Unilateral cease-fire begins.*
1997	**September.** *Final peace talks begin.*
1998	**April.** *Major agreement reached between U.K. and Ireland.* **May.** *Peace referendum approved by voters in Ireland and Northern Ireland.*

While most of Ireland is an independent country, the six counties of Northern Ireland remain part of the United Kingdom. The Irish Catholics have never accepted the partition of their island into Ireland and Northern Ireland to accommodate the Protestant descendants of the British. The Protestant majority in Northern Ireland insists that the region remain part of the U.K. rather than reunite with Ireland. Radical groups from both sides have engaged in bloody violence and terrorism, claiming 3,200 lives since 1969. In 1994 a cease-fire was implemented, and in May 1998 a peace referendum was passed by voters in both Ireland and Northern Ireland. The inhabitants of the Emerald Isle are hopeful that this stormy chapter of their history is finally over.

Issues and Events
The conflict between the IRA and various Protestant loyalist groups escalated during the 1990s as the number of British troops sent to Northern Ireland increased to 11,000. In 1992 the IRA launched a bombing campaign in England, targeting police stations, airports, rail stations, and London's theater and financial districts.

A major breakthrough for peace occurred in late 1993 when, after many years of negotiations, the U.K. and Ireland signed the Downing Street Declaration. This accord set guidelines for peace

talks, barring violent groups from participating in the peace process. The IRA responded by declaring a unilateral cease-fire in September 1994. At first this was greeted with skepticism, but after several weeks loyalist militia groups that oppose the IRA joined the cease-fire. Hopes for peace soared when the U.K. and Ireland signed another pact in 1995 as a framework for future talks.

The negotiations suffered a setback in 1996, however, when the IRA detonated a truck bomb in London that killed two people, injured 100, and caused more than $100 million in damage. Then, in December 1997, an imprisoned loyalist paramilitary leader was murdered by inmates who were members of a left-wing militia group. This caused a rash of retaliatory killings. In February 1998 the IRA was implicated in at least two revenge killings, and the group was temporarily suspended from the peace talks.

In April 1998 a major agreement was reached between the governments of the U.K. and Ireland. Under its terms, Northern Ireland is to have a National Assembly in which both Catholics and Protestants are represented, based on their percentage of the population. A North-South Ministerial Council will join leaders of Ireland and Northern Ireland to resolve issues that involve the entire island, including tourism, transportation, and the environment. A Council of the Isles will represent all areas of the British Isles in one body. This restructuring will better represent all major ethnic groups and political entities. Ireland and the U.K. also agreed to give Northern Ireland the right of self-determination, and Ireland relinquished its claim to Northern Ireland.

On May 22 this agreement was put to a referendum in Ireland and Northern Ireland, and citizens voted overwhelmingly in its favor. The election for members of the new Northern Ireland Assembly was held on June 25.

Background
The seeds of the Irish conflict were sown by the British in the seventeenth century. In an attempt to consolidate control over Ireland, the British seized land from the Irish and gave it to English and Scottish settlers. The dispute had religious overtones because the Irish were traditionally Roman Catholic and the British invaders were Protestant.

Although they suffered under British occupation, the people of Northern Ireland did not organize for more than 200 years. The 1846 potato crop failure, famine, and subsequent unrest led to the birth of Ireland's first terrorist organization, the Irish Republican Brotherhood. When the Irish began to push for independence, the Protestants in Northern Ireland demanded continued ties to Great Britain, and the country was partitioned. The Irish Republican Army was formed in 1919 to drive the British from the Island. Its terrorist tactics have been emulated by rebel groups worldwide.

Basque Separatism: SPAIN

Perspective

1937	**October.** *General Francisco Franco defeats the semi-autonomous Basque Republic during the Spanish Civil War.*
1959	*Basque Fatherland and Liberty Party (ETA) founded.*
1968	*ETA endorses armed struggle.*
1973	**December 20.** *Basque terrorists assassinate Prime Minister Carrero Blanco.*
1975	**November 20.** *Franco dies.*
1978	**December 6.** *Democratic constitution allows for regional autonomy.*
1980	**March 9.** *Moderates win first Basque Provinces elections.*
1989	**January.** *Peace talks begin; terrorism continues.*
1996	**February 19.** *One million people demonstrate against Basque terrorism after a university professor is shot.*
1997	**July 13.** *Shooting of a young Spanish politician provokes national outrage.*

The Basques are culturally and racially distinct from their neighbors in the rest of northern Spain and adjacent areas of France. Numbering about two million, the Basques have been trying to achieve independence from Spain since the 1930s, and in the late 1960s the struggle turned violent. Since then hundreds have been killed, and Basque terrorism has become the European mainland's most enduring security problem.

Issues and Events

Although many different factions fight for Basque independence, the most feared is the Basque Fatherland and Liberty Party (ETA), which was formed in 1959 and adopted a policy of armed violence in 1968. The ETA has been responsible for thousands of meticulously planned kidnappings, assassinations, and bombings directed at Spanish police, military personnel, and government officials. One of the most infamous attacks was the assassination of Spanish Prime Minister Carrero Blanco in 1973.

The violence peaked in 1980 with 85 deaths: the most people killed in a single year by Basque ethnic violence. In recent years there have been fewer ETA attacks and casualties, in part because the Basque Provinces have been granted increased political autonomy over the years by the Spanish government. In addition, virtually all of the original leadership and members of the ETA have been arrested. Finally, the ETA, which originally financed its operations through ransom demands and robbery, has failed to secure other more stable forms of funding.

Throughout the years the ETA has become increasingly unpopular, even among the Basque community, and the Spanish government is encouraging the Basques to pressure the terrorists to stop their campaign of violence. Originally the ETA went to great pains to avoid unnecessary deaths during their attacks, but in recent years more civilians have been killed in ETA violence. During 1997 and 1998 several popular politicians were targeted by the ETA. Terrorists kidnapped a young city councilman named Miguel Angel Blanco and threatened to kill him unless Basque prisoners were moved to prisons closer to home within 48 hours. Hundreds of thousands across the country demonstrated for his release, and the Pope made a plea on his behalf, but Blanco was found dead two days later. Over the next few months other elected councilmen were killed, and each incident was followed by massive public outcry within the Basque community. Although many Basques still long for an independent Basque nation, they want to establish it through legal action.

Certainly the current government will not be intimidated into changing the status of the Basque Provinces. The prime minister, José Maria Aznar, was the target of an unsuccessful car bombing in 1995, and he has aggressively pursued and prosecuted Basque terrorists. Basques have long accused the Spanish government of using excessively harsh counter-terrorism tactics, and recently released government documents from the 1980s indicate that death squads were authorized to kill suspected ETA sympathizers. While the government admits that it has dealt with the situation inappropriately, it firmly refuses to negotiate with the ETA until they surrender their weapons.

Background

The Basques live primarily in the coastal provinces of Gipuzkoako and Bizkaiko, and in the inland provinces of Arabako and Navarra. Gipuzkoako, Bizkaiko, and Arabako make up the autonomous community known as the Basque Provinces, while Navarra is both an autonomous community and a province.

In the tenth century the Basque region was part of the kingdom of Navarre, and by the sixteenth century it was overtaken by the kingdom of Castile. For the next 300 years the Basque Provinces enjoyed a certain amount of autonomy. By the end of the nineteenth century Spanish centralization began to erode Basque self-rule, and after the Spanish Civil War General Francisco Franco tried to abolish all traces of Basque cultural identity. It was during this period that the ETA was formed.

After Franco's death the Basques and other ethnic groups regained some measure of home rule, but ambitions for a country of their own remain strong.

South America

The South American republics have often been characterized by political instability. The military plays an important role in political life, and civilian governments frequently rule only with military approval. Popularly elected democratic governments are often overthrown and replaced by military juntas. Human rights abuses are commonplace as these military governments cling to the reins of power and authority despite a lack of popular support.

Recent political reforms throughout the region have done little to improve the economic situation. In most South American countries there is dramatic economic polarity: a politically and economically elite class that enjoys luxury and privilege, contrasted with the oppressed masses who survive in dire poverty. This large, underprivileged majority has often been systematically exploited by a succession of rulers interested only in personal wealth and power.

The patterns of inequity in South America's wealth distribution were set down hundreds of years ago during the region's colonial period, and the situation in modern South America is partly a result of Euro-pean colonial influences upon an indigenous population. The dominant colonial power in South America was Spain, although Portugal, the Netherlands, Britain, and France also acquired possessions in the area. Portugal's influence is most evident in Brazil, where Portuguese is the predominant language.

Prior to the arrival of the Europeans around the sixteenth century, various indigenous peoples inhabited the region. Among these were the Inca, whose sophisticated civilization flourished in the areas of present-day Ecuador, Peru, and Bolivia.

The first major wave of European settlement occurred in the 1500s with the arrival of the Spanish conquistadors. The resistance offered by most indigenous groups was ineffectual, and their lands quickly fell to the invaders.

Many of the early settlers were drawn to South America by the promise of wealth. As word of the continent's natural riches spread back to Europe, fortune-seeking colonists flocked to the region. Oftentimes the promise of gold and silver remained unfulfilled, but most settlers stayed on, establishing large plantations that laid the basis for much of South America's present economy. The colonists took the conquered Amerindians as slaves to work their farmlands, and soon a thriving agricultural society was established.

During the colonial period, much of the indigenous population disappeared. Wars with the settlers, hard labor at the plantations, and exposure to European diseases claimed thousands of Amerindian lives. In addition, many of the Amerindians who managed to survive intermarried with the Europeans. Modern South America's large mestizo population of mixed Spanish and Amerindian blood is a result of these relationships.

As the indigenous population was decimated by colonial rule, blacks were brought from Africa to continue slave labor on the plantations. South America continued to develop, and the descendants of the early settlers soon established a unique South American culture, combining influences of their ancestors with a lifestyle evolved from the plantations.

Prosperity for the ruling class also continued, and in time the large-estate holders, many of them mestizos, found themselves wielding economic influence but enjoying few of the benefits of their profits. Native-born South Americans of Spanish descent were equally dissatisfied with colonial status. Political power remained in the hands of the mother country, whose people and government now had little in common with South American life. Resentment toward the ruling powers grew, along with the colonies' demands for a voice in their government. During the nineteenth century, wars in Europe weakened Spain and Portugal both politically and economically. Consequently, all Spanish and Portuguese holdings in South America became independent before 1900.

The region remained politically unstable following independence. A class that already possessed a certain amount of influence won the fight for self-rule during the 1800s, and the change in government only shifted power from the European rulers to the South American elite. Thus the change in leadership did not bring beneficial reforms to the many people outside the small circle of economic influence. Subsequent economic development concentrated wealth more solidly in the hands of the rich. Land ownership remains a critical issue throughout South America: Most of the arable land is held by a few, while most of the rural population holds none.

Great inequities in the distribution of wealth led to the emergence of left-wing guerrilla groups such as the Shining Path in Peru and the Revolutionary Armed Forces in Colombia. The rich, having a vested interest in maintaining the status quo, supported the rise of military governments and right-wing vigilante groups throughout the region to fight these leftist movements. The governments developed ruthless tactics to stay in power, such as the use of "disappearances," or kidnappings followed by secret executions. Military governments also terrorized the populace by using "death squads," or government-sanctioned vigilante groups, to eliminate their opposition.

The emergence of elected governments throughout South America has reduced but not ended the struggle between right-wing terrorists and various Marxist groups. However, there is no doubt that if democratically elected governments fail to bring reform and economic prosperity, South Americans may once again fall prey to dictatorships or military regimes. In Peru, democracy and freedom of the press have been all but eliminated by President Fujimori in his attempt to thwart a terrorist takeover. Chile's tenuous democracy is also threatened by growing friction between the government and the country's powerful military over human rights issues.

Political problems have been compounded by growing economic instability in the region. During the 1960s, South American countries began taking out loans from foreign banks and governments to finance major development programs, such as roads, airports, and hydroelectric projects. Much of the money was wasted through mismanagement and corruption, and by the early 1980s many of the countries were unable to keep up their payments on the loans. Suddenly the flow of foreign capital dried up and the region began a period of runaway inflation, rising poverty, unemployment, and severe economic recession. This economic failure and growing concern for human rights led to the establishment of civilian governments in most countries by the end of the decade, but the problems created by the previous governments endure.

Political stability in the region will largely depend upon whether the civilian governments will be able to improve the overall standard of living. Argentina is a prime example of a country that was governed by a series of military or civilian dictatorships until 1983, when the junta fell to a democratically elected government. In an attempt to reduce triple-digit inflation and to amass capital to keep up its debt payments, the government was forced to implement a severe austerity program. The result was recession, unemployment, and a drastic reduction in social services. By the early 1990s, however, the economy was showing signs of improvement. Although unemployment remained high, both inflation and foreign debt were significantly reduced. Major elections proceeded as planned, and it seemed that the Argentinean government was on firm footing. As a result, Argentina has become a model for other countries in the region that are attempting to create economic and political stability.

South America's economic malaise has been a boon for the lucrative drug trafficking industry. Cocaine is the main source of income for thousands of peasant farmers in Peru, Bolivia and neighboring countries. Colombia's mammoth cocaine processing industry has resulted in economic vitality, but the cocaine trade generates such huge profits that corruption and violence are the law of the land in some areas, and governmental authority is widely flouted. The United States, the major market for the illicit drug, has tried without much success to pressure the South American countries to stop the production and exportation of cocaine.

Perhaps the most far-reaching consequence of the South American debt crisis is the over-exploitation of the area's resources, such as the rain forest. Throughout the region, vast tracts of virgin forest have fallen prey to those who would put the land to alternative uses. In Brazil, poverty and the largest foreign debt in South America led to a drive to convert the Amazonian rain forest to agricultural and other uses. International outcry has subsequently forced the government to come up with a rational plan to develop and exploit the rain forest without destroying it. But Brazil's own problems with widespread corruption have hampered these efforts, and the initiative has had disastrous results.

Threatened Rain Forest: BRAZIL

Perspective

1960	*Capital of Brazil moved from Rio de Janeiro to Brasília.*
1973	*Trans-Amazon highway completed.*
1979	*Gold at Serra Pelada draws miners to Amazonia.*
1987	*Roraima gold rush begins.*
1988	**October 13.** *Government halts incentives for Amazon development.*
1989	**April 6.** *"Our Nature" program begins.*
1990	**January.** *Miners barred from Yanomami homeland.* **March.** *Government orders bombing of miners' airstrips.*
1991	**June 24.** *Brazil agrees to "debt-for-nature" swaps.* **November.** *Government creates several huge Amerindian reserves.*
1992	**June 3.** *Earth Summit convenes in Rio de Janeiro.*
1993	**August.** *Reports surface about a massacre of Yanomami people by gold miners.*
1994	**December.** *Farmers protest creation of a new Amerindian reservation.*
1995	**August 9.** *Peasant farmers and the military clash in Rondonia.*
1996	**January 8.** *Government relaxes laws that prevent people from claiming Amerindian lands.* **April 17.** *Nineteen peasants killed in land reform demonstration.*
1997-1998	*Drought contributes to massive forest fires.*

The burning season in the Amazonian rain forest traditionally begins in August. Every year cattlemen burn down trees to create rangeland for their herds, and farmers burn their lands to make the earth more fertile. Because rain forest soils are very poor, however, heavy Amazonian rains quickly leach valuable nutrients out of the soil. Without the protection of the forest canopy, what remains of the soil is washed away and the terrain becomes a permanent wasteland.

In 1997 this unfortunate situation was ripe for disaster. The El Niño weather system caused a serious drought and the annual fires soon raged out of control, devastating huge areas of virgin forest that are normally too wet to burn. It may be years before the actual damage to the rain forest can be fully assessed, but scientists agree that what occurred was surely a major ecological catastrophe. They also agree that the Brazilian government is to blame for irresponsibility and the mismanagement of the rain forest.

Issues and Events

The great rain forests of the world cover only about seven percent of Earth's surface, yet they contain about 80 percent of the planet's vegetation. Scientists have long warned that the destruction of the rain forest could cause a global warming trend called the "greenhouse effect" that could ultimately render the planet uninhabitable.

About one-third of the world's rain forests are located in Brazil. In an unprecedented move, the government of Brazil admitted in 1988, after more than 6,000 man-made fires were reported in a single day in Rondonia, along one of Brazil's new roads through Amazonia, that development of the rain forest had gotten out of hand. This startling information inspired the wrath of environmentalists throughout the world, and Brazil was subjected to mounting international criticism for its environmental policies at a time when it desperately needed foreign investment.

The government tried to subdue its critics by enacting legislation to control—but not curtail—Amazonian development. Efforts to curb rain forest destruction included the discontinuation of subsidies for cattle ranchers, miners, and lumber concerns in the region. The first comprehensive Amazonian forest management program—"Our Nature"—was launched the following year. It included 49 new environmental laws concerning zoning, nature reserves, and mandatory burning permits. These measures, although conservative, met with violent resistance from ranchers and miners. Several of the government's enforcement agents, as well as many environmental leaders, were assassinated.

No group has suffered more from Amazonian development than the region's indigenous populations, which have often been devastated. Reports of Amerindians being slaughtered at the hands of cattle ranchers and gold miners have filtered out of the jungle for decades. The Brazilian government has tried to set aside large portions of land exclusively for these people, but their proposals have met with particularly vehement resistance by individual state governments and developers.

In 1990, international attention turned to the plight of the Yanomami, one of the world's last isolated tribes. In 1987, some 45,000 gold miners began pouring into the Yanomami's homelands in Roraima state. More than ten percent of the Yanomami have subsequently perished as a result of the invasion. The government tried to bar miners from the area, but when this proved ineffective, they bombed the miners' airstrips to cut off their supply lines.

In 1991 the Brazilian government stepped up its conservation efforts by agreeing to a "debt-for-nature" swap, whereby a portion of Brazil's massive foreign debt would be forgiven if Brazil used the money for environmental protection. Also, a huge reserve the size of Indiana was created for the Yanomami. This was one of more than 70 reserves created during the year. In addition, Brazil began encouraging environmental tourism and marketing rain forest products to help the region's fragile economy.

These measures have further angered the region's miners, farmers, and loggers. Tensions between the government and developers remain high. In 1994, some 10,000 angry farmers gathered to protest the decision to create a new Amerindian reservation in northern Brazil. In 1992 Brazil tried to improve its image by hosting the Earth Summit, the largest gathering of world leaders ever assembled. Their goal was to discuss ways to save the environment from further damage due to industrialization and uncontrolled development. Environmentalists later claimed that after the summit Brazil did not honor its commitment, and indeed deforestation reached record levels only three years later in 1995. During that year satellite imagery detected more than 75,000 fires, and smoke blanketed huge areas of the country.

Environmentalists assert that Brazil's programs to save the rain forest are ineffective because the government has failed to provide funding for enforcement. Thus, the farmers, ranchers, loggers, and miners who are responsible for most of the environmental damage are free to ignore new laws. Monitoring the situation is also expensive, and Brazil claims that it cannot afford to continually assess the status of rain forest destruction. The destruction of huge tracts of forest can go undetected for up to five years.

In Brazil, concerns about the fate of the Amazonian forest are tempered by more immediate concerns such as politics, the economy, and individual rights. Because Brazil has a 41 percent poverty rate, the pressures for development are enormous. It is virtually impossible for the government to effectively set aside land as long as there are millions of poor peasants who need the land for their survival. In 1995, 13 people, including two police officers, were killed when the government tried to evict 700 landless families from a plot of land in Amazonia, a scene that repeated in 1996 when another 19 peasants were killed in Pará state.

Some Brazilians believe that the wilderness is somehow too vast to be destroyed and that international concerns about the rain forest are a ruse to allow the developed countries to control and plunder Brazil's natural resources. Many generals in the army have publicly stated that the U.S. and other countries are looking for an excuse to invade the Amazon and steal it from Brazil.

Background

Brazil was colonized during the early 1500s by Portuguese settlers, most of whom grew sugar along the northeast coast. The discovery of gold in 1693 started a gold rush to the central highlands in the present-day state of Minas Gerais. By the mid-1800s, coffee had become the country's leading export as people flocked to the São Paulo region to work on the new plantations. During the late 1800s, the rubber boom prompted limited migration to the Amazonian region. Each of these economic booms resulted in the establishment of large new plantations controlled by a few wealthy landowners. Land ownership patterns have changed very little over the years: More than 60 percent of the arable land in Brazil is still owned by less than two percent of the population, and 70 percent of all rural families have no land at all.

After World War II, Amazonia was hailed as the land of opportunity for landless Brazilians, and in 1960 the country officially moved its capital from Rio de Janeiro to the futuristic new city of Brasília to serve as a base for the development of Amazonia. The Trans-Amazon Highway opened up the area to ranching, farming, forestry, and mining. Peasants were lured to the wilderness by offers of free land, and the rich made even bigger fortunes by exploiting the free land. The government hoped to relocate 100,000 property-less families to Amazonia by 1974, but poor farming conditions and a lack of facilities hindered development. By 1977, only about 7,000 families had been established along the highway, which is rendered impassable for six months of the year by seasonal rains.

In 1979, thousands of poor peasants flocked to Amazonia to find gold at Serra Pelada. In a few short years, more than 60,000 prospectors using crude hand tools dug a crater 250 feet deep in search of instant wealth. Tremendous quantities of gold, iron ore, bauxite, and manganese are all currently being mined at various locations in Amazonia.

For scientists, the Amazon, with its incredible diversity of plant and animal life, is like a big drugstore whose contents are waiting to be discovered. More than one-third of all pharmaceuticals used today have been developed from compounds found in nature. Environmentalists who argue for rain forest preservation point out that the cure for cancer could be growing right now in the rain forest.

Scientists also fear that global warming will be accelerated by destruction of the Amazon, which many call the "lungs of the Earth." Its vast area of vegetation is a major source of oxygen in the atmosphere. Ironically, the fires that clear the rain forest produce enormous amounts of smoke and carbon dioxide. In death, the Amazon sucks out the very oxygen it produced in life.

Terrorism Continues: PERU

Perspective

1824	*Peru gains independence from Spain.*
1968	*Military government adopts socialist policies.*
1979	*Country returns to democracy and capitalism.*
1980	*Abimael Guzman founds Shining Path terrorist group.*
1984	*Tupac Amaru Revolutionary Movement formed.*
1990	**June 10.** *Alberto Fujimori elected president.*
1991	**April 5.** *Shining Path launches an urban terrorism campaign.*
1992	**April 6.** *Fujimori dismisses government and suspends the constitution.* **September 12.** *Guzman is arrested.*
1993	**August 19.** *Shining Path kills 60 villagers.*
1995	**May 24.** *Shining Path bombs a Lima tourist hotel.*
1996	**December 17.** *Tupac Amaru Revolutionary Movement hostage crisis begins.*
1997	**April 22.** *Hostages rescued during a bloody raid.*

At the time of Alberto Fujimori's election to the presidency in 1992, the Peruvian economy was in a shambles following 30 years of corruption and mismanagement. Terrorist groups, especially the powerful Shining Path, controlled more than half of the country and were responsible for tens of thousands of deaths. Although Fujimori quickly brought both situations under control, he did so only by sacrificing Peru's democratic institutions. Authoritarian rule didn't succeed for the long-term. After a few years of relative calm, renewed rebel attacks shattered hopes for permanent peace and prosperity.

Issues and Events

After years of attacking villages in the countryside, the Shining Path struck at the heart of Peru when it moved its terrorism campaign to the country's urban areas in 1991. In a single day in April, it bombed several embassies and banks and knocked out electrical power in cities throughout the country, including Lima. The Shining Path's tactics were matched in ruthlessness only by those of the Peruvian security

forces. The government's crackdown on terrorism resulted in more than 3,700 "disappearances": people who were probably kidnapped and secretly killed.

Peru's human rights record is condemned as one of the worst in the world. Like the Shining Path, the Peruvian army is also accused of raiding villages and killing innocent people. Civilians caught in the crossfire represent by far the largest number of casualties in the war between the Shining Path and the government.

Although Fujimori managed to bring rampant inflation under control, he argued that political and economic reform could not be accomplished until the terrorist insurgency was defeated. Frustrated with congressional opposition to measures he claimed were necessary to end the terrorism, Fujimori dismissed the government in April 1992 and assumed dictatorial powers. Five months later Fujimori was vindicated when his security forces managed to capture the Shining Path's elusive leader, Abimael Guzman. In the months that followed, hundreds of other Shining Path leaders and followers were jailed.

The arrests hindered the Shining Path, but the movement refused to die and by 1995 the group bombed a major tourist hotel in Lima. In 1996 the Tupac Amaru Revolutionary Movement stormed a party at the Japanese embassy and captured hundreds of hostages. Although most were promptly released, 70 men were held captive for four months.

Stability will continue to elude Peru as long as the conditions that brought the country to the brink of disaster in the 1980s still exist. Until economic equality is achieved, democracy will remain elusive and Peru will continue to teeter on the edge of chaos.

Background

During Spanish rule, Peru's indigenous population was ruthlessly exploited and all wealth was concentrated in the hands of the Spanish aristocracy who lived in Lima, the capital. The land was rich in gold and silver, and the treasures of Peru made Spain one of the world's richest countries.

After Peru gained independence in 1824 the Spanish aristocracy held on to power and wealth. Today, 80 percent of the people are either native American or mestizo, but the country remains in the hands of a very small, white ruling class that controls the government and the economy.

About half of the people of Peru live in poverty. The ever-expanding chasm between the rich and the poor has provided a breeding ground for radical terrorist groups that find sympathy among the poor. The most powerful of these groups is the Shining Path, or Sendero Luminoso, modeled after the Khmer Rouge in Cambodia whose short reign of terror in the 1970s left more than one million dead. Another rebel group is the Tupac Amaru Revolutionary Movement, named after a famous Inca revolutionary who fought against Spanish rule in Peru.

Society Under Siege: COLOMBIA

Perspective

1899-1902	*War of A Thousand Days between Liberals and Conservatives kills 100,000 people.*
1948-1957	*Second war, called* La Violencia, *kills 300,000 people.*
1964	*Army of National Liberation (ELN) founded.*
1966	*Revolutionary Armed Forces of Colombia (FARC) emerges.*
1984	**March 24.** *Drug war begins when government raids Tranquilandia.* **April 30.** *Minister of Justice killed by Medellin drug cartel.*
1985	**November 6.** *Guerrillas kill 11 Supreme Court justices in a single attack.*
1988	**January 25.** *Attorney General murdered by drug dealers.*
1992	**November 8.** *Rising terrorist attacks prompt a state of emergency.*
1993	**December 2.** *Death of Pablo Escobar breaks up the Medellin drug cartel.*
1996	**August 30.** *FARC captures 60 soldiers.*
1998	**March 2.** *Seventy soldiers killed in heavy fighting with FARC.*

In many ways Colombia differs greatly from its Latin American neighbors. While other countries struggle to rid themselves of military governments, Colombia is an oasis of democracy and enjoys prosperity and economic growth. And yet, Colombia is one of the world's most violent countries. Over the years the reasons for bloodshed have changed, but today the country continues to be plagued by leftist guerrillas, right-wing terrorists, violent drug-dealing organizations, murderers, kidnappers, and an army infamous for human rights violations.

Issues and Events

Violence in Colombia continues to escalate. The number of murders has risen from 9,000 in 1979, to 23,000 in 1989, to about 31,000 in 1997. While the 1997 murder rate was about one per 1,000 people, Colombia is among the most dangerous countries in the world. (By comparison, the number of murders in the United States was 19,645 in 1996, a rate of one offense per 13,500 people.)

Many of those killed in Colombia are casualties of an ongoing war between the government and various leftist guerrilla groups. The largest of these groups is the Revolutionary Armed Forces of Colombia (FARC), which routinely attacks police outposts and government installations. Another leftist group, the Army of National Liberation (ELN), specializes in the destruction of the country's oil pipelines and facilities. In 1997 a single pipeline was blown up 66 times. Both of these groups are also involved in kidnapping and robbery to finance their operations.

In response to these attacks by leftist rebels, right-wing paramilitary organizations have sprung up in support of the country's wealthy landowners. The objective of these death squads, responsible for heinous crimes against civilians, is to terrorize rural peasants into ending their support for the guerrillas.

Both the guerrillas and paramilitary groups finance their operations by protecting Colombia's drug dealers and their operations. Since the 1980s the powerful drug-dealer cartels have been able to buy or intimidate Colombia's police, armed forces, politicians, and judges into doing their bidding. Unrelenting pressure from the United States, along with the capture or arrest of the worst narcotics dealers, has weakened the cartels, but they remain a powerful force in Colombian society. Some of the worst violence in recent years has occurred in the Uraba region where the rebels, paramilitaries, drug dealers, and the military are all fighting for control of a lucrative drug trafficking corridor into Panama.

Surprisingly, most of the murders in Colombia cannot be attributed to any organized effort. The government claims that in 1996 less than 6,000 of the killings were politically motivated. In this violent society most of the murdered are victims of common crimes and personal vendettas.

Background

In 1899 the War of A Thousand Days was fought between the Conservatives, who wanted a strong, centralized government, and the Liberals, who promoted a decentralized government. This conflict, which killed 100,000 people, ended in a victory for the Conservatives. After the war the Liberals began to work for socialist reforms, while the Conservatives wanted the ruling class to retain power. The two sides went to war again in 1948 after Jorge Gaitan, a populist leader, was killed. This era of terror, known as *La Violencia,* was even worse than the first war. Three hundred thousand people were murdered before a power-sharing arrangement was reached in 1957.

Soon after the war Communist insurgency groups began to spring up. The ELN was the first, founded in 1961 with the help of Cuba. FARC came into existence two years later and advocated a Soviet-style political system. There are currently about 12,000 armed guerrillas in Colombia.

North America

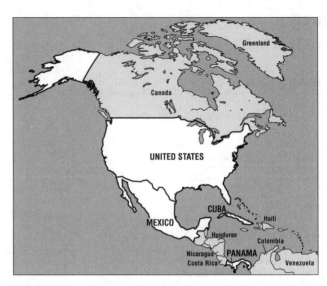

Since the mid-1800s, the United States has played a dominant role in shaping the political and economic landscape of the North American continent. Although the North American Free Trade Agreement (NAFTA) binds the U.S., Canada and Mexico closer than ever, the U.S. remains the overwhelmingly dominant force not just in North America but elsewhere in the hemisphere. Although the countries of Central America are linked to their neighbors in the Southern Hemisphere by culture, language, and history, the U.S. has had a profound effect on their development, and has long considered Central America to be within its sphere of influence.

U.S. intervention in Central American affairs began with the Monroe Doctrine of 1823, when President James Monroe stated that no further European colonization or intervention in the New World would be tolerated. The statement was made primarily to warn Spain not to try to recapture any of America's newly independent colonies and also to ward off further Russian expansion in Alaska.

The U.S.' first military action in Central America took place in 1846 during the Mexican-American War. More than 21,000 were killed in the fighting over the territory of Texas, which resulted in an American victory and Mexico's loss of nearly half its territory. By 1860 the U.S. had entered a period of isolationism that lasted until 1889, when it announced a new "good neighbor" policy, calling for political and military alliance among all of the countries in the Western Hemisphere. The year 1898 saw the beginning of the Spanish-American War and the transfer of Puerto Rico to American sovereignty. In 1899 an American entrepreneur founded the United Fruit Company, initiating an era of economic domination of Central America by U.S. interests. Within a short time, the company had acquired vast tracts of land for its banana plantations. Although the host countries initially benefited from the construction of new railroads and shipping facilities, the profits of these operations went to stockholders in the U.S. and proved to be a drain on the local economies.

In 1903 an agreement was reached to build the Panama Canal, which opened in 1914. The Canal Zone was established as a U.S. territory without Panama's permission, effectively separating the country into two separate pieces. Expanding American interests in the area prompted the adoption of the Roosevelt Corollary of the Monroe Doctrine, stating U.S. intentions to exercise international police power in Latin America and effectively placing the entire region under United States military authority. Between 1904 and 1933, the U.S. repeatedly sent troops to the Dominican Republic, Cuba, Honduras, Nicaragua, and Haiti. Troops were sent to Mexico in 1914 after the Mexican Revolution and again in 1916 to try to capture Pancho Villa.

By the 1930s, the countries of Central America began to resent the U.S. intervention in their internal affairs, and America renounced the Roosevelt Corollary. After World War II, the "good neighbor" policy was reintroduced and prompted the founding of the Organization of American States (OAS), designed to establish cooperation and create a defensive alliance. Throughout the 1950s and 1960s, the United Fruit Company experienced decline as more and more of its land was nationalized by host governments. In 1959 Cuba nationalized American sugar interests, which led to an embargo and break in diplomatic relations in 1960. In 1961 Castro's Communist government came to power. Cuba turned to the Soviet Union for economic assistance, a move that further infuriated the United States and led to the Cuban missile crisis of 1962. Since then, the U.S. has done everything in its power to isolate Cuba economically, which has been especially effective since the island nation lost its flow of Soviet aid. In addition, the U.S. has generally welcomed Cuban refugees, who tend to be from the Cuban upper classes. It has not extended these rights to other Latin American refugees, who tend to be much poorer.

After the Cuban revolution, the U.S. generally tried to back right-wing or military governments in an effort to prevent any further Communist takeovers. During the years of the Reagan administration, intervention in Central America increased as leftist factions in Nicaragua and El Salvador gained strength. In Nicaragua, Daniel Ortega's leftist government was voted out in free elections in favor of U.S.-backed Violeta Chamorro. In El Salvador, the civil war raged on until the two sides negotiated a shaky peace in 1992. The U.S. invaded the tiny island country of Grenada in 1983 to oust a Marxist government. In 1994 the U.S. invaded Haiti to oversee the restoration to power of the country's exiled president.

The U.S. has always maintained a high level of involvement in the affairs of Panama, site of the Panama Canal. In 1989, an invasion of Panama resulted in the arrest of the country's dictator, Manual Noriega, for his involvement in international drug smuggling. From the beginning Panamanians resented the U.S. Canal Zone, and in 1977 the area reverted to Panamanian sovereignty. Ironically, the Panamanians are reluctant to take full responsibility for control of the Panama Canal when it is transferred to them in 1999.

Relations between Mexico and the U.S. have been strained repeatedly over the issues of drug traffic, the environment, and trade. Despite this, the two countries enjoy substantial foreign exchange, and tourists from the U.S. provide Mexico with additional revenues.

The biggest problem facing the U.S. and Mexico has been the issue of illegal immigration to the United States. Several million Mexicans live illegally in the U.S., where the federal government claims they steal jobs from American workers and place a strain on social services, especially education. On the other hand, many argue that Mexican workers perform the low-level jobs many Americans do not want. In 1986 the U.S. passed the Immigration Reform and Control Act, which threatened U.S. employers with fines for employing illegals and offered amnesty to three million illegals who could prove that they had been in the U.S. since 1981. The Mexican government denounced the passage of the act as racist and repressive although Mexican leaders may have been more concerned that a crackdown on illegals would result in a loss of foreign exchange. Many illegals send back most of their wages to Mexico, and the country can ill afford to lose any of its revenues in this time of economic crisis. Enforcement of the law has been difficult, as ille-gals have become an integral part of many sectors of the American economy.

The North American Free Trade Agreement, which was implemented in 1994, eliminated trade barriers between the U.S., Mexico, and Canada. While people in the U.S. feared that NAFTA would result in a shift of jobs from the U.S. to Mexico, people in Canada envisioned that they would lose their jobs to people in the U.S. Three years later, there is still a lot of debate about the impact of NAFTA on the economies of the three countries. One reason NAFTA has been difficult to evaluate is that Mexico experienced a severe economic crisis in 1995 that profoundly affected Mexican imports and exports. It will probably be several years before the real effects of NAFTA can be assessed.

In the meantime, informal Mexican-American cooperation thrives in cross-border urban areas such as El Paso and Ciudad Juarez where thousands of workers and tons of goods cross the borders each day. The leaders of these cities work closely not only on economic issues, but also on regional concerns such as the provision of human services and the elimination of pollution.

While U.S. relations with Canada have been more peaceful than those with countries to the south, the Canadians still are wary of their American neighbors. Canada has enjoyed a shared history with the U.S., but despite a long and fruitful trade relationship, many Canadians regard Americans with suspicion, worrying that America's economic strength will overwhelm the Canadian market. Fears about economic and cultural domination by the U.S. prompted renewed nationalism during NAFTA negotiations and implementation. Canada and the U.S. are both large agricultural producers, and Canadians are concerned about their ability to maintain their system of providing subsidies to Canadian farmers. Also, Canada has always insisted that American firms conducting business in Canada should be required to invest in Canadian businesses. The legality and feasibility of these kinds of laws under NAFTA remains an issue.

A more pressing concern for most Canadians is their own country's future, given the renewed vigor shown by separatists in Quebec. Should the country split, there are fears that the individual parts will be even more prone to American dominance than the whole.

Welfare Reform:
THE UNITED STATES

Perspective

1929	*Stock market crash ushers in the Great Depression.*
1933	*Tennessee Valley Authority (TVA) creates jobs and promotes regional development.*
1935	**May.** *Works Progress Administration (WPA) creates jobs nationwide.* **August.** *Social Security Act passed.*
1941	*Economy improves in preparation for World War II.*
1949	*President Truman continues to build welfare programs through Fair Deal legislation.*
1952	*President Eisenhower bolsters social security, public housing, education aid, and civil rights.*
1960	*President Kennedy increases minimum wage, begins urban renewal programs, and establishes antidrug enforcement.*
1964	*President Johnson begins War on Poverty, including improved unemployment insurance.*
1965	*Johnson's Great Society campaign increases spending for education, housing, and the environment.*
1980	*President Reagan cuts social programs and begins federal "trickle down" tax-cut policy.*
1996	*President Clinton signs the Personal Responsibility and Work Opportunity Reconciliation Act.*

Between the 1960s and the 1990s the welfare system of the United States saw few meaningful changes. The system was highly criticized, however, for the nearly continual increase in the welfare budget and bureaucracy, and for highly publicized cases of fraud.

Major problems with the welfare system were widely recognized, including the lack of firm demands on recipients to reduce their welfare dependency. In fact, some families had been on welfare continually for two or more generations. The system was structured so that any outside income would cause a corresponding decrease in benefits. Too often, the easiest way for a family to maintain its economic standing was for it to remain on welfare.

Unfortunately, the system did not support the traditional family structure. It was much easier for a single mother to receive aid than it was for a married couple with children. Sometimes, a teenage couple would have a child out of wedlock and the young woman and child would start receiving aid, only to have the young man expect a cut of each check. Though most welfare recipients were law-abiding citizens trying to cope with difficult circumstances, it was obvious that the welfare environment, from its deteriorating public housing to its support of a "sit back and let the checks roll in" mentality, was not working in the recipients' best interest. For the system to truly improve lives, it would need radical changes.

For decades, it was considered risky for a political leader to suggest an overhaul of the welfare system. By the time Bill Clinton ran for President in 1992, public opinion had finally swayed in favor of reform, and he made a promise to "end welfare as we know it." In August 1996, after a few reform bill drafts by both his administration and Congress were rejected, Clinton signed the Personal Responsibility and Work Opportunity Reconciliation Act into law. The result has been the most widespread reform of the American welfare system in 60 years.

Issues and Events

In 1996 more than 27 million Americans—nearly one in ten—lived in a family with an income below the poverty line. Of all families, those most likely to be poor consisted of a single mother and her children. Almost 36 percent of these households were impoverished in 1996.

The 1996 welfare law was designed to address welfare dependency, impoverished single motherhood, and permissive eligibility for benefits. It replaced the major federal welfare programs with block grants to the states, making each state responsible for distributing funds to qualified recipients in the form of cash or services.

The new law requires state welfare departments to put clients to work or train them in job skills while they receive benefits. By the end of the first 24 months of assistance, a welfare recipient must be ready to work at a regular job. There is a 60-month lifetime maximum time limit for receiving federal welfare benefits, though these time limits can be waived for recipients legitimately incapable of working.

Other changes include a five-year waiting period for immigrants to receive aid; they must also become United States citizens. States can also forbid extra benefits for children born to a mother after she has begun receiving welfare. The law waives any reduction in benefits that would endanger an abused spouse or child, and provides funding for child care while parents are in training or at work.

One of the assumptions behind the law is that the most persistent welfare cases are single teenage mothers who have dropped out of high school. Therefore, the new law includes provisions to discourage teen pregnancy. States are required to implement programs to reduce illegitimate births, and a teen parent must live at home and stay in school to receive benefits. The law also requires the collection of child support from absentee fathers.

State welfare agencies develop their own rules for eligibility, specific benefits, and restrictions. Typically, if a recipient is not immediately able to find a job, an agency will place him or her into a training or work program. States can cut benefits for recipients who, without an acceptable excuse, refuse to participate in work or training.

Many states have taken advantage of the flexibility in the new law to start innovative programs. In Maine, a separate state-funded welfare program was developed to support college students as they continue their education while fulfilling new work requirements. Louisiana now guarantees transportation to jobs for some of its welfare recipients. Many other states have made surplus government cars available at low cost to those on welfare. State welfare programs vary widely, not only in their innovations but also in their ability to overhaul the entire welfare system.

Wisconsin, which has radically overhauled its system, has been held up as either a success story or a potential disaster. The state's 1995 pilot program required recipients in two counties to begin looking for work or enter a job-training program within 30 days of starting on welfare. By March 1998, Wisconsin became the first state to complete its transfer from the old welfare system to their new system. The transition has not been entirely smooth. There have been reports of increased homelessness and of children receiving inadequate care while parents are working or training. To alleviate this, the state has increased funding for homeless shelters and child care. In Wisconsin, the number of welfare recipients has decreased by more than 40 percent since the new federal welfare law was enacted in 1996.

Nationwide, between 1996 and 1998, the number of welfare dependents decreased by 27 percent. An estimated 40 percent of this decline is attributed to the expanding economy. Training and job placement due to welfare reform account for 31 percent of the decline. The rest of the decline was due to related government policies, including the Earned Income Tax Credit, the collection of child support from absentee fathers, and increased funding for child care.

The fate of those who leave the welfare system, either after finding a job or after being sanctioned for not following the rules, is very uncertain. An estimated 40 to 60 percent of former welfare recipients find work at poverty-level wages; some people even become homeless, as evidenced by Wisconsin's need to increase funding for shelters. There have been few real success stories. In Minnesota, the system was redesigned so that it reduces poverty itself, rather than leaving welfare recipients in jobs that pay poverty wages. This system supplements wages until the recipient's work income rises to 20 percent above the official poverty level.

Critics of welfare reform point out that those who leave welfare tend to remain poor, and are very likely to lose their jobs, become underemployed, and return to the welfare system—as long as they have not reached their 60-month maximum time limit. If the new system continues to emphasize pushing people off of welfare and into low-wage employment instead of addressing their overall poverty, it risks creating a new underclass with nowhere to turn for help.

Background

The "welfare state" as we know it was originally intended to relieve widespread poverty caused by the Great Depression. The New Deal, conceived by President Franklin Roosevelt, was the first major increase in government spending to dispel poverty and improve public welfare. In 1933, Roosevelt started the Tennessee Valley Authority (TVA) with the goal of creating jobs and developing the region. The success of the TVA spurred the establishment of other work programs, such as the Works Progress Administration (WPA). Roosevelt's Social Security Act of 1935 provided pensions for the elderly, unemployment compensation, and Aid to Families with Dependent Children (AFDC).

By 1941, the country was mobilizing for war. This effort spurred an economic recovery that continued through World War II. Afterward, President Harry Truman enacted the Fair Deal legislation, which included an increase in the minimum wage set by Roosevelt, and extended Social Security benefits. The social spending trend continued under John Kennedy, who strengthened Social Security, public housing, education, and civil rights programs. The Kennedy Administration enacted legislation for urban renewal, additional increases for the minimum wage, and antidrug enforcement. In 1964 Lyndon Johnson began his $1 billion War on Poverty, including improved unemployment insurance, food stamps, and special assistance to the Appalachian region. In 1965 he launched the Great Society program, which included more opportunities for education and housing, and he established Medicare and Medicaid. After the Vietnam war ended in 1963, poor economic conditions prompted a reduction in spending on social programs. By the time Ronald Reagan was elected in 1980, unemployment was 7.5 percent, and inflation was 12.5 percent. Reagan instituted new economic policies, including tax cuts and increased government spending, which stimulated the economy enough to cut unemployment to 5.2 percent and lower inflation to 4.2 percent. However, many believe that his "trickle down" policy of reducing taxes on the rich widened the gap between the rich and the poor. President Bush, who was elected in 1988, held welfare spending constant and suggested that charitable organizations increase their role in helping the poor. The Persian Gulf War soon drew his attention away from domestic issues, and was followed by an economic expansion that began in 1991 and continues to this day.

Surviving the Embargo: CUBA

Perspective

1898	*The United States takes possession of Cuba from Spain.*
1902	*Cuba gains independence.*
1959	**January 1.** *Fidel Castro becomes president.*
1961	**January 3.** *U.S. and Cuba break diplomatic relations.* **April.** *Bay of Pigs invasion fails.* **December 2.** *Castro embraces Marxist-Leninist policies.*
1962	**October.** *Cuban missile crisis brings U.S. and Soviet Union to brink of nuclear war.*
1963	**March.** *U.S. imposes Cuban embargo.*
1992	**January 17.** *Trade with Russia collapses.* **November 24.** *United Nations calls on the U.S. to lift the embargo.*
1994	**August 5.** *Rioting erupts in Havana.* **August 11.** *Massive exodus of Cubans to U.S. begins.* **September.** *U.S. and Cuba reach refugee accord.*
1996	**February 25.** *Two unarmed U.S. planes are shot down near Cuba.* **March 12.** *Helms-Burton law passes.*
1997	**September 4.** *Hotel bombing kills an Italian tourist.*
1998	*Pope John Paul II visits Cuba.*

Separated by only 90 miles (145 kilometers), Cuba and the United States enjoyed close relations until 1960 when Cuba asserted its independence from its powerful neighbor. Since then, Cuba and the U.S. have been worlds apart.

Issues and Events

The year 1991 brought hard times to Cuba. Not since the original imposition of the U.S. embargo in 1963 had Cuba faced such economic uncertainty. For decades Cuba had relied on the Soviet Union and the countries of Eastern Europe for more than three-quarters of its international trade. The collapse of Communism and the break-up of the Soviet Union were devastating blows to the Cuban economy.

In 1994, growing poverty resulted in the first-ever anti-government riot against the Castro regime. After the riot, Castro encouraged tens of thousands of Cubans to move to the U.S. The U.S. refused entry to these "boat" people and

tried to prevent a recurrence by signing an accord with Castro allowing more people to emigrate legally.

The deteriorating economy ultimately forced Castro to compromise his socialist principles and open up the country to foreign investors and tourists. By 1995 it seemed that the worst was over. In 1996 Cuba hosted more than one million visitors, and tourism surpassed the sugar industry as the largest source of foreign revenue.

Cuba's relations with the U.S. were damaged in early 1996 when two planes owned and piloted by American civilians were shot down near Cuba. Cuba insisted that the planes were owned by Cuban exiles who were trying to create an international incident. When the international community failed to condemn Cuba for the incident, the U.S. passed the Helms-Burton bill, which penalized foreign companies and individuals doing business with Cuba. The bill infuriated U.S. allies, most of whom had already voted repeatedly in the United Nations for the U.S. to end the embargo.

Despite growing international support, new cracks in Castro's totalitarian state continue to appear. In 1997 there were several bombings at tourist hotels. In 1998, Castro invited Pope John Paul II to visit Cuba, an event that would have been unthinkable only a few years earlier. The Pope's visit attracted large crowds and revived Catholicism throughout the country, which was officially atheist until 1992.

As long as the embargo continues, Castro has a scapegoat for Cuba's economic and political problems. If the embargo were lifted, Castro would face a tough decision: either to let Cuba continue to suffer economically or to expose it to an inevitable flood of Americans with capitalist ideas. Either alternative would end Cuba's dreams of a socialist utopia.

Background

The U.S. gained sovereignty over Cuba in 1898 following the Spanish-American War. Although the U.S. set Cuba free in 1902, it continued to intervene in Cuban affairs. Under corrupt leadership, Cuba became a mecca for organized crime, gambling, drugs, and prostitution.

At first the U.S. supported the revolution led by Fidel Castro, who pledged to restore democracy and end corruption. However, Cubans resented the continuing U.S. involvement in their internal affairs. In 1961 the U.S. engineered the failed Bay of Pigs invasion by anti-Castro Cubans who had fled to the United States. Several months later, Castro announced Cuba's conversion to Communism, and established a Soviet-style government and economy.

Castro's actions infuriated the U.S., and the Soviets responded to Cuba's pleas for help by sending nuclear missiles to Cuba, an act which brought the U.S. and the Soviet Union to the brink of nuclear war. The Soviets eventually withdrew the missiles, but a U.S. embargo imposed shortly after the crisis still remains in effect.

Dissent in Chiapas: MEXICO

Perspective

1821	**September 27.** *Spain grants Mexico independence.*
1910	**November 10.** *Popular uprising sparks the Mexican Revolution.*
1929	*Institutional Revolutionary Party (PRI) founded.*
1994	**January 1.** *North American Free Trade Agreement (NAFTA) takes effect; Zapatista National Liberation Army (EZLN) stages armed rebellion in Chiapas.*
1995	**February 9.** *Government launches offensive against EZLN.*
1996	**February 16.** *Peace treaty signed between EZLN and the government is unsuccessful.*
1997	**July 6.** *PRI defeated in election upset.* **December 22.** *Paramilitary groups massacre 45 villagers in Acteal.*

The year 1994 held great economic promise for Mexico. The North American Free Trade Agreement (NAFTA) was designed to develop closer links with the United States and Canada, Mexico's economically powerful neighbors to the north. Instead, 1994 brought the most dramatic series of political and military events since the Mexican Revolution.

Issues and Events

On January 1, 1994, Mexico planned to celebrate the implementation of NAFTA. Instead, national attention was focused on an armed rebellion that broke out in the impoverished southern state of Chiapas. Amerindians, angered by economic and political discrimination, ambushed Mexican army units, took control of several towns, and became instantly symbolic of the gulf that exists between Mexico's haves and have-nots. At least 140 people, and perhaps many more, died.

The rebels, calling themselves the Zapatista National Liberation Army (EZLN), claimed that NAFTA would bring economic ruin to Mexico's poor. They claimed that the wealthy farmers in Chiapas would benefit from free trade of their high-value crops to the U.S., while small farmers would lose government subsidies for staple crops like corn.

The Zapatistas also focused on political reform and challenged the ruling Industrial Revolutionary Party (PRI) to hold open, fair elections. In southern Mexico, PRI politicians often stayed in office for life, conspiring with wealthy landowners for mutual gain. The Zapatistas' call for fair elections and a truly representative government struck a national chord.

In early 1995 the government installed a military sweep of Chiapas, but the guerrillas fled to jungle strongholds where they continued to plan their campaign. Captured rebel leaders notified international human rights organizations that they were tortured in prison and forced to confess to crimes they did not commit.

A peace agreement was forged in early 1996 but it broke down in a matter of months. After that the two sides reached an uneasy stalemate. Mexican troops continue to surround EZLN-controlled areas—considered war zones.

While the EZLN lacks the military strength to defeat the Mexican army, it has strongly influenced Mexican politics. The Chiapas rebellion affected the outcome of 1997 elections in which the ruling PRI party lost control of the Mexican legislature in its worst electoral defeat ever, after a 70-year monopoly on power.

Soon after the PRI's defeat, paramilitary organizations began to emerge, some of which allegedly had ties to PRI officials. In December 1997, 45 unarmed villagers, including ten children, were killed in the Chiapas village of Acteal by masked gunmen. Among those later arrested for involvement in the massacre were a mayor and several police officers. Both the Governor of Chiapas and the Interior Minister resigned from office after the incident, and the government renewed its efforts to reach a peaceful settlement with the EZLN.

The Zapatistas and the people of Chiapas want their own government and legal system. The Mexican government, although willing to provide more financial aid to the region, claims that Chiapas autonomy would compromise Mexican unity. The real source of the conflict, however, is the disparity of wealth distribution that has resulted in poverty and powerlessness for Mexico's indigenous population.

Background

Before the arrival of Spanish conquistadors, Mexico was the home of the Aztecs and the Maya, probably the greatest and most advanced civilizations in the New World. In Mexico today, more than one-third of the people are indigenous Mexicans and 90 percent are of mixed European and Amerindian ancestry.

Under Spanish rule, wealthy Europeans built huge estates and vast mineral empires with the help of indigenous slave labor. This pattern continued after Mexico became independent. The indigenous population was brutally repressed until the Mexican Revolution of 1910. Leaders of the revolution, including Emiliano Zapata, sought to bring about social reform and justice for the country's peasant farmers and laborers. It was another leader of the revolution, Lazaro Cardenas, who founded the PRI party to carry out the principles of the Revolution.

Canal Takeover: PANAMA

Perspective

1903	**November 3.** *Panama gains its independence from Colombia.*
1904	**February 23.** *Panama becomes a United States protectorate.*
1914	**August 15.** *Panama Canal opens.*
1936	*Hull Alfaro Treaty recognizes Panamanian independence.*
1959	**November.** *Student riots result in the building of a fence along the Canal Canal Zone.*
1964	**January 9.** *Three days of rioting leave 20 people dead.*
1977	**September 7.** *Panama Canal Treaty abolishes the Canal Zone and transfers the canal to Panama in 1999.*
1989	**December 20.** *U.S. invades Panama and overthrows Noriega.*
1992	**April 9.** *A U.S. court convicts Noriega of drug-trafficking and racketeering.*
1997	**December 23.** *Tentative agreement allows U.S. troops to remain in Panama beyond 1999.*

As the site of the Panama Canal, this small Central American country has been under the shadow of the American flag since the late 1800s. The U.S. owned and operated the 51-mile-long canal, and for more than 70 years the Canal Zone, a ten-mile-wide strip of U.S. territory surrounding the canal, has divided Panama into two unconnected parts. In 1977 a treaty abolished the Canal Zone and transferred canal ownership to the Panamanians in 1999. As the deadline approaches, the future of the canal under Panamanian stewardship is under hot debate.

Issues and Events

To Panamanians the canal has been both a blessing and a curse. Americans living in Panama have injected half a billion dollars annually into the Panamanian economy, but Panamanians gave up independence and national sovereignty in exchange.

The U.S. helped Panama gain its independence from Colombia in 1903, but freedom was short-lived. The treaty that authorized canal construction created the Canal Zone, established an annuity for Panama, and declared Panama a U.S. protectorate was signed by the U.S. and France. Panama's consent to the agreement was considered inconsequential.

The next decades brought political upheaval, repeated anti-American protests, and revised treaties. Riots in 1927 led to a new treaty in 1936 that guaranteed Panamanian independence. During World War II, however, the U.S. built new military bases near the canal without Panama's permission (although the bases were eventually included in a treaty signed in 1955). In 1959, and again in 1960, serious unrest resulted in millions of dollars in property damage, hundreds of injuries, and 20 deaths.

In 1977 the U.S. agreed to transfer ownership of the canal to Panama at noon on December 31, 1999. The Panama Canal Treaty also abolished the Canal Zone and called for the closure of the U.S. military bases. Another agreement called the Neutrality Treaty, however, allows the U.S. to invade the country if the canal were rendered inoperable for any reason.

Shipping companies are skeptical about Panama's ability to manage the canal after 1999. Although the Panamanians have the expertise to run the canal, there are concerns about their ability to properly maintain it. Many of the structures on property turned over to Panama have already decayed from lack of maintenance in the harsh jungle climate. There are also serious concerns about Panama's long history of corruption and political instability. The country is known for its ties with drug dealers and its involvement in money-laundering. In 1989 the U.S. invaded Panama and arrested Panama's President Manuel Noriega, brought him to the U.S., and then tried and convicted him for drug smuggling and related charges.

There are signs that Panama is nervous about the transfer. Panamanians hope they can offset the loss of revenue from the American exodus by establishing new regional universities, retirement communities, and luxury resorts in the former Canal Zone. But security concerns still abound. In late 1997 Panama reportedly intended to allow U.S. troops to remain after 1999 as part of a regional anti-drug effort.

Background

The Spanish, who arrived in Panama in 1501, were the first to establish rule over this strategically located country. By 1821 Spain's power had declined, and Panama became a dependency of Colombia.

In 1513 Vasco Nuñez de Balboa became the first to lead a land expedition from the Atlantic Ocean to the Pacific Ocean through the dense jungles of the Isthmus of Panama. By 1520 Spain was exploring the possibility of building a canal, but construction did not begin until 1879 when the French, under the leadership of the builder of the Suez Canal, began the project. Ten years later construction was abandoned as a result of disease, design flaws, and lack of financing.

The French transferred rights to the project to the U.S. in 1904, and the Panama Canal was officially opened in 1914.

World Gazetteer:
Profiles of Countries & Places

Masai woman standing in the doorway of a mud hut in Masai Mara, Kenya

The following World Gazetteer presents an up-to-date overview of the world's independent countries and their possessions. Geographic, political, and population-related information is derived from the most current Rand McNally data available. Ethnic groups, religions, trade partners, exports, and imports are listed in order of decreasing size and/or importance. Languages are similarly organized, with official language(s) listed first. Political parties are cited alphabetically, as are membership entries, which represent member countries of the following organizations:

Arab League (AL)

Association of South East Asian Nations (ASEAN)

Commonwealth of Nations (CW)

European Union (EU)

North Atlantic Treaty Organization (NATO)

Organization for Economic Cooperation and Development (OECD)

Organization of African Unity (OAU)

Organization of American States (OAS)

Organization of Petroleum Exporting Countries (OPEC)

United Nations (UN)

AFGHANISTAN

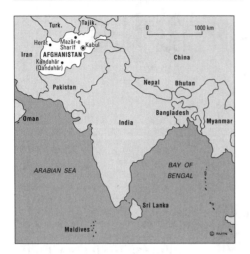

Official name Islamic State of Afghanistan

PEOPLE
Population 24,290,000. **Density** 96/mi² (37/km²).
Urban 20%. **Capital** Kabul, 1,424,400. **Ethnic groups**
Pathan 38%, Tajik 25%, Hazara 19%, Uzbek 6%.
Languages Dari, Pashto, Uzbek, Turkmen. **Religions**
Sunni Muslim 84%, Shiite Muslim 15%. **Life**
expectancy 46 female, 45 male. **Literacy** 32%.

POLITICS
Government Islamic council. **Parties** Islamic, Islamic
Revolutionary Movement, Islamic Society, Islamic
Union, Taliban, others. **Suffrage** None. **Memberships**
UN. **Subdivisions** 29 provinces.

ECONOMY
GDP $12,800,000,000. **Per capita** $562. **Monetary**
unit Afghani. **Trade partners** Exports: Former Soviet
republics, Pakistan, India. Imports: Former Soviet
republics, Japan, Singapore. **Exports** Fruits and nuts,
carpets, wool, cotton, hides, pelts, gems. **Imports**
Food, petroleum, manufactures.

LAND
Description Southern Asia, landlocked. **Area** 251,826
mi² (652,225 km²). **Highest point** Nowshāk, 24,557 ft
(7,485 m). **Lowest point** Along Amu Darya River, 850 ft
(259 m).

People. Afghanistan shares borders with China,
Iran, Pakistan, Tajikistan, Turkmenistan, and
Uzbekistan. This crossroads position has created
a population that is ethnically and linguistically
diverse. Religion plays a strong unifying role,
however. Most Afghans are Muslim, and Islamic
laws and customs determine lifestyles and
beliefs, both religious and secular. The population is mainly rural, consisting primarily of
farmers and a small nomadic group.

Economy and the Land. Afghanistan's economy
is in a shambles as a result of an ongoing civil
war. Subsistence agriculture and animal husbandry are the main economic activities. A terrain of mountains and valleys, including the

Hindu Kush, separates the desert region of the
southwest from the more fertile north, an area of
higher population density and the site of natural
gas deposits. Winters are generally cold, and
summers are hot and dry.

History and Politics. Once part of the Persian
Empire, the area of present-day Afghanistan has
seen invasions by Persians, Macedonians,
Greeks, Turks, Arabs, Mongols, and other peoples. An Arab invasion in A.D. 652 introduced
Islam. In 1747, Afghan tribes led by Ahmad Shah
Durrani united the area and established present-
day Afghanistan. Power remained with the
Durrani tribe for more than two centuries. In the
19th and early 20th centuries, Britain controlled
Afghanistan's foreign affairs. A Durrani tribe
member and former prime minister led a military
coup in 1973 and set up a republic. The new government's failure to improve economic and
social conditions led to a 1978 revolution that
established a Marxist government and brought
Soviet aid. Intraparty differences and citizenry
dissent led to a Soviet invasion in 1979. Fighting
erupted between government forces and the
mujahidin (holy warrior) guerrillas. In 1991 the
United States and Russia stopped all military
assistance to the warring factions. Currently, the
Islamic fundamentalist *Taliban* controls two-
thirds of the country, including the capital of
Kabul. ∎

ALBANIA

Official name Republic of Albania

PEOPLE
Population 3,314,000. **Density** 299/mi² (115/km²).
Urban 38%. **Capital** Tiranë, 243,000. **Ethnic groups**
Albanian (Illyrian) 95%, Greek 3%. **Languages**
Albanian, Greek. **Religions** Muslim 70%, Greek
Orthodox 20%, Roman Catholic 10%. **Life expectancy**
76 female, 70 male. **Literacy** 72%.

POLITICS

Government Republic. **Parties** Democratic, Socialist. **Suffrage** Universal, 18 and over. **Memberships** UN. **Subdivisions** 26 districts.

ECONOMY

GDP $4,100,000,000. **Per capita** $1,194. **Monetary unit** Lek. **Trade partners** Italy, Macedonia, Germany. **Exports** Asphalt, metals and metallic ores, electricity, crude oil, produce, tobacco. **Imports** Machinery, consumer goods, grains.

LAND

Description Southeastern Europe. **Area** 11,100 mi² (28,748 km²). **Highest point** Korabit Peak, 9,035 ft (2,754 m). **Lowest point** Sea level.

People. A homogeneous native population characterizes Albania, where Greeks are the main minority. Five centuries of Turkish rule shaped much of the culture and led many Albanians to adopt Islam. Since 1944 an increased emphasis on education has more than tripled the literacy rate. From 1967 until 1990 religious institutions were banned.

Economy and the Land. The poorest country in Europe, Albania has tried to shift its economy from a centrally planned system to an open market economy. Although the economy rebounded after a severe depression in 1990-91, unemployment remains high. Living conditions are poor, but land has been privatized and the economy has begun to grow. Mineral resources make mining the chief industry. The terrain consists of forested hills and mountains, and the climate is mild.

History and Politics. Early invaders and rulers included Greeks, Romans, and Goths. In 1468 the Ottoman Turks conquered the area, and it remained part of their empire until the First Balkan War in 1912. Albania was invaded by Italy and occupied by Germany during World War II. A Communist government was established after the war. The failure of Soviet Communism increased instability, and in 1991 the Communist government resigned. There was some violence as a democratic process was installed. In 1992 Albanians elected their first democratic president. Relations with Greece have been deteriorating as a result of an ongoing border dispute. ■

ALGERIA

Official name Democratic and Popular Republic of Algeria

PEOPLE

Population 30,150,000. **Density** 33/mi² (13/km²). **Urban** 56%. **Capital** Algiers, 1,507,241. **Ethnic groups** Arab-Berber 99%. **Languages** Arabic, Berber dialects, French. **Religions** Sunni Muslim 99%, Christian and Jewish 1%. **Life expectancy** 70 female, 68 male. **Literacy** 62%.

POLITICS

Government Republic. **Parties** Democratic National Rally, Movement of Peaceful Society, National Liberation Front, others. **Suffrage** Universal, 18 and

over. **Memberships** AL, OAU, OPEC, UN. **Subdivisions** 48 departments.

ECONOMY

GDP $108,700,000,000. **Per capita** $3,767. **Monetary unit** Dinar. **Trade partners** Exports: France, U.S., Italy. Imports: France, Germany, U.S. **Exports** Petroleum, natural gas. **Imports** Machinery, manufactures, food.

LAND

Description Northern Africa. **Area** 919,595 mi² (2,381,741 km²). **Highest point** Tahat, 9,541 ft (2,908 m). **Lowest point** Chott Melrhir, -131 ft (-40 m).

People. Indigenous Berbers and invading Arabs shaped modern Algeria's culture, and today most of the population is Muslim and of Arab-Berber descent. European cultural influences, evidence of more than a century of French control, exist in urban areas. Since it became independent in 1962, Algeria has instituted free medical care and greatly improved its educational system.

Economy and the Land. A member of the Organization of Petroleum Exporting Countries (OPEC), Algeria produces oil and natural gas. Agriculture is divided between state and privately owned farms. After a recession in the mid-1980s, Algeria began to abandon its centrally planned economy and to implement free market reforms. Algeria's terrain is varied. The Tell, Arabic for hill, is a narrow Mediterranean coastal region that contains the country's most fertile land and highest population. South of this lie high plateaus and the Atlas Mountains, which give way to the Sahara Desert. The climate is temperate along the coast and dry and cool in the plateau region.

History and Politics. In the 8th and 11th centuries, invading Arabs brought their language and religion to the native Berbers. France began to conquer Algeria in 1830, and by 1902 the entire country was under French control. The revolution against French rule began in 1954, and in 1962 the country was declared independent. Since a bloodless coup in 1965, the political situation has been relatively stable. A 1989 referendum approved a new constitution allowing multiparty elections. The first free national elections since independence were held in 1991. The fundamentalist Islamic Salvation Front (ISF) won in a landslide victory, prompting a military take-over. In 1992 the government banned ISF and jailed its leaders. In 1996 citizens approved a new constitution that strengthened the government and banned religion-based political parties. The resulting repression prompted violence across the country, which has resulted in approximately 80,000 deaths so far, mostly innocent villagers. Muslim militants continue their opposition. ■

AMERICAN SAMOA

Official name Territory of American Samoa

PEOPLE
Population 63,000. **Density** 818/mi² (317/km²). **Urban** 51%. **Capital** Pago Pago, 3,519. **Ethnic groups** Samoan 89%, Caucasian 2%, Tongan 4%. **Languages** Samoan, English. **Religions** Congregationalist 50%, Roman Catholic 20%, Protestant and other 30%. **Life expectancy** 75 female, 71 male. **Literacy** 97%.

POLITICS
Government Unincorporated territory (U.S.). **Suffrage** Universal, 18 and over. **Memberships** None. **Subdivisions** 3 districts.

ECONOMY
GDP $128,000,000. **Per capita** $3,048. **Monetary unit** U.S. dollar. **Trade partners** U.S., Japan, New Zealand. **Exports** Canned tuna, manufactures. **Imports** Machinery, food, petroleum products.

LAND
Description South Pacific islands. **Area** 77 mi² (199 km²). **Highest point** Lata Mtn., 3,160 ft (963 m). **Lowest point** Sea level.

People. Ethnically and linguistically, the people of American Samoa are the same as those of Samoa: mainly Samoan-speaking Polynesians, with a minority of Samoan-European descent. The majority of American Samoans are bilingual, speaking English in addition to Samoan. Most live in rural villages on Tutuila—the main island and location of the capital of Pago Pago—but more American Samoans live on the United States mainland and in Hawaii than live on the islands themselves.

Economy and the Land. American Samoa's industry is based on fishing, and activities include tuna canning and producing fish products. Most farming is on the subsistence level. In the 1960s an economic expansion program, funded by the U.S., improved transportation systems, medical and educational facilities, and the tourist and fish industries. Many benefits were short-lived, however. The seven islands are part of the South Pacific island chain that includes Samoa. Tutuila, Aunuu, and the Manua group—Tau, Ofu, and Olosega—are volcanic in origin, and Rose and Swains islands are coral atolls. The terrain is mostly mountainous, and the climate is tropical.

History and Politics. More than 2,000 years ago, the first inhabitants of the Samoan islands probably migrated from eastern Melanesia. The first Europeans arrived at the islands in the early 1700s. Foreign competition for influence resulted in the division of the islands between the United States and Germany in 1900, with the U.S. receiving the eastern islands of Tutuila, Aunuu, and the Manua group. Swains Island was annexed in 1925. In 1976 American Samoans voted to elect their own governor, who had previously been appointed by the Secretary of the Interior. ■

ANDORRA

Official name Principality of Andorra

PEOPLE
Population 76,000. **Density** 434/mi² (168/km²) **Urban** 95%. **Capital** Andorra, 20,437. **Ethnic groups** Spanish 61%, Andorran 30%, French 6%. **Languages** Catalan, Spanish (Castilian), French. **Religions** Roman Catholic. **Life expectancy** 82 female, 76 male.

POLITICS
Government Parliamentary co-principality (Spanish and French protection). **Parties** Liberal Union, National Democratic Group. **Suffrage** Universal, 18 and over. **Memberships** UN. **Subdivisions** 7 parishes.

ECONOMY
GDP $1,000,000,000. **Per capita** $16,949. **Monetary unit** French franc, Spanish peseta. **Trade partners** France, Spain. **Exports** Electricity, tobacco products, furniture. **Imports** Manufactures, food.

LAND
Description Southwestern Europe, landlocked. **Area** 175 mi² (453 km²). **Highest point** Pic de Coma Pedrosa, 9,652 ft (2,942 m). **Lowest point** Along Valira River, 2,749 ft (838 m).

People. Much of Andorran life and culture has been shaped by its mountainous terrain and governing countries, France and Spain. Population is concentrated in the valleys, and despite a tourism boom in past decades, the peaks and valleys of the Pyrenees have isolated the small country from many 20th-century changes. Catalan is the official language, and cultural and historic ties exist with the Catalonian region of northern Spain. The majority of the population is Spanish; Andorran citizens are a minority.

Economy and the Land. The terrain has established Andorra's economy as well as its lifestyle. Improved transportation routes, together with other factors, have resulted in a thriving tourist industry—a dramatic shift from traditional sheepherding and tobacco growing. In addition, duty-free status has made the country a European shopping mecca. Due to Andorra's "tax haven" status, banking is also a significant part of its economy. Because only 2 percent of the land is arable, most food must be imported. Climate varies with altitude; winters are cold and summers are cool and pleasant.

History and Politics. Tradition indicates that Charlemagne freed the area from the Moors in A.D. 806. A French count and the Spanish bishop of Seo de Urgel signed an agreement in the 1200s to act as co-princes of the country, establishing the political status and boundaries that exist today. The co-principality is governed by the president of France and the bishop of Seo de Urgel. In 1994 Andorra adopted a new constitution, ending a system of government in effect since the 13th century. ■

ANGOLA

Official name Republic of Angola

PEOPLE
Population 10,760,000. **Density** 22/mi² (8.6/km²). **Urban** 32%. **Capital** Luanda, 1,459,900. **Ethnic groups** Mbundu 62%, Kongo 13%, mulatto 2%, European 1%. **Languages** Portuguese, indigenous. **Religions** Animist 47%, Roman Catholic 38%, Protestant 15%. **Life expectancy** 51 female, 47 male. **Literacy** 41%.

POLITICS
Government Republic. **Parties** National Union for the Total Independence of Angola, Popular Movement for Liberation, others. **Suffrage** Universal, 18 and over. **Memberships** OAU, UN. **Subdivisions** 18 provinces.

ECONOMY
GDP $7,400,000,000. **Per capita** $666. **Monetary unit** Kwanza. **Trade partners** Exports: U.S., Bahamas. Imports: U.S., France, Brazil, Portugal. **Exports** Petroleum, natural gas, diamonds, coffee, sisal, fish, lumber, cotton. **Imports** Machinery and electrical equipment, food, transportation equipment.

LAND
Description Southern Africa. **Area** 481,354 mi² (1,246,700 km²). **Highest point** Morro do Môco, 8,596 ft (2,620 m). **Lowest point** Sea level.

People. Angola is made up mostly of various Bantu peoples—mainly Ovimbundu, Mbundu, and Kongo. Despite influences from a half-century of Portuguese rule, Angolan traditions remain strong, especially in rural areas. Each group has its own language, and although Portuguese is the official language, it is spoken by a minority. Many Angolans, retaining traditional indigenous beliefs, worship ancestral spirits.

Economy and the Land. Although blessed with rich natural resources, the Angolan economy has suffered as a result of an ongoing civil war. Not a member of the Organization of Petroleum Exporting Countries (OPEC), Angola is, nevertheless, a large oil producer. Cabinda, an enclave separated from the rest of the country by the Democratic Republic of the Congo and the Congo River (formerly the Zaire), is the main site of oil production. Diamond mining remains an important activity, as does agriculture. Much of the land is forested, however, and is therefore not suited for commercial farming. About 85 percent of the population engages in subsistence agriculture. The flat coastal area gives way to inland plateaus and uplands. The climate varies from tropical to subtropical.

History and Politics. Bantu groups settled in the area prior to the first century A.D. In 1483, a Portuguese explorer became the first European to arrive in Angola, and slave trade soon became a major activity. Portuguese control expanded and continued almost uninterrupted for several centuries. In the 1960s ignored demands for popular rule led to two wars for independence. Three nationalist groups emerged, each with its own ideology and supporters. In 1974, a coup in Portugal resulted in independence for all Portuguese territories in Africa, and Angola became independent in 1975. A civil war ensued, with the three groups fighting for power. By 1976, with the assistance of Cuban military personnel, the Popular Movement for the Liberation of Angola (PMLA) had established control. Angola, Cuba, and South Africa signed an accord in 1988 providing for Cuban troop withdrawals by July 1991. The country's first democratic elections were held in 1992 but were disputed. In 1994 a

UN-sponsored peace process began; it led to the formation of a unity government in 1997 that brought together the leaders of the main rebel group and the 1992 elected government. ■

ANGUILLA See UNITED KINGDOM.

ANTARCTICA

Official name Antarctica
Capital None. **Memberships** None.

LAND
Description Continent in Southern Hemisphere. **Area** 5,400,000 mi² (14,000,000 km²). **Highest point** Vinson Massif, 16,066 ft (4,897 m). **Lowest point** Deep Lake, -184 ft (-56 m).

People. Antarctica, which surrounds the South Pole, is the southernmost continent, the coldest place on Earth, and one of the last frontiers. There are no native inhabitants, and its temporary population is made up mainly of scientists from various countries operating research stations.

Economy and the Land. Harsh climate and terrain have inhibited resource exploration and development. Antarctica's natural resources include coal, various ores, iron, offshore oil, and natural gas. Fishing for krill, a marine protein source, is another activity. Crossed by several ranges collectively known as the Transantarctic Mountains, Antarctica can be roughly divided into a mountainous western region and a larger eastern sector consisting of an icy plain rimmed by mountains. With its tip about 700 miles (1,127 kilometers) from southern South America, the mountainous Antarctic Peninsula and its offshore islands jut northward. Nearly all Antarctica is ice-covered, precipitation is minimal, and the continent is actually a desert.

History and Politics. In the 1770s, Captain James Cook of Britain set out in search of the southernmost continent and sailed completely around Antarctica without sighting land. Explorations beginning in 1820 resulted in sightings of the mainland or offshore islands by the British, Russians, and Americans. British explorer Sir James C. Ross conducted the first extensive explorations. After a lull of several decades, interest in Antarctica was renewed in the late 19th and early 20th centuries. Captain Robert F. Scott and Ernest Shackleton of Britain and Roald Amundsen of Norway led the renewed interest. Amundsen won the race to the South Pole in 1911. An Antarctic Treaty signed in 1959 permitted only peaceful scientific research to be conducted in the region. It also delayed settlement of overlapping claims to the territory held by Norway, Australia, France, New Zealand, Chile, Britain, and Argentina. In 1996, it was found that the depletion of atmospheric ozone over Antarctica had increased to record levels. ■

ANTIGUA AND BARBUDA

Official name Antigua and Barbuda

PEOPLE
Population 67,000.
Density 392/mi² (152/km²). **Urban** 36%.
Capital St. John's, Antigua I., 24,359.
Ethnic groups Black, British, Portuguese, Lebanese, Syrian.
Languages English, local dialects. **Religions** Anglican, Protestant, Roman Catholic. **Life expectancy** 76 female, 71 male. **Literacy** 89%.

POLITICS
Government Parliamentary state.
Parties Labor, United Progressive. **Suffrage** Universal, 18 and over.
Memberships CW, OAS, UN. **Subdivisions** 7 parishes.

ECONOMY
GDP $425,000,000. **Per capita** $6,343. **Monetary unit** East Caribbean dollar. **Trade partners** Exports: U.S., U.K., Canada. Imports: U.S., U.K., Yugoslavia. **Exports** Petroleum products, manufactures, food, machinery, transportation equipment. **Imports** Food, livestock, machinery, transportation equipment, manufactures, chemicals.

LAND
Description Caribbean islands. **Area** 171 mi² (442 km²). **Highest point** Boggy Pk., 1,319 ft (402 m). **Lowest point** Sea level.

People. Most Antiguans are descendants of black African slaves brought by the British to work sugarcane plantations. The largest urban area is St. John's, but most Antiguans live in rural areas. British rule has left its imprint; most people are Protestant and speak English.

Economy and the Land. The dry, tropical climate and white-sand beaches attract many visitors, making tourism the economic mainstay. Once dependent on sugar cultivation, the country has shifted to a multicrop agriculture. The country is composed of three islands: Antigua, Barbuda, and uninhabited Redondo. Formed by volcanoes, the low-lying islands are mostly flat.

History and Politics. The original inhabitants of Antigua and Barbuda were the Caribs. Columbus arrived at Antigua in 1493, and after unsuccessful Spanish and French attempts at colonization, the British began settlement in the 1600s. The country remained a British colony until 1967, when it became an associated state of the United Kingdom. Antigua gained independence in 1981. In March 1994, the Antigua Labour Party was returned to power for the third time, pledging a more open political system. ■

ARGENTINA

Official name Argentine Republic

PEOPLE
Population 36,065,000. **Density** 34/mi² (13/km²). **Urban** 88%. **Capital** Buenos Aires (de facto), 2,960,976; Viedma (future) 40,452. **Ethnic groups** White 85%; mestizo, Amerindian, and others 15%. **Languages** Spanish, English, Italian, German, French. **Religions** Roman Catholic 90%, Jewish 2%, Protestant 2%. **Life expectancy** 77 female, 70 male. **Literacy** 96%.

POLITICS
Government Republic. **Parties** Front for a Country in Solidarity (Frepaso), Justicialist (Peronista), Radical Civic Union, others. **Suffrage** Universal, 18 and over. **Memberships** OAS, UN. **Subdivisions** 22 provinces, 1 district, 1 national territory.

ECONOMY
GDP $278,500,000,000. **Per capita** $8,081. **Monetary unit** Peso. **Trade partners** Exports: U.S., Brazil, Netherlands. Imports: U.S., Brazil, Germany. **Exports** Meat, wheat, corn, oilseed, manufactures. **Imports** Machinery, chemicals, metals, fuel, agricultural products.

LAND
Description Southern South America. **Area** 1,073,519 mi² (2,780,400 km²). **Highest point** Cerro Aconcagua, 22,831 ft (6,959 m). **Lowest point** Salinas Chicas, -138 ft (-42 m).

People. An indigenous population, Spanish settlement, and a turn-of-the-century influx of immigrants have made Argentina an ethnically diverse country. Today, most Argentines are descendants of Spanish and Italian immigrants. Other Europeans, mestizos of mixed Amerindian and Spanish blood, Middle Easterners, and Latin American immigrants diversify the population further. A strong Spanish influence is evident in the major religion, Roman Catholicism; the official language, Spanish; and many aspects of cultural life.

Economy and the Land. Political difficulties beginning in the 1930s have resulted in economic problems and have kept this one-time economic giant from realizing its potential. The most valuable natural resource is the rich soil of the *pampas,* fertile plains in the east-central region. The greatest contributors to the economy, however, are food processing, manufacturing, and services. The second-largest country in South America, Argentina has a varied terrain, with northern lowlands, the east-central *pampas,* the Andes Mountains in the west, and the southern Patagonian steppe. The climate also varies, from subtropical in the north to subarctic in the south.

History and Politics. The earliest inhabitants of the area were Amerindians. In the 1500s silver-seeking Spaniards arrived, and by 1580 they had established a colony on the site of present-day Buenos Aires. In 1816 Argentina officially announced its independence from Spain. A successful struggle for independence ensued, and in 1853 a constitution was adopted and a president elected. Prosperity continued through the 1920s, and immigration and foreign investment increased. Unsatisfactory power distribution and concern over foreign investment resulted in a military coup in 1930. Thus began a series of civil and military governments; coups; the election, overthrow, and reelection of Juan Perón; and controversial human-rights violations. In 1982 Argentina lost a war with Britain over the Falkland Islands. Years of struggling with human rights transgressions followed. Since winning the election in 1989, the Perónistas have introduced austere economic reforms and rescheduled foreign debts. In the 1990s, these actions began to noticeably improve in the economy. ■

ARMENIA

Official name Republic of Armenia

PEOPLE
Population 3,465,000. **Density** 301/mi² (116/km²). **Urban** 69%. **Capital** Yerevan, 1,199,000. **Ethnic groups** Armenian 93%, Azerbaijani 3%, Russian 2%. **Languages** Armenian, Russian. **Religions** Armenian Orthodox 94%. **Life expectancy** 76 female, 70 male. **Literacy** 99%.

POLITICS
Government Republic. **Parties** Communist, Democratic Liberal, National Movement, Shamiram Women's Movement, other. **Suffrage** Universal, 18 and over. **Memberships** UN. **Subdivisions** None.

ECONOMY
GDP $9,100,000,000. **Per capita** $2,548. **Monetary unit** Dram. **Trade partners** Former Soviet republics. **Exports** Gold, jewelry, machinery, transportation equipment, metals, chemicals. **Imports** Food, energy, fuel.

LAND
Description Southwestern Asia, landlocked. **Area** 11,506 mi² (29,800 km²). **Highest point** Mt. Aragats, 13,419 ft (4,090 m). **Lowest point** Along Debed River, 1,280 ft (390 m).

People. The Armenians are among Europe's oldest and most distinct ethnic groups, having inhabited the area east and south of the Black Sea and west of the Caspian Sea since the 7th century B.C. Both the Armenian alphabet and the Armenian church date back to the 4th century and remain substantially unchanged today. Early Armenia left a historical legacy of many gifted artists, writers, and philosophers over the centuries.

Economy and the Land. Most of Armenia is mountainous and dry. Despite fertile soils in some of the mountain valleys, agriculture is of little importance. Armenia's great rivers have provided hydroelectric power for an important machine-building industry. Armenia is subject to severe earthquakes, and the country is still rebuilding from a 1988 earthquake that killed 25,000 people and destroyed one-tenth of Armenia's industrial capacity and housing. Transportation is not well developed, and in recent years blockades imposed against Armenia by neighboring Azerbaijan have crippled the economy.

History and Politics. Armenia traces its beginnings to the first millennium B.C. when the Urartu empire fell to the Armens. Alexander the Great conquered Armenia around 300 B.C., but its independence was restored 100 years later. By the early part of the first century A.D., Armenia encompassed parts of present-day Turkey, Syria, Iraq, Iran, and the former Soviet Union. Later, various groups invaded Armenia, including the Arabs, Turks, and Persians. The Russians gained control over the country in 1828. Continued calls for independence led to the massacre of more than 200,000 Armenians by the Turks in the 1890s. Armenians tried to assert their independence in 1918, but the Soviets took full control in 1920. Protests by ethnic Armenians in the enclave of Nagorno-Karabakh within Azerbaijan led to escalating violence between Armenia and Azerbaijan. The struggle fueled rising Armenian nationalism, and Armenia first declared its independence from the Soviet Union in August 1990. The country did not achieve true sovereignty until the breakup of the Soviet Union in September 1991. The Nagorno-Karabakh dispute continues to plague relations between Armenia and Azerbaijan. ■

ARUBA

Official name Aruba

PEOPLE
Population 68,000. **Density** 907/mi² (352/km²). **Urban** 68%. **Capital** Oranjestad, 19,800. **Ethnic groups** mixed European and West Indian 80%. **Languages** Dutch, Papiamento, English, Spanish. **Religions** Roman Catholic 86%, Protestant 4%. **Life expectancy** 80 female, 73 male.

POLITICS
Government Self-governing territory (Netherlands protection). **Parties** Electoral Movement, People's, others. **Suffrage** Universal, 18 and over. **Memberships** None. **Subdivisions** None.

ECONOMY
GDP $1,200,000,000. **Per capita** $18,182. **Monetary unit** Florin. **Trade partners** U.S., European countries. **Exports** Petroleum products. **Imports** Food, manufactures.

LAND
Description Caribbean island. **Area** 75 mi² (193 km²). **Highest point** Jamanota, 617 ft (188 m). **Lowest point** Sea level.

People. Aruba's population combines descendants of the original West Indian population, black Africans, Spanish invaders, and Dutch settlers. Spoken here are Dutch, English, Spanish, and Papiamento—a language that combines elements of Spanish, Portuguese, English, and Dutch with West Indian words.

Economy and the Land. Aruba is dry with soils unsuited for agriculture. In the 20th century, however, nearby Venezuela began producing crude oil, and companies were attracted to Aruba as an economical site to establish their refinery centers. Tourism, too, has grown, with visitors attracted by the coral reefs, white sand beaches, and tropical climate moderated by trade winds. Aruba's landscape is rocky, with giant boulders and monoliths scattered across the island.

History and Politics. Early in Aruba's history, the Caribs replaced the peaceful Arawaks, and caves on the island are marked with signs and symbols made by these early peoples. In 1499, sometime after the first arrival of the Spanish, the island was claimed for the Spanish crown. Aruba was a center of activity for pirates until the 1600s, when the Netherlands obtained possession following long years of war with the Spanish. For a brief time during the Napoleonic Wars the British occupied Aruba, but the island remained in Dutch hands. Until 1986, Aruba was part of the Netherlands Antilles, two groups of West Indies islands that belong to the Netherlands. In 1986, in preparation for its planned 1996 independence, Aruba was made a self-governing territory equal in status to the remainder of the Netherlands Antilles. Since the island's economy has not yet recovered from the 1985 closing of its oil refinery, however, Aruba was allowed to remain a dependent territory beyond 1996. ■

ASCENSION See UNITED KINGDOM.

AUSTRALIA

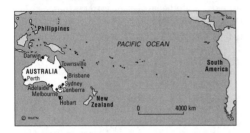

Official name Commonwealth of Australia

PEOPLE
Population 18,535,000. **Density** 6.2/mi² (2.4/km²).
Urban 85%. **Capital** Canberra, 276,162. **Ethnic groups** Caucasian 95%, Asian 4%, Aboriginal and other 1%. **Languages** English, indigenous. **Religions** Catholic 27%, Anglican 22%, other Christian 22%.
Life expectancy 81 female, 75 male. **Literacy** 100%.

POLITICS
Government Federal parliamentary state. **Parties** Labor, Liberal, National. **Suffrage** Universal, 18 and over. **Memberships** CW, OECD, UN. **Subdivisions** 6 states, 2 territories.

ECONOMY
GDP $405,400,000,000. **Per capita** $21,997. **Monetary unit** Dollar. **Trade partners** Exports: Japan, U.S., New Zealand, Korea. Imports: U.S., Japan, U.K. **Exports** Metals, minerals, wool, grain, meat, machinery, transportation equipment. **Imports** Manufactures, machinery, transportation equipment, petroleum products.

LAND
Description Continent between South Pacific and Indian Oceans. **Area** 2,966,155 mi² (7,682,300 km²).
Highest point Mt. Kosciusko, 7,313 ft (2,229 m).
Lowest point Lake Eyre (North), -52 ft (-16 m).

People. Australia's culture reflects a unique combination of British, other European, and Aboriginal influences. Settlement and rule by the United Kingdom gave the country a distinctly British flavor, and many Australians trace their roots to early British settlers. Planned immigration also played a major role in Australia's development, bringing more than three million Europeans since World War II. Refugees, most recently from Southeast Asia, make up another group of incoming peoples. The country is home to a small number of Aborigines. Australia's size and a relatively dry terrain have resulted in un-even settlement patterns, with people concentrated in the rainier southeastern coastal area. The population is mainly urban, though overall population density remains low.

Economy and the Land. Australia's economy is similar to economies in other developed countries, and is characterized by a postwar shift from agriculture to industry and services. Australia is the world's largest producer of wool and the largest exporter of beef. Livestock raising is concentrated on a fertile southeastern plain. Plentiful mineral resources provide for a strong mining industry. Australia is the world's smallest continent but one of its largest countries. The climate is varied, and part of the country lies within the tropics.

History and Politics. Aboriginal peoples probably arrived about 40,000 years ago and established a hunter-gatherer society. The Dutch explored the area in the 17th century, but no claims were made until the 18th century when British Captain James Cook found his way to the fertile east and annexed the land to Britain. The first colony, New South Wales, was founded in 1788, and many of its early settlers were British convicts. During the 1800s, a squatter movement spread the population to other parts of the continent, and the discovery of gold led to a population boom. Demands for self-government soon began, and by the 1890s all the colonies were self-governing, with Britain maintaining control of foreign affairs and defense. Nationalism continued to increase, and a new country, the Commonwealth of Australia, was created in 1901. Participation in international affairs has expanded since World War II, with attention turned particularly to Asian countries. Currently a move-

Places and Possessions of AUSTRALIA

Entity	Status	Area	Population	Capital/Population
Ashmore and Cartier Islands (Indian Ocean; north of Australia)	External territory	1.9 mi² (5.0 km²)	None	None
Christmas Island (Indian Ocean)	External territory	52 mi² (135 km²)	2,000	Settlement
Cocos (Keeling) Islands (Indian Ocean)	External territory	5.4 mi² (14 km²)	700	West Island
Coral Sea Islands (South Pacific)	External territory	1.0 mi² (2.6 km²)	None	None
Heard and McDonald Islands (Indian Ocean)	External territory	154 mi² (400 km²)	None	None
Norfolk Island (South Pacific)	External territory	14 mi² (36 km²)	2,200	Kingston

ment is underway to declare Australia a republic and thus loosen ties with Britain. ■

AUSTRIA

Official name Republic of Austria

PEOPLE
Population 8,073,000. **Density** 249/mi² (96/km²). **Urban** 64%. **Capital** Vienna, 1,539,848. **Ethnic groups** German 99%. **Languages** German. **Religions** Roman Catholic 85%, Protestant 6%. **Life expectancy** 80 female, 74 male. **Literacy** 99%.

POLITICS
Government Federal republic. **Parties** Freedom, People's, Social Democratic, others. **Suffrage** Universal, 18 and over. **Memberships** EU, OECD, UN. **Subdivisions** 9 states.

ECONOMY
GDP $152,000,000,000. **Per capita** $18,993. **Monetary unit** Schilling. **Trade partners** Exports: Germany, Italy, Switzerland. Imports: Germany, Italy, Japan. **Exports** Machinery, equipment, iron, steel, wood, textiles, paper products, chemicals. **Imports** Petroleum, food, machinery, transportation equipment, chemicals, textiles.

LAND
Description Central Europe, landlocked. **Area** 32,377 mi² (83,856 km²). **Highest point** Grossglockner, 12,461 ft (3,798 m). **Lowest point** Neusiedler See, 377 ft (115 m).

People. The majority of Austrians are native born, German-speaking, and Roman Catholic, a homogeneity belying a history of invasions by diverse peoples. With a long cultural tradition, the country has contributed greatly to music and the arts. Vienna, the capital, is one of the great cultural centers of Europe.

Economy and the Land. Austria maintains a strong economy as a result of its natural resources and skilled labor force. Unemployment is low, and the economy remains relatively strong. The economic mainstays are services and manufacturing. Agriculture is limited because of the overall mountainous terrain, with the Danube River basin in eastern Austria containing the most productive soils. Despite its limitations, Austria is able to produce almost enough food to feed itself. In addition to the country's cultural heritage, its alpine landscape attracts many tourists. The climate is generally moderate.

History and Politics. Early in its history, Austria was settled by Celts, ruled by Romans, and invaded by Germans, Slavs, Magyars, and others. Long rule by the Hapsburg family began in the 13th century, and in time Austria became the center of a vast empire. In 1867, Hungarian pressure resulted in the formation of the dual monarchy of Austria-Hungary. Nationalist movements against Austria culminated in the 1914 assassination of the heir to the throne, Archduke Francis Ferdinand, and set off the conflict that became World War I. In 1918 the war ended, the Hapsburg emperor was overthrown, Austria became a republic, and present-day boundaries were established. Political unrest and instability followed. In 1938 Adolf Hitler incorporated Austria into the German Reich. A period of occupation after World War II was followed by Austria's declaration of neutrality. Austria joined the European Union in 1994. ■

AZERBAIJAN

Official name Azerbaijani Republic

PEOPLE
Population 7,767,000. **Density** 232/mi² (90/km²). **Urban** 56%. **Capital** Baku (Bakı), 1,080,500. **Ethnic groups** Azerbaijani 90%, Dagestani peoples 3%, Russian 3%, Armenian 2%. **Languages** Azerbaijani, Russian, Armenian. **Religions** Muslim 93%, Russian Orthodox 3%, Armenian Orthodox 2%. **Life expectancy** 76 female, 68 male. **Literacy** 97%.

POLITICS
Government Republic. **Parties** Musavat, National

Independence, Popular Front, Social Democratic, others. **Suffrage** Universal, 18 and over. **Memberships** UN. **Subdivisions** 1 republic.

ECONOMY
GDP $11,500,000,000. **Per capita** $1,467. **Monetary unit** Manat. **Trade partners** Former Soviet republics, European countries. **Exports** Oil and gas, chemicals, oil-field equipment, textiles, cotton. **Imports** Machinery and parts, consumer durables, food, textiles.

LAND
Description Southwestern Asia, landlocked. **Area** 33,436 mi² (86,600 km²). **Highest point** Mt. Bazarduzu, 14,652 ft (4,466 m). **Lowest point** Caspian Sea, -92 ft (-28 m).

People. The Azeris are Turkish people and account for more than 90 percent of the population. There are also small Armenian and Russian minorities. Most Azeris are Shiite Muslims, although the Armenians in the enclave of Nagorno-Karabakh are Christian. About one-half of the inhabitants of Azerbaijan live in urban areas.

Economy and the Land. Azerbaijan's landscape varies from the cool slopes of the Caucasus to flat, dry steppes. Cotton is produced in abundance. Sheep and cattle are also raised on the dry, grassy pasture of the steppes. The Lenkoran lowland in the extreme southeast part of the country is semitropical and produces many fruits and vegetables. The area around Baku is a major oil-producing and refining center, although production has been steadily declining. Like many other former Soviet republics, Azerbaijan suffers from high unemployment and a low standard of living.

History and Politics. Azerbaijan is part of a larger historical region of the same name, which includes parts of neighboring Iran. Arabs conquered the region and brought Islam to the people in A.D. 642. Later, Mongols, Turks, and Persians invaded the region. Russian interest in the area began during the reign of Peter the Great and led to several wars with Persia. In 1828, Azerbaijan was formally divided between Russia and Persia (now Iran). The country enjoyed a brief period of independence from 1918 until 1920, when a Soviet invasion forced the incorporation of Azerbaijan into the Soviet Union. Fighting between Azerbaijan and neighboring Armenia over the Armenian enclave of Nagorno-Karabakh began in 1987, and prompted a renewed Soviet invasion of the capital city of Baku in early 1990. Azerbaijan declared its independence in August 1991. The country attained real independence, however, after the dissolution of the Soviet Union at the end of 1991. The ongoing war in Nagorno-Karabakh continues to contribute to general political instability. ■

AZORES See PORTUGAL.

BAHAMAS, THE

Official name Commonwealth of The Bahamas

PEOPLE
Population 263,000. **Density** 49/mi² (19/km²). **Urban** 87%. **Capital** Nassau, New Providence I., 141,000. **Ethnic groups** Black 85%, white 15%. **Languages** English, Creole. **Religions** Baptist 32%, Anglican 20%, Roman Catholic 19%, Methodist 6%. **Life expectancy** 79 female, 70 male. **Literacy** 98%.

POLITICS
Government Parliamentary state. **Parties** Free National Movement, Progressive Liberal. **Suffrage** Universal, 18 and over. **Memberships** CW, OAS, UN. **Subdivisions** 21 districts.

ECONOMY
GDP $4,800,000,000. **Per capita** $17,455. **Monetary unit** Dollar. **Trade partners** Exports: U.S., U.K., Japan. Imports: Saudi Arabia, U.S., Nigeria. **Exports** Pharmaceuticals, cement, rum, crawfish, petroleum products. **Imports** Petroleum, motor vehicles, electronics, food, manufactures.

LAND
Description Caribbean islands. **Area** 5,382 mi² (13,939 km²). **Highest point** Mt. Alvernia, 206 ft (63 m). **Lowest point** Sea level.

People. Only about 29 of the 700 Bahamian islands are inhabited, and most of the people live on Grand Bahama and New Providence. The majority blacks are mainly descendants of slaves routed through the area or brought by British Loyalists fleeing the American colonies during the Revolutionary War.

Economy and the Land. Because the thin soils of these flat coral islands are not suited for agriculture, the country struggled for years to develop a strong economic base. Tourism capitalized on the islands' semitropical climate. Because it is a tax haven, the country is also an international finance center.

History and Politics. Christopher Columbus's first stop on his way to America in 1492, the

Bahamas were originally the home of the Lucayo people, whom the Spaniards took for slave trade. The British arrived in the 1600s, and the islands became a British colony in 1717. The country achieved independence in 1973. The 25-year entrenchment of Prime Minister Lynden Pindling ended in 1992. A new government has made no major changes. ■

BAHRAIN

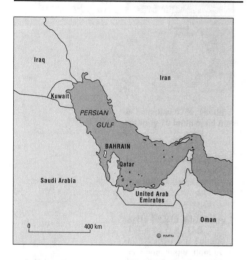

Official name State of Bahrain

PEOPLE
Population 619,000. **Density** 2,318/mi² (896/km²). **Urban** 91%. **Capital** Manama, Bahrain I., 127,578. **Ethnic groups** Bahraini 63%, Asian 13%, other Arab 10%. **Languages** Arabic, English, Farsi, Urdu. **Religions** Shiite Muslim 75%, Sunni Muslim 25%. **Life expectancy** 75 female, 71 male. **Literacy** 85%.

POLITICS
Government Monarchy. **Parties** None. **Suffrage** None. **Memberships** AL, UN. **Subdivisions** 12 regions.

ECONOMY
GDP $7,300,000,000. **Per capita** $12,521. **Monetary unit** Dinar. **Trade partners** Exports: Saudi Arabia, Japan, United Arab Emirates. Imports: Saudi Arabia, U.K., U.S. **Exports** Petroleum products, aluminum. **Imports** Crude petroleum, machinery and transportation equipment, manufactures.

LAND
Description Southwestern Asian islands (in Persian Gulf). **Area** 267 mi² (691 km²). **Highest point** Mt. Dukhan, 440 ft (134 m). **Lowest point** Sea level.

People. Most residents of Bahrain are native-born Muslims, with the Sunni sect predominating in urban areas and Shiites in the countryside. Many of the country's 33 islands are barren, and population is concentrated in the capital city—Manama, on Bahrain Island—and on the smaller island of Muharraq. The oil economy has resulted in an influx of foreign workers and considerable westernization, and Bahrain is a Persian Gulf leader in free health care and education.

Economy and the Land. The one-time pearl-and-fish economy was reshaped by exploitation of oil and natural gas, careful management, and diversification. A major refinery processes crude oil piped from Saudi Arabia, as well as the country's own oil, and Bahrain's aluminum industry is the Gulf's largest non-oil activity. Because of its location, Bahrain is able to provide Gulf countries with services such as dry docking, and the country has become a Middle Eastern banking center. Agriculture exists on northern Bahrain Island, where natural springs provide an irrigation source. Their newest industry is tourism, providing a "playground" for Saudis and American military. Much of the state is desert. Summers are hot and dry and winters are mild.

History and Politics. From about 2000 to 1800 B.C., the area of Bahrain flourished as a center for trade. After early periods of Portuguese and Iranian rule, the Al Khalifa family came to power in the 18th century, and it has governed ever since. Bahrain became a British protectorate in the 19th century and gained independence in 1971. Growing unrest has been sparked by Shiite opposition groups who feel they do not share equally in the country's wealth. ■

BALEARIC ISLANDS
See SPAIN.

BANGLADESH

Official name People's Republic of Bangladesh

PEOPLE
Population 126,470,000. **Density** 2,275/mi² (878/km²). **Urban** 19%. **Capital** Dhaka, 3,637,892. **Ethnic groups** Bengali 98%. **Languages** Bangla, English. **Religions** Muslim 88%, Hindu 11%. **Life expectancy** 58 female, 58 male. **Literacy** 38%.

POLITICS
Government Republic. **Parties** Awami League, Jatiyo, Nationalist, others. **Suffrage** Universal, 18 and over. **Memberships** CW, UN. **Subdivisions** 5 divisions.

ECONOMY
GDP $14,450,000,000. **Per capita** $112. **Monetary unit** Taka. **Trade partners** Exports: U.S., Italy, Japan, U.K. Imports: Japan, U.S., United Arab Emirates. **Exports** Clothing, jute goods, leather, shrimp. **Imports** Machinery, petroleum, food, textiles.

LAND
Description Southern Asia. **Area** 55,598 mi² (143,998 km²). **Highest point** Mowdak Mtn., 3,292 ft (1,003 m). **Lowest point** Sea level.

People. Bangladesh's population is characterized by extremes. The people, mostly peasant farmers, are among Asia's and the world's poorest and most rural. With a relatively small area and a high birthrate, the country is also one of the world's most densely populated. Many Bangladeshis are victims of disease, floods, and ongoing medical and food shortages. Islam, the major religion, has influenced almost every aspect of life. Bangla is the official language.

Economy and the Land. Fertile floodplain soil is the chief resource of this primarily flat, river-crossed country, and farming is the main activity. Rice and jute are among the major crops. Farm output fluctuates greatly, however, subject to the frequent monsoons, floods, and droughts of a semitropical climate. Because of this and other factors, foreign aid, imports, and an emphasis on agriculture have not assuaged the continuing food shortage.

History and Politics. Most of Bangladesh lies in eastern Bengal, an Asian region whose western sector encompasses India's Bengal province. Early religious influences included Buddhist rulers in the 8th century A.D. and Hindus in the 11th. In A.D.1200, Muslim rule introduced the religion to which the majority of eastern Bengalis eventually converted, while most western Bengalis retained their Hindu beliefs. British control in India, beginning in the 17th century, expanded until all Bengal was part of British India by the 1850s. When British India gained independence in 1947, Muslim population centers were united into the single country of Pakistan in an attempt to end Hindu-Muslim hostilities. More than 1,000 miles (1,600 kilometers) separated West Pakistan, formed from northwest India, from East Pakistan, comprised mostly of eastern Bengal. The bulk of Pakistan's population resided in the eastern province and felt the west wielded political and economic power at its expense. A civil war began in 1971, and the eastern province declared itself an independent country called Bangladesh, or "Bengal nation." The state has seen numerous political crises since independence, including two assassinations and numerous coups. Elections in 1996 were heavily boycotted and the results were challenged, further destabilizing the country. Fragile economic growth has been damaged by the uncertain political climate, but there is great potential for development. ■

BARBADOS

Official name Barbados

PEOPLE
Population 258,000. **Density** 1,554/mi² (600/km²). **Urban** 48%. **Capital** Bridgetown, 5,928. **Ethnic groups** Black 80%, mixed 16%, white 4%. **Languages** English, local dialects. **Religions** Anglican 40%, Pentecostal 8%, Methodist 7%, Roman Catholic 4%. **Life expectancy** 79 female, 74 male. **Literacy** 97%.

POLITICS
Government Parliamentary state. **Parties** Democratic Labor, Labor, National Democratic. **Suffrage** Universal, 18 and over. **Memberships** CW, OAS, UN. **Subdivisions** 11 parishes.

ECONOMY
GDP $2,500,000,000. **Per capita** $9,766. **Monetary unit** Dollar. **Trade partners** Exports: U.S., U.K., Trinidad and Tobago. Imports: U.S., Trinidad and Tobago, U.K. **Exports** Sugar, molasses, food, drink, chemicals, electrical equipment, clothing, rum. **Imports** Food, consumer goods, machinery, chemicals, construction materials, fuel.

LAND
Description Caribbean island. **Area** 166 mi² (430 km²). **Highest point** Mt. Hillaby, 1,115 ft (340 m). **Lowest point** Sea level.

People. A history of British rule is reflected in the Anglican religion and English language of this easternmost West Indian island. It is one of the world's most densely populated countries, and most citizens are black descendants of African slaves.

Economy and the Land. Barbados' pleasant tropical climate and its land have determined its economic mainstays: tourism and sugar. Sunshine and year-round warmth attract thousands of visitors and, in conjunction with the soil, provide an excellent environment for sugarcane cultivation. Traditionally, manufacturing was based on sugar processing, but recent efforts to diversify have been successful. The coral island's terrain is mostly flat, rising to a central ridge.

History and Politics. Originally settled by South American Arawaks, followed by the Caribs, Barbados was uninhabited when the first British settlers arrived in the 1600s. More colonists followed, developing sugar plantations and bringing slaves from Africa to work them. The country remained under British control until it became independent in 1966. ∎

BELARUS

Official name Republic of Belarus

PEOPLE
Population 10,445,000. **Density** 130/mi² (50/km²).
Urban 72%. **Capital** Minsk, 1,661,000. **Ethnic groups**
Belarussian 78%, Russian 13%, Polish 4%, Ukrainian
3%. **Languages** Belorussian, Russian. **Religions**
Russian Orthodox, Roman Catholic. **Life expectancy**
75 female, 65 male. **Literacy** 98%.

POLITICS
Government Republic. **Parties** Agrarian, Civic Accord
Bloc, Communist. **Suffrage** Universal, 18 and over.
Memberships UN. **Subdivisions** 6 oblasts.

ECONOMY
GDP $49,200,000,000. **Per capita** $4,744. **Monetary
unit** Rubel. **Trade partners** Former Soviet republics.
Exports Food, machinery and equipment, chemicals.
Imports Steel, raw materials, textiles, sugar, fuel,
natural gas.

LAND
Description Eastern Europe, landlocked. **Area**
80,155 mi² (207,600 km²). **Highest point** Mt.
Dzerzhinsk, 1,132 ft (345 m). **Lowest point** Along
Neman River, 279 ft (85 m).

People. Most people speak Belarussian, a Slavic
language closely related to Russian and
Ukrainian, and belong to the Orthodox church.
There is also a substantial Roman Catholic
minority. Belarussian people also predominate
in a large area of surrounding Russian territory.

Economy and the Land. Belarus is one of the
most highly developed of the former Soviet
republics. Both the agricultural and manufacturing sectors are relatively modern. The country is
a net exporter of food, including meat, milk, eggs,
flour, and potatoes. Peat is the major mineral
resource and is used to fuel several major electrical power plants. Most of the land is either forest
or swamp, and the terrain is flat.

History and Politics. The Belarussians are
descendants of Slavic peoples who came to the
area around the 7th century. The area was conquered first by Kiev, then by Lithuania, and later
by Poland. Russia gained control of what was
then known as Belorussia in the late 1700s.
Emancipation of the serfs did not come until
1861, and the area remained underdeveloped
and poor. Following the Bolshevik Revolution,
Belorussia enjoyed a short period of independence before joining the Soviet Union in 1922.
Poland controlled part of Belorussia from 1921
until 1939, and the country suffered vast devasta-
tion under German occupation during World
War II. Belorussia became known as Belarus after
it gained its independence following the demise
of the Soviet Union in 1991. Since then, the
Communist Party has been returned to power,
and in 1996 Belarus signed an agreement that
strengthens its economic, political, and cultural
ties with Russia. The economy has been in
decline, and current President Lukashenko is on
the brink of dictatorship. The government refuses to give up the nuclear arms that were left
behind by the former Soviet Union. ∎

BELGIUM

Official name Kingdom of Belgium

PEOPLE
Population 10,220,000. **Density** 867/mi² (335/km²).
Urban 97%. **Capital** Brussels, 136,424. **Ethnic groups**
Fleming 55%, Walloon 33%, mixed and others 12%.
Languages Dutch (Flemish), French, German.
Religions Roman Catholic 75%. **Life expectancy**
81 female, 74 male. **Literacy** 99%.

POLITICS
Government Constitutional monarchy. **Parties**
Flemish: Christian Democrats, Liberal Democrats,
Socialist. Francophone: Liberal Reformation. others.
Suffrage Universal, 18 and over. **Memberships** EU,
NATO, OECD, UN. **Subdivisions** 9 provinces.

ECONOMY
GDP $197,000,000,000. **Per capita** $19,361. **Monetary**

unit Franc. **Trade partners** Exports: France, Germany, Netherlands. Imports: Germany, Netherlands, France. **Exports** Iron, steel, transportation equipment, tractors, diamonds, petroleum products. **Imports** Fuel, grains, chemicals, food.

LAND
Description Western Europe. **Area** 11,783 mi² (30,518 km²). **Highest point** Botrange, 2,277 ft (694 m). **Lowest point** Sea level.

People. Language separates Belgium into two main regions. Northern Belgium, known as Flanders, is dominated by Flemings, or Flemish-speaking descendants of Germanic Franks. French-speaking Walloons, descendants of the Celts, inhabit southern Belgium, or Wallonia. Both groups are found in centrally located Brussels. In addition, a small German-speaking population is concentrated in the east. Flemish and French divisions often result in discord, but diversity has also been a source of cultural richness. Belgium has often been at the hub of European cultural movements.

Economy and the Land. The economy, as well as the population, was affected by Belgium's location at the center of European activity. Flanders, formerly a poor, rural area, is now more prosperous than the southern Wallonia. Industry was established early as the economic base, and today the country is heavily industrialized. Although agriculture plays a minor economic role, Belgium is nearly self-sufficient in food production. The north and west are dominated by a flat fertile plain, the central region by rolling hills, and the south by the Ardennes Forest, often a tourist destination. The climate is cool and temperate.

History and Politics. Belgium's history began with the settlement of the Belgae tribe in the 2nd century B.C. The Romans invaded the area around 50 B.C. and were overthrown by Germanic Franks in the A.D. 400s. Trade, manufacturing, and art prospered as various peoples invaded, passed through, and ruled the area. In 1794 Napoleon annexed Belgium to France. He was defeated at Waterloo in Belgium in 1815, and the country passed into Dutch hands. Dissatisfaction under Netherlands rule led to revolt and, in 1830, the formation of the independent country of Belgium. Linguistic divisions mark nearly all political activity, from parties split by language to government decisions based on linguistic rivalries. ■

BELIZE

Official name Belize

PEOPLE
Population 227,000. **Density** 26/mi² (9.9/km²). **Urban** 46%. **Capital** Belmopan, 5,256. **Ethnic groups** Mestizo 44%, Creole 30%, Mayan 11%, Garifuna 7%. **Languages** English, Spanish, Mayan, Garifuna, Ketchi. **Religions** Roman Catholic 62%, Anglican 12%, Methodist 6%, Mennonite 4%. **Life expectancy** 76 female, 73 male. **Literacy** 70%.

POLITICS
Government Parliamentary state. **Parties** National Alliance, People's United, United Democratic. **Suffrage** Universal, 18 and over. **Memberships** CW, OAS, UN. **Subdivisions** 6 districts.

ECONOMY
GDP $575,000,000. **Per capita** $2,650. **Monetary unit** Dollar. **Trade partners** U.S., U.K., Mexico. **Exports** Sugar, clothing, seafood, molasses, fruit, wood. **Imports** Machinery, transportation equipment, food, manufactures, fuels, chemicals.

LAND
Description Central America. **Area** 8,867 mi² (22,963 km²). **Highest point** Victoria Pk., 3,675 ft (1,120 m). **Lowest point** Sea level.

People. With the lowest population of any Central American country, Belize has a mixed populace, including descendants of black Africans, mestizos of Spanish-Amerindian ancestry, and indigenous peoples. Population is concentrated in six urban areas along the coast. Most people are poor, but participation in the educational system has led to a high literacy rate.

Economy and the Land. An abundance of timberland resulted in an economy based on forestry until woodlands began to be depleted in the 20th century. Today the economy focuses on agriculture, with sugar the major crop and export. Arable land is the primary resource, but only a small portion has been cultivated. Industrial activity is limited. The recipient of much foreign aid, Belize hopes to expand its export of agricultural surpluses and to develop a tourist industry based on its climate and sandy beaches. The coastal region consists of swampy lowlands rising to the Maya Mountains inland. The hot, humid climate is offset by sea breezes.

History and Politics. Until about the 11th century A.D., Belize was the site of a flourishing Mayan civilization. Spain claimed the region in the 16th century. A British shipwreck in 1638 resulted in the first European settlement and began a process of British colonization, accompanied by extensive logging, piracy, and occasional Spanish and Indian attacks. In 1862 the area officially became the crown colony of British Honduras. Its name was changed to Belize in 1973, and independence was achieved in 1981. A July 1993 election resulted in an upset victory for the opposition United Democratic Party. ∎

BENIN

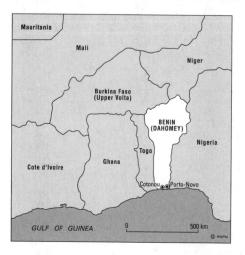

Official name Republic of Benin

PEOPLE
Population 5,994,000. **Density** 138/mi² (53/km²).
Urban 39%. **Capital** Porto-Novo (designated), 179,138; Cotonou (de facto), 536,827. **Ethnic groups** Fon 42%, Adja 16%, Yoruba 12%. **Languages** French, Fon, Yoruba, indigenous. **Religions** Voodoo and other African religions 70%, Muslim 15%, Christian. **Life expectancy** 51 female, 47 male. **Literacy** 37%.

POLITICS
Government Republic. **Parties** Action for Renewal and Development, Democratic Renewal, Renaissance, others. **Suffrage** Universal, 18 and over. **Memberships** OAU, UN. **Subdivisions** 6 provinces.

ECONOMY
GDP $7,600,000,000. **Per capita** $1,353. **Monetary unit** CFA franc. **Trade partners** Exports: Netherlands, U.S., Spain. Imports: France, U.K., Netherlands. **Exports** Oil, cotton, palm products, cocoa. **Imports** Food, beverages, tobacco, petroleum, manufactures.

LAND
Description Western Africa. **Area** 43,475 mi² (112,600 km²). **Highest point** 2,234 ft (681 m). **Lowest point** Sea level.

People. Numerous peoples comprise the mostly black population of Benin. The main groups are the Fon, the Adja, the Yoruba, and the Bariba. The country's linguistic diversity reflects its ethnic variety; French is the official language, a result of former French rule. Most Beninese are farmers, although urban migration is increasing. Indigenous beliefs predominate, but there are

also Christians, especially in the south, and Muslims in the north. In 1996 voodoo was designated as an official religion.

Economy and the Land. The economy of Benin is dependent on subsistence agriculture, and cotton is the main cash crop. The industrial sector accounts for less than 10 percent of Benin's GDP. Some economic relief may be found in the exploitation of offshore oil. The predominately flat terrain features coastal lagoons and dense forests, with mountains in the northwest. Heat and humidity characterize the coast, with less humidity and varied temperatures in the north.

History and Politics. In the 1500s Dahomey, a Fon kingdom, became the power center of the Benin area. European slave traders came to the coast in the 17th and 18th centuries, establishing posts and bartering with Dahomey royalty for slaves. As the slave trade prospered, the area became known as the Slave Coast. France defeated Dahomey's army in the 1890s and subsequently made the area a territory of French West Africa. In 1960 the country gained independence, which was followed by political turmoil, various coups, and a military overthrow that installed a socialist government in 1972. In 1975 the country changed its name from Dahomey to Benin. Economic difficulties in the late 1980s led the country away from socialism and toward private enterprise. In March 1991, elections resulted in the first popularly elected president, and the country is becoming a model of openness and multiparty participation. ∎

BERMUDA See UNITED KINGDOM.

BHUTAN

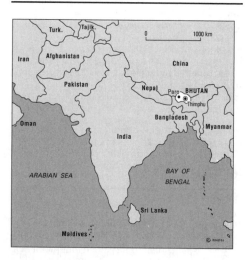

Official name Kingdom of Bhutan

PEOPLE

Population 1,886,000. **Density** 105/mi² (41/km²).
Urban 6%. **Capital** Thimphu, 12,000. **Ethnic
groups** Bhotia 50%, Nepalese 35%, indigenous 15%.
Languages Dzongkha, Tibetan and Nepalese dialects.
Religions Buddhist 75%, Hindu 25%. **Life expectancy**
55 female, 52 male. **Literacy** 42%.

POLITICS

Government Monarchy (Indian protection). **Parties**
None. **Suffrage** One vote per family. **Memberships**
UN. **Subdivisions** 18 districts.

ECONOMY

GDP $1,300,000,000. **Per capita** $739. **Monetary unit**
Ngultrum, Indian rupee. **Trade partners** India. **Exports**
Cardamom, gypsum, wood, handicrafts, cement, fruit,
gems, electricity, spices. **Imports** Fuel, grain, machinery, transportation equipment, textiles.

LAND

Description Southern Asia, landlocked. **Area**
17,954 mi² (46,500 km²). **Highest point** Kula Kangri,
24,784 ft (7,554 m). **Lowest point** Along Manãs River,
318 ft (97 m).

People. A mountainous terrain long isolated
Bhutan from the outside world and limited internal mingling of its peoples. The population is
ethnically divided into the Bhotia, Nepalese, and
various tribes. Of Tibetan ancestry, the Bhotes
are a majority and as such have determined the
major religion, Buddhism, and major language,
Dzongkha, a Tibetan dialect. The Nepalese are
mostly Hindu and speak Nepalese; tribal dialects
diversify language further. A largely rural population, many villages grew up around *dzongs*, or
monastery fortresses built in strategic valley locations during Bhutan's past. In 1989 a controversial program began to evict settlers who could
not prove their Bhutanese descent.

Economy and the Land. Partially because of
physical isolation, Bhutan has one of the world's
least developed economies and remains dependent on foreign aid. There is potential for success, however. Forests cover much of the land,
limiting agricultural area but offering opportunity for the expansion of forestry. Farming is concentrated in the more densely populated, fertile
valleys of the Himalayas, and the country is self-
sufficient in food production. The climate varies
with altitude; the icy Himalayas in the north
give way to temperate central valleys and a
subtropical south.

History and Politics. Bhutan's early history
remains mostly unknown, but it is thought that
by the early 16th century, descendants of Tibetan
invaders were ruling their lands from strategically located *dzongs*. In the 1600s a Tibetan lama
consolidated the area and became the political
and religious leader. Proximity to and interaction
with British India resulted in British control of
Bhutan's foreign affairs in the 19th and early 20th
centuries. In 1907, the current hereditary monarchy was established. India gained independence
from Britain in 1947 and soon assumed the role
of adviser in Bhutan's foreign affairs. Bhutan

became independent in 1949, but ties with India
were strengthened in the late 1950s to counter
Chinese influence. In recent years the King has
instituted a policy of expelling people he consid-
ers refugees, causing widespread hardship. ∎

BOLIVIA

Official name Republic of Bolivia

PEOPLE

Population 8,112,000. **Density** 19/mi² (7.4/km²). **Urban**
62%. **Capital** La Paz (seat of government), 713,378;
Sucre (legal capital), 131,769. **Ethnic groups** Quechua
30%, Aymara 25%, mixed 25-30%, European 5-15%.
Languages Aymara, Quechua, Spanish. **Religions**
Roman Catholic 95%, Methodist and other Protestant.
Life expectancy 63 female, 60 male. **Literacy** 83%.

POLITICS

Government Republic. **Parties** Civic Solidarity Union,
Nationalist Democratic Action, Nationalist
Revolutionary Movement, others. **Suffrage** Universal,
18 and over (married), 21 and over (single).
Memberships OAS, UN. **Subdivisions** 9 departments.

ECONOMY

GDP $20,000,000,000. **Per capita** $2,671. **Monetary
unit** Boliviano. **Trade partners** Exports: Argentina,
U.S., U.K. Imports: U.S., Brazil, Argentina. **Exports**
Metals, natural gas, soybeans, jewelry, lumber. **Imports**
Food, petroleum, consumer goods, capital goods,
chemicals.

LAND

Description Central South America, landlocked. **Area**
424,165 mi² (1,098,581 km²). **Highest point** Nevado
Sajama, 21,463 ft (6,542 m). **Lowest point** Along
Paraguay River, 226 ft (69 m).

People. The Quecho and Aymara compose the
majority of the population; minorities include
mestizos of Spanish-Amerindian descent and
Europeans. Most people live at a subsistence
level, but Bolivia has a rich cultural heritage,
evidenced by Spanish-influenced mestizo art;
early Aymaran and Quechuan artifacts; and
20th-century achievements. Roman Catholicism,

the major religion, is frequently combined with indigenous beliefs.

Economy and the Land. Although underdeveloped Bolivia is among South America's poorest countries, it is rich in natural resources. Most people are engaged in agriculture, but mining and the production of illicit drugs are also major economic activities. Population, industry, and major cities are concentrated on the western *altiplano*, an Andean high plateau where many continue to practice agriculture using ancestral methods. The eastern *llano*, or lowland plain, contains fuel deposits and is the site of commercial farming. The *yungas* (hills and valleys) between the *altiplano* and the *llano* form the most developed agricultural region. The climate varies from tropical to semiarid and cool, depending on altitude.

History and Politics. The Aymara culture flourished in the area that is now Bolivia between the 7th and 10th centuries. In the mid-1400s the area was absorbed into the expanding empire of the Incas, who controlled the region until ousted by the Spanish in 1535. Simón Bolívar, the Venezuelan organizer of the South American movement to free Spanish colonies, helped lead the way to independence, which was gained in 1825. Although Bolivia developed economically, its indigenous population remained in poverty and enjoyed few rights. After years of turmoil, a 1952 revolution installed a government that introduced suffrage, land and educational reforms. Several military coups followed, and civilian control was reestablished in 1982. The government elected in 1993 has created stability and reduced foreign debt. Relations with the United States have been strained due to Bolivia's continued drug production and trafficking. ■

BOSNIA AND HERZEGOVINA

Official name Republic of Bosnia and Herzegovina

PEOPLE
Population 2,543,000. **Density** 129/mi² (50/km²). **Urban** 42%. **Capital** Sarajevo, 341,200. **Ethnic groups** Serb 40%, Muslim 38%, Croat 22%. **Languages** Serbo-Croatian. **Religions** Muslim 40%, Orthodox 31%, Roman Catholic 15%. **Life expectancy** 76 female, 71 male. **Literacy** 86%.

POLITICS
Government Republic. **Parties** Bosnia and Herzegovina, Croatian Democratic Union, Party of Democratic Changes, Serbian Democratic, others. **Suffrage** Universal, 18 and over, 16 if employed. **Memberships** UN. **Subdivisions** None.

ECONOMY
GDP $1,000,000,000. **Per capita** $223. **Monetary unit** Convertible Marka. **Trade partners** Former Yugoslavian republics. **Exports** Manufactures, machinery and transportation equipment, raw materials. **Imports** Fuels, machinery and transportation equipment, chemicals, raw materials, food.

LAND
Description Eastern Europe. **Area** 19,741 mi² (51,129 km²). **Highest point** Maglić, 7,828 ft (2,386 m). **Lowest point** Sea level.

People. The recent war strongly impacted the ethnic structure of Bosnia and Herzegovina. Currently the country's population is 40 percent Serbian, while Muslims, formerly the majority group, make up 38 percent of the population. Croatians make up the remaining 22 percent—a larger percentage than they did before the war.

Economy and the Land. The three years of war after Bosnia and Herzegovina's secession from Yugoslavia have left the economy in disarray. Before the war, the main activity was agriculture, and there was limited industrial development. The country has ample mineral and hydroelectric resources, but the region is one of the poorest of the former Yugoslavian republics. Bosnia, in the north, is a land of mountains and dense forests, while the Herzegovina region, in the south, is a rocky plateau. Bosnia and Herzegovina has many spas, which have historically been popular tourist destinations.

History and Politics. The Serbs and the Croats settled Bosnia in the 7th century, and the country later became part of the Roman Empire. Bosnia established itself as a self-governing country under Hungarian rule in the 1100s. Bosnia and Herzegovina were joined when they were conquered by the Ottoman Turks in the 15th century. Bosnia and Herzegovina was one of the few areas of Europe that converted to Islam during this period. The region was annexed by Austria-Hungary in 1908. Following World War I, both Bosnia and Herzegovina were incorporated into Serbia, and later into Yugoslavia. When Yugoslavia began to break up in the early 1990s, ethnic Muslims and Croatians overwhelmingly favored independence, but most of the region's ethnic Serbians resisted the notion and boycotted the referendum. Fighting over independence broke out following the country's secession from

Yugoslavia in 1992. The bitter war and its many broken cease-fire agreements have left the survival of the country in doubt. In 1995 the Dayton Peace Accord was signed, and elections were held later that year. A multinational military force will enforce the fragile peace indefinitely. ■

BOTSWANA

Official name Republic of Botswana

PEOPLE
Population 1,514,000. **Density** 6.7/mi² (2.6/km²). **Urban** 63%. **Capital** Gaborone, 133,468. **Ethnic groups** Tswana 95%; Kalanga, Baswara, and Kgalagadi 4%; white 1%. **Languages** English, Tswana. **Religions** Tribal religionist 50%, Roman Catholic and other Christian 50%. **Life expectancy** 69 female, 65 male. **Literacy** 70%.

POLITICS
Government Republic. **Parties** Democratic, National Front. **Suffrage** Universal, 21 and over. **Memberships** CW, OAU, UN. **Subdivisions** 10 districts.

ECONOMY
GDP $4,500,000,000. **Per capita** $3,010. **Monetary unit** Pula. **Trade partners** Switzerland, U.K., Southern African countries. **Exports** Diamonds, copper, nickel, meat. **Imports** Food, motor vehicles, textiles, petroleum, paper products.

LAND
Description Southern Africa, landlocked. **Area** 224,711 mi² (582,000 km²). **Highest point** 4,969 ft (1,515 m). **Lowest point** Confluence of Shashe and Limpopo Rivers, 1,684 ft (513 m).

People. The population of this sparsely populated country is composed mostly of Tswana, Bantu peoples of various groups. Following settlement patterns laid down centuries ago, Tswana predominate in the more fertile eastern region, and the minority Bushmen are concentrated in the Kalahari Desert. There is also a white minority population. English is an official language, reflecting years of British rule, but the majority

speak Tswana. Half of the people follow tribal religions, while the rest are Christian.

Economy and the Land. Agriculture and livestock raising are the primary activities, although they are limited by the southwestern Kalahari Desert. The most productive farmland lies in the east and north, where rainfall is higher and grazing lands are plentiful. Since the early 1970s, when increased exploitation of natural resources began, the economy has developed rapidly. Diamond mining is the main focus of this growth, together with development of copper, nickel, and coal. The climate is mostly subtropical.

History and Politics. In Botswana's early history, Bushmen, the original inhabitants, retreated into the Kalahari region when the Tswana invaded and established their settlements in the more fertile east. Intertribal wars in the early 19th century were followed by conflicts with the Boers, settlers of Dutch or Huguenot descent. These conflicts led the Tswana to seek British assistance, and the area of present-day Botswana became part of the British protectorate of Bechuanaland. When the Union of South Africa was created in 1910, those living in Bechuanaland (later Botswana), Basutoland (later Lesotho), and Swaziland requested and were granted exclusion from the Union. British rule continued until 1966, when the protectorate of Bechuanaland became the Republic of Botswana. With outstanding leadership and a tribal history of democracy, Botswana has developed into Africa's oldest and most prosperous democracy. ■

BRAZIL

Official name Federative Republic of Brazil

PEOPLE
Population 165,490,000. **Density** 50/mi² (19/km²). **Urban** 79%. **Capital** Brasília, 1,513,470. **Ethnic groups** White 55%, mixed 38%, black 6%. **Languages**

Portuguese, Spanish, English, French. **Religions** Roman Catholic 70%. **Life expectancy** 70 female, 66 male. **Literacy** 85%.

POLITICS
Government Federal republic. **Parties** Democratic Movement, Liberal Front, Social Democracy, others. **Suffrage** Universal, 16 and over, compulsory over 18 and under 70. **Memberships** OAS, UN. **Subdivisions** 26 states, 1 federal district.

ECONOMY
GDP $976,800,000,000. **Per capita** $6,041. **Monetary unit** Real. **Trade partners** Exports: U.S., Netherlands, Japan. Imports: U.S., Germany, Argentina, Iraq. **Exports** Iron ore, soybeans, orange juice, shoes, coffee, vehicle parts. **Imports** Petroleum, machinery, chemicals, food, coal.

LAND
Description Eastern South America. **Area** 3,300,171 mi² (8,547,404 km²). **Highest point** Pico da Neblina, 9,888 ft (3,014 m). **Lowest point** Sea level.

People. The largest South American country, Brazil is also the most populous. Native South Americans, Portuguese colonists, black African slaves, and European and Japanese immigrants shaped the mixed population. Today, indigenous people compose less than 1 percent of the population, and the group is disappearing rapidly due to contact with modern cultures and other factors. Brazil is the only Portuguese-speaking country in the Americas, and Roman Catholicism is the major religion.

Economy and the Land. Brazil's ample natural resources are a major strength, but the diversified base of agriculture, mining, and industry suffers from inequitable ownership and distribution. Sweeping market-oriented reform is aimed at improving this situation. Most commercial farms and ranches lie in the southern plateau region, and coffee, cocoa, soybeans, and beef are important products. Mineral resources include iron ore deposits. Forests cover about half the country, and the Amazon River basin is the site of the world's largest rain forest. The northeast consists of semiarid grasslands, and the central west and south are marked by hills, mountains, and rolling plains. Overall, the climate is semitropical to tropical, with heavy rains.

History and Politics. Portugal obtained rights to the region in a 1494 treaty with Spain and claimed Brazil in 1500. As the indigenous population died out, blacks were brought from Africa to work the plantations. In the 1800s, during the Napoleonic Wars, the Portuguese royal family fled to Rio de Janeiro, and in 1815 the colony became a kingdom. In 1821, the Portuguese king departed for Portugal, leaving Brazil's rule to his son, who declared Brazil an independent country and himself emperor in 1822. Economic development in the mid-1800s brought an influx of Europeans. Following a military takeover in 1889, Brazil became a republic. In recent years key political issues have been the massive foreign debt, land reform, and worldwide concern over the destruction of the rain forest. Corruption at high government levels has been extensive. However, fiscal reform has lowered Brazil's annual inflation rate from 2,500 percent in 1994 to eight percent in 1997. ■

BRITISH INDIAN OCEAN TERRITORY See UNITED KINGDOM.

BRUNEI

Official name Negara Brunei Darussalam

PEOPLE
Population 312,000. **Density** 140/mi² (54/km²). **Urban** 70%. **Capital** Bandar Seri Begawan, 45,867. **Ethnic groups** Malay 64%, Chinese 20%, indigenous 8%, Tamil 3%. **Languages** Malay, English, Chinese, Tamil. **Religions** Muslim 67%, Buddhist 13%, Roman Catholic and other Christian 10%. **Life expectancy** 77 female, 73 male. **Literacy** 88%.

POLITICS
Government Monarchy. **Parties** None. **Suffrage** None. **Memberships** ASEAN, CW, UN. **Subdivisions** 4 districts.

ECONOMY
GDP $4,600,000,000. **Per capita** $15,917. **Monetary unit** Dollar. **Trade partners** Exports: Japan, Thailand, Korea. Imports: Singapore, Japan, U.S. **Exports** Petroleum, petroleum products, natural gas. **Imports** Machinery and transportation equipment, manufactures, food, chemicals.

LAND
Description Southeastern Asia (island of Borneo). **Area** 2,226 mi² (5,765 km²). **Highest point** Mt. Pagon, 6,070 ft (1,850 m). **Lowest point** Sea level.

People. The majority of Brunei's population is Malay, with minorities of Chinese and indigenous peoples. Most Malays are Muslim, and the Chinese are mainly Christian or Buddhist. Many Chinese are unable to become citizens due to language-proficiency exams and strict residency requirements.

Economy and the Land. Brunei is one of Asia's wealthiest countries. Oil and natural gas are the economic mainstays, giving Brunei a high per capita gross domestic product. Much food is imported, however, and the country has failed to diversify. The standard of living is high because of Brunei's oil-based economy, yet wealth is not equally distributed. Situated on northeastern Borneo, Brunei is generally flat and covered with dense rain forests. The climate is tropical.

History and Politics. Historical records of Brunei date back to the 7th century. The country was an important trading center, and by the 16th century the sultan of Brunei ruled Borneo and parts of nearby islands. In 1888 Brunei became a British protectorate, and in 1984 it gained independence from Great Britain. The country is ruled by a sultan who has been on the throne since 1967. ∎

BULGARIA

Official name Republic of Bulgaria

PEOPLE
Population 8,672,000. **Density** 202/mi² (78/km²). **Urban** 69%. **Capital** Sofia, 1,190,126. **Ethnic groups** Bulgarian (Slavic) 85%, Turkish 9%, Gypsy 3%, Macedonian 3%. **Languages** Bulgarian, Turkish. **Religions** Bulgarian Orthodox 85%, Muslim 13%. **Life expectancy** 75 female, 68 male. **Literacy** 98%.

POLITICS
Government Republic. **Parties** Socialist, Union of Democratic Forces, others. **Suffrage** Universal, 18 and over. **Memberships** UN. **Subdivisions** 9 regions.

ECONOMY
GDP $43,200,000,000. **Per capita** $5,140. **Monetary unit** Lev. **Trade partners** Exports: EU countries, former Soviet republics, central and eastern European countries. Imports: Former Soviet republics, Germany, Poland. **Exports** Machinery, agricultural products, textiles, metals and ores, chemicals. **Imports** Fuel and minerals, machinery and equipment, manufactures, food.

LAND
Description Eastern Europe. **Area** 42,855 mi² (110,994 km²). **Highest point** Musala, 9,596 ft (2,925 m). **Lowest point** Sea level.

People. Bulgaria's ethnic composition was determined early in its history when Bulgar tribes conquered the area's Slavic inhabitants. Bulgarians, descendants of these peoples, are a majority today, while Turks, Gypsies, and Macedonians compose the main minority groups. Postwar development is reflected in an agriculture-to-industry shift in employment and a resultant rural-to-urban population movement. Ethnic tension between Bulgarians and ethnic Turks has eased somewhat since the collapse of Communism.

Economy and the Land. A market economy is the declared goal of the post-Soviet government. The pace of reform is slow, however, with 90 percent of the economy still under control of the state. Rich soils in river valleys, as well as a climate similar to that of the American Midwest, make the area well suited for raising livestock, growing grain and other crops. The overall terrain is mountainous.

History and Politics. The area of modern Bulgaria was absorbed by the Roman Empire by A.D. 15, and was subsequently invaded by the Slavs. In the 7th century, Bulgars conquered the region and settled alongside Slavic inhabitants. Rule by the Ottoman Turks began in the late 14th century and lasted until 1878, when the Bulgarians defeated the Turks with the aid of Russia and Romania. The Principality of Bulgaria emerged in 1885, with boundaries approximating those of today, and in 1908 Bulgaria was declared an independent kingdom. Increased territory and a desire for access to the Aegean Sea were partially responsible for Bulgaria's involvement in the Balkan Wars of 1912 and 1913 and alliances with Germany during both world wars. Following Bulgaria's declaration of war on the United States and Britain in World War II, the Soviet Union declared war on Bulgaria. Defeat came in 1944, when the monarchy was overthrown and a Communist government was established shortly thereafter. In 1989, pressure from the people for more participation in the government resulted in the resignation of General Zhivkov, Bulgaria's leader for 35 years. A severe economic downturn forced multiparty elections in 1990, with the Bulgarian Socialist (formerly Communist) Party retaining control. Worsening economic conditions in late 1990 led to their collapse, however, and elections in late 1991 were won by the Union of Democratic Forces, in forced coalition with the Muslim Turkish minority. The Bulgarian Socialist Party regained control in 1994 after years of disheartening economic hardship. In recent years the economy was near collapse. ∎

BURKINA FASO

Official name Burkina Faso

PEOPLE
Population 11,025,000. **Density** 104/mi² (40/km²).
Urban 16%. **Capital** Ouagadougou, 441,514. **Ethnic groups** Mossi 24%, Fulani, Lobi, Malinke, Bobo, Senufo, Gurunsi, others. **Languages** French, indigenous. **Religions** Muslim 50%, Animist 40%, Roman Catholic and other Christian 10%. **Life expectancy** 48 female, 45 male. **Literacy** 19%.

POLITICS
Government Republic. **Parties** Congress for Democracy and Progress, others. **Suffrage** None. **Memberships** OAU, UN. **Subdivisions** 30 provinces.

ECONOMY
GDP $7,400,000,000. **Per capita** $700. **Monetary unit** CFA franc. **Trade partners** Exports: France, Cote d'Ivoire, Switzerland. Imports: France, Cote d'Ivoire, U.S. **Exports** Cotton, animal products, gold. **Imports** Grain and other food, petroleum, machinery.

LAND
Description Western Africa, landlocked. **Area** 105,869 mi² (274,200 km²). **Highest point** Téna Kourou, 2,451 ft (747 m). **Lowest point** Along Pendjari River, 443 ft (135 m).

People. The agricultural Mossi, descendants of warrior migrants, are Burkina Faso's majority population. Other groups include the Fulani, Lobi, Malinke, Bobo, Senufo, and Gurunsi. Ethnic languages vary, although French is the official language.

Economy and the Land. Burkina Faso's agricultural economy suffers from frequent droughts and an underdeveloped transportation system. Most people engage in subsistence farming or livestock raising, and industrialization is minimal. Resources are limited but include gold and manganese. The country remains dependent on foreign aid, much of it from France. The land is marked by northern desert, central savanna, and southern forests, while the climate is generally tropical.

History and Politics. The Mossi arrived from central or eastern Africa during the 11th century and established their kingdom in the area of Burkina Faso. The French came in the late 19th century. In 1919, France united various provinces and created the colony of Upper Volta. The colony was divided among other French colonies in 1932, reinstituted in 1937 as an administrative unit called the Upper Coast, and returned to territorial status as Upper Volta in 1947. It gained independence in 1960. Economic problems and accusations of government corruption led to leadership changes and military rule, including numerous coups. In 1984 the country changed its name from Upper Volta to Burkina Faso. It has since functioned under a civilian, multiparty government. ■

BURMA See MYANMAR.

BURUNDI

Official name Republic of Burundi

PEOPLE
Population 6,080,000. **Density** 566/mi² (218/km²).
Urban 8%. **Capital** Bujumbura, 226,628. **Ethnic groups** Hutu 85%, Tutsi 14%, Twa (Pygmy) 1%.
Languages French, Kirundi, Swahili. **Religions** Roman Catholic 62%, Animist 32%, Protestant 5%, Muslim 1%. **Life expectancy** 53 female, 49 male. **Literacy** 35%.

POLITICS
Government Republic. **Parties** Burundi Democratic Front, Unity for National Progress, others. **Suffrage** Universal adult. **Memberships** OAU, UN. **Subdivisions** 15 provinces.

ECONOMY
GDP $4,000,000,000. **Per capita** $646. **Monetary unit** Franc. **Trade partners** Exports: Germany, Finland. Imports: Belgium, Germany, Iran, France. **Exports** Coffee, tea, hides, cotton. **Imports** Machinery, petroleum products, food, manufactures.

LAND
Description Eastern Africa, landlocked. **Area** 10,745 mi^2 (27,830 km^2). **Highest point** Mt. Heha, 8,760 ft (2,670 m). **Lowest point** Lake Tanganyika, 2,534 ft (772 m).

People. One of Africa's most densely populated countries, Burundi is composed mainly of three Bantu groups. The Hutu are a majority, but the Tutsi, descendants of invaders from Ethiopia, wield most of the power. The Twa are Pygmy hunters, probably descended from the area's inhabitants prior to the influx of the Hutu. Most Burundians are subsistence farmers and Roman Catholic, evidence of foreign influence and rule.

Economy and the Land. An undeveloped country, Burundi relies mainly on agriculture, although undependable rainfall, depleted soil, and erosion occasionally combine for famine. Coffee is a major export. Exploitation of nickel deposits, industrial development through foreign investment, and expansion of tourism offer potential for growth. Although the country is situated near the equator, its high altitude and hilly terrain result in a pleasant climate.

History and Politics. In the 14th century, invading pastoral Tutsi warriors conquered the Hutu and Pygmy Twa and established themselves as the region's power base. The areas of modern Burundi and Rwanda were absorbed into German East Africa in the 1890s. In 1919, following Belgian occupation during World War I, the League of Nations placed present-day Burundi and Rwanda under Belgian rule as part of Ruanda-Urundi. After World War II, Ruanda-Urundi was made a United Nations trust territory under Belgian administration. In 1962, Urundi became Burundi, an independent monarchy, and political turmoil soon followed. A Tutsi-dominated government replaced the monarchy in 1966. The country's first multiparty elections were held in 1993. The new president, a member of the majority Hutu ethnic tribe, was assassinated four months later. Violence ensued between the Hutu and the Tutsi, causing more than 150,000 deaths and creating 500,000 refugees. In 1996 a Tutsi military coup reinstated a former president. Neighboring countries responded by imposing an embargo on Burundi. Sporadic violence continues in rural areas. ∎

CAMBODIA

Official name Kingdom of Cambodia

PEOPLE
Population 11,310,000. **Density** 162/mi^2 (62/km^2). **Urban** 21%. **Capital** Phnom Penh, 620,000. **Ethnic groups** Khmer 90%, Vietnamese 5%. **Languages** Khmer, French. **Religions** Buddhist 95%. **Life expectancy** 55 female, 53 male. **Literacy** 65%.

POLITICS
Government Constitutional monarchy. **Parties** Buddhist Liberal Democratic, FUNCINPEC, People's. **Suffrage** Universal, 18 and over. **Memberships** UN. **Subdivisions** 20 provinces.

ECONOMY
GDP $7,000,000,000. **Per capita** $654. **Monetary unit** Riel. **Trade partners** Vietnam, former Soviet republics, Eastern European countries. **Exports** Rubber, soybeans, sesame, wood. **Imports** Manufactures, machinery, vehicles, construction materials, petroleum products.

LAND
Description Southeastern Asia. **Area** 69,898 mi^2 (181,035 km^2). **Highest point** Mt. Aoral, 5,948 ft (1,813 m). **Lowest point** Sea level.

People. The Khmer, one of the oldest peoples in Southeast Asia, constitute the major ethnic group in Cambodia. The population has declined significantly since the mid-1970s due to war, famine, human rights abuses, and emigration. Because of an urban evacuation campaign initiated by the Khmer Rouge, Cambodia's previous regime, most Cambodians live in rural areas, working as farmers or laborers. Although religious activity was often punished by death during the Khmer Rouge era and discouraged by the Communists, the practice of Buddhism, the main religion, is on the rise.

Economy and the Land. Cambodia's flat central region and wet climate make it well suited for rice production. Along with rubber, rice was the mainstay of the economy before the 1970s, but the Vietnam and civil wars all but destroyed agriculture. This sector of the economy has begun to recover recently, but a shortage of skilled labor, combined with the effects of war, have limited development. The terrain is marked by the central plain, forests, and mountains in the south, west, and along the Thai border. The climate is tropical, with high rainfall and humidity.

History and Politics. Cambodia traces its roots to the Hindu kingdoms of Funan and Chenla, which reigned in the early centuries A.D. The Khmer Empire dominated until the 15th century, incorporating much of present-day Laos, Thailand, and Vietnam and constructing the stone temples of Angkor Wat, considered one of Southeast

Asia's greatest architectural achievements. By 1431 the Siamese had overrun the region, and subsequent years saw the rise of the Siamese, Vietnamese, and Lao. By the mid-1700s Cambodia's boundaries approximated those of today. During the 1800s, as French control in Indochina expanded, the area became a French protectorate. Cambodia gained independence in 1953 under King Sihanouk, who, after changing his title to "prince," became prime minister in 1955 and head of state in 1960. In 1970, after Sihanouk was ousted, Lon Nol was installed as prime minister, and the monarchy of Cambodia changed to the Khmer Republic. During this time the Vietnam War spilled over the Khmer Republic's borders, as United States forces made bombing raids against North Vietnamese bases. Resulting anti-American sentiment gave rise to discontent with Lon Nol's pro-U.S. regime. The Khmer Communists, or Khmer Rouge, seized power in 1975 and, led by Pol Pot, exiled most Cambodians to the countryside. An estimated three million people died under the Khmer Rouge; many were executed because they were either educated or had links to the former government. Vietnamese troops supported by some Cambodian Communists invaded Cambodia in late 1978, and by early 1979 had overthrown the Khmer Rouge. In 1993, elections and a new constitution resulted in Prince Sihanouk again becoming King of Cambodia. The Khmer Rouge resumed its campaign of terror in 1994, but in 1996 it was severely weakened by a split into a political group and a military faction. The Cambodian army is battling the militant Khmer Rouge in northeastern Cambodia. ∎

CAMEROON

Official name Republic of Cameroon

PEOPLE
Population 14,880,000. **Density** 81/mi² (31/km²).

Urban 46%. **Capital** Yaoundé, 560,785. **Ethnic groups** Cameroon Highlander 31%, Equatorial Bantu 19%, Kirdi 11%, Fulani 10%. **Languages** English, French, indigenous. **Religions** Bangwa and other African religions 51%, Christian 33%, Muslim 16%. **Life expectancy** 60 female, 57 male. **Literacy** 63%.

POLITICS
Government Republic. **Parties** National Union for Democracy and Progress, People's Democratic Movement, Social Democratic Front, others. **Suffrage** Universal, 21 and over. **Memberships** OAU, UN. **Subdivisions** 10 provinces.

ECONOMY
GDP $16,500,000,000. **Per capita** $1,202. **Monetary unit** CFA franc. **Trade partners** Exports: France, Belgium, U.S. Imports: France, Netherlands, Japan, Germany. **Exports** Petroleum, petroleum products, aluminum, coffee, cocoa, lumber, manufactures. **Imports** Machinery, electrical equipment, food, manufactures, transportation equipment.

LAND
Description Central Africa. **Area** 183,568 mi² (475,440 km²). **Highest point** Cameroon Mtn., 13,451 ft (4,100 m). **Lowest point** Sea level.

People. Immigration and foreign rule shaped Cameroon's diverse population, composed of more than 200 groups speaking 24 major African languages. Both English and French are official languages, resulting from the merging of former French-ruled eastern and British-ruled western territories. Population is concentrated in the French-speaking eastern region. The majority of people practice indigenous beliefs that often influence Islamic and Christian practices as well.

Economy and the Land. Recent economic plans have focused on agriculture, industry, and the development of oil deposits. Agriculture is still the country's economic base, but oil is a major export. A varied terrain features southern coastal plains and rain forests, central plateaus, mountainous western forests, and northern savanna and marshes. Although this has hindered transportation development and thus slowed economic growth, improvements are being made. Climate varies from hot and humid along the coast to fluctuating temperatures and less humidity northward.

History and Politics. The Sao people reached the Cameroon area in the 10th century. The Portuguese arrived in the 1500s, and the following three centuries saw an influx of European and African peoples and an active slave trade along the coast. In 1884 Germany set up a protectorate that included modern Cameroon by 1914. During World War I British and French troops occupied the area. In 1919, following the war, the League of Nations divided Cameroon into eastern French and western British mandates. The Cameroons became trust territories in 1946, and French Cameroon became an independent republic in 1960. In 1961 the northern region of British Cameroon elected to join Nigeria, and the southern area chose to unite with the eastern Republic of Cameroon. This resulted in a two-state Federal Republic of Cameroon. A 1972 referendum combined the states into the United Republic of Cameroon and, in 1984, the official name was changed to the Republic of Cameroon. An election in October 1992 returned an authoritarian government to power despite widespread claims of electoral fraud by foreign observers. Following the election, rioting and mass arrests ensued. ■

CANADA

Official name Canada

PEOPLE
Population 29,280,000. **Density** 7.6/mi² (2.9/km²). **Urban** 77%. **Capital** Ottawa, 323,340. **Ethnic groups** European descent 43%, mixed European and indigenous 10%, indigenous 20%. **Languages** English, French. **Religions** Roman Catholic 46%, United Church 11%, Anglican 8%, other Christian. **Life expectancy** 81 female, 75 male. **Literacy** 97%.

POLITICS
Government Federal parliamentary state. **Parties** Bloc Quebecois, Liberal, New Democratic, Progressive Conservative, Reform. **Suffrage** Universal, 18 and over. **Memberships** CW, NATO, OAS, OECD, UN. **Subdivisions** 10 provinces, 2 territories.

ECONOMY
GDP $694,000,000,000. **Per capita** $23,347. **Monetary unit** Dollar. **Trade partners** U.S., Japan, U.K. **Exports** Newsprint, wood pulp, timber, petroleum, machinery, natural gas, aluminum. **Imports** Petroleum, chemicals, transportation equipment, manufactures, computers.

LAND
Description Northern North America. **Area** 3,849,674 mi² (9,970,610 km²). **Highest point** Mt. Logan, 19,551 ft (5,959 m). **Lowest point** Sea level.

People. Canada was greatly influenced by French and British rule, and its culture reflects this dual nature. Descendants of British and French settlers compose the two main population groups, and languages include both English and French. French-speaking inhabitants are concentrated in the province of Quebec. Canada does not have a single majority ethnic group. The largest groups are the indigenous peoples and those of European descent. Because of the rugged terrain and harsh climate of northern Canada, the country's population is concentrated near the United States border in such large cities of Vancouver, Toronto, Ottawa, Montréal, and Quebec.

Economy and the Land. Rich and varied natural resources—including extensive mineral deposits, fertile land, forests, and lakes—helped shape Canada's diversified economy, which ranks among the world's most prosperous. Economic problems are those common to most modern industrial countries. Agriculture, mining, and industry are highly developed. Canada is a major wheat producer; mineral output includes asbestos, zinc, silver, and nickel; and crude petroleum is an important export. The service sector is also active. Second only to Russia in land area, Canada has a terrain that varies from eastern rolling hills and plains to massive mountain ranges in the west. The Canadian Shield consists of ancient rock and extends from Labrador to the Arctic Islands. It is covered by thick forests in the south and tundra in the north. Overall, summers tend to be moderate and winters long and cold.

History and Politics. Canada's first inhabitants were Asian peoples and the Inuit, an Arctic people. Around the year 1000, Vikings were the first Europeans to reach North America, and in 1497 John Cabot claimed the Newfoundland coastal area for Britain. Jacques Cartier established the French claim when he landed at the Gaspé Peninsula in the 1500s. Subsequent French and British rivalry culminated in several wars during the late 17th and 18th centuries. The wars ended with the 1763 Treaty of Paris, by which France lost Canada and other North American territory to Britain. To aid in resolving the continued conflict between French and English residents, the British North America Act of 1867 united the colonies into the Dominion of Canada. Canada fought on the side of the British during World War I. In 1926, along with other dominions, Canada declared itself an independent member of the British Commonwealth and, in 1931, Britain recognized the declaration through the Statute of Westminster. Canada once again allied itself with Britain during World War II. In 1989, Canada saw vigorous debate over a free trade pact with the United States, which narrowly won approval. The Quebec separatist movement is striving for independent status for French-speaking Quebec. ■

CANARY ISLANDS See SPAIN.

CAPE VERDE

Official name Republic of Cape Verde

PEOPLE
Population 469,000. **Density** 301/mi² (116/km²). **Urban** 56%. **Capital** Praia, São Tiago I., 61,644. **Ethnic groups** Creole (mulatto) 71%, African 28%, European 1%. **Languages** Portuguese, Crioulo. **Religions** Roman Catholic. **Life expectancy** 68 female, 66 male. **Literacy** 72%.

POLITICS
Government Republic. **Parties** African Party for Independence, Movement for Democracy, others. **Suffrage** Universal, 18 and over. **Memberships** OAU, UN. **Subdivisions** 14 districts.

ECONOMY
GDP $440,000,000. **Per capita** $1,026. **Monetary unit** Escudo. **Trade partners** Exports: Algeria, Portugal. Imports: Portugal, Netherlands, Japan. **Exports** Bananas, fish. **Imports** Food, manufactures, industrial products, transportation equipment.

LAND
Description Western African islands. **Area** 1,557 mi² (4,033 km²). **Highest point** Pico, 9,281 ft (2,829 m). **Lowest point** Sea level.

People. The Portuguese-African heritage of Cape Verde's population is a result of Portuguese rule and the forced transmigration of Africans for slavery. Although Portuguese is an official language, the majority speaks Crioulo, a creole dialect. Most people are Roman Catholic, but indigenous practices exist. The mainly poor population is largely undernourished and plagued by unemployment. The country consists of five islets and ten main islands, and all but one are inhabited.

Economy and the Land. Agriculture on the rugged Cape Verde islands is difficult, so almost all food must be imported. The volcanic mountainous islands have few natural resources and low rainfall, and drought is a frequent problem. Fishing is a potential but undeveloped resource. Cape Verde's location and tropical climate provide the potential for an expanded tourist industry, but until there is more development, the country will remain dependent upon foreign aid.

History and Politics. The islands that make up Cape Verde were uninhabited when the Portuguese arrived around 1460. Settlement began in 1462, and by the 16th century Cape Verde had become a shipping center for the African slave trade. Until 1879 Portugal ruled Cape Verde and present-day Guinea-Bissau as a single colony. An independence movement began in the 1950s, and a 1974 coup in Portugal resulted in autonomy for both countries, with Cape Verde proclaiming independence in 1975. A 1980 coup in Guinea-Bissau quelled plans to unify Cape Verde and Guinea-Bissau. ■

CAYMAN ISLANDS
See UNITED KINGDOM.

CENTRAL AFRICAN REPUBLIC

Official name Central African Republic

PEOPLE
Population 3,376,000. **Density** 14/mi² (5.4/km²). **Urban** 40%. **Capital** Bangui, 451,690. **Ethnic groups** Baya 34%, Banda 27%, Mandjia 21%, Sara 10%. **Languages** French, Sango, Arabic, indigenous. **Religions** Protestant 25%, Roman Catholic 25%, Animist 24%, Muslim 15%. **Life expectancy** 53 female, 48 male. **Literacy** 60%.

POLITICS
Government Republic. **Parties** Central African Democratic Assembly, Movement for the Liberation of the Central African People, others. **Suffrage** Universal, 21 and over. **Memberships** OAU, UN. **Subdivisions** 16 prefectures, 1 autonomous commune.

ECONOMY
GDP $2,500,000,000. **Per capita** $787. **Monetary unit** CFA franc. **Trade partners** Exports: Belgium, France, Switzerland. Imports: France, Cameroon, Japan. **Exports** Diamonds, cotton, coffee, lumber, tobacco. **Imports** Food, textiles, petroleum products, machinery, electrical equipment, drugs.

LAND
Description Central Africa, landlocked. **Area** 240,535 mi² (622,984 km²). **Highest point** Mont Ngaoui, 4,626 ft (1,410 m). **Lowest point** Along Ubangi River, 1,100 ft (335 m).

People. Lying near Africa's geographical center, the Central African Republic was the stopping point for many pre-colonial nomadic groups. The resultant multiethnic populace was further diversified by migrations during the slave trade era. Of the country's many languages, Sango is most widely used. Overall, the population is rural and suffers from poverty and a low literacy rate.

Economy and the Land. Fertile land, extensive forests, and mineral deposits provide adequate bases for agriculture, forestry, and mining. Economic development remains minimal, however, impeded by poor transportation routes, a landlocked location, lack of skilled labor, and political instability. Subsistence farming continues as the major activity, and agriculture is the chief contributor to the economy. The country consists of a plateau region with southern rain forests and a northeastern semidesert. The climate is temperate.

History and Politics. Little is known of the area's early history except that it was the site of many migrations. European slave trade in the 19th century led to the 1894 creation of a French territory called the Ubangi-Chari. This in turn combined with the areas of the present-day Congo, Chad, and Gabon in 1910 to form French Equatorial Africa. The Central African Republic gained independence in 1960. A 1966 military coup installed military chief Jean-Bedel Bokassa, who in 1976 assumed the title of emperor, changed the republic to a monarchy, and renamed the country the Central African Empire. A 1979 coup ended the monarchy and reinstated the name Central African Republic. The country was governed by either a military council or a single political party until a 1992 constitution provided for political pluralism. A military mutiny in 1996 required the intervention of French troops to restore the government, though some fighting continues. ∎

CHAD

Official name Republic of Chad

PEOPLE
Population 7,079,000. **Density** 14/mi² (5.5/km²). **Urban** 23%. **Capital** N'Djamena, 546,572. **Ethnic groups** Sara and other African, Arab. **Languages** Arabic, French, indigenous. **Religions** Muslim 50%, Christian 25%, Animist 25%. **Life expectancy** 51 female, 48 male. **Literacy** 48%.

POLITICS
Government Republic. **Parties** Patriotic Salvation Movement, Union for Renewal and Democracy, others. **Suffrage** Universal adult. **Memberships** OAU, UN. **Subdivisions** 14 prefectures.

ECONOMY
GDP $3,300,000,000. **Per capita** $516. **Monetary unit** CFA franc. **Trade partners** Exports: France, Nigeria, Cameroon. Imports: U.S., France, Nigeria. **Exports** Cotton, cattle, textiles, fish. **Imports** Machinery, transportation equipment, industrial goods, petroleum, food, cloth.

LAND
Description Central Africa, landlocked. **Area** 495,755 mi² (1,284,000 km²). **Highest point** Mt. Koussi, 11,204 ft (3,415 m). **Lowest point** Bodélé, 525 ft (160 m).

People. Centuries ago, Islamic Arabs mixed with indigenous black Africans and established Chad's diverse population. Descendants of Arab invaders mainly inhabit the north, where Islam predominates and nomadic farming is the major activity. In the south—traditionally the economic and political center—the black Sara predominate, operating small farms and practicing indigenous or Christian beliefs. Chad's many languages also reflect its ethnic variety.

Economy and the Land. Natural features and instability arising from ethnic and regional conflict have combined to prevent Chad from prospering. Agriculture and fishing are economic mainstays and are often conducted at subsistence levels. The Sahara extends into Chad's northern region, and the southern grasslands with their heavy rains compose the primary agricultural area. The relative prosperity of the region, in conjunction with its predominantly Sara population, has fueled much of the political conflict. Climate varies from the hot, dry northern desert to the semiarid central region and rainier south.

History and Politics. African and Arab societies began prospering in the Lake Chad region around the 8th century A.D. Subsequent centuries saw the landlocked area become an ethnic crossroads for Muslim nomads and African groups. European traders arrived in the late 1800s, and by 1900 France had gained control. When created in 1910, French Equatorial Africa's boundaries included modern Chad, Gabon, the Congo, and the Central African Republic. Following Chad's independence in 1960, the southern Sara gained dominance over the government. A northern rebel group emerged and government-rebel conflict ensued. Libyan troops entered Chad in 1980, and a cease-fire was implemented in 1987.

Isolated incursions continue. The pro-Western government fell to rebel forces in December 1990. A 1993 national conference established an interim constitution and a transitional government. In 1996, the first democratic election since independence from France was held. ∎

CHANNEL ISLANDS

See UNITED KINGDOM.

CHILE

Official name Republic of Chile

PEOPLE
Population 14,850,000. **Density** 51/mi² (20/km²). **Urban** 84%. **Capital** Santiago, 4,295,593. **Ethnic groups** White and mestizo 95%, Amerindian 3%. **Languages** Spanish. **Religions** Roman Catholic 77%, Pentecostal and other Protestant 13%. **Life expectancy** 78 female, 71 male. **Literacy** 95%.

POLITICS
Government Republic. **Parties** Christian Democratic, Democracy, National Renewal, Socialist, others. **Suffrage** Universal, 18 and over. **Memberships** OAS, UN. **Subdivisions** 13 regions.

ECONOMY
GDP $113,200,000,000. **Per capita** $7,938. **Monetary unit** Peso. **Trade partners** Exports: U.S., Japan, Germany. Imports: U.S., Japan, Brazil, Germany. **Exports** Copper and other metals, minerals, lumber, fish, fruit. **Imports** Petroleum, wheat, manufactures, raw materials.

LAND
Description Southern South America. **Area** 292,135 mi² (756,626 km²). **Highest point** Nevado Ojos del Salado, 22,615 ft (6,893 m). **Lowest point** Sea level.

People. Chile's land barriers—the eastern Andes, western coastal range, and northern desert—have resulted in a mostly urban population concentrated in a central valley. Mestizos, of Spanish-Amerindian heritage, and descendants of Spanish immigrants predominate. In addition to an Amerindian minority, the population includes those who trace their roots to Irish and English colonists or 19th-century German immigrants. The country enjoys a relatively high literacy rate, but poverty remains a problem.

Economy and the Land. Chile's land provides the natural resources necessary for a successful economy. Economic growth has been high in the post-Pinochet era, but there is concern over the increasing gap between the rich and the poor. The northern desert region is the site of mineral deposits, and mining is a major component of trade, making Chile vulnerable to outside market forces. An agricultural zone lies in the central valley, while the South offers forests, grazing land, and some petroleum deposits. The climate varies from region to region but is generally mild.

History and Politics. Upon their arrival in the 1500s, the Spanish defeated the northern Inca, although many years were spent in conflict with the Araucanian people of the central and southern regions. From the 16th through the 19th centuries, Chile received little attention from ruling Spain, and colonists established a successful agriculture. In 1818, Bernardo O'Higgins led the way to victory over the Spanish and became ruler of independent Chile. By the 1920s, dissent arising from unequal power and land distribution united the middle and working classes, but social welfare, education, and economic programs were unable to eliminate inequalities rooted in the past. A 1960 earthquake and tidal wave added to the country's problems. Leftist Salvador Allende Gossens was elected to power in 1970, governing until his death in 1973 in a military coup, which installed Augusto Pinochet. Civil disturbances and grave human-rights abuses marked his right-wing government. This dictatorship ended in 1989, although Pinochet continued as the army's commander-in-chief until March 1998. Soon after, he was sworn in by the Chilean legislature as dictator for life—a post created for him in the constitution that he had adopted for the country. ∎

CHINA

Official name People's Republic of China

PEOPLE
Population 1,234,260,000. **Density** 334/mi² (129/km²).

Urban 31%. **Capital** Beijing (Peking), 6,690,000. **Ethnic groups** Han Chinese 92%, Zhuang, Uygur, Hui, Yi, Tibetan, miao, Manchu, others. **Languages** Chinese dialects. **Religions** Taoist, Buddhist, and Muslim 3%. **Life expectancy** 72 female, 68 male. **Literacy** 82%.

POLITICS
Government Socialist republic. **Parties** Communist. **Suffrage** Universal, 18 and over. **Memberships** UN. **Subdivisions** 22 provinces, 5 autonomous regions, 3 municipalities.

ECONOMY
GDP $3,500,000,000,000. **Per capita** $2,895. **Monetary unit** Yuan. **Trade partners** Japan, U.S. **Exports** Textiles, clothing, machinery, equipment, toys, footwear. **Imports** Machinery, plastics, communications equipment, manufactures, steel, textiles.

LAND
Description Eastern Asia. **Area** 3,690,045 mi^2 (9,557,172 km^2). **Highest point** Mt. Everest, 29,028 ft (8,848 m). **Lowest point** Turfan Depression, -505 ft (-154 m).
The above information excludes Taiwan.

People. China is the world's most populous country. Its population is concentrated in the east, and Han Chinese are the majority group. Zhuang, Hui, Uygur, Yi, Miao, Manchu, and Tibetan peoples compose minorities. Many Chinese languages are spoken, but the national language is Modern Standard Chinese, or Mandarin, based on a northern dialect. Following a Communist revolution in 1949, religious activity was discouraged. It is now on the increase, and religions include Taoism and Buddhism, as well as Islam and Christianity. China's population has soared to more than 1.2 billion, and family-planning programs have been implemented to aid population control. With a recorded civilization going back about 3,500 years, China has contributed much to world culture.

Economy and the Land. Economic progress dates from 1949, when the new People's Republic of China faced a starving, war-torn, and unemployed population. As of 1993, the Chinese economy was the third-largest in the world. Industry is expanding, but agriculture continues as the major activity. Natural resources include coal, oil, natural gas, and minerals, many of which remain to be explored. China's terrain is varied: Two-thirds consists of mountainous or semiarid land, with fertile plains and deltas in the east. The climate is marked by hot, humid summers and cold, dry winters.

History and Politics. China's civilization ranks among the world's oldest. The first dynasty, the Shang, began sometime during the second millennium B.C. Kublai Khan's 13th-century invasion brought China the first of its various foreign rulers. In the 19th century, foreign influence and intervention grew. The government was weakened by the Opium War with Britain in the 1840s; the Taiping Rebellion, a civil war; and a war with Japan from 1894-1895. Opposition to foreign influences erupted in the anti-foreign and anti-

Christian Boxer Rebellion of 1900. After China became a republic in 1912, the death of the president in 1916 triggered the warlord period, in which conflicts were widespread and power was concentrated among military leaders. Attempts to unite the country began in the 1920s with Sun Yat-sen's Nationalist party, initially allied with the Communist party. Under the leadership of Chiang Kai-shek, the Nationalist party overcame the warlords, captured Beijing, and executed many Communists. Remaining Communists reorganized under Mao Zedong, and the Communist-Nationalist conflict continued, along with Japanese invasion and occupation. By 1949 the Communists controlled most of the country, and the People's Republic of China was proclaimed. Chiang Kai-shek fled to Taiwan, proclaiming T'aipei as China's provisional capital. After Mao's death in 1976, Deng Xiaopeng introduced capitalism to China's Communist environment. This began a vast increase in the domestic economy through foreign trade and contact. In 1979 the United States recognized Beijing, rather than T'aipei, as China's capital. When a retrenchment of the government from liberalization erupted violently in student demonstrations in 1989, many people were killed or arrested. There has been an increase in violence protesting China's continued political repression. Despite this, China is experiencing burgeoning economic growth. In 1997 Hong Kong, formerly a British colony, was returned to China under an agreement whereby its present economic system would remain in place for 50 years. The agreement also permitted citizens to retain most of the freedoms they enjoyed under British rule. See also TAIWAN. ∎

CHRISTMAS ISLAND
See AUSTRALIA.

COCOS ISLANDS See AUSTRALIA.

COLOMBIA
Official name Republic of Colombia

PEOPLE
Population 37,730,000. **Density** 86/mi^2 (33/km^2). **Urban** 73%. **Capital** Bogotá, 3,974,813. **Ethnic groups** Mestizo 58%, white 20%, mulatto 14%, black 4%. **Languages** Spanish. **Religions** Roman Catholic 95%. **Life expectancy** 73 female, 67 male. **Literacy** 91%.

POLITICS
Government Republic. **Parties** Conservative, Liberal, others. **Suffrage** Universal, 18 and over. **Memberships** OAS, UN. **Subdivisions** 32 departments, 1 capital district.

ECONOMY
GDP $192,500,000,000. **Per capita** $5,438. **Monetary unit** Peso. **Trade partners** Exports: U.S.,

became president. By 1830 Venezuela and Ecuador had seceded from the republic, followed by Panama in 1903. Conflict between the two dominant political parties, the Conservative and the Liberal, led to a civil war from 1899 to 1902. From the 1940s to the 1960s, Conservative-Liberal tension caused another civil disturbance called *La Violencia* (The Violence), resulting in about 300,000 deaths. From the late 1950s through the 1970s, the government alternated between conservative and liberal rule. Political unrest reduced the effectiveness of both parties. By the 1980s growing drug traffic presented Colombia with new problems. Colombia's government has a history of both cooperating with the United States in fighting cocaine production as well as giving in to the violence and bribery of the drug cartels and overlooking the illicit activities. The government is now faced with widespread corruption and violence. ∎

Germany, Netherlands. Imports: U.S., Japan, Germany. **Exports** Petroleum, coffee, coal, bananas, flowers. **Imports** Industrial and transportation equipment, manufactures, chemicals, paper.

LAND
Description Northern South America. **Area** 440,831 mi^2 (1,141,748 km^2). **Highest point** Pico Cristóbal Colón, 18,947 ft (5,775 m). **Lowest point** Sea level.

People. Colombia's mixed population traces its roots to indigenous peoples, Spanish colonists, and black African slaves. Most numerous today are mestizos, those of Spanish-Amerindian descent. Roman Catholicism, the Spanish language, and Colombia's overall culture evidence the long-lasting effect of Spanish rule. Over the past decades, the population has shifted from mainly rural to urban as the economy has expanded into industry.

Economy and the Land. Industry now keeps pace with traditional agriculture in economic contributions, and mining is also important. Natural resources include oil, coal, natural gas, most of the world's emeralds, plus fertile soils. The traditional coffee crop also remains important for Colombia, a leading coffee producer. The most valuable cash crop, however, is coca, and the chief export is cocaine, both of which are illegal. The terrain features a flat coastal region, central highlands, and wide eastern *llanos*, or plains. The climate is tropical on the coast and in the west, with cooler temperatures in the highlands.

History and Politics. In the 1500s Spaniards conquered the indigenous peoples and established the area as a Spanish colony. In the early 1700s, Bogotá became the capital of the viceroyalty of New Granada, which included modern Colombia, Venezuela, Ecuador, and Panama. Rebellion in Venezuela in 1796 sparked revolts elsewhere in New Granada, including Colombia, and in 1813 independence was declared. In 1819, the Republic of Greater Colombia was formed and included all the former members of the Spanish viceroyalty. Independence leader Simón Bolívar

COMOROS

Official name Federal Islamic Republic of the Comoros

PEOPLE
Population 599,000. **Density** 694/mi^2 (268/km^2). **Urban** 31%. **Capital** Moroni, Njazidja I., 23,432. **Ethnic groups** Antalote, Cafre, Makoa, Oimatsaha, Sakalava. **Languages** Arabic, French, Comoran. **Religions** Sunni Muslim 86%, Roman Catholic 14%. **Life expectancy** 59 female, 58 male. **Literacy** 57%.

POLITICS
Government Federal Islamic republic. **Parties** Rassemblement National pour le Development, Front National pour la Justice. **Suffrage** Universal, 18 and over. **Memberships** OAU, UN. **Subdivisions** 3 islands.

ECONOMY
GDP $370,000,000. **Per capita** $685. **Monetary unit** Franc. **Trade partners** Exports: France, U.S., Mauritius. Imports: France and other European countries. **Exports** Vanilla, cloves, perfume essence, copra. **Imports** Rice, food, cement, petroleum products, manufactures.

LAND
Description Southeastern African islands. **Area** 863 mi² (2,235 km²). **Highest point** Kartala, 7,746 ft (2,361 m). **Lowest point** Sea level.
The above information excludes Mayotte.

People. The ethnic groups of Comoros' Njazidja, Nzwani, and Mwali islands are mainly of Arab-African descent, practice Islam, and speak Comoran, a Swahili dialect. Arab culture, however, predominates throughout the island group. Poverty, disease, a shortage of medical care, and low literacy continue to plague the country.

Economy and the Land. Comoros' economic mainstay is agriculture, and most Comorans practice subsistence farming and fishing. Plantations employ workers to produce the main cash crops, which include spices and essential (perfume) oils. Of volcanic origin, the islands have soils of varying quality, and some are unsuited for farming. Terrain varies from the mountains of Njazidja to the hills and valleys of Mwali. The climate is cool and dry, with a winter rainy season.

History and Politics. The Comoro Islands saw invasions by coastal African, Persian Gulf, Indonesian, and Malagasy peoples. Portuguese explorers landed in the 1500s, around the same time Arab Shirazis, most likely from Persia, introduced Islam. The French took Mayotte in 1843 and had established colonial rule over the four main islands by 1912. Comoros declared unilateral independence in 1975. Mayotte, however, voted to remain under French administration. Ongoing political instability is evidenced by repeated military coups. In August 1997 two separate secessionist movements occurred on the Comoran islands of Anjouan and Mwali with the goal of restoring French rule. The islands are currently negotiating with the Comoran government. ■

CONGO

Official name Republic of the Congo

PEOPLE
Population 2,556,000. **Density** 19/mi² (7.5/km²). **Urban** 59%. **Capital** Brazzaville, 693,712. **Ethnic groups** Kongo 48%, Sangho 20%, Bateke 17%, Mbochi 12%. **Languages** French, Lingala, Kikongo, indigenous. **Religions** Christian 50%, Animist 48%, Muslim 2%. **Life expectancy** 52 female, 48 male. **Literacy** 57%.

POLITICS
Government Republic. **Parties** Movement for Democracy and Integral Development, Pan-African Union for Social Development, others. **Suffrage** Universal, 18 and over. **Memberships** OAU, UN. **Subdivisions** 9 regions, 1 federal district.

ECONOMY
GDP $7,700,000,000. **Per capita** $3,191. **Monetary unit** CFA franc. **Trade partners** Exports: U.S., Spain, France. Imports: France, Spain, U.S. **Exports** Petroleum, lumber, coffee, cocoa, sugar, diamonds. **Imports** Food, manufactures, machinery, construction materials, petroleum products.

LAND
Description Central Africa. **Area** 132,047 mi² (342,000 km²). **Highest point** Mt. Nabeba, 3,219 ft (981 m). **Lowest point** Sea level.

People. The Congo's main groups—the Kongo, Sangho, Bateke, and Mbochi—create an ethnically and linguistically diverse populace. The official language, French, reflects former colonial rule. Population is concentrated in the south, away from the dense forests, heavy rainfall, and hot climate of the north. Educational programs have improved, although rural inhabitants remain relatively isolated.

Economy and the Land. Brazzaville was the commercial center of the former colony called French Equatorial Africa. The Congo now benefits from the early groundwork laid for service and transport industries. Subsistence farming occupies most Congolese, however, and takes most of the cultivated land. Low productivity and a growing populace create a need for foreign aid, much of it from France. Offshore petroleum is the most valuable mineral resource and a major economic contributor. The land is marked by coastal plains, a south-central valley, a central plateau, and the Congo River basin in the north. The climate is tropical.

History and Politics. Several tribal kingdoms existed in the area during its early history. The Portuguese arrived on the coast in the 1400s, and slave trade flourished until it was banned in the 1800s. A Teke king then signed a treaty placing the area, known as Middle Congo, under French protection. In 1910 Middle Congo, the present-day Central African Republic, Gabon, and Chad were joined to form French Equatorial Africa. The Republic of the Congo became independent in 1960. Subsequent years saw unrest, including coups, a presidential assassination, and accusations of corruption and human rights violations. In 1991 Congo's dictatorial president, Col. Denis Sassou-Nguessou, responded to growing unrest by legalizing opposition political parties. In the

1992 election a former president was re-elected, sparking tribal and ethnic violence. In 1997 the fighting escalated into a civil war, and Sassou-Nguessou returned to power. ■

CONGO, DEMOCRATIC REPUBLIC OF THE

Official name Democratic Republic of the Congo

PEOPLE
Population 47,660,000. **Density** 53/mi² (20/km²). **Urban** 29%. **Capital** Kinshasa, 3,000,000. **Ethnic groups** Kongo, Luba, Mongo, Mangbetu-Azande, others. **Languages** French, Kikongo, Lingala, Swahili, Tshiluba, Kingwana. **Religions** Roman Catholic 50%, Protestant 20%, Kimbanguist 10%, Muslim 10%. **Life expectancy** 53 female, 50 male. **Literacy** 77%.

POLITICS
Government Republic. **Parties** Popular Movement of the Revolution, Union for Democracy and Social Progress, others. **Suffrage** Universal, 18 and over. **Memberships** None. **Subdivisions** 10 regions, 1 independent town.

ECONOMY
GDP $16,500,000,000. **Per capita** $380. **Monetary unit** Franc. **Trade partners** Exports: U.S., Belgium, Germany. Imports: Belgium, Brazil, France. **Exports** Copper, coffee, diamonds, cobalt, petroleum. **Imports** Manufactures, food, machinery, transportation equipment, fuel.

LAND
Description Central Africa. **Area** 905,446 mi² (2,345,095 km²). **Highest point** Margherita Pk., 16,762 ft (5,109 m). **Lowest point** Sea level.

People. The diverse population of Democratic Republic of the Congo (D.R.C.) is composed of more than 200 African ethnic groups, with Bantu peoples in the majority. Belgian settlers introduced French, but hundreds of indigenous languages are more widely spoken. Much of the population is Christian, another result of former European rule. Many non-Christians practice traditional or syncretic faiths such as Kimbanguism. The majority of the people are rural farmers.

Economy and the Land. D.R.C. is rich in mineral resources, particularly copper, cobalt, diamonds, and petroleum; mining has supplanted agriculture in economic importance. Agriculture continues to employ most people, however, and subsistence farming is practiced in nearly every region. Industrial activity—especially petroleum refining and hydroelectric production—was once a growing part of the economy but has suffered during the recent civil war. D.R.C.'s terrain is composed of mountains and plateaus. The climate is equatorial, with hot and humid weather in the north and west, and cooler and drier conditions in the south and east.

History and Politics. The earliest inhabitants of the modern D.R.C. were probably Pygmies who settled in the area thousands of years ago. By the A.D. 700s, sophisticated civilizations had developed in what is now southeastern D.R.C. In the early 1500s, the Portuguese began the forced emigration of black Africans for slavery. Other Europeans came to the area as the slave trade grew, but the interior remained relatively unexplored until the 1870s. Belgian King Leopold II realized the potential value of the region, and in 1885 his claim was recognized. Belgium took control from Leopold in 1908, renaming the colony the Belgian Congo. Nationalist sentiment grew until rioting broke out in 1959. The country, which was then called the Democratic Republic of the Congo, gained independence in 1960, and a weak government assumed control. Violent civil disorder, provincial secession, and a political assassination characterized the next five years. The country became stabilized under the rule of Mobuto Sese Seko, a former army general, who changed its name to Zaire. Later, a rebel movement arose in response to government corruption and human rights abuses. In May 1997, after a seven-month rebellion, forces led by Laurent Désiré Kabila took control of Zaire. Soon after, Kabila assumed the role of president and changed the name of the country to the Democratic Republic of the Congo. Despite his early promises to install a democratic government, Kabila has behaved like a dictator, jailing his detractors and impeding UN investigations into alleged atrocities committed by his rebel forces during the war. His international support has dwindled, limiting his ability to rebuild his war-torn country with foreign aid. ■

COOK ISLANDS
See NEW ZEALAND.

CORSICA See FRANCE.

COSTA RICA

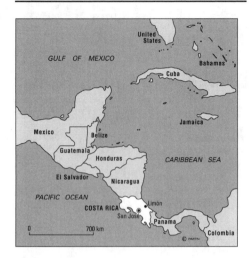

Official name Republic of Costa Rica

PEOPLE
Population 3,570,000. **Density** 181/mi² (70/km²).
Urban 50%. **Capital** San José, 318,765. **Ethnic groups**
White and mestizo 96%, black 2%, Amerindian 1%.
Languages Spanish. **Religions** Roman Catholic 95%.
Life expectancy 79 female, 74 male. **Literacy** 95%.

POLITICS
Government Republic. **Parties** National Liberation,
Social Christian Unity, others. **Suffrage** Universal,
18 and over. **Memberships** OAS, UN. **Subdivisions**
7 provinces.

ECONOMY
GDP $18,400,000,000. **Per capita** $5,916. **Monetary
unit** Colon. **Trade partners** Exports: U.S., Germany,
Italy. Imports: U.S., Venezuela, Japan. **Exports** Coffee,
bananas, textiles, sugar. **Imports** Petroleum, manufactures, machinery, food, capital equipment, raw
materials.

LAND
Description Central America. **Area** 19,730 mi²
(51,100 km²). **Highest point** Cerro Chirripó, 12,530 ft
(3,819 m). **Lowest point** Sea level.

People. Compared with most other Central
American countries, Costa Rica has a relatively
large population of European descent, mostly
Spanish with minorities of German, Dutch, and
Swiss ancestry. Together with mestizos—people
of Spanish-Amerindian heritage—they compose
the bulk of the population. Descendants of black
Jamaican immigrants inhabit mainly the Caribbean coastal region. Indigenous peoples in scattered enclaves continue traditional lifestyles;
some, however, have assimilated the country's
majority culture.

Economy and the Land. Costa Rica's economy,
one of the most prosperous in Central America,
has not been without problems, some resulting
from falling coffee prices and rising oil costs.
Agriculture remains important, producing tradi-

tional coffee and banana crops, while the country
attempts to expand industry. Population and
agriculture are concentrated in the central highlands. Much of the country is forested, and the
mountainous central area is bordered by coastal
plains on the east and west. The climate is
semitropical to tropical.

History and Politics. In 1502, Christopher
Columbus arrived and claimed the area for
Spain. Spaniards named the region Rich Coast,
and settlers soon flocked to the new land to seek
their fortune. Rather than riches, they found an
Amerindian population unwilling to surrender its
land. But many Spaniards remained, establishing
farms in the central area. In 1821, the Central
American provinces of Costa Rica, Guatemala,
El Salvador, Honduras, and Nicaragua declared
themselves independent from Spain, and by 1823
they had formed the Federation of Central
America. Despite efforts to sustain it, the federation was in a state of virtual collapse by 1838, and
Costa Rica became an independent republic.
Since the first free elections in 1889, Costa Rica
has experienced a presidential overthrow in 1919
and a civil war in 1948, which arose over a disputed election. In the 1980s, the country worked to
promote peaceful solutions to armed conflicts in
the region. It is Central America's oldest and
most stable democracy. ■

COTE D'IVOIRE

Official name Republic of Cote d'Ivoire

PEOPLE
Population 15,410,000. **Density** 124/mi² (48/km²).
Urban 44%. **Capital** Abidjan (de facto), 1,929,079;
Yamoussoukro (future), 106,786. **Ethnic groups**
Baule 23%, Bete 18%, Senoufou 15%, Malinke 11%,
other African. **Languages** French, Dioula and other
indigenous. **Religions** Muslim 39%, Roman Catholic
21%, Animist 17%. **Life expectancy** 51 female,
49 male. **Literacy** 40%.

POLITICS
Government Republic. **Parties** Democratic, Popular Front, Rally of the Republicans, others. **Suffrage** Universal, 21 and over. **Memberships** OAU, UN. **Subdivisions** 49 departments.

ECONOMY
GDP $21,900,000,000. **Per capita** $1,521. **Monetary unit** CFA franc. **Trade partners** Exports: Netherlands, France, U.S. Imports: France, Nigeria. **Exports** Cocoa, coffee, wood, cotton, bananas, pineapples, palm oil. **Imports** Food, manufactures, raw materials and fuel.

LAND
Description Western Africa. **Area** 124,518 mi^2 (322,500 km^2). **Highest point** Mont Nimba, 5,748 ft (1,752 m). **Lowest point** Sea level.

People. Cote d'Ivoire is composed almost entirely of black Africans from more than 60 ethnic groups. As a result of former French rule, French is the country's official language, but many indigenous languages are also spoken. Traditional religions predominate, though a significant number of Ivorians are either Muslim or Christian. Most Ivorians live in small villages, but increased numbers have moved to the cities to find work. Overcrowding is a major problem in the cities.

Economy and the Land. Once solely dependent upon the export of cocoa and coffee, Cote d'Ivoire now produces and exports a variety of agricultural goods. Forest land, when cleared, provides rich soil for agriculture—still the country's main activity. Petroleum, textile, and apparel industries also contribute to the strong economy. Cote d'Ivoire pursues a policy of economic liberalism in which foreign investment is encouraged. As a result, foreigners hold high-level positions in most Cote d'Ivoire industries. The hot, humid coastal region gives way to inland tropical forest. Beyond the forest lies savanna, and to the northwest are highlands.

History and Politics. Cote d'Ivoire once consisted of many African kingdoms. French sailors gave the region its present name when they began trading for ivory and other goods in 1483. Missionaries arrived in 1637, but European settlement was hindered by the rugged coastline and intertribal conflicts. Cote d'Ivoire became a French colony in 1893. Movements toward autonomy began after World War II, and in 1960 Cote d'Ivoire declared itself an independent republic. The country enjoyed many years of political stability under its first president, Felix Houphouet-Boigny. His death in 1993 resulted in a peaceful transition of power to his legal successor. ■

CROATIA

Official name Republic of Croatia

PEOPLE
Population 5,048,000. **Density** 231/mi^2 (89/km^2). **Urban** 56%. **Capital** Zagreb, 867,865. **Ethnic groups** Croat 78%, Serb 12%, Muslim 1%. **Languages** Serbo-

Croatian. **Religions** Roman Catholic 77%, Orthodox 11%, Muslim 1%. **Life expectancy** 77 female, 68 male. **Literacy** 97%.

POLITICS
Government Republic. **Parties** Democratic Union, Peasants', Social Democratic, Social Liberal, others. **Suffrage** Universal, 18 and over, 16 if employed. **Memberships** UN. **Subdivisions** 21 counties.

ECONOMY
GDP $20,100,000,000. **Per capita** $4,303. **Monetary unit** Kuna. **Trade partners** Former Yugoslav republics. **Exports** Machinery, transportation equipment, manufactures, chemicals, food, fuels. **Imports** Machinery, transportation equipment, petroleum products, food, chemicals.

LAND
Description Eastern Europe. **Area** 21,829 mi^2 (56,538 km^2). **Highest point** Dinara, 6,007 ft (1,831 m). **Lowest point** Sea level.

People. Despite a common heritage with the Serbian people of Yugoslavia, the Croats have their own distinct culture and traditions. The basis of the continuing friction between the Croats and Serbs is religious in origin: The Croats are Roman Catholic, while the Serbs are mainly Orthodox. The religious difference resulted in a more Western European cultural orientation for the Croats and an eastern affiliation for the Serbs. Most of Croatia's Serbian minority lives in northwestern Croatia.

Economy and the Land. Croatia is a land of extremely varied terrain, and includes the historic regions of Croatia, Dalmatia, Slavonia, and part of Istria. Croatia's fertile plains produce ample supplies of grains. Grapes, olives, and citrus fruits are grown along the mountainous coast. Croatia has a well-developed industrial sector, and leading industries include petrochemicals, food processing, and shipbuilding. The Adriatic coast attracts tourists from all over the world.

History and Politics. Slavic people settled in Croatia in the 7th century and established their own independent state. The original tribal organization of the people was eventually replaced by a feudal one. In 1102 the country chose to merge with Hungary. Turkey invaded Croatia in 1463, but in 1699 Croatia was reclaimed by the Austro-Hungarian Hapsburg Empire. Tiring of foreign rule, the Croats began to agitate for independence in the mid-1800s, but Croatia nevertheless joined the Serbs and Slovenes in the new state of Yugoslavia in 1918. In 1941 Germany invaded Yugoslavia, and Croatia was set up as an independent state. Allied with the Nazis, this government was responsible for the deaths of thousands of Serbs and Jews. Croatian independence ended in 1946 after World War II when it became a state of the new Yugoslavia, united under the dictator Tito. Enmity between the Croats and Serbs continued to simmer in the postwar period, and terrorism was common. Tito's death in 1980 plunged the country into a political and economic crisis, and Croats began to demand greater autonomy. Croatia claimed home rule in February 1991, and fighting between the Croats and the Yugoslavian army began shortly thereafter. Along with Slovenia, Croatia declared its independence on June 25, 1991. The war between Croatia and Serbian Yugoslavia continued to escalate throughout 1991. More than 10,000 people were killed by the time a cease-fire was reached in 1992, when a United Nations peacekeeping force was sent in. Croatia recently resumed full control of Eastern Slavonia, the last Serbian enclave within its borders. ■

CUBA

Official name Republic of Cuba

PEOPLE
Population 11,025,000. **Density** 258/mi² (99/km²). **Urban** 76%. **Capital** Havana, 2,119,059. **Ethnic groups** Mulatto 51%, white 37%, black 11%,

Chinese 1%. **Languages** Spanish. **Religions** Roman Catholic, Pentecostal, Baptist, Jehovah's Witnesses. **Life expectancy** 78 female, 74 male. **Literacy** 96%.

POLITICS
Government Socialist republic. **Parties** Communist. **Suffrage** Universal, 16 and over. **Memberships** UN. **Subdivisions** 13 provinces, 1 city, 1 municipality.

ECONOMY
GDP $14,700,000,000. **Per capita** $1,339. **Monetary unit** Peso. **Trade partners** Former Soviet republics, Germany. **Exports** Sugar, nickel, medical supplies, shellfish, fruit, tobacco, coffee. **Imports** Petroleum, machinery, chemicals, food.

LAND
Description Caribbean island. **Area** 42,804 mi² (110,861 km²). **Highest point** Pico Turquino, 6,470 ft (1,972 m). **Lowest point** Sea level.

People. Most Cubans are descendants of Spanish colonists, African slaves, or a blend of the two. The government provides free education and health care. Although religious practices are discouraged, most people belong to the Roman Catholic church. Personal income, health, education, and housing have improved since the 1959 revolution, but most food products and consumer goods remain in short supply.

Economy and the Land. Cuba's economy is largely dependent on sugar, although other agricultural products are also important. The most fertile soils lie in the central region between mountain ranges, while mineral deposits, including oil and nickel, are found in the northeast. In addition to agriculture and mining, industry is an economic contributor. Most economic activity is nationalized, and has, until recently, been dependent on aid from the former Soviet Union. Mountains, plains, and a scenic coastline make Cuba one of the most beautiful islands in the West Indies. The climate is tropical.

History and Politics. Christopher Columbus claimed Cuba for Spain in 1492, and Spanish settlement began in 1511. When the indigenous population died out, African slaves were brought to work plantations. The United States joined with Cuba against Spain in the Spanish-American War in 1898. Cuba gained full independence in 1902. Unrest continued, however, and the U.S. again intervened from 1906 to 1909 and in 1917. A government overthrow in 1934 ushered in an era dominated by Sergeant Fulgencio Batista. After ruling through other presidents and serving an elected term himself, Batista seized power in a 1952 coup that established an unpopular and oppressive regime. Led by lawyer Fidel Castro, a revolutionary group gained quick support, and Batista fled the country on January 1, 1959. Early U.S. support of Castro soured when nationalization of American businesses began. American aid soon ceased, and Cuba looked to the Soviet Union for assistance. The U.S. ended diplomatic relations with Cuba in 1961. In 1962 the U.S. and the Soviet Union became embroiled in a dispute over Soviet missile bases in Cuba that ended with removal of the missiles. In the 1990s, Cuba-U.S. relations were strained by Castro's encouragement of illegal emigration to the U.S. and Cuba's military strike against two U.S. citizen-owned planes that Cuba claimed violated its airspace. In 1995, Cuba's economy began to recover through non-U.S. foreign investment and tourism. Political and economic sanctions continue to sour relations with the U.S., however. ■

CURAÇAO See NETHERLANDS.

CYPRUS

Official name Republic of Cyprus

PEOPLE
Population 619,000. **Density** 272/mi² (105/km²). **Urban** 55%. **Capital** Nicosia (Levkosía), 47,036. **Ethnic groups** Greek. **Languages** Greek, English. **Religions** Greek Orthodox. **Life expectancy** 80 female, 76 male. **Literacy** 94%.

POLITICS
Government Republic. **Parties** Democratic, Democratic Rally, Progressive Party of the Working People, others. **Suffrage** Universal, 18 and over. **Memberships** CW, UN. **Subdivisions** 6 districts.

ECONOMY
GDP $7,800,000,000. **Per capita** $12,893. **Monetary unit** Pound. **Trade partners** Exports: U.K., Greece, Lebanon. Imports: U.K., Japan, Italy. **Exports** Fruit, potatoes, grapes, wine, cement, clothing and shoes. **Imports** Manufactures, petroleum, lubricants, food, feed grains, machinery.

LAND
Description Southern part of the island of Cyprus. **Area** 2,276 mi² (5,896 km²). **Highest point** Ólimbos, 6,401 ft (1,951 m). **Lowest point** Sea level.

People. Most Cypriots occupying the southern two thirds of the island are of Greek ancestry, and their religion, language, and general culture reflect this heritage. Family and religion are a dominant influence in the community. Decades of British rule had little impact.

Economy and the Land. Conflict between the Greek and Turkish Cypriots has severely disrupted the economy of the island. With foreign assistance, Greek Cypriots have made considerable progress, expanding traditional southern agriculture to light manufacturing and tourism. Known for its scenic beauty and tourist appeal, southern

Cyprus is marked by a fertile southern plain bordered by the rugged Troodos Mountains to the southwest. Sandy beaches dot the coastline. The Mediterranean climate brings hot, dry summers and damp, cool winters.

History and Politics. History of Cyprus and North Cyprus follows NORTH CYPRUS. ■

CYPRUS, NORTH

Official name Turkish Republic of Northern Cyprus

PEOPLE
Population 138,000. **Density** 107/mi² (41/km²). **Capital** Nicosia (Lefkoşa), 37,400. **Ethnic groups** Turkish 99%, Greek, Maronite, and others 1%. **Languages** Turkish. **Religions** Sunni Muslim. **Life expectancy** 75 female, 71 male. **Literacy** 99%.

POLITICS
Government Republic. **Parties** Communal Liberation, Democratic, National Unity, Republican Turkish, others. **Suffrage** Universal, 18 and over. **Memberships** None. **Subdivisions** 3 districts.

ECONOMY
GDP $520,000,000. **Per capita** $3,852. **Monetary unit** Turkish lira. **Trade partners** Turkey, U.K., Germany. **Exports** Citrus, potatoes, textiles. **Imports** Manufactures, machinery, petroleum and lubricants, food and feed grains.

LAND
Description Northern part of the island of Cyprus. **Area** 1,295 mi² (3,355 km²). **Highest point** 3,360 ft (1,024 m). **Lowest point** Sea level.

People. The northern part of the island is occupied by Cypriots of Turkish ancestry who speak Turkish and are Sunni Muslims. The 1974 Turkish invasion resulted in a formal segregation of this settlement pattern. The Turkish Cypriot ancestors first arrived on the island during the three centuries of Ottoman rule.

Economy and the Land. Since the partition of the island, North Cyprus has become somewhat isolated. Lacking in capital, foreign aid, and official recognition, it remains agriculturally based and dependent upon Turkey for tourism, trade, and assistance. The mostly barren Kyrenia Range dominates North Cyprus.

History and Politics. In the Late Bronze Age—from 1600 to 1050 B.C.—a Greek culture flourished in Cyprus. Rule by various peoples followed, including Assyrians, Egyptians, Persians, Romans, Byzantines, French, and Venetians. The Ottoman Turks invaded in 1571. In the 19th century Turkey ceded the island to the British as security for a loan. Although many Turks remained on Cyprus, the British declared it a crown colony in 1925. A growing desire for *enosis*, or union, with Greece led to rioting and guerrilla activity by Greek Cypriots. The Turkish government, opposed to absorption by Greece, desired separation into Greek and Turkish sectors. Cyprus became independent in 1960, with treaties forbidding either *enosis* or partition, but Greek-Turkish conflicts continued. A 1974 coup by pro-enosis forces led to an invasion by Turkey. The partition resulting from this invasion runs east-west across the island dividing Nicosia, which serves as a capital for both countries. North Cyprus, which is not recognized internationally, maintains a separate government with a prime minister and a president. The United Nations, in an attempt to force a resolution of the continuing conflict, is threatening to withdraw its peacekeeping forces. Peace talks have been stalled by many disagreements, including whether Greek Cyprus should be admitted to the European Union. ■

CZECH REPUBLIC

Official name Czech Republic

PEOPLE
Population 10,315,000. **Density** 339/mi² (131/km²). **Urban** 66%. **Capital** Prague, 1,214,174. **Ethnic groups** Czech 94%, Slovak 3%. **Languages** Czech, Slovak. **Religions** Roman Catholic 39%, Protestant 5%, Orthodox 3%. **Life expectancy** 75 female, 68 male. **Literacy** 99%.

POLITICS
Government Republic. **Parties** Civic Democratic, Civic Democratic Alliance, Communist, Social Democrats, others. **Suffrage** Universal, 18 and over. **Memberships** OECD, UN. **Subdivisions** 8 regions.

ECONOMY
GDP $106,200,000,000. **Per capita** $10,158. **Monetary unit** Koruna. **Trade partners** Exports: Slovakia, Germany, Poland. Imports: Slovakia, former Soviet republics, Germany. **Exports** Manufactures, machinery, transportation equipment, chemicals, fuels, minerals. **Imports** Machinery, transportation equipment, fuel, manufactures, raw materials.

LAND
Description Eastern Europe, landlocked. **Area** 30,450 mi² (78,864 km²). **Highest point** Sněžka, 5,256 ft (1,602 m). **Lowest point** Along Elbe River, 377 ft (115 m).

People. Although the Czechs are Slavic in origin, their culture has been profoundly influenced by the Germans as a result of centuries of Austrian rule. By eastern European standards, the people are well-educated and highly skilled. The language is Czech, and the predominate religion is Roman Catholic. There is a small Slovak minority.

Economy and the Land. An industrial country, the Czech Republic has moved aggressively since 1991 to establish a free market economy. Unlike other eastern European countries, the Czech Republic has managed to keep unemployment and government spending in check during the transition from Communism to capitalism. Coal deposits have traditionally formed the base for the development of glass, chemical, and machine industries. Most of the land is low hills and plateaus bounded on three sides by mountain ranges. The climate is temperate.

History and Politics. Slavic tribes were established in the region by the 5th century, and the area fell under the rule of the Roman Empire. An important Moravian state rose in the 9th century, followed by the advent of a strong Bohemian kingdom that reached its zenith in the 13th century. Austria gained control of the area in the 1500s, and sovereignty later passed to Austria-Hungary. With the collapse of Austria-Hungary at the end of World War I, an independent Czechoslovakia, consisting of Bohemia, Moravia, Silesia, and Slovakia, was formed. Nazi Germany invaded Czechoslovakia in 1939, and the Soviet Union liberated the country from German occupation during 1944 and 1945. By 1948, Communists controlled the government, and political purges continued from 1949 to 1952. When the Czechoslovakian Communist party leader introduced liberal reforms in 1968, an invasion by the Soviet Union, Bulgaria, Hungary, Poland, and East Germany resulted. Demonstrations forced the Communist party to relinquish its power in 1989. Growing economic differences between the rural east and the industrialized west led to the breakup of Czechoslovakia into the Czech Republic and Slovakia in 1993. The Czech Republic is expected to join NATO in 1999. ■

DENMARK

Official name Kingdom of Denmark

PEOPLE
Population 5,280,000. **Density** 317/mi² (123/km²). **Urban** 85%. **Capital** Copenhagen, 471,300. **Ethnic groups** Danish (Scandinavian), German. **Languages** Danish. **Religions** Lutheran 91%. **Life expectancy** 79 female, 73 male. **Literacy** 99%.

POLITICS
Government Constitutional monarchy. **Parties** Conservative, Liberal, Social Democratic, others. **Suffrage** Universal, 18 and over. **Memberships** EU, NATO, OECD, UN. **Subdivisions** 14 counties, 2 cities.

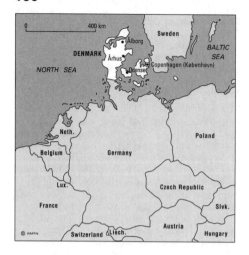

ECONOMY
GDP $112,800,000,000. **Per capita** $21,580. **Monetary unit** Krone. **Trade partners** Germany, Sweden, U.K. **Exports** Meat, dairy products, ships, fish, chemicals, machinery. **Imports** Petroleum, machinery, equipment, chemicals, food, grain, textiles, paper.

LAND
Description Northern Europe. **Area** 16,639 mi² (43,094 km²). **Highest point** Yding Skovhøj, 568 ft (173 m). **Lowest point** Lammefjord, -23 ft (-7 m). *The above information excludes Greenland and the Faroe Islands.*

People. Denmark is made up of the Jutland Peninsula and more than 400 islands, about 100 of which are inhabited. Greenland, which is situated northeast of Canada, and the Faroe Islands, which are located between Scotland and Iceland in the North Atlantic, are also part of Denmark. Lutheran, Danish-speaking Scandinavians constitute the homogenous population of the peninsula and surrounding islands, although a German minority is concentrated near the German border. The government provides extensive social services and programs. The literacy rate is high, and Denmark has made significant contributions to science, literature, and the arts.

Economy and the Land. Despite limited natural resources, Denmark has a diversified economy. Agriculture contributes to trade, and pork and bacon are important products. Postwar expansion focused on industry, and the country now imports the raw materials it lacks and exports finished products. The North Sea is the site of oil and natural gas deposits. On the Faroe Islands, traditional fishing continues as the economic mainstay. Most of Denmark's terrain is rolling, with hills covering much of the peninsula and the nearby islands. Coastal regions are marked by fjords and sandy beaches, especially in the west. The climate is temperate, with North Sea winds moderating temperatures. The rugged Faroe Islands are damp, cloudy, and windy.

History and Politics. By the first century, access to the sea had brought contact with other civi-

lizations. This led to the Viking era, which lasted from the 9th to 11th centuries and resulted in temporary Danish rule of England. In the 14th century, Sweden, Norway, Finland, Iceland, the Faroe Islands, and Greenland were united under Danish rule. Sweden and Finland withdrew from the union in the 1500s, and Denmark lost Norway to Sweden in 1814. A constitutional monarchy was instituted in 1849. Late 19th-century social reform, reflected in a new constitution in 1915, laid the groundwork for Denmark's current welfare state. The country remained neutral in World War I. Iceland gained independence following the war but maintained its union with Denmark until 1944. Despite declared neutrality in World War II, Denmark was invaded and occupied by Germany from 1940 to 1945. Compromise and gradual change characterize Danish politics. ■

DJIBOUTI

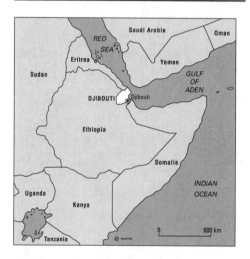

Official name Republic of Djibouti

PEOPLE
Population 438,000. **Density** 49/mi² (19/km²). **Urban** 82%. **Capital** Djibouti, 329,337. **Ethnic groups** Somali 60%, Afar 35%. **Languages** French, Arabic, Somali, Afar. **Religions** Muslim 94%, Christian 6%. **Life expectancy** 52 female, 49 male. **Literacy** 46%.

POLITICS
Government Republic. **Parties** Democratic National, Democratic Renewal, People's Progress Assembly, others. **Suffrage** Universal adult. **Memberships** AL, OAU, UN. **Subdivisions** 5 districts.

ECONOMY
GDP $500,000,000. **Per capita** $898. **Monetary unit** Franc. **Trade partners** Exports: France, Yemen, Somalia. Imports: France, Ethiopia, Italy. **Exports** Hides and skins, coffee (in transit). **Imports** Food, beverages, transportation equipment, chemicals, petroleum products.

LAND
Description Eastern Africa. **Area** 8,958 mi² (23,200 km²).

Highest point Moussa 'Ali, 6,631 ft (2,021 m).
Lowest point Lac 'Assal, -515 ft (-157 m).

People. Characterized by strong cultural unity, Islamic religion, and ethnic ties to Somalia, Somali Issas compose Djibouti's majority. Afars, another main group, are also mostly Muslim and are linked ethnically with Afars in Ethiopia. Rivalry between the two groups is strong. Because of unproductive land, much of the population is concentrated in the capital city of Djibouti.

Economy and the Land. Traditional nomadic herding is a way of life, despite heat, aridity, and limited grazing area. Several assets promote Djibouti as a port and trade center: free trade status, a strategic position on the Gulf of Aden, an improved harbor, and a railway linking the city of Djibouti with Addis Ababa in Ethiopia. Marked by mountains that divide a coastal plain from a plateau, the terrain is mostly desert. The climate is hot and dry.

History and Politics. In the 9th century, Arab missionaries introduced Islam to the population, and by the 1800s a pattern of conflict between the Issas and Afars had developed. The French purchased the port of Obcock from Afar sultans in 1862, and their territorial control expanded until the region became French Somaliland. The goal of the pro-independence Issas was defeated in elections in 1958 and 1967 when the country became the French Territory of Afars and Issas. As the Issa population grew, so did demands for independence. A 1977 referendum created the independent Republic of Djibouti. The country has been involved in ethnic conflict since 1991. ∎

DOMINICA

Official name Commonwealth of Dominica

PEOPLE
Population 83,000. **Density** 272/mi2 (105/km2). **Urban** 70%. **Capital** Roseau, 9,348. **Ethnic groups** Black 91%, mixed 6%, West Indian 2%. **Languages** English, Creole French. **Religions** Roman Catholic 77%, Methodist 5%, Pentecostal 3%. **Life expectancy** 80 female, 74 male. **Literacy** 94%.

POLITICS
Government Republic. **Parties** Freedom, Labor, United Workers. **Suffrage** Universal, 18 and over. **Memberships** CW, OAS, UN. **Subdivisions** 10 parishes.

ECONOMY
GDP $200,000,000. **Per capita** $2,410. **Monetary unit** East Caribbean dollar. **Trade partners** Exports: U.K., U.S., Jamaica. Imports: U.S., U.K., Trinidad and

Tobago. **Exports** Bananas, coconuts, citrus, vegetables, bay oil, soap. **Imports** Food, chemicals, manufactures, machinery and equipment.

LAND
Description Caribbean island. **Area** 305 mi2 (790 km2). **Highest point** Morne Diablotins, 4,747 ft (1,447 m). **Lowest point** Sea level.

People. Dominica's population consists of descendants of black Africans, brought to the island as slaves, and Caribs descended from early inhabitants. The Carib population is concentrated in the northeastern part of the island, and maintains its own customs and lifestyle. English is widely spoken in urban areas, but villagers, who compose a majority, speak mainly a French-African blend, resulting from French rule and the importation of Africans.

Economy and the Land. Of volcanic origin, the island has soil suitable for farming, but a mountainous and densely-forested terrain limits cultivable land. Agriculture is the economic mainstay, although hurricanes have hindered production. Forestry and fishing offer potential for expansion, and a tropical climate and scenic landscape create a basis for tourism.

History and Politics. In the 14th century Caribs conquered the Arawak, who originally inhabited the island. Although Christopher Columbus arrived at Dominica in 1493, Carib hostilities discouraged Spanish settlement. French and British rivalry for control of the island followed, and British possession was recognized in 1783. Dominica gained independence in 1978. ∎

DOMINICAN REPUBLIC

Official name Dominican Republic

PEOPLE
Population 8,299,000. **Density** 444/mi2 (171/km2). **Urban** 63%. **Capital** Santo Domingo, 2,411,900. **Ethnic groups** Mulatto 73%, white 16%, black 11%.

Languages Spanish. **Religions** Roman Catholic 95%.
Life expectancy 73 female, 69 male. **Literacy** 82%.

POLITICS

Government Republic. **Parties** Liberation,
Revolutionary, Social Christian Reformist, others.
Suffrage Universal, 18 and over, married persons
regardless of age. **Memberships** OAS, UN.
Subdivisions 29 provinces, 1 district.

ECONOMY

GDP $26,800,000,000. **Per capita** $3,389. **Monetary
unit** Peso. **Trade partners** Exports: U.S., Netherlands.
Imports: U.S., western European countries. **Exports**
Sugar, coffee, cocoa, gold, ferronickel. **Imports** Food,
petroleum, cotton and fabrics, chemicals and
pharmaceuticals.

LAND

Description Caribbean island (eastern Hispaniola).
Area 18,704 mi² (48,442 km²). **Highest point** Pico
Duarte, 10,417 ft (3,175 m). **Lowest point** Lago
Enriquillo, -131 ft (-40 m).

People. Occupying eastern Hispaniola Island,
the Dominican Republic borders Haiti and has a
population of mixed ancestry. Haitians, other
blacks, Spaniards, and European Jews compose
minority groups. Population growth has resulted
in unemployment and has made it difficult for
the government to meet food and service needs.

Economy and the Land. Agriculture remains
important. Sugar is a main component of trade,
and sugar refining is a major manufacturing
activity. Farmland is limited by a northwest-to-
southeast mountain range and an arid region
west of the range. Mineral exploitation and iron
exports contribute to trade, and a number of
American firms have subsidiaries here. Tourism
is growing, aided by the tropical climate.

History and Politics. In 1492 Christopher
Columbus arrived at Hispaniola Island. Spanish
colonists followed, and the indigenous population was virtually wiped out, although some
intermingling with Spanish probably occurred.
In 1697 the western region of the island, which
would become Haiti, was ceded to France. The
entire island came under Haitian control as the
Republic of Haiti in 1822, and an 1844 revolution
established the independent Dominican
Republic. Since independence, the country has
experienced instability, evidenced by military
coups, United States military intervention, and
human rights abuses. In May 1994, an aged and
ill President Balaguer was re-elected for a seventh term. Political unrest following claims of
vote fraud forced Balaguer to agree to a reduced
mandate of 18 months. ∎

ECUADOR

Official name Republic of Ecuador

PEOPLE

Population 11,805,000. **Density** 112/mi² (43/km²).
Urban 60%. **Capital** Quito, 1,100,847. **Ethnic groups**
Mestizo 55%, Amerindian 25%, Spanish 10%, black
10%. **Languages** Spanish, Quechua, indigenous.

Religions Roman Catholic 95%. **Life expectancy**
73 female, 67 male. **Literacy** 90%.

POLITICS

Government Republic. **Parties** Popular Democracy,
Roldosist, Social Christian, others. **Suffrage** Universal,
18 and over. **Memberships** OAS, UN. **Subdivisions**
21 provinces.

ECONOMY

GDP $44,600,000,000. **Per capita** $4,223. **Monetary
unit** Sucre. **Trade partners** Exports: U.S., Peru, Chile.
Imports: U.S., Japan, Germany. **Exports** Petroleum,
bananas, cocoa, coffee, shrimp, fish. **Imports**
Transportation equipment, manufactures, machinery,
chemicals.

LAND

Description Western South America. **Area** 105,037 mi²
(272,045 km²). **Highest point** Chimborazo, 20,702 ft
(6,310 m). **Lowest point** Sea level.

People. Ecuador's ethnicity was established by
an indigenous Amerindian population and
Spanish colonists. Minority whites, of Spanish or
other European descent, live mainly in urban
areas or operate large farms called haciendas.
Of mixed Spanish-Amerindian blood, mestizos
compose over half the population, although
economic and political power is concentrated
among whites. Minority Amerindians speak
Quechua or other indigenous languages and
maintain traditional customs in Andean villages
or nomadic jungle tribes. Blacks are concentrated on the northern coastal plain. Recent trends
show a movement from the interior highlands to
the fertile coastal plain and a rural-to-urban
shift. A history of economic inequality has produced a literary and artistic tradition that has
focused on social reform.

Economy and the Land. Despite an oil boom in
the 1970s, Ecuador remains underdeveloped.
Minor oil production began in 1911, but since a
1967 petroleum discovery in the *oriente*, a jungle
region east of the Andes, Ecuador has become an
oil exporter. Agriculture remains important for
much of the population, although inefficient

practices continue among the poor. Rich soils of the *costa*, extending from the Pacific Ocean to the Andes, support most of the export crops. Forestry and fishing have growth potential, and the waters around the Galapagos Islands are rich in tuna. Manufacturing is mainly devoted to meeting domestic needs. The oriente and costa lie on either side of the *sierra*, a region of highland plateaus between the two Andean chains. Varied altitudes result in a climate ranging from tropical in the lowlands to temperate in the plateaus and cold in the high mountains. A variety of wildlife inhabits the Galapagos Islands, five large and nine small islands about 600 miles (966 kilometers) off Ecuador's coast in the Pacific Ocean.

History and Politics. In the 15th century, Incas conquered and united the area's various tribes. In the 1500s the Spanish gained control, using natives and African slaves to work the plantations. Weakened by the Napoleonic Wars, Spain lost control of Ecuador in 1822, and Simón Bolívar united the independent state with the Republic of Greater Colombia. Ecuador left the union as a separate republic in 1830, and subsequent years saw instability and rule by presidents, dictators, and juntas. From 1925 to 1948, no leader was able to complete a full term in office. A new constitution was established in 1978. Elections in 1992 were won by the right-wing United Republican Party, committed to a privatization policy. After the 1993 drop in world crude oil prices, Ecuador underwent a long period of austerity aimed at curbing inflation and stabilizing the economy. In 1995, the president was forced out of office amidst claims of mismanagement. ■

EGYPT

Official name Arab Republic of Egypt

PEOPLE
Population 65,390,000. **Density** 169/mi² (65/km²).

Urban 45%. **Capital** Cairo, 6,068,695. **Ethnic groups** Egyptian, Berber, Bedouin. **Languages** Arabic. **Religions** Muslim 94%, Coptic Christian and others 6%. **Life expectancy** 67 female, 65 male. **Literacy** 51%.

POLITICS
Government Republic. **Parties** National Democratic. **Suffrage** Universal, 18 and over. **Memberships** AL, OAU, UN. **Subdivisions** 26 governorates.

ECONOMY
GDP $171,000,000,000. **Per capita** $2,846. **Monetary unit** Pound. **Trade partners** Exports: Italy, former Soviet republics, France. Imports: U.S., Germany, France. **Exports** Petroleum, petroleum products, cotton, textiles, metal products, chemicals. **Imports** Machinery and equipment, food, fertilizer, wood products, manufactures.

LAND
Description Northeastern Africa. **Area** 386,662 mi² (1,001,449 km²). **Highest point** Mt. Katrina, 8,668 ft (2,642 m). **Lowest point** Qattara Depression, -436 ft (-133 m).

People. Egypt's population is relatively homogeneous, and Egyptians compose the largest group. Descended from ancient Nile Valley inhabitants, Egyptians have intermixed somewhat with Mediterranean and Asiatic peoples in the north and with black Africans in the south. Minorities include Bedouins, Arabic-speaking desert nomads; Nubians, black descendants of migrants from the Sudan; and Copts, a Christian group. Islam, the major religion, is also a cultural force; many Christians and Muslims lead Islamic lifestyles. A desert terrain confines about 99 percent of the population to less than four percent of the land, in the fertile Nile River valley and along the Suez Canal.

Economy and the Land. Egypt's economy has suffered from wars, shifting alliances, and limited natural resources. Government-sponsored expansion and reform in the 1950s concentrated on manufacturing, and most industry was nationalized during the 1960s. Agriculture, centered in the Nile Valley, remains an economic mainstay, and cotton, a principal crop, is both exported and processed. Petroleum is found mainly in the Gulf of Suez. Tourism is one of the country's most important economic activities. Much of Egypt is desert, with hills and mountains in the east and along the Nile River, while the climate is warm and dry.

History and Politics. Egypt's recorded history began when King Menes united the region around 3100 B.C., and began a series of Egyptian dynasties. Art and architecture flourished during the Age of the Pyramids, from 2700 to 2200 B.C. In time native dynasties gave way to foreign conquerors, including Alexander the Great in the 4th century B.C. The Coptic Christian church emerged between the 4th and 6th centuries A.D., but in the 600s Arabs conquered the area and established Islam as the main religion. Ruling parties changed frequently, and in 1517 the Ottoman Turks added Egypt to their empire.

Upon completion of the strategically important Suez Canal in 1869, foreign interest in Egypt increased. In 1875 Egypt sold its share of the canal to Britain, and British occupation in 1882 ended a rebellion against foreign intervention. Turkey sided with Germany in World War I, and the United Kingdom made Egypt a British protectorate in 1914. The country became an independent monarchy in 1922, but the British presence remained. In 1945 Egypt and six other countries formed the Arab League. The founding of Israel in 1948 initiated an era of Arab-Israeli hostilities, including periodic warfare in which Egypt often had a major role. Dissatisfaction over dealings with Israel and continued British occupation of the Suez Canal led to the overthrow of the king, and Egypt became a republic in 1953. Following a power struggle, Gamal Abdel Nasser was elected president in 1956, and the British agreed to remove their troops. Upon the death of Nasser in 1970, Vice President Anwar Sadat came to power. Negotiations between Egyptian president Sadat and Israeli prime minister Menachem Begin began in 1977, and in 1979 the leaders signed a peace treaty ending conflicts between Egypt and Israel. As a result, Egypt was suspended from the Arab League until 1989. In 1981 President Sadat was assassinated and was succeeded by Hosni Mubarak, who faces a growing fundamentalist Muslim campaign of violence targeting tourists and government officers. ∎

EL SALVADOR

Official name Republic of El Salvador

PEOPLE
Population 5,988,000. **Density** 737/mi² (285/km²). **Urban** 45%. **Capital** San Salvador, 415,346. **Ethnic groups** Mestizo 94%, Amerindian 5%, white 1%. **Languages** Spanish, Nahua. **Religions** Roman Catholic 75%, Protestant 18%. **Life expectancy** 71 female, 66 male. **Literacy** 74%.

POLITICS
Government Republic. **Parties** National Conciliation, National Liberation Front, National Republican Alliance, others. **Suffrage** Universal, 18 and over. **Memberships** OAS, UN. **Subdivisions** 14 departments.

ECONOMY
GDP $11,400,000,000. **Per capita** $1,923. **Monetary unit** Colon. **Trade partners** Exports: U.S., Guatemala, Germany. Imports: U.S., Guatemala, Mexico. **Exports** Coffee, sugar cane, shrimp. **Imports** Manufactures, machinery, raw materials.

LAND
Description Central America. **Area** 8,124 mi² (21,041 km²). **Highest point** Cerro El Pital, 8,957 ft (2,730 m). **Lowest point** Sea level.

People. Most Salvadorans are Spanish-speaking mestizos, people of Spanish-Amerindian descent. An Amerindian minority is mainly descended from the Pipil, a Nahuatl group related to the Aztecs. The Nahuatl dialect is still spoken by some. El Salvador, the smallest Central American country in area, has the highest population density in mainland Latin America, with inhabitants concentrated in a central valley-and-plateau region.

Economy and the Land. El Salvador's economy has been plagued by political instability, low literacy, high population density, and high unemployment. Agriculture remains the economic mainstay of the region, and most arable land has been cultivated. Coffee, cotton, and sugar are produced on large commercial plantations, while subsistence farmers rely on corn, bean, and sorghum crops. In the 1990s the economy began to improve, becoming increasingly oriented toward manufacturing and services. East-to-west mountain ranges divide El Salvador into a southern coastal region, central valleys and plateaus, and northern mountains. El Salvador's climate is subtropical.

History and Politics. Maya and Pipil groups predominated the area of El Salvador prior to Spanish arrival. In the 1500s, Pipil defeated invading Spaniards but were conquered in a later invasion. In 1821, the Spanish-controlled Central American colonies declared independence, and in 1823 they united as the Federation of Central America. By 1838, the problem-ridden federation was in a state of collapse, and as the union dissolved, El Salvador became independent. With independence, however, soon came instability and revolution. The expansion of the coffee economy in the late 1800s exacerbated economic problems by further concentrating wealth and power among large estate holders. A dictatorship from 1931 to 1944 was followed by political instability under various military rulers. In 1969, a brief war with Honduras arose from resentment toward land-ownership laws, border disputes, and nationalistic feelings following a series of soccer games between the two countries. During the 1980s, the United States provided extensive military and economic aid in an attempt to moderate the El Salvadoran government. A 12-year civil war erupted and lasted until 1992. The transfer of land from a few major landowners to subsistence farmers has been an important and difficult part of the peace process. ■

EQUATORIAL GUINEA

Official name Republic of Equatorial Guinea

PEOPLE
Population 448,000. **Density** 41/mi² (16/km²). **Urban** 43%. **Capital** Malabo, Bioko I., 31,630. **Ethnic groups** Fang, Bubi. **Languages** Spanish, indigenous, English. **Religions** Roman Catholic and other Christian. **Life expectancy** 52 female, 48 male. **Literacy** 79%.

POLITICS
Government Republic. **Parties** Democratic, others. **Suffrage** Universal adult. **Memberships** OAS, UN. **Subdivisions** 7 provinces.

ECONOMY
GDP $325,000,000. **Per capita** $825. **Monetary unit** CFA franc. **Trade partners** Exports: Spain, Italy, Netherlands. Imports: France, Spain, Italy. **Exports** Coffee, wood, cocoa, petroleum. **Imports** Petroleum, food, beverages, clothing, machinery.

LAND
Description Central Africa. **Area** 10,831 mi² (28,051 km²). **Highest point** Pico de Santa Isabel, 9,869 ft (3,008 m). **Lowest point** Sea level.

People. Several ethnic groups inhabit Equatorial Guinea's five islands, as well as the mainland region of Río Muni. Although the majority Fang, a Bantu people, are concentrated in Río Muni, they also inhabit Bioko, the largest island. Found mainly on Bioko Island are the minority Bubi, also a Bantu people. Coastal groups known as *playeros*, or "those who live on the beach," live on both the mainland and the small islands. The Fernandino, of mixed African heritage, are concentrated on Bioko. Equatorial Guinea is the only black African state with Spanish as its official language.

Economy and the Land. Equatorial Guinea's economy is based on agriculture and forestry; cocoa, coffee, and wood are the main products. Cocoa production is centered on fertile Bioko Island, and coffee in Río Muni. The mainland's rain forests also provide for forestry. Mineral exploration has revealed petroleum and natural gas in the waters north of Bioko, and petroleum, iron ore, and radioactive materials exist in Río Muni. Bioko is of volcanic origin, and Río Muni consists of a coastal plain and interior hills. The climate is tropical, with high temperatures and humidity.

History and Politics. Pygmies most likely inhabited the Río Muni area prior to the 13th century, when mainland Bubi came to Bioko. From the 17th to the 19th centuries, Bantu migrations brought first the coastal tribes and then the Fang. Portugal claimed Bioko and part of the mainland in the 1400s, then ceded them to Spain in 1778. From 1827 to 1843, British antislavery activities were based on Bioko, which became the home of many former slaves, the ancestors of the Fernandino population. In 1959 the area became the Spanish Territory of the Gulf of Guinea, and the name was changed to Equatorial Guinea in 1963. Independence was achieved in 1968. November 1993 elections were boycotted by opposition parties and a dictatorship remains in place. ■

ERITREA

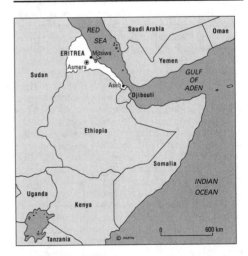

Official name State of Eritrea

PEOPLE
Population 3,571,000. **Density** 99/mi² (38/km²). **Urban** 17%. **Capital** Asmera, 358,100. **Ethnic groups** Tigray 50%, Tigre and Kunama 40%, Afar 4%, Saho 3%. **Languages** Arabic, Tigrinya, Amharic, Kunama, Tigre, other. **Religions** Muslim, Coptic Christian, Roman Catholic, Protestant. **Life expectancy** 55 female, 51 male.

POLITICS
Government Republic. **Parties** Peoples Front for Democracy and Justice. **Memberships** OAU, UN. **Subdivisions** 3 administrative regions.

ECONOMY
GDP $2,000,000,000. **Per capita** $578. **Monetary unit** Nakfa. **Exports** Livestock, sorghum, textiles. **Imports** Processed goods, machinery, petroleum products.

LAND
Description Eastern Africa. **Area** 36,170 mi² (93,679 km²). **Highest point** Soira, 9,806 ft (2,989 m). **Lowest point** Unnamed, -246 ft (-75 m).

People. Eritrea is a land of diverse languages and religions. The main ethnic groups are the Tigre and Afar, although there are also Kunama, Saho, Agau, and others. Tigre and Kunama are two of the predominate languages, along with Arabic. About half of the population is Coptic Christian, and the other half practices Islam.

Economy and the Land. Eritrea's climate is dry and the region suffers from chronic drought. Some cotton and oilseed crops are grown, but fish provide the major source of food. Crop failure resulted in severe food shortages in 1994. Thirty years of war with Ethiopia left Eritrea's infrastructure in disrepair, but the rebuilding process has been swift. Despite many advances, the country is still dependent on foreign aid. Eritrea hopes to develop its Red Sea coastline as a tourist attraction and develop offshore oil production in the Red Sea.

History and Politics. Eritrea was originally settled by people who migrated across the Red Sea from Yemen. In 950 A.D. the region now known as Eritrea was part of the Ethiopian empire. In 1557, the city of Massawa and surrounding areas were captured by the Ottoman Turks, who established loose control of the region until it was overtaken by the Egyptians in 1846. Sovereignty shifted between Turkey and Egypt until 1890, when the Italians invaded the region and established the colony of Eritrea in 1890. Fifty years of Italian rule left Eritrea with sound industrial, educational, governmental, and transportation systems that were rare elsewhere in Africa. It also left the Eritreans with a strong sense of national identity, despite their cultural diversity. After the British captured the region from the Italians in World War II, the United Nations handed it over to Ethiopia in 1952, despite claims by some that Eritrea should be granted its independence. The Ethiopians were instructed to administer Eritrea as a self-governing territory within Ethiopia, but they violated the arrangement by annexing Eritrea in 1962. This action ignited a civil war which lasted for more than 30 years. After defeating the Marxist regime in 1991, the Eritreans agreed to wait almost two years before legalizing their status as an independent country. In May 1993 Eritrea became independent, and a transitional government was elected to function until a constitution is drafted. The country has moved forward painstakingly to rebuild an economy that was heavily damaged during the long years of warfare. Eritrea has become a model of development and self-sacrifice, accepting outside help judiciously in its determination to rebuild from within. ■

ESTONIA

Official name Republic of Estonia

PEOPLE
Population 1,434,000. **Density** 82/mi² (32/km²). **Urban** 73%. **Capital** Tallinn, 452,665. **Ethnic groups** Estonian 64%, Russian 29%, Ukrainian 3%. **Languages** Estonian, Latvian, Lithuanian, Russian. **Religions** Lutheran, Baptist, Methodist. **Life expectancy** 75 female, 64 male. **Literacy** 100%.

POLITICS
Government Republic. **Parties** Center, Coalition and Rural Union, Reform-Liberals, others. **Suffrage** Universal, 18 and over. **Memberships** UN. **Subdivisions** 15 counties, 6 municipalities.

ECONOMY
GDP $12,300,000,000. **Per capita** $8,205. **Monetary unit** Kroon. **Trade partners** Former Soviet republics. **Exports** Textiles, food products, vehicles, metals. **Imports** Machinery, fuels, vehicles, textiles.

LAND
Description Eastern Europe. **Area** 17,413 mi² (45,100 km²). **Highest point** Suur Munamägi, 1,043 ft (318 m). **Lowest point** Sea level.

People. The Estonians have retained their own unique language and culture for centuries, despite almost continuous foreign intervention. Before the Soviet invasion in 1940, the Estonians, who are related to the Finns, accounted for almost all of the population. Since then, massive immigration has increased the Russians' share of the population to almost one-third. Estonia has a relatively high urban population, and most people are engaged in industry.

Economy and the Land. Most of Estonia's industry is centered on shale oil, its only major industrial raw material. Shale oil has permitted Estonia to develop a sound manufacturing base. Agriculture is based on livestock and dairy products, and most crops are grown to supply animal feed. Estonia's natural landscape is plains and poorly drained marshes, although much of the land has been drained for agriculture. More than one third of the land is forested.

History and Politics. Prior to incorporation into the Soviet Union, Estonia enjoyed only 20 years of independence during its long history. Danes conquered the territory in 1219 and sold it to the Teutonic Knights in 1346. The Swedes invaded in 1561 and domination alternated between Sweden and Poland until Peter the Great of Russia conquered Estonia in 1721. The country was granted independence in 1918, but freedom lasted only until the Soviet invasion of 1940, after which Estonia was forced to become a Soviet Socialist Republic. Estonians enjoyed the highest overall standard of living in the Soviet Union. Estonia's "home rule" legislation led the Baltic states' drive for independence following the introduction of glasnost in the Soviet Union. International recognition as an independent country was achieved in 1991, several months before the breakup of the Soviet Union. The first free elections in any former Soviet Union country were held in late 1992. Tensions exist between Estonians and ethnic Russians over discrimination and language laws. A 1995 election voted out the youthful Fatherland Party in favor of older, more cautious politicians, but this was not expected to slow the rapid economic growth. ∎

ETHIOPIA

Official name Ethiopia

PEOPLE
Population 59,510,000. **Density** 133/mi² (51/km²). **Urban** 16%. **Capital** Addis Ababa, 1,912,500. **Ethnic groups** Oromo (Galla) 40%, Amhara and Tigrean 32%, Sidamo 9%, Shankella 6%, Somali 6%. **Languages** Amharic, Tigrinya, Orominga, Guaraginga, Somali, Arabic. **Religions** Muslim 45-50%, Ethiopian Orthodox 35-40%, Animist 12%. **Life expectancy** 52 female, 48 male. **Literacy** 36%.

POLITICS
Government Federal Republic. **Parties** Ethiopian People's Revolutionary Democratic Front, Oromo Liberation Front, others. **Suffrage** Universal, 18 and over. **Memberships** OAU, UN. **Subdivisions** 14 administrative regions.

ECONOMY
GDP $24,200,000,000. **Per capita** $439. **Monetary unit** Birr. **Trade partners** Exports: Germany, Japan, U.S. Imports: Italy, former Soviet republics, U.S. **Exports** Coffee, animal hides, gold. **Imports** Capital goods, fuel, consumer goods.

LAND
Description Eastern Africa, landlocked. **Area** 446,953 mi² (1,157,603 km²). **Highest point** Ras Dashen Mtn., 15,157 ft (4,620 m). **Lowest point** Āsale, -410 ft (-125 m).

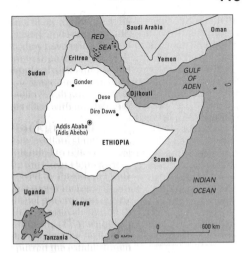

People. Ethiopia is ethnically, linguistically, and religiously diverse, but the Oromo, Amhara, and Tigre ethnic groups predominate. The Oromo include agricultural Muslims, Christians, and nomadic herders with traditional religions. Mainly Christian and agricultural, the Amhara have dominated the country politically. The official language is Amharic; Arabic and indigenous languages are also spoken. Ethiopia's boundaries encompass more than 40 ethnic groups.

Economy and the Land. Political instability, soil erosion, deforestation, and drought have plagued Ethiopia's agriculture-based economy. In 1982, a devastating drought occurred when planting season rains failed to arrive in much of the country. The consequences of this drought are still felt in the north and the west. Despite recent good harvests, Ethiopia has not yet received enough rainfall to eliminate the possibility of recurring drought. Subsistence farming remains a major activity, though much arable land is uncultivated. Mines produce gold, copper, and platinum, and there is potential for expansion. A central plateau is split diagonally by the Great Rift Valley, with lowlands on the west and plains in the southeast. The climate is temperate on the plateau and hot in the lowlands.

History and Politics. Ethiopia's history is one of the oldest in the world. Its ethnic patterns were established by indigenous Cushites and Semite settlers, who probably arrived from Arabia about 3,000 years ago. Christianity was introduced in the early 4th century. During the 1800s, modern Ethiopia began to develop under Emperor Menelik II. Ras Tafari Makonnen became emperor in 1930, taking the name Haile Selassie. Italians invaded in the 1930s and occupied the country until 1941, when Selassie returned to the throne. Discontent with feudal society increased until Selassie was ousted by the military in 1974. Reform programs and the change in leadership did little to ease political tensions, which sometimes erupted in governmental and civilian violence. Government troops continued their battle with separatists in Eritrea, a former Italian colony and autonomous province incorporated into Ethiopia in 1962. Since the 1980s, widespread famine and drought aggravated political problems. Civil war hampered worldwide relief efforts. More than 250,000 people died in the war which ended in 1991 when the country's Marxist regime fell to Eritrean and Tigrean rebels. Eritrea gained full independence in 1993, leaving Ethiopia a landlocked country. A new constitution adopted in December 1994 established a federal system of government. Food shortage, high population growth, and inadequate infrastructure are among the biggest challenges facing the government. ■

FAROE ISLANDS See DENMARK.

FALKLAND ISLANDS

Official name Colony of the Falkland Islands

PEOPLE
Population 2,000. **Density** 0.4/mi² (0.2/km²). **Urban** 86%. **Capital** Stanley, East Falkland I., 1,557. **Ethnic groups** British descent. **Languages** English. **Religions** Anglican, Roman Catholic, United Free Church.

POLITICS
Government Dependent territory (U.K.). **Suffrage** Universal, 18 and over. **Memberships** None. **Subdivisions** None.

ECONOMY
Monetary unit Pound. **Trade partners** Exports: U.K., Netherlands, Japan. Imports: U.K., Netherlands Antilles, Japan. **Exports** Wool, animal hides, meat. **Imports** Food, clothing, timber, machinery.

LAND
Description South Atlantic islands (east of Argentina). **Area** 4,700 mi² (12,173 km²). **Highest point** Mt. Usborne, 2,312 ft (705 m). **Lowest point** Sea level.

People. Most Falkland Island inhabitants are of British descent, an ancestry reflected in their official language, English, and majority Anglican religion.

Economy and the Land. Sheep raising is the main activity, supplemented by fishing. In 1982 Britain funded the Falkland Islands Development Corporation, which began operation in 1984. In 1993 offshore oil was detected. Situated about 300 miles (482 kilometers) east of southern Argentina, East and West Falkland compose the main and largest islands. Numerous small islands are also part of the Falklands. The climate is cool, damp, and windy.

History and Politics. Although the British sighted the islands in 1592, the French established the first settlement in 1764, on East Falkland. The British settled on West Falkland the next year. Spain, which ruled the Argentinean territories to the west, purchased the French area and drove out the British in 1770. When Argentina gained independence from Spain in 1816, it took over Spain's claim on the islands. Britain reasserted its rule over the islands in the 1830s. The Falklands became a British colony in 1892, with dependencies annexed in 1908. Continued Argentinean claims resulted in a 1982 Argentine invasion and occupation. The British won the subsequent battle and continue to govern the Falklands. The dependencies of South Georgia and the South Sandwich Islands became a separate British colony in 1985. ■

FIJI

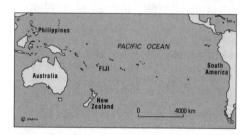

Official name Republic of Fiji

PEOPLE
Population 787,000. **Density** 112/mi² (43/km²). **Urban** 41%. **Capital** Suva, Viti Levu I., 69,665. **Ethnic groups** Indian 49%, Fijian 46%. **Languages** English, Fijian, Hindustani. **Religions** Hindu 38%, Methodist 37%, Roman Catholic 9%, Muslim 8%. **Life expectancy** 75 female, 71 male. **Literacy** 92%.

POLITICS
Government Republic. **Parties** Fijian Political, National Federation, others. **Suffrage** Universal, 21 and over. **Memberships** CW, UN. **Subdivisions** 4 divisions.

ECONOMY
GDP $4,700,000,000. **Per capita** $6,041. **Monetary unit** Dollar. **Trade partners** Exports: EU countries, Australia, Japan. Imports: Australia, New Zealand, Japan. **Exports** Sugar, clothing, gold, fish, lumber. **Imports** Machinery, transportation equipment, petroleum products, food, manufactures.

LAND
Description South Pacific islands. **Area** 7,056 mi² (18,274 km²). **Highest point** Tomanivi (Victoria), 4,341 ft (1,323 m). **Lowest point** Sea level.

People. Almost half of Fiji's population is descended from laborers brought from British India between 1879 and 1916. Most Indians are Hindu, but a Muslim minority also exists. Native Fijians are of Melanesian and Polynesian heritage, and most are Christian. English is the official language, a result of British rule; but Indians speak Hindustani, and the main Fijian dialect is Bauan. Tensions between the two groups occasionally arise because plantation owners, who are mainly Indian, must often lease their land from Fijians, the major landowners. About 100 of the 330 islands are inhabited.

Economy and the Land. The traditional sugar-cane crop continues as the basis of Fiji's economy, and agricultural diversification is a current goal. Tourism is another economic contributor, and expansion of forestry is planned. Terrain varies from island to island and is characterized by mountains, valleys, rain forests, and fertile plains. The tropical islands are cooled by ocean breezes.

History and Politics. Little is known of Fiji's history prior to the arrival of Europeans. Melanesians probably migrated from Indonesia, followed by Polynesian settlers in the second century. After a Dutch navigator sighted Fiji in 1643, Captain James Cook of Britain visited the island in the 18th century. The 19th century saw the arrival of European missionaries, traders, whalers, and the outbreak of several native wars. In 1874, tribal chiefs ceded Fiji to the British, who established sugar plantations and brought indentured indigenous laborers. The country became independent in 1970. Fiji was ejected from the British Commonwealth in 1987 after declaring itself a republic and limiting participation by Indians in the government. A new constitution in 1990 institutionalized the domination of ethnic Fijians. ∎

FINLAND

Official name Republic of Finland

PEOPLE
Population 5,113,000. **Density** 39/mi² (15/km²). **Urban** 64%. **Capital** Helsinki, 501,514. **Ethnic groups** Finnish (mixed Scandinavian and Baltic) 93%, Swedish 6%. **Languages** Finnish, Swedish, Lapp, Russian. **Religions** Evangelical Lutheran 90%, Greek Orthodox 1%. **Life expectancy** 80 female, 73 male. **Literacy** 100%.

POLITICS
Government Republic. **Parties** Center, Leftist Alliance, National Coalition, Social Democratic, others. **Suffrage** Universal, 18 and over. **Memberships** EU, OECD, UN. **Subdivisions** 12 provinces.

ECONOMY
GDP $92,400,000,000. **Per capita** $18,057. **Monetary unit** Markka. **Trade partners** Exports: Former Soviet republics, Sweden, Germany. Imports: Germany, Sweden, former Soviet republics. **Exports** Lumber, paper, wood pulp, ships, machinery, chemicals, metals. **Imports** Food, petroleum, chemicals, transportation equipment, iron, steel, machinery.

LAND
Description Northern Europe. **Area** 130,559 mi² (338,145 km²). **Highest point** Haltiatunturi, 4,357 ft (1,328 m). **Lowest point** Sea level.

People. The primarily Finnish population includes a minority population of Swedes—a result of past Swedish rule—and indigenous Lapps. Since part of northern Finland lies within the Arctic Circle, population is concentrated in the south. Finland's rich cultural tradition has contributed much to the arts. Its highly developed social welfare programs provide free education through the university level, as well as national health insurance.

Economy and the Land. Much of Finland's economy is based on its rich forests, which support trade and manufacturing activities. The steel industry is also important to the economy. Agriculture in Finland focuses on dairy farming and livestock raising; hence many fruits and vegetables must be imported. Coastal islands and lowlands, a central lake region, and northern hills mark Finland's scenic terrain. Summers in the south and central regions are warm, and winters long and cold.

History and Politics. The indigenous nomadic Lapps migrated north in the first century when the Finns arrived, probably from west-central Russia. Russia and Sweden struggled for control of the area, resulting in Swedish rule of Finland in the 1100s. Finland was united with Denmark from the 14th through the 16th centuries. Russia and Sweden fought several wars for control of the country. In 1809, Finland became an autonomous grand duchy within the Russian Empire. After the Russian czar was overthrown in the 1917 Bolshevik Revolution, the new Russian government recognized Finland's declaration of independence. During World War II, Finland fought against the Soviets and, when the peace treaty was signed in 1947, Finland lost a portion of its land to the Soviet Union. During the postwar years, Finland and the Soviet Union developed strong economic ties that resulted in prosperity for Finland. The dissolution of the Soviet Union and a worldwide recession have recently threatened Finland's economic stability. ∎

FRANCE

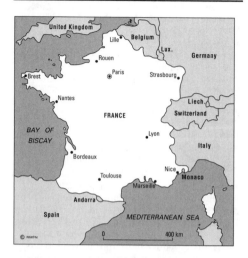

Official name French Republic

PEOPLE
Population 58,340,000. **Density** 276/mi² (107/km²). **Urban** 75%. **Capital** Paris, 2,152,423. **Ethnic groups** French (mixed Celtic, Latin, and Teutonic). **Languages** French. **Religions** Roman Catholic 90%, Protestant 2%, Jewish 1%, Muslim 1%. **Life expectancy** 81 female, 74 male. **Literacy** 99%.

POLITICS
Government Republic. **Parties** Communist, Rally for the Republic, Socialist, Union for Democracy, others. **Suffrage** Universal, 18 and over. **Memberships** EU, NATO, OECD, UN. **Subdivisions** 96 departments.

ECONOMY
GDP $1,173,000,000,000. **Per capita** $20,127.

Monetary unit Franc. **Trade partners** Germany, Italy, Belgium. **Exports** Machines, transportation equipment, chemicals, food, metal products, textiles. **Imports** Petroleum, machines, agriculture products, chemicals, iron and steel products.

LAND
Description Western Europe. **Area** 211,208 mi² (547,026 km²). **Highest point** Mt. Blanc, (Monte Bianco), 15,774 ft (4,808 m). **Lowest point** Étang de Cazaux et de Sanguinet, -10 ft (-3 m).
The above information excludes French overseas departments.

People. Many centuries ago, Celtic and Teutonic tribes and Latins established France's current ethnic patterns. The French language developed from the Latin tongue of invading Romans, but includes Celtic and Germanic influences as well. Language and customs vary somewhat from region to region, but most people who speak dialects also speak French. France has long contributed to learning and the arts, and Paris is a world cultural center. In addition to mainland divisions, the country has overseas departments and territories.

Economy and the Land. The French economy is highly developed. The country is a leader in agriculture and industry; its problems of inflation and unemployment are common to other developed countries. Soils in the north and northeast are especially productive, and grapes are grown in the south. Minerals include iron ore and bauxite. Industry is diversified, centered in the Paris manufacturing area, and tourism is important. About two thirds of the country is flat to rolling, and about one third is mountainous, including the Pyrenees in the South and the Alps in the east. In the west and north, winters are cool and summers mild. Climate varies with altitude. The

Places and Possessions of FRANCE

Entity	Status	Area	Population	Capital/Population
Corsica (Mediterranean island)	Part of France	3,367 mi² (8,720 km²)	258,000	None
French Guiana (Northeastern South America)	Overseas department	32,253 mi² (83,534 km²)	161,000	Cayenne, 41,067
French Polynesia (South Pacific islands)	Overseas territory	1,359 mi² (3,521 km²)	226,000	Papeete, 23,555
Guadeloupe (Caribbean islands)	Overseas department	657 mi² (1,702 km²)	415,000	Basse-Terre, 14,003
Kerguelen Islands (Indian Ocean)	Overseas territory	2,700 mi² (6,993 km²)	100	None
Martinique (Caribbean island)	Overseas department	436 mi² (1,128 km²)	406,000	Fort-de-France, 100,080
Mayotte (Southeastern African islands)	Territorial collectivity	144 mi² (374 km²)	107,000	Mamoudzou, 20,274
New Caledonia (South Pacific islands)	Overseas territory	7,172 mi² (18,575 km²)	193,000	Nouméa, 65,110
Reunion (Indian Ocean island)	Overseas department	967 mi² (2,504 km²)	699,000	Saint-Denis, 121,999
St. Pierre and Miquelon (North Atlantic islands)	Territorial collectivity	93 mi² (242 km²)	7,000	Saint-Pierre, 5,580
Wallis and Futuna (South Pacific islands)	Overseas territory	98 mi² (255 km²)	15,000	Matâ'utu, 1,222

southern coast has a Mediterranean climate with hot summers and mild winters.

History and Politics. In ancient times, Celtic tribes inhabited the area that encompasses present-day France. The Romans, who called the region Gaul, began to invade about 200 B.C., and by the 50s B.C. the entire region had come under Roman rule. Northern Germanic tribes—including the Franks, Visigoths, and Burgundians—spread throughout the region as Roman control weakened. The Franks defeated the Romans in A.D. 486. In the 800s, Charlemagne greatly expanded Frankish-controlled territory, which was subsequently divided into three kingdoms. The western kingdom and part of the central kingdom included modern France. In 987 the Capetian dynasty began when Hugh Capet came to the throne, an event which is often considered the start of the French nation. During subsequent centuries, the power of the kings increased and France became a leading world power. Ambitious projects, such as the palace built by Louis XIV at Versailles, and several military campaigns, resulted in financial difficulties. The failing economy and divisions between rich and poor led to the French Revolution in 1789 and the First French Republic in 1792. Napoleon Bonaparte, who had gained prominence during the revolution, overthrew the government in 1799 and established the First Empire, which ended in 1815 with his defeat at Waterloo in Belgium. The subsequent monarchy resulted in discontent, and an 1848 revolution established the Second French Republic with an elected president, who in turn proclaimed himself emperor and set up the Second Empire in 1852. Following a war with Prussia in 1870, the emperor was ousted and the Third Republic began. This republic repulsed Germany's invasion in World War I but ended in 1940 when invading Germans defeated the French. By 1942 the Nazis controlled the entire country. The Allies liberated France in 1944, and General Charles de Gaulle headed a provisional government until 1946, when the Fourth Republic was established. Colonial revolts in Africa and French Indochina took their toll on the economy during the 1950s. Controversy over a continuing Algerian war for independence brought de Gaulle to power once more and resulted in the Fifth Republic in 1958. Dissension and national strikes erupted during the 1960s, a result of dissatisfaction with the government, and de Gaulle resigned in 1969. In 1987, François Mitterand was re-elected, giving the Socialists a plurality until 1993. Since then the country has moved steadily to the right. Conservative President Jacques Chirac took office in 1995, replacing the ailing Mitterand. In response to France's continued military and political presence in its former colony of Algeria, Algerian terrorist groups have been increasingly active in France. ■

FRENCH GUIANA

Official name Department of Guiana

PEOPLE
Population 161,000. **Density** 5.0/mi² (1.9/km²). **Urban** 77%. **Capital** Cayenne, 41,067. **Ethnic groups** Black or mulatto 66%; white 12%; East Indian, Chinese, and Amerindian 12%. **Languages** French. **Religions** Roman Catholic. **Life expectancy** 79 female, 72 male. **Literacy** 83%.

POLITICS
Government Overseas department (France). **Parties** Democratic Front, Rally for the Republic, Socialist, others. **Suffrage** Universal, 18 and over. **Memberships** None. **Subdivisions** 2 arrondissements.

ECONOMY
GDP $800,000,000. **Per capita** $6,107. **Monetary unit** French franc. **Trade partners** Exports: France, Guadeloupe, Spain. Imports: France, Trinidad and Tobago, Germany. **Exports** Shrimp, timber, rum, rosewood essence. **Imports** Food, manufactures, petroleum.

LAND
Description Northeastern South America. **Area** 32,253 mi² (83,534 km²). **Highest point** 2,723 ft (830 m). **Lowest point** Sea level.

People. French Guiana has a majority population of black descendants of African slaves and people of mixed African-European ancestry. Population is concentrated on the coast, but the interior wilderness is home to minority Indians and the descendants of slaves who fled to pursue traditional African lifestyles. French is the predominant language, but a French-English creole is also spoken. Two Indo-Chinese refugee settlements were established in 1977 and 1979.

Economy and the Land. Shrimp production and a growing timber industry are French Guiana's economic mainstays. The land remains largely undeveloped, however, and reliance on French aid continues. The fertile coastal plains of the north give way to hills and mountains along the Brazilian border. Rain forests cover the land, which has a tropical climate.

History and Politics. Indigenous peoples and a hot climate defeated France's attempt at settlement in the early 1600s. The first permanent French settlement was established in 1634, and the area became a French colony in 1667. Beginning in the 1850s, penal colonies brought an influx of European prisoners. The region became a French overseas department in 1946. A minority nationalist group strives for autonomy. ■

FRENCH POLYNESIA

Official name Territory of French Polynesia

PEOPLE
Population 226,000. **Density** 166/mi² (64/km²). **Urban** 56%. **Capital** Papeete, Tahiti I., 23,555. **Ethnic groups** Polynesian 78%, Chinese 12%, French descent 6%. **Languages** French, Tahitian. **Religions** Evangelical and other Protestant 54%, Roman Catholic 30%. **Life expectancy** 74 female, 69 male. **Literacy** 98%.

POLITICS
Government Overseas territory (France). **Parties** New Fatherland, People's, Rally for the Republic, Polynesian Liberation Front, others. **Suffrage** Universal, 18 and over. **Memberships** None. **Subdivisions** 5 circumscriptions.

ECONOMY
GDP $1,760,000,000. **Per capita** $8,111. **Monetary unit** CFP franc. **Trade partners** Exports: France, U.S. Japan. Imports: France, U.S., Greece. **Exports** Coconut products, cultured pearls, mother-of-pearl, vanilla, shark meat. **Imports** Fuel, food, equipment.

LAND
Description South Pacific islands. **Area** 1,359 mi² (3,521 km²). **Highest point** Mont Orohena, 7,352 ft (2,241 m). **Lowest point** Sea level.

People. Most inhabitants are Polynesian, with minorities including Chinese and French. More than 100 islands compose the five archipelagoes, and population and commercial activity are concentrated in Papeete on Tahiti. Although per capita income is relatively high, wealth is not equally distributed. Emigration from the poorer islands to Tahiti is common. Polynesia's reputation as a tropical paradise has attracted many European and American writers and artists, including French painter Paul Gauguin.

Economy and the Land. Since France stationed military personnel in French Polynesia in 1963, the economy has evolved from subsistence to service. Much of the work force is now employed by the military or in tourism. Coconut and mother-of-pearl still play an important part in the export economy. This South Pacific territory, located south of the equator and midway between South America and Australia, is spread over roughly 1.5 million square miles (3.9 million square kilometers) and is made up of the Marquesas Islands, the Society Islands, the Tuamotu Archipelago, the Gambier Islands, and the Austral Islands. The Marquesas, known for their beauty, form the northernmost group. The Society Islands, southwest of the Marquesas, include Tahiti and Bora-Bora, both popular tourist spots. The Tuamoto Archipelago lies south of the Marquesas and east of the Society Islands, the Gambier Islands are situated at the southern tip of the Tuamotu group, and the Austral Islands lie to the southwest. The region includes both volcanic and coral islands, and the climate is tropical, with a rainy season extending from November to April.

History and Politics. The original settlers probably came from Micronesia and Melanesia in the east. Europeans arrived around the 16th century. By the late 1700s they had reached the five island groups, and visitors to the area included mutineers from the British vessel *Bounty*. By the 1880s, the islands came under French rule and become an overseas territory in 1946. The country has since moved toward autonomy with discussion of eventual independence. Anti-French sentiments grew in 1995 when France resumed nuclear testing in the Pacific. ■

GABON

Official name Gabonese Republic

PEOPLE
Population 1,199,000. **Density** 12/mi² (4.5/km²). **Urban** 51%. **Capital** Libreville, 337,700. **Ethnic groups** Fang, Eshira, Bapounou, Bateke. **Languages** French, Fang, indigenous. **Religions** Roman Catholic and other Christian 55-75%, Muslim, tribal religionist. **Life expectancy** 57 female, 54 male. **Literacy** 63%.

POLITICS
Government Republic. **Parties** Democratic, National Recovery Movement-Lumberjacks, others. **Suffrage** Universal, 21 and over. **Memberships** OAU, UN. **Subdivisions** 9 provinces.

ECONOMY
GDP $6,000,000,000. **Per capita** $5,155. **Monetary unit** CFA franc. **Trade partners** Exports: France, U.S., Spain. Imports: France, U.S., Japan. **Exports** Petroleum, manganese, wood, uranium. **Imports** Food, chemicals, petroleum, construction materials, manufactures, machinery.

LAND

Description Central Africa. **Area** 103,347 mi²
(267,667 km²). **Highest point** 3,360 ft (1,024 m).
Lowest point Sea level.

People. Of Gabon's more than 40 ethnic groups,
the Fang are a majority and inhabit the area
north of the Ogooué River. Other major groups
include the Eshira, Bapounou, and Bateke. The
French, who colonized the area, compose a larger group today than during colonial times. Each
of the groups has its own distinct language and
culture, but French remains the official language.

Economy and the Land. Gabon is located astride
the equator, and its many resources include
petroleum, manganese, uranium, and dense rain
forests. The most important activities are oil
production, forestry, and mining. The economy
depends greatly on foreign investment and
imported labor, however, and many native
Gabonese continue as subsistence farmers.
While the labor shortage hinders economic
development, the country has a high per capita
income. The terrain is marked by a coastal plain,
inland forested hills, and savanna in the east and
south. The climate is hot and humid.

History and Politics. First inhabited by Pygmies,
Gabon was the site of migrations by numerous
Bantu peoples during its early history. The thick
rain forests isolated the migrant groups from one
another and thus preserved their individual cultures. The Portuguese arrived in the 15th century,
followed by the Dutch, British, and French in the
1700s. The slave and ivory trades flourished, and
the Fang, drawn by the prosperity, migrated to
the coast in the 1800s. A group of freed slaves
founded Libreville, which later became the capital. By 1885 France had gained control of the
area, and in 1910 it was united with present-day
Chad, the Congo, and the Central African
Republic as French Equatorial Africa. Gabon
became independent in 1960, and in 1964 French
assistance thwarted a military takeover. After
anti-government protests in 1990, opposition
parties were legalized. ■

GALAPAGOS ISLANDS

See ECUADOR.

GAMBIA, THE

Official name Republic of the Gambia

PEOPLE

Population 1,269,000. **Density** 307/mi² (119/km²).
Urban 30%. **Capital** Banjul, 42,407. **Ethnic groups**
Malinke 42%, Fulani 18%, Wolof 16%, Jola 10%,
Serahuli 9%. **Languages** English, Malinke, Wolof, Fula,
indigenous. **Religions** Muslim 90%, Christian 9%, tribal
religionist 1%. **Life expectancy** 49 female, 45 male.
Literacy 39%.

POLITICS

Government Republic. **Parties** Alliance for Patriotic

Reorientation and Construction, United Democratic,
others. **Suffrage** Universal, 18 and over. **Memberships**
CW, OAU, UN. **Subdivisions** 5 divisions, 1 city.

ECONOMY

GDP $1,100,000,000. **Per capita** $1,017. **Monetary
unit** Dalasi. **Trade partners** Exports: Japan, European
countries, African countries. Imports: European
countries, Asian countries. **Exports** Peanuts, peanut
products, fish, cotton, palm kernels. **Imports** Food,
manufactures, raw materials, fuel, machinery,
transportation equipment.

LAND

Description Western Africa. **Area** 4,127 mi²
(10,689 km²). **Highest point** 174 ft (53 m). **Lowest
point** Sea level.

People. The Gambia's population includes the
Mandingo, or Malinke; Fulani; Wolof; Jola; and
Serahuli. Most people are Muslim, and language
differs from group to group, although the official
language of The Gambia is English. Gambians are
mainly rural farmers, and literacy is low, with
educational opportunities focused in the Banjul
area. The population's size varies with the arrival
and departure of seasonal Senegalese farm
laborers.

Economy and the Land. The Gambia's economy
relies on peanut production, and crop diversification is a goal. Subsistence crops include rice,
and the government hopes increased rice production will decrease dependence on imports
and foreign aid. Fishing and tourism have
expanded in the past years. In addition, the
Gambia River, which provides a route to the
African interior, offers potential for an increased
role in trade. Dense mangrove swamps border
the river, giving way to flat ground that floods in
the rainy season. Behind this lie sand hills and
plateaus. The Gambia is low-lying with a subtropical climate, and is virtually an enclave within Senegal.

History and Politics. From the 13th to the 15th
centuries, the flourishing Mali Empire included
the Gambia area. The Portuguese arrived in the

15th century, established slave trading posts, and sold trade rights to Britain in 1588. During the 17th and 18th centuries France and Britain competed for control of the Gambia River trade. By the late 1800s, the Banjul area had become a British colony and the interior a British protectorate. The Gambia achieved independence as a monarchy in 1965 and became a republic in 1970. After independence, the country was ruled by President Dawda Jawara, who was returned to office by popular vote for 24 years. Jawara was overthrown in a bloodless coup in July 1994, however, and the country is now ruled by a military council. ■

GEORGIA

Official name Republic of Georgia

PEOPLE
Population 5,140,000. **Density** 191/mi² (74/km²).
Urban 59%. **Capital** Tbilisi, 1,279,000. **Ethnic groups** Georgian 70%, Armenian 8%, Russian 6%, Azerbaijani 6%, Ossetian 3%, Abkhaz 2%. **Languages** Georgian, Russian, Armenian, Azerbaijani. **Religions** Georgian Orthodox 65%, Muslim 11%, Russian Orthodox 10%. **Life expectancy** 78 female, 70 male. **Literacy** 99%.

POLITICS
Government Republic. **Parties** Citizen's Union, National Democratic, others. **Suffrage** Universal, 18 and over. **Memberships** UN. **Subdivisions** 2 republics.

ECONOMY
GDP $6,200,000,000. **Per capita** $1,078. **Monetary unit** Lari. **Trade partners** Exports: Russia, Turkey, Armenian. Imports: Russia, Azerbaijan, Turkey. **Exports** Fruit, tea, wine, agriculture products, machines, metals, textiles, chemicals. **Imports** Fuel, grain, food, machinery and parts, transportation equipment.

LAND
Description Southwestern Asia. **Area** 26,911 mi² (69,700 km²). **Highest point** Mt. Shkhara, 16,627 ft (5,068 m). **Lowest point** Sea level.

People. Georgians are the descendants of the original inhabitants of the Caucasus region, and are proud of their ancient culture and language. Georgians have been Christians since the 4th century, and are world renowned for their many important contributions to the arts. Georgia is also home to Armenian, Russian, Abkhazian, and Ossetian minorities.

Economy and the Land. Despite its small size, Georgia has a variety of climates and terrains. Most of Georgia is mountainous or forested, but there are also fertile plains and valleys that are highly suitable for agriculture. Vineyards and orchards are scattered throughout the country. The area on the shores of the Black Sea is subtropical and is used for growing tea and citrus fruit. Georgia also has a well-developed industrial base as a result of its enormous hydroelectric power resources. The country has abundant mineral deposits, including coal and manganese. Georgia also has an active tourism industry that has been weakened recently by political instability.

History and Politics. Civilization has flourished in the Georgian region since 3000 B.C. The country's great wealth attracted a variety of invaders, including the Roman, Byzantine, and Persian empires. Arabs invaded the region in the 7th century. The early 13th century marked a high point in Georgia's cultural influence throughout the region, but this era was brought to a sudden end by the invasion of the Mongols. The country was later divided between the Turks and the Persians before it was annexed by Russia in 1801. Georgia, the birthplace of Joseph Stalin, played an important role in the Russian revolution of 1917. After the revolution, Georgia declared its independence, but Soviet troops invaded the country and forced its surrender in 1921. Resistance continued until great purges in the late 1930s eliminated Georgia's enemies of communism. After Soviet troops attacked Georgian demonstrators with poison gas in 1990, Georgia declared its independence in April 1991. It achieved full independence after the Soviet Union fell the following December. Fighting immediately resumed as pro-democracy elements battled to force the resignation of the country's first elected president, the controversial Zviad Gamsakhurdia. In 1992, the former Soviet foreign minister Eduard Shevardnadze was elected head of state. Georgia has been troubled by secessionist wars ignited by ethnic minorities in the Georgian territory of Abkhazia. Russia has lent military aid to the government in exchange for agreements that extend Russia's influence in the economic and military affairs of Georgia. Abkhazia and South Ossetia each held unauthorized elections in 1996, and now operate as if they were independent. Though there is presently no open warfare, the situation is unstable. ■

GERMANY

Official name Federal Republic of Germany

PEOPLE
Population 83,870,000. **Density** 609/mi² (235/km²). **Urban** 87%. **Capital** Berlin (designated), 3,475,392; Bonn (de facto), 296,859. **Ethnic groups** German (Teutonic) 95%, Turkish 2%. **Languages** German. **Religions** Evangelical and other Protestant 45%, Roman Catholic 37%. **Life expectancy** 80 female, 74 male. **Literacy** 99%.

POLITICS
Government Federal republic. **Parties** Christian Democratic Union, Social Democratic, others. **Suffrage** Universal, 18 and over. **Memberships** EU, NATO, OECD, UN. **Subdivisions** 16 states

ECONOMY
GDP $1,452,200,000,000. **Per capita** $17,944. **Monetary unit** Mark. **Trade partners** Exports: France, Italy, Netherlands, U.K. Imports: France, Netherlands, Italy, Belgium. **Exports** Machinery, chemicals, transportation equipment, iron, steel, raw materials. **Imports** Manufactures, agricultural products, raw materials, fuel.

LAND
Description Northern Europe. **Area** 137,822 mi² (356,955 km²). **Highest point** Zugspitze, 9,718 ft (2,962 m). **Lowest point** Freepsum Lake, -7 ft (-2 m).

People. Germany has a homogeneous, German-speaking population with a very small Turkish minority. Roman Catholics, Evangelicals, and other Protestants are the largest religious groups. Germans are well-educated and boast a rich cultural heritage of achievements in music, literature, philosophy, and science. Germany has the largest population of any European country, excluding Russia.

Economy and the Land. Despite the devastating effects of World War II and Germany's 45-year division into two countries, the country has one of the world's strongest economies. Industry is the basis of its prosperity, with mining, manufacturing, construction, and utilities as important contributors. The Ruhr district, which is the country's most important industrial region, is located near the Rhine River in west-central Germany and includes cities such as Essen and Dortmund. Agriculture remains important in the southern and central regions. Germany's terrain varies from northern plains to central uplands to the southern Bavarian Alps. A mild climate is tempered by the sea in the north; in the south the winters are colder because of the Alps.

History and Politics. In ancient times, Germanic tribes overcame Celtic inhabitants in the area of Germany and established a northern stronghold against Roman expansion of Gaul. As the Roman Empire weakened, the Germanic peoples invaded, deposing the Roman governor of Gaul in the 5th century A.D. The Franks composed the most powerful tribe, and in the 9th century Frankish-controlled territory was expanded and united under Charlemagne. Unity did not last, however, and Germany remained a disjointed territory of warring feudal states, duchies, and independent cities. The Reformation, a movement led by German monk Martin Luther, began in 1517 and evolved into the Protestant branch of Christianity. The rise of Prussian power and growing nationalism eventually united the German states into the German Empire in 1871, and Prussian chancellor Otto von Bismarck installed Prussian King Wilhelm I as emperor. In a few short years, Germany rose to become Europe's foremost industrial and military power. In 1914 Germany allied with Austria; their subsequent invasions of France and Russia led to World War I. Hardships imposed by the victors against Germany led to instability and economic collapse. Promising prosperity, Adolf Hitler and his National Socialist, or Nazi, party rose to power in 1933. Hitler's ruthless nationalist policies included a genocidal program to eliminate Jews and many other peoples, and his ambitions to conquer all of Europe led to World War II. The Allied Forces defeated Germany in 1945 only after enormous casualties had been inflicted on both sides. After the ware, the United States, Britain, the Soviet Union, and France divided Germany into four zones of occupation. The eastern, Soviet-occupied zone became a Communist country called the German Democratic Republic, or East Germany. The three remaining zones of Germany were combined to form the capitalist Federal Republic of Germany, or West Germany. Berlin, not included in occupation zones, was divided between the east and west. The Berlin Wall became a symbol of the Cold War between the U.S. and the Soviet Union. In the late 1980s the Soviet Union began to loosen its grip on its satellite countries, and in 1989 East Germans began a mass exodus to West Germany. In October 1990 East Germany was officially absorbed into West Germany. Elation over reunification has been followed by unforeseen economic problems and resentments between the two sections of the country. ∎

GHANA

Official name Republic of Ghana

PEOPLE
Population 18,305,000. **Density** 199/mi² (77/km²).
Urban 36%. **Capital** Accra, 949,113. **Ethnic groups**
Akan 52%, Moshi-Dagomba 16%, Ewe 13%, Ga 8%.
Languages English, Akan and other indigenous.
Religions Tribal religionist 38%, Muslim 30%,
Christian 24%. **Life expectancy** 60 female, 56 male.
Literacy 64%.

POLITICS
Government Republic. **Parties** National Democratic
Congress, New Patriotic, others. **Suffrage** Universal, 18
and over. **Memberships** CW, OAU, UN. **Subdivisions**
10 regions.

ECONOMY
GDP $25,100,000,000. **Per capita** $1,392. **Monetary
unit** Cedi. **Trade partners** Exports: Switzerland, U.S.
Imports: Nigeria, U.S., Germany. **Exports** Cocoa, gold,
timber, tuna, metal ores, metals, diamonds. **Imports**
Petroleum, manufactures, food, machinery.

LAND
Description Western Africa. **Area** 92,098 mi²
(238,533 km²). **Highest point** Afadjoto, 2,905 ft
(885 m). **Lowest point** Sea level.

People. Nearly all Ghanaians are black Africans.
The Akan, the majority group, are further divided
into the Fanti, who live mainly along the coast,
and the Ashanti, who inhabit the forests north of
the coast. The Ewe and Ga live in the south and
southeast. Other groups include the Guan, living
on the Volta River plains, and the Moshi-
Dagomba in the North. Ghana's more than 50
languages and dialects reflect this ethnic diversity, and English, the official language, is spoken
by a minority. Islam and traditional African religions predominate, but a Christian minority also
exists. Most people live in rural areas, and the literacy rate is low.

Economy and the Land. Agriculture is the economic base, but Ghana's natural resources are
diverse. Production of cocoa, the most important

export, is concentrated in the Ashanti region, a
belt of tropical rain forest extending north from
the coastal plain. Resources include forests and
mineral deposits. Bauxite, gold, diamonds, and
manganese are being mined currently. Ghana
has enjoyed steady economic growth since the
1980s. Its coastal lowlands give way to scrub and
plains, the Ashanti rain forest, and northern
savanna. A dam on the Volta River has created
the world's largest reservoir. The
climate is tropical.

History and Politics. The ancestors of today's
Ghanaians probably migrated from the northern
areas of Mauritania and Mali in the 13th century.
The Portuguese reached the shore around 1470
and called the area the Gold Coast. Many countries competed for the region, but in 1874 the
Gold Coast was made a British colony. By 1901
Britain had extended its control to the inland
Ashanti area, which became a colony, and the
northern territories, which became a protectorate. The three regions were merged with
British Togoland, a onetime German colony
under British administration since 1922. In 1957
the four regions united as independent Ghana.
Instability resulted, arising from a history of dis-
unity and economic problems. The parliamentary state became a republic in 1960, and civilian
rule has alternated with military governments.
The leader of the 1979 military coup was elected
as a civilian president in 1992 and has overseen
a successful but fragile economic recovery program. Ongoing tribal conflicts are a continuing
problem. ∎

GIBRALTAR

Official name Gibraltar

PEOPLE
Population 29,000. **Density** 12,609/mi² (4,833/km²).
Urban 100%. **Capital** Gibraltar, 29,000. **Ethnic groups**
Gibraltarian (mixed Italian, English, Maltese,
Portuguese, and Spanish) 72%, British 16%.
Languages English, Spanish. **Religions** Roman
Catholic 74%, Anglican 8%, Muslim 8%, Jewish 2%,
Hindu 1%. **Life expectancy** 79 female, 74 male.

POLITICS
Government Dependent territory (U.K.). **Parties** Social
Democratic, Socialist Labor. **Suffrage** Universal, 18
and over. **Memberships** None. **Subdivisions** None.

ECONOMY
GDP $205,000,000. **Per capita** $6,406. **Monetary unit**
Pound. **Trade partners** Exports: U.K., Morocco,
Portugal. Imports: U.K., Spain, Japan. **Exports**
Petroleum re-export, manufactures re-export. **Imports**
Fuel, manufactures, food.

LAND
Description Southwestern Europe (peninsula on
Spain's southern coast). **Area** 2.3 mi² (6.0 km²).
Highest point 1,398 ft (426 m). **Lowest point** Sea level.

People. Occupying a narrow peninsula on
Spain's southern coast, the British colony of
Gibraltar has a mixed population of Italian,

English, Maltese, Portuguese, and Spanish descent. A number of British residents—many of whom are military personnel—also reside here. Most are bilingual in English and Spanish.

Economy and the Land. With land unsuitable for agriculture and a lack of mineral resources, Gibraltar's economy depends mainly on the British military and tourism. Shipping-related activities and a growing service industry also provide jobs and income. Connected to Spain by an isthmus, Gibraltar consists mainly of the limestone-and-shale ridge known as the Rock of Gibraltar. The climate is mild.

History and Politics. Drawn by Gibraltar's strategic location at the Atlantic entrance to the Mediterranean Sea, Phoenicians, Carthaginians, Romans, Vandals, Visigoths, and Moors all played a role in the land's history. After nearly 300 years under Spanish control, Gibraltar was captured by Britain in 1704, during the War of the Spanish Succession. It was officially ceded to the British in the 1713 Peace of Utrecht. In a 1967 referendum, residents voted to remain under British control. British-Spanish competition for the colony continues. ■

GREECE

Official name Hellenic Republic

PEOPLE
Population 10,605,000. **Density** 208/mi² (80/km²). **Urban** 59%. **Capital** Athens, 772,072. **Ethnic groups** Greek 98%. **Languages** Greek, English, French. **Religions** Greek Orthodox 98%, Muslim 1%. **Life expectancy** 81 female, 76 male. **Literacy** 95%.

POLITICS
Government Republic. **Parties** New Democracy, Panhellenic Socialist Movement, others. **Suffrage** Universal, 18 and over. **Memberships** EU, NATO, OECD, UN. **Subdivisions** 13 regions.

ECONOMY
GDP $101,700,000,000. **Per capita** $9,654.

Monetary unit Drachma. **Trade partners** Germany, Italy, France. **Exports** Manufactures, food, fuel. **Imports** Manufactures, food, fuel.

LAND
Description Southeastern Europe. **Area** 50,949 mi² (131,957 km²). **Highest point** Mt. Olympus, 9,570 ft (2,917 m). **Lowest point** Sea level.

People. Greece has played a central role in European, African, and Asian cultures for thousands of years, but today its population is almost homogeneous. Native Greek inhabitants are united by a language that dates back 3,000 years and a religion that influences many aspects of everyday life. Athens, the capital, was the cultural center of an ancient civilization that produced masterpieces of art and literature and broke ground in philosophy, political thought, and science.

Economy and the Land. The economy of Greece takes its shape from terrain and location. Dominated by the sea and long a maritime trading power, Greece has one of the largest merchant fleets in the world and depends greatly on commerce. The mountainous terrain and poor soil limit agriculture, although Greece is a leading producer of lemons and olives. The service sector, including tourism, provides most of Greece's national income. Inhabitants enjoy a temperate climate, with mild, wet winters, and hot, dry summers.

History and Politics. Greece's history begins with the early Bronze Age cultures of the Minoans and the Mycenaeans. The city-state, or polis, began to develop around the 10th century B.C., and Athens, a democracy, and Sparta, an oligarchy, gradually emerged as Greece's leaders. The Persian Wars, in which the city-states united to repel a vastly superior army, ushered in the Golden Age of Athens, a cultural explosion in the 5th century B.C. The Parthenon, perhaps Greece's most famous building, was built at this time. Athens was defeated by Sparta in the Peloponnesian War, and by 338 B.C. Philip II of Macedon had conquered all of Greece. His son, Alexander the Great, defeated the Persians and spread Greek civilization and language all over the known world. Greece became a Roman province in 146 B.C. and part of the Byzantine Empire in A.D. 395, but its traditions had a marked influence on these empires. Absorbed into the Ottoman Empire in the 1450s, Greece gained independence by 1830 and became a constitutional monarchy 15 years later. For much of the 20th century, the country was divided between republicans and monarchists. During World War II Germany occupied Greece, and postwar instability led to a civil war, which Communist rebels eventually lost. A repressive military junta ruled Greece from 1967 until 1974, followed by a civilian government. The Greeks voted for a republic over a monarchy, and in 1993 Socialists regained power. ■

GREENLAND

Official name Greenland

PEOPLE

Population 59,000. **Density** 0.7/mi² (0.3/km²). **Urban** 81%. **Capital** Godthåb, 12,909. **Ethnic groups** Greenlander (Inuit and native-born whites) 87%, Danish 13%. **Languages** Danish, Greenlandic, Inuit dialects. **Religions** Lutheran. **Life expectancy** 72 female, 63 male.

POLITICS

Government Self-governing territory (Danish protection). **Parties** Forward (Siumut), Inuit Ataqatigiit, Solidarity (Atassut), others. **Suffrage** Universal, 18 and over. **Memberships** None. **Subdivisions** 3 municipalities.

ECONOMY

GDP $892,000,000. **Per capita** $15,649. **Monetary unit** Danish krone. **Trade partners** Exports: Denmark, U.K., Germany. Imports: Denmark, Norway, U.S. **Exports** Fish, fish products. **Imports** Manufactures, machinery, transportation equipment, food, petroleum products.

LAND

Description North Atlantic island. **Area** 840,004 mi² (2,175,600 km²). **Highest point** Gunnbjorn Mtn., 12,139 ft (3,700 m). **Lowest point** Sea level.

People. Most Greenlanders are native-born descendants of mixed Inuit-Danish ancestry. Lutheranism, the predominant religion, reflects Danish ties. Descended from an indigenous Arctic people, pure Inuit are a minority and usually follow traditional lifestyles. Most of the island lies within the Arctic Circle, and population is concentrated along the southern coast.

Economy and the Land. Since lead and zinc mining was discontinued in 1989, fishing has been the main economic activity. There are also deposits of iron, coal, uranium, and molybdenum that remain undeveloped due to difficulties with the Arctic environment. The largest island in the world, Greenland is composed of an inland plateau, coastal mountains and fjords, and off-shore islands. More than 80 percent of the island lies under permanent ice cap. The climate is cold, with warmer temperatures and more precipitation in the southwest.

History and Politics. Following the early migration of Arctic Inuit, Norwegian Vikings sighted Greenland in the 9th century, and in the 10th century Erik the Red brought the first settlers from Iceland. Greenland united with Norway in the 1200s, and the two regions, along with several others, came under Danish rule in the 1300s. Denmark retained control of Greenland when Norway left the union in 1814. American troops defended the island during World War II. In 1953 the island became a province of Denmark, and in 1979 it gained home rule. ■

GRENADA

Official name Grenada

PEOPLE

Population 96,000. **Density** 722/mi² (279/km²). **Urban** 36%. **Capital** St. George's, 4,439. **Ethnic groups** Black 82%, mixed 13%, East Indian 3%. **Languages** English, French. **Religions** Roman Catholic 53%, Anglican 14%, Seventh Day Adventist 8%. **Life expectancy** 73 female, 68 male. **Literacy** 98%.

POLITICS

Government Parliamentary state. **Parties** National Democratic Congress, New National, United Labor, others. **Suffrage** Universal, 18 and over. **Memberships** CW, OAS, UN. **Subdivisions** 7 parishes.

ECONOMY

GDP $284,000,000. **Per capita** $3,021. **Monetary unit** East Caribbean dollar. **Trade partners** Exports: U.K., Netherlands, Germany. Imports: U.S., U.K., Trinidad and Tobago. **Exports** Nutmeg, cocoa beans, fruits and vegetables, clothing, mace. **Imports** Food, manufactures, machinery, chemicals, fuel.

LAND

Description Caribbean island. **Area** 133 mi² (344 km²). **Highest point** Mt. St. Catherine, 2,756 ft (840 m). **Lowest point** Sea level.

People. Grenada's culture bears the influences of former British and French rule. The most widely spoken language in Grenada is English, although a French patois is also spoken, and the majority of the population is Roman Catholic. Most Grenadians are black, descended from African slaves brought to the island by the British. In addition there are small East Indian and European populations.

Economy and the Land. Rich volcanic soils and heavy rainfall have made agriculture the chief economic activity. Also known as the Isle of Spice, Grenada is one of the world's leading producers of nutmeg and mace. Many tropical fruits are also raised, and the small plots of peasant farms dot the hilly terrain. Another mainstay of the economy is tourism, with visitors drawn by the beaches and tropical climate. Grenada has little industry; high unemployment has plagued the country in recent years.

History and Politics. The Caribs resisted European attempts to colonize Grenada for more than 100 years after Christopher Columbus discovered the island in 1498. The French established the first settlement in 1650 and slaughtered the Caribs, but the British finally gained control in 1783. In 1974, Grenada achieved full independence under Prime Minister Eric Gairy, despite widespread opposition to his policies. In 1979, foes of the regime staged a coup and installed a Marxist government headed by Maurice Bishop. Power struggles resulted, and a military branch of the government seized power in 1983 and executed Bishop, along with several of his ministers. The United States led a subsequent invasion that deposed the Marxists. A centrist government has ruled since 1984. ■

GUADELOUPE

Official name Department of Guadeloupe

PEOPLE
Population 415,000. **Density** 632/mi² (244/km²). **Urban** 100%. **Capital** Basse-Terre, 14,003. **Ethnic groups** Black or mulatto 90%, white 5%. **Languages** French, Creole. **Religions** Roman Catholic 95%. **Life expectancy** 79 female, 72 male. **Literacy** 90%.

POLITICS
Government Overseas department (France). **Parties** Rally for the Republic, Socialist, others. **Suffrage** Universal, 18 and over. **Memberships** None. **Subdivisions** 3 arondissements.

ECONOMY
GDP $3,700,000,000. **Per capita** $8,565. **Monetary unit** Franch franc. **Trade partners** Exports: France, Martinique. Imports: France, U.S., Italy. **Exports** Bananas, sugar, rum. **Imports** Transportation equipment, food, clothing, manufactures, petroleum.

LAND
Description Caribbean islands. **Area** 657 mi² (1,702 km²). **Highest point** Soufrière, 4,813 ft (1,467 m). **Lowest point** Sea level.
The above information includes dependencies.

People. Most of the people of these French islands in the Caribbean are black or of mixed black and white ancestry. A white community in the Îles des Saintes island group is descended from the original French settlers.

Economy and the Land. Important economic activities include tourism, agriculture, sugar refining, and rum distilling. A drawbridge crossing a narrow strait connects the volcanic island of

Basse-Terre, or Guadeloupe proper, to Grand-Terre, part of a limestone island chain. Together, these two islands are known as Guadeloupe. Other islands include the Îles des Saintes group, Marie-Galante, La Désirade, St. Barthélemy, the northern section of St. Martin, and Îles de la Petite Terre. The climate is warm with moderating trade winds.

History and Politics. Around A.D. 1000, the Carib tribes took the main island from the Arawaks. In 1493 Christopher Columbus arrived, but the first French settlers did not come to the islands until 1635. About ten years later the sugar economy was underway, and slaves were imported from Africa to work the plantations. In 1946 France changed Guadeloupe's status to an overseas department. Hurricane Hugo hit Guadeloupe in 1989, causing extensive damage to structures and destroying much of the vegetation, including most coconut palms. ■

GUAM See UNITED STATES.

GUATEMALA

Official name Republic of Guatemala

PEOPLE
Population 11,700,000. **Density** 278/mi² (107/km²). **Urban** 39%. **Capital** Guatemala, 823,301. **Ethnic groups** Ladino (mestizo) 56%, Amerindian 44%. **Languages** Spanish, Amerindian. **Religions** Roman Catholic, Protestant, tribal religionist. **Life expectancy** 70 female, 65 male. **Literacy** 56%.

POLITICS
Government Republic. **Parties** National Advancement, New Democratic Front, Republican Front, others. **Suffrage** Universal, 18 and over. **Memberships** OAS, UN. **Subdivisions** 22 departments.

ECONOMY
GDP $36,700,000,000. **Per capita** $3,294. **Monetary unit** Quetzal. **Trade partners** Exports: U.S.,

El Salvador, Germany. Imports: U.S., Venezuela, Germany, Japan. **Exports** Coffee, sugar, bananas, cardamom, beef. **Imports** Petroleum products, machinery, grain, fertilizer, transportation equipment.

LAND
Description Central America. **Area** 42,042 mi^2 (108,889 km^2). **Highest point** Volcán Tajumulco, 13,845 ft (4,220 m). **Lowest point** Sea level.

People. Guatemala's population is made up of majority ladinos and minority Amerindians. Ladinos include both mestizos, those of Spanish-Amerindian origin, and westernized Amerindians of Mayan descent. Classified on the basis of culture rather than race, ladinos follow a Spanish-American lifestyle and speak Spanish. Non-ladino Amerindians are of Mayan descent and speak several Mayan dialects. Many are poor, uneducated, and suffer from persecution. Roman Catholicism here often combines with traditional Mayan religious practice. Population is concentrated in the central highlands.

Economy and the Land. Most Guatemalans practice agriculture in some form. Amerindians generally operate small subsistence farms. Export crops are produced mainly on large plantations on the fertile southern plain that borders the Pacific. Although light industry is growing, it is unable to absorb rural immigrants seeking employment in the cities. Much of the landscape is mountainous, with the Pacific plain and Caribbean lowlands bordering central highlands. Northern rain forests and grasslands are sparsely populated and largely undeveloped. The climate is tropical in low areas and temperate in the highlands.

History and Politics. Indigenous Amerindians in the region were absorbed into the Mayan civilization that flourished in Central America by the fourth century. In 1523, the Spanish defeated the Maya and went on to establish one of the most influential colonies in Central America. Guatemala joined Costa Rica, El Salvador, Nicaragua, and Honduras in 1821 to declare independence from Spain, and the former Spanish colonies formed the Federation of Central America in 1823. Almost from the start, the federation was marked by dissension, and by 1838 it had, in effect, been dissolved. Following a series of dictatorships, social and economic reform began in 1944 and continued under two successive presidents. The government was ousted in a United States-backed 1954 coup, and military rule was established. In 1985, the country returned to a civilian government. The years since then have been marked by corruption and some of the worst human rights abuses in Central America. After 35 years of civil war, leftist guerrillas signed a peace accord in 1996 when the government agreed to more financial support and political power for the rural poor. ■

GUERNSEY See UNITED KINGDOM.

GUINEA

Official name Republic of Guinea

PEOPLE
Population 7,618,000. **Density** 80/mi^2 (31/km^2). **Urban** 30%. **Capital** Conakry, 950,000. **Ethnic groups** Fulani 35%, Malinke 30%, Susu 20%, others. **Languages** French, indigenous. **Religions** Muslim 85%, Christian 8%, Animist 7%. **Life expectancy** 47 female, 46 male. **Literacy** 36%.

POLITICS
Government Republic. **Parties** Party for Unity and Progress, Rally for the Guinean People, Union for a New Republic, others. **Suffrage** Universal, 18 and over. **Memberships** OAU, UN. **Subdivisions** 33 regions.

ECONOMY
GDP $6,500,000,000. **Per capita** $981. **Monetary unit** Franc. **Trade partners** Exports: U.S., European countries, former Soviet republics. Imports: U.S., France, Brazil. **Exports** Alumina, bauxite, diamonds, gold, coffee, pineapples, bananas, palm kernels. **Imports** Petroleum products, metals, machinery and transportation equipment, food.

LAND
Description Western Africa. **Area** 94,926 mi^2 (245,857 km^2). **Highest point** Mont Nimba, 5,748 ft (1,752 m). **Lowest point** Sea level.

People. Guinea's population is composed of several ethnic groups, with three—the Fulani, Malinke, and Susu—forming the majority. Most Guineans are rural farmers, living in hamlets, and the only true urban center is Conakry. Mortality as well as emigration rates are high. Eight languages besides French, the language of the colonial power, are taught in the schools.

Economy and the Land. Rich soil and a varied terrain suited for diverse crop production have made agriculture an important economic activity. Guinea also has vast mineral reserves, including one of the world's largest bauxite deposits. Centralized economic planning and state enterprise have characterized the republic, but Guinea now encourages private and foreign investments. The terrain is mostly flat along the coast and mountainous in the interior. The climate is tropical on the coast, hot and dry in the north and northeast, and cooler with less humidity in the highlands.

History and Politics. As part of the Ghana, Mali, and Songhai empires that flourished in West Africa between the 4th and 15th centuries, Guinea was a trading center for gold and slaves. The Portuguese arrived on the coast in the 1400s, and European competition for Guinean trade soon began. In the 1890s France declared the area a colony and named it French Guinea. After World War II a movement for autonomy began with a series of reforms by the French and the growth of a labor movement headed by Sékou Touré, later the country's first president. The first of the French colonies in West Africa to attain independence, in 1958 Guinea was also the only colony to reject membership in the French Community. The country's first multiparty elections were held in December 1993 amid violence and confusion. The results were not accepted by opposition leaders and the winner, President Lansana Conte, has since resumed a military title. ∎

GUINEA-BISSAU

Official name Republic of Guinea-Bissau

PEOPLE
Population 1,192,000. **Density** 85/mi² (33/km²). **Urban** 22%. **Capital** Bissau, 125,000. **Ethnic groups** Balanta 30%, Fulani 20%, Manjaca 14%, Malinke 13%, Papel 7%. **Languages** Portuguese, Crioulo, indigenous. **Religions** Tribal religionist 65%, Muslim 30%, Christian 5%. **Life expectancy** 47 female, 44 male. **Literacy** 55%.

POLITICS
Government Republic. **Parties** African Party for Independence, Resistance-Bah Fatah Movement, Social Renovation, others. **Suffrage** Universal, 15 and over. **Memberships** OAU, UN. **Subdivisions** 9 regions.

ECONOMY
GDP $1,000,000,000. **Per capita** $878. **Monetary unit** Peso. **Trade partners** Exports: Portugal, Senegal, France. Imports: Portugal, Netherlands, Senegal. **Exports** Cashews, fish, peanuts, palm kernels. **Imports** Food, transportation equipment, petroleum products, machinery, equipment.

LAND
Description Western Africa. **Area** 13,948 mi² (36,125 km²). **Highest point** 860 ft (262 m). **Lowest point** Sea level.

People. Guinea-Bissau's largest ethnic group, the Balanta, mainly inhabit the coastal area. Most practice traditional beliefs, although some are Christian. Predominately Muslim peoples, the Fulani and Malinke are concentrated in the northwest. The Manjaca inhabit the northern and central coastal regions. Although the official language is Portuguese, many speak Crioulo, a creole dialect also spoken in Cape Verde.

Economy and the Land. Guinea-Bissau's economy is underdeveloped and dependent upon agriculture. Peanuts, cotton, corn, and sorghum are grown in the north, and palm oil production is concentrated along the coast. Timber is produced primarily in the south. Fishing, especially shrimp production, has increased since 1976. Bauxite deposits have been located, and exploration for additional resources continues. Mineral exploitation is hindered by a lack of transportation routes, however. A swamp-covered coastal plain rises to an eastern savanna. The climate is tropical. The country includes the Bijagos Archipelago, which lies just off the coast.

History and Politics. The area of Guinea-Bissau was inhabited by diverse peoples prior to the arrival of the Portuguese in 1446. Ruled as a single colony with Cape Verde, the region soon developed into a base for the Portuguese slave trade. In 1879 it was separated from Cape Verde as Portuguese Guinea, and its status changed to overseas province in 1951. A movement for the independence of Guinea-Bissau and Cape Verde developed in the 1950s, and a coup in Portugal in 1974 resulted in independence the same year. Attempts to unite Guinea-Bissau and Cape Verde were unsuccessful, and a 1980 coup installed an anti-unification government. The country's first multiparty presidential elections were held in July 1994, and the incumbent party retained power. ∎

GUYANA

Official name Co-operative Republic of Guyana

PEOPLE
Population 702,000. **Density** 8.5/mi² (3.3/km²). **Urban** 36%. **Capital** Georgetown, 78,500. **Ethnic groups** East Indian 51%, black and mixed 43%, Amerindian 4%. **Languages** English, Hindi, Urdu.

Britain feared a Communist victory at the polls. In the early 1960s, racial tensions erupted into riots between East Indians and blacks. In 1966, the country became independent and adopted the name Guyana. Guyana became a republic in 1970 and has pursued socialist policies. The two main political parties continue to reflect its ethnic divisions: the People's National Congress (PNC) is supported by blacks, and the People's Progressive Party (PPP) by East Indians. A 1992 election was won by the PPP. ∎

HAITI

Official name Republic of Haiti

Religions Anglican and other Christian 57%, Hindu 33%, Muslim 9%. **Life expectancy** 70 female, 64 male. **Literacy** 98%.

POLITICS
Government Republic. **Parties** People's National Congress, People's Progressive, others. **Suffrage** Universal, 18 and over. **Memberships** CW, OAS, UN. **Subdivisions** 10 regions.

ECONOMY
GDP $1,600,000,000. **Per capita** $2,219. **Monetary unit** Dollar. **Trade partners** Exports: U.K., U.S., Trinidad and Tobago. Imports: Trinidad and Tobago, U.S., U.K. **Exports** Bauxite, alumina, sugar, rice, shrimp, molasses. **Imports** Manufactures, machinery, food, petroleum.

LAND
Description Northeastern South America. **Area** 83,000 mi² (214,969 km²). **Highest point** Mt. Roraima, 9,432 ft (2,875 m). **Lowest point** Sea level.

People. Guyana's population includes descendants of black African slaves and East Indian, Chinese, and Portuguese laborers who were brought to work sugar plantations. Amerindians, the indigenous peoples of Guyana, are a minority. Ninety percent of the people live along the fertile coastal plain, where farming and manufacturing are concentrated.

Economy and the Land. Agriculture and mining compose the backbone of the Guyanese economy. Sugar and rice continue to be important crops, and mines produce bauxite, manganese, diamonds, and gold. Guyana's inland forests give way to savanna and a coastal plain. The climate is tropical.

History and Politics. First gaining European notice in 1498 with the voyages of Christopher Columbus, Guyana was the stage for competing colonial interests—British, French, and Dutch— until it officially became British Guiana in 1831. Slavery was abolished several years later, causing the British to import indentured laborers, the ancestors of today's majority group. A constitution, adopted in 1953, was suspended when

PEOPLE
Population 6,911,000. **Density** 645/mi² (249/km²). **Urban** 32%. **Capital** Port-au-Prince, 846,247. **Ethnic groups** Black 95%, mulatto and white 5%. **Languages** Creole, French. **Religions** Roman Catholic 80%, Baptist 10%, Pentecostal 4%. **Life expectancy** 60 female, 57 male. **Literacy** 45%.

POLITICS
Government Republic. **Parties** Lavalas, Movement for the Organization of the Country, National Front for Change and Democracy, Others. **Suffrage** Universal, 18 and over. **Memberships** OAS, UN. **Subdivisions** 9 departments.

ECONOMY
GDP $6,500,000,000. **Per capita** $903. **Monetary unit** Gourde. **Trade partners** Exports: U.S., Italy. Imports: U.S., Canada, Japan. **Exports** Manufactures, coffee, agricultural products. **Imports** Machines, food, drink, manufactures, petroleum products, chemicals, fat, oils.

LAND
Description Caribbean island (western Hispaniola). **Area** 10,714 mi² (27,750 km²). **Highest point** Morne La Selle, 8,773 ft (2,674 m). **Lowest point** Sea level.

People. The world's oldest black republic, Haiti has a population composed mainly of descendants of African slaves. Most people are poor and rural. Although French is an official language, Haitian Creole, a combination of French and

West African languages, is more widely spoken. Roman Catholicism is the major religion. Voodooism, which blends Christian and African beliefs, is also practiced.

Economy and the Land. Haiti's economy remains underdeveloped. Most people rely on subsistence farming, though productivity is hampered by high population density in productive regions. Coffee is a main commercial crop and export. Recent growth of light industry is partially attributable to tax exemptions and low labor costs. Occupying the western third of Hispaniola Island, Haiti has an overall mountainous terrain and a tropical climate.

History and Politics. Christopher Columbus reached Hispaniola in 1492, and the indigenous Arawaks almost completely died out during subsequent Spanish settlement. Most Spanish settlers had gone to seek their fortunes in other colonies by the 1600s, and western Hispaniola came under French control in 1697. Slave importation increased rapidly, and in less than 100 years black Africans far outnumbered the French. In a 1791 revolution led by Henri Christophe, Toussaint L'Ouverture, and Jean Jacques Dessalines, the slaves rose against the French. By 1804 the country achieved independence from France, and the area was renamed Haiti. In the 1820s Haitians conquered the eastern region of the island, now the Dominican Republic, and it remained part of Haiti until 1844. Instability increased under various dictatorships from 1843 to 1915, and United States marines occupied the country from 1915 to 1934. After a time of alternating military and civilian rule, François Duvalier came to office in 1957, declaring himself president-for-life in 1964. His rule was marked by repression, corruption, and human rights abuses. His son, Jean-Claude, succeeded him as president-for-life in 1971. The Duvalier dictatorship ended in 1986 when Jean-Claude fled the country. There were six different governments between 1987 and 1990. An internationally monitored election in 1990 failed to bring peace and democracy. A coup in September 1991 forced the winner, Jean-Bertrand Aristide, into exile. International pressure and sanctions resulted in his 1994 return. After a period of calm, political violence has recently increased, destabilizing the government. ■

HONDURAS

Official name Republic of Honduras

PEOPLE
Population 5,824,000. **Density** 135/mi² (52/km²). **Urban** 44%. **Capital** Tegucigalpa, 576,661. **Ethnic groups** Mestizo 90%, Amerindian 7%, black 2%, white 1%. **Languages** Spanish, indigenous. **Religions** Roman Catholic 97%. **Life expectancy** 72 female, 68 male. **Literacy** 73%.

POLITICS
Government Republic. **Parties** Liberal, National,

others. **Suffrage** Universal, 18 and over. **Memberships** OAS, UN. **Subdivisions** 18 departments.

ECONOMY
GDP $10,800,000,000. **Per capita** $1,799. **Monetary unit** Lempira. **Trade partners** Exports: U.S., Germany, Japan. Imports: U.S., Japan, Mexico. **Exports** Bananas, coffee, shrimp, lobster, minerals, meat, lumber. **Imports** Machinery, transportation equipment, chemicals, manufactures, fuel, oil, food.

LAND
Description Central America. **Area** 43,277 mi² (112,088 km²). **Highest point** Cerro Las Minas, 9,347 ft (2,849 m). **Lowest point** Sea level.

People. Most Hondurans are mestizos—people of Spanish-Amerindian descent. Other groups include Amerindians and descendants of black Africans and Europeans. Most Amerindians have been assimilated into the majority culture, but a minority continues to practice traditional lifestyles. The Spanish language predominates, and English is spoken by a small population of British descent on the northern coast and Bay Islands. Poverty is an ongoing problem for the mainly rural population, and economic and educational improvements mostly affect urban inhabitants.

Economy and the Land. Honduras has an underdeveloped economy based on banana cultivation. Other activities include livestock raising, coffee production, forestry, and some mining. Honduras's terrain is mostly mountainous, with lowlands along some coastal regions. The climate varies from tropical in the lowlands to temperate in the mountains.

History and Politics. Early in its history Honduras was part of the Mayan Empire. By 1502, when Christopher Columbus arrived to claim the region for Spain, the decline of the Maya had rendered them weak and unable to resist Spanish settlement. The Spanish colonial period introduced gold and silver mines, cattle ranches, and African slaves. In 1821 Honduras, El Salvador, Nicaragua, Costa Rica, and Guatemala declared independence from Spain and, in 1823, formed the Federation of Central America. The unstable union had virtually collapsed by 1838, and the member states became independent as the federation dissolved. Instability, Guatemalan political influence, and the development of a banana economy based on United States-owned plantations marked the 1800s and early 1900s. Frequent revolutions have characterized the 20th century, and a dictator governed from 1933 to 1948. Since the 1950s, civilian governments have alternated with military coups and rule. Honduras and El Salvador waged a brief war in 1969. Contro-versies focus on issues of poverty and land distribution. There have been reports of extensive human rights abuses. Presidential elections in 1993 brought to power reformers who promise to confront the military and to stop abuses. ■

HONG KONG See CHINA.

HUNGARY

Official name Republic of Hungary

PEOPLE
Population 9,901,000. **Density** 276/mi² (106/km²). **Urban** 65%. **Capital** Budapest, 1,906,798. **Ethnic groups** Hungarian (Magyar) 90%, Gypsy 4%, German 3%, Serb 2%. **Languages** Hungarian. **Religions** Roman Catholic 68%, Calvinist 20%, Lutheran 5%. **Life expectancy** 74 female, 65 male. **Literacy** 99%.

POLITICS
Government Republic. **Parties** Alliance of Free Democrats, Democratic Forum, Socialist, others. **Suffrage** Universal, 18 and over. **Memberships** OECD, UN. **Subdivisions** 19 counties, 1 autonomous city.

ECONOMY
GDP $72,500,000,000. **Per capita** $7,080. **Monetary unit** Forint. **Trade partners** Former Soviet republics, Germany, Austria. **Exports** Raw materials, manu-

factures, food, agricultural products, fuels and energy. **Imports** Fuel, raw materials, manufactures, food, agricultural products.

LAND
Description Eastern Europe, landlocked. **Area** 35,919 mi² (93,030 km²). **Highest point** Kékes, 3,327 ft (1,014 m). **Lowest point** Along Tisza River, 256 ft (78 m).

People. Hungary's major ethnic group and language evolved from Magyar tribes who settled the region in the 9th century. Gypsies, Germans, and other peoples compose minorities. Most people are Roman Catholic and the literacy rate is high. Growth of industry since the 1940s has caused a rural-to-urban population shift.

Economy and the Land. Following World War II, Hungary pursued a program of industrialization, which is now in the process of being privatized. Agriculture, socialized under Communist rule, will also be returned to private ownership. Farming remains important, with productivity aided by fertile soils and a mild climate. Economic planning was decentralized in 1968, differentiating Hungary's economic structure from that of other Soviet-bloc countries and permitting some private enterprise. A flat plain dominates the landscape, and the lack of varied terrain results in a temperate climate throughout the country.

History and Politics. In the late 800s Magyar tribes from the east overcame Slavic and Germanic residents and settled the area. Invading Mongols caused much destruction in the 13th century. In the early 1500s, after repeated attacks, the Ottoman Turks dominated central Hungary. By the late 17th century, the entire region had come under the rule of Austria's Hapsburgs. Hungary succeeded in obtaining equal status with Austria in 1867, and the dual monarchy of Austria-Hungary emerged. Discontent and nationalistic demands increased until 1914 when a Bosnian Serb killed the heir to the Austro-Hungarian throne. Austria-Hungary declared war on Serbia, and World War I began, resulting in both territory and population losses for Hungary. At the end of the war, in 1918, Hungary became a republic, only to revert to monarchical rule in 1919. Hungary entered World War II on the side of Germany, and Adolf Hitler set up a pro-Nazi government in Hungary in 1944. The Soviet Union invaded that same year, and a Hungarian-Allied peace treaty was signed in 1947. Coalition rule evolved into a Communist government in 1949. In 1956 discontent erupted into rebellion, a new premier declared Hungary neutral, and Soviet forces entered Budapest to quell the uprising. A new constitution, which went into effect in 1990, helped move the country away from Communist domination. After several difficult years, the government's free market reforms are beginning to bear fruit. Hungary is expected to join NATO in 1999. ■

ICELAND

Official name Republic of Iceland

PEOPLE
Population 273,000. **Density** 6.9/mi² (2.7/km²).
Urban 92%. **Capital** Reykjavík, 100,850. **Ethnic groups** Icelander (mixed Norwegian and Celtic).
Languages Icelandic. **Religions** Lutheran 96%, other Christian 3%. **Life expectancy** 81 female, 76 male.
Literacy 100%.

POLITICS
Government Republic. **Parties** Independence, Progressive, Social Democratic, others. **Suffrage** Universal, 18 and over. **Memberships** NATO, OECD, UN. **Subdivisions** 8 regions.

ECONOMY
GDP $5,000,000,000. **Per capita** $18,727. **Monetary unit** Krona. **Trade partners** Exports: U.K., Germany, U.S. Imports: U.S., Germany, Netherlands. **Exports** Fish, animal products, aluminum, ferrosilicon, diatomite. **Imports** Machinery and transportation equipment, petroleum products, food, textiles.

LAND
Description North Atlantic island. **Area** 39,769 mi² (103,000 km²). **Highest point** Hvannadalshnúkur, 6,952 ft (2,119 m). **Lowest point** Sea level.

People. Most Icelanders are of Norwegian or Celtic ancestry, live in coastal cities, and belong to the Lutheran church. Icelandic, the predominant language, has changed little from the Old Norse of the original settlers and still resembles the language of 12th-century Nordic sagas.

Economy and the Land. Fish, found in the island's rich coastal waters, are the main natural resource and export. Iceland has a long tradition based on fishing, but the industry has recently suffered from decreasing markets and catches. Glaciers, lakes, hot springs, volcanoes, and a lava desert limit agricultural land but provide a scenic terrain. Although the island lies just south of the Arctic Circle, the climate is moderated by the Gulf Stream. Summers are damp and cool, and winters relatively mild but windy.

History and Politics. Norwegians began settlement of Iceland around the ninth century. The world's oldest parliament, the Althing, was established in Iceland in A.D. 930. Civil wars and instability during the 13th century led to the end of independence in 1262, when Iceland came under Norwegian rule. In the 14th century Norway was joined to Denmark's realm, and rule of Iceland passed to the Danes. The Althing was abolished in 1800 but re-established in 1843. In the 1918 Act of Union, Iceland became a sovereign state but retained its union with Denmark under a common king. Germany occupied Denmark in 1940 during World War II. British troops, replaced by Americans in 1941, protected Iceland from invasion. Following a 1944 plebiscite, Iceland left its union with Denmark and became an independent republic. ∎

INDIA

Official name Republic of India

PEOPLE
Population 975,530,000. **Density** 789/mi² (304/km²).
Urban 27%. **Capital** New Delhi, 301,297. **Ethnic groups** Indo-Aryan 72%, Dravidian 25%, Mongoloid and other 3%. **Languages** English, Hindi, Telugu, Bengali, indigenous. **Religions** Hindu 82%, Muslim 12%, Christian 2%, Sikh 2%. **Life expectancy** 63 female, 63 male. **Literacy** 52%.

POLITICS
Government Federal republic. **Parties** Bharatiya Janata, Congress (I), Janata Dal, others. **Suffrage** Universal, 18 and over. **Memberships** CW, UN. **Subdivisions** 25 states, 7 union territories.

ECONOMY
GDP $1,408,700,000,000. **Per capita** $1,491.
Monetary unit Rupee. **Trade partners** Exports: U.S., former Soviet republics, Japan. Imports: U.S., Japan, Germany. **Exports** Gems, jewelry, engineering goods, clothing, textiles, chemicals, tea. **Imports** Oil, petroleum products, machinery, gems, fertilizer, chemicals, iron, steel.

LAND
Description Southern Asia. **Area** 1,237,062 mi² (3,203,975 km²). **Highest point** Kānchenjunga, 28,209 ft (8,598 m). **Lowest point** Sea level. *The above information includes part of Jammu and Kashmir.*

People. India's population is composed of two main ethnic groups: the Indo-Aryans and the Dravidians. Found mostly in the north are the Indo-Aryans, a central Asian people who arrived in India around 1500 B.C., pushing the Dravidians to the south, where they remain concentrated today. A Mongoloid minority inhabits the mountains of the far north, and aboriginal groups live in the central forests and mountains. There are 15 official indigenous languages, as well as English, which is spoken by the majority of educated people. India is second only to China in population, and although Hindus are the religious majority, the country also has one of the world's largest Muslim populations. Christians, Sikhs, Jains, and Buddhists comprise additional religious minorities.

Economy and the Land. Economic conditions have improved since India became independent in 1947. Agriculture, upon which most Indians depend, is now more efficient, a result of modernization programs. Industry has expanded as well, and the country ranks high in its number of scientists and skilled laborers. Poverty, unemployment, and underemployment continue, however, partly due to rapid population growth and improved life expectancy. Many natural resources, including coal, iron ore, bauxite, and manganese, remain undeveloped. India comprises three land regions: the Himalayas along the northern border; the Gangetic plain, a fertile northern region; and the peninsula, made up mostly of the Deccan, a plateau region. The climate in India ranges from temperate to tropical monsoon.

History and Politics. India's civilization dates back to 2500 B.C. when the Dravidians flourished. Aryan tribes invaded 1,000 years later, bringing the beliefs that evolved into Hinduism, and various empires followed. Invasions beginning around A.D. 450 brought the Huns and, during the 7th and 8th centuries, Arab conquerors introduced Islam. The Mogul Empire, under a series of Muslim rulers, began in the 1500s, and the British East India Company established trading posts in the 1600s. By 1757 the East India Company had become India's major power, and by the 1850s the company controlled nearly all present-day India, Pakistan, and Bangladesh. An Indian rebellion in 1857 caused Britain to take over the East India Company's rule. Demands for independence increased after a controversial massacre of Indians by British troops in 1919. By 1920, Mohandas Gandhi had emerged as the leader of an independence campaign based on nonviolent disobedience and noncooperation. The country gained independence in 1947 and

established Pakistan as a separate Muslim state. Ongoing disputes include a border conflict with China that erupted into fighting in 1959 and 1962, and a disagreement with Pakistan over the Muslim region of Kashmir. In 1974, India held its first underground nuclear test. Since then, both India and Pakistan have worked to develop their nuclear weapons capability. In the state of Kashmir, which had been under direct presidential rule for six years, the local government was restored, sparking separatist violence. In 1998 India defied the world's nuclear superpowers by conducting underground nuclear tests. Pakistan soon reciprocated, with its own nuclear test, increasing the risk of nuclear proliferation in the area. Throughout India, violence between Hindus and Muslims has increased since a coalition government was formed in 1998. ∎

INDONESIA

Official name Republic of Indonesia

PEOPLE
Population 211,340,000. **Density** 281/mi² (108/km²). **Urban** 36%. **Capital** Jakarta, Java I., 8,227,746. **Ethnic groups** Javanese 45%, Sundanese 14%, Madurese 8%, coastal Malay 8%. **Languages** Bahasa Indonesia (Malay), English, Dutch, indigenous. **Religions** Muslim 87%, Protestant 6%, Catholic 3%, Hindu 2%. **Life expectancy** 67 female, 63 male. **Literacy** 84%.

POLITICS
Government Republic. **Parties** Democracy, Golkar, Development Unity. **Suffrage** Universal, 17 and over or married. **Memberships** ASEAN, OPEC, UN. **Subdivisions** 27 provinces.

ECONOMY
GDP $710,900,000,000. **Per capita** $3,612. **Monetary unit** Rupiah. **Trade partners** Exports: Japan, U.S., Singapore. Imports: Japan, U.S., Germany. **Exports** Petroleum and natural gas, timber, textiles, rubber, coffee. **Imports** Machinery, chemicals, manufactures.

LAND

Description Southeastern Asian islands. **Area** 752,410 mi² (1,948,732 km²). **Highest point** Jaya Pk., 16,503 ft (5,030 m). **Lowest point** Sea level.

People. Indonesia is the fourth most populous country in the world. The majority of the people are Malay, which includes several subgroups, such as Javanese, Sundanese, Madurese, and coastal Malay. There are more than 200 indigenous languages, but the official language is Bahasa Indonesia, a Malay dialect. Most people live in small farm villages and follow ancient customs that emphasize cooperation. Muslim traders brought Islam to Indonesia, and most of the population is Muslim. Many Indonesians combine spirit worship with Islam or Christianity. Indonesia's rich cultural heritage includes many ancient temples.

Economy and the Land. Indonesia is a leading producer of petroleum in the Far East. The area also has large deposits of minerals and natural gas. Agriculture is still a major economic activity, and rice remains an important crop, though overpopulation threatens the economy and food supply. The country's more than 13,600 islands form a natural barrier between the Indian and Pacific oceans, making the straits between the islands important for world trade and military strategy. Java, the most industrial and heavily populated island, has volcanic mountains and narrow fertile plains along the northern coast. Indonesia includes most of Borneo, the third largest island in the world. Other major Indonesian islands are Sulawesi, Sumatra, and Irian Jaya (the western half of New Guinea), which also feature inland mountains and limited coastal plains. The climate is tropical, with seasonal monsoons.

History and Politics. Indonesian civilization is more than 2,500 years old and has produced two major empires with influence throughout Southeast Asia. The Portuguese arrived in the 16th century but were outnumbered by the Dutch, who eventually gained control of most of the islands and established a plantation colony. An independence movement began early in the 20th century, and Japan encouraged Indonesian nationalism during World War II. Shortly after the Japanese surrendered in 1945, Indonesia proclaimed itself an independent republic. Economic and political instability led to an attempted Communist coup in 1965. In 1975, Indonesia invaded and annexed East Timor. It is believed that 100,000 (one in seven) East Timorese were killed during the invasion. The government has outlawed the Communist party and strengthened relations with the West, at the same time establishing trade talks with China. In East Timor, reports of human rights abuses continue. In July 1997, an economic crisis in Thailand caused the value of Indonesia's currency to plummet, creating extreme inflation. The government was forced to ask the International

Monetary Fund for more than $53 billion in aid; in return the government would be required to make drastic economic reforms. Food prices rose even further after a drought caused crop failures. These problems sparked rioting and attacks on individuals of Chinese descent, many of whom own businesses in Indonesia. In May 1998 the legislature called for Suharto's resignation, and he soon stepped down. Bacharuddin Jusuf Habibie, Vice President and a close friend of Suharto's, was immediately sworn in as interim President. ■

IRAN

Official name Islamic Republic of Iran

PEOPLE

Population 68,280,000. **Density** 108/mi² (42/km²). **Urban** 60%. **Capital** Tehrān, 6,475,527. **Ethnic groups** Persian 51%, Azerbaijani 24%, Kurdish 7%. **Languages** Farsi, Turkish dialects, Kurdish. **Religions** Shiite Muslim 89%, Sunni Muslim 10%. **Life expectancy** 70 female, 69 male. **Literacy** 72%.

POLITICS

Government Islamic republic. **Parties** Militant Clerics Association, Tehran Militant Clergy Association, Others. **Suffrage** Universal, 15 and over. **Memberships** OPEC, UN. **Subdivisions** 24 provinces.

ECONOMY

GDP $323,500,000,000. **Per capita** $4,951. **Monetary unit** Rial. **Trade partners** Exports: Japan, Italy, France. Imports: Germany, Japan, Italy. **Exports** Petroleum, carpets, fruit, nuts, hides, iron, steel. **Imports** Machinery, military supplies, metal works, food, drugs, technical services.

LAND

Description Southwestern Asia. **Area** 630,578 mi² (1,633,189 km²). **Highest point** Mt. Demavend, 18,386 ft (5,604 m). **Lowest point** Caspian Sea, -92 ft (-28 m).

People. Most Iranians are of Aryan ancestry, descended from an Asiatic people who migrated to the area in ancient times. The Aryan groups include majority Persians and minority Gilani, Mazanderani, Kurds, Lur, Bakhtiari, and Baluchi. Turks and Azeries are the major non-Aryan minorities. Nearly all Iranians are Muslim, mainly of the Shiite sect, and the country is an Islamic republic, with law based on Islamic teachings. Minority religious groups, especially Baha'is, have been persecuted. Due to aridity and a harsh mountain-and-desert terrain, the population is concentrated in the west and north.

Economy and the Land. Iran's previously rapid economic development has slowed as a result of a 1979 revolution and a war with Iraq. Small-scale farming, manufacturing, and trading are the current economic trends. Oil remains the most important export, although output has decreased due to changes in economic policy and other factors. Persian carpets also continue as elements of trade. Iran's terrain consists mainly of a central plateau marked by desert and surrounded by mountains; thus agriculture is limited, and the country remains dependent on imported food. The central region is one of the most arid areas on Earth, and summers throughout most of the country are long, hot, and dry, with higher humidity along the Persian Gulf and Caspian coast. Winters are cold in the mountains of the northwest, but mild on the plain. The Caspian coastal region is generally subtropical.

History and Politics. Iran's history is one of the world's oldest, with a civilization dating back several thousand years. Around 1500 B.C., Aryan immigrants began arriving from central Asia, calling the region Iran, or land of the Aryans, and splitting into two groups: the Medes and the Persians. In the 6th century B.C., Cyrus the Great founded the Persian, or Achaemenian, Empire, which came to encompass Babylonia, Palestine, Syria, and Asia Minor. Alexander the Great conquered the region in the 4th century B.C. Various dynasties followed, and Muslim Arabs invaded in the A.D. 600s and established Islam as the major religion. The following centuries saw Iran's boundaries expand and recede under various rulers, and increasing political awareness resulted in a 1906 constitution and parliament. In 1908 oil was discovered in the region, and modernization programs began during the reign of Reza Shah Pahlavi, who came to power in 1925. In 1935 the name of the country, formerly Persia, was officially changed to Iran. Despite Iran's declared neutrality in World War II, the Allies invaded and obtained rights to use the country as a supply route to the Soviet Union. The presence of foreign influences caused nationalism to increase sharply after the war. Mohammad Reza Pahlavi—who succeeded his father as shah—instituted social and economic reforms during the 1960s. Many Muslims felt the reforms violated religious law and resented the increasing Western orientation of the country and the absolute power of the shah. Led by Muslim leader Ayatollah Ruholla Khomeini, revolutionaries

seized the government in 1979, declaring Iran an Islamic republic. Khomeini remained the religious leader of Iran until his death in 1989. In 1988 a long and destructive war with Iraq ended. Hashemi Rafsanjani was elected president two years later. Recent signs of military buildup and the growing strength of the fundamentalist movement throughout the world continue to cause concern in the West. The United States imposed a trade embargo against Iran in 1995 and added more sanctions in 1996. In 1997 Mohammed Khatami, a moderate, was elected President. Though the President has little power, his election demonstrated the people's desire for a less conservative government. ■

IRAQ

Official name Republic of Iraq

PEOPLE
Population 22,610,000. **Density** 134/mi² (52/km²). **Urban** 75%. **Capital** Baghdād, 3,841,268. **Ethnic groups** Arab 75%-80%; Kurdish 15-20%; Turkoman, Assyrian, or other 5%. **Languages** Arabic, Kurdish, Assyrian, Armenian. **Religions** Shiite Muslim 60-65%, Sunni Muslim 32-37%, Christian and others 3%. **Life expectancy** 70 female, 67 male. **Literacy** 71%.

POLITICS
Government Republic. **Parties** Ba'th. **Suffrage** Universal, 18 and over. **Memberships** AL, OPEC, UN. **Subdivisions** 15 governorates, 3 autonomous regions.

ECONOMY
GDP $41,100,000,000. **Per capita** $1,956. **Monetary unit** Dinar. **Trade partners** Exports: U.S., Brazil, Turkey, Japan. Imports: Germany, U.S., Turkey, France, U.K. **Exports** Petroleum, petroleum products, fertilizer, sulphur. **Imports** Manufactures, food.

LAND
Description Southwestern Asia. **Area** 169,235 mi² (438,317 km²). **Highest point** 11,835 ft (3,607 m). **Lowest point** Sea level.

People. The descendants of one of the world's oldest civilizations inhabit Iraq. Most Iraqis are Muslim Arabs and speak Arabic. In the northwest are the minority Kurds, who are predominantly Muslim, speak Kurdish, and follow a non-Arab lifestyle. Kurdish demands for self-rule have led to occasional rebellion.

Economy and the Land. Oil is the mainstay of Iraq's economy, and nearly all economic development has focused on the petroleum industry, nationalized in the 1970s. Despite its oil wealth, Iraq, like Iran, was economically drained by the Iran-Iraq war. Most farmland lies near the Tigris and Euphrates Rivers. The terrain is marked by northeastern mountains, southern and western deserts, and the plains of upper and lower Iraq, between the Tigris and Euphrates rivers. The climate is generally hot and dry.

History and Politics. In ancient times, civilizations such as the Sumerian, Babylonian, and Parthian flourished in the area of the Tigris and Euphrates. Once known as Mesopotamia, the region was the setting for many biblical events. After coming under Persian rule in the 6th century B.C., Mesopotamia fell to Alexander the Great in the 4th century B.C. Invading Arabs brought the Muslim religion in the 7th century A.D., and for a time Baghdād was the capital and cultural center of the Arab empire. Thirteenth-century Mongol invaders were followed by Ottoman Turks in the 16th century. Ottoman rule continued and, following a British invasion during World War I, Mesopotamia became a British mandate at the end of the war. In 1921 the monarchy of Iraq was established, and independence was gained in 1932. Iraq and other countries formed the Arab League in 1945 and participated in a war against Israel in 1948. Opposition to monarchical rule increased during the 1950s and the country was declared a republic, after a 1958 military coup. Instability, evidenced by coups, continued into the 1970s. The political climate was further complicated by occasional uprisings by Kurds demanding autonomy. War with Iran, which caused heavy losses on both sides, continued intermittently through the early 1980s, ending in a 1988 cease-fire agreement. In August 1990 Iraq invaded Kuwait and forced the government into exile. A coalition of countries under the military direction of the United States forced Iraq to withdraw in early 1991. After the war the United Nations established "no-fly" zones in northern and southern Iraq to protect Kurdish and Shiite rebels. Despite this, Turkey has attacked the Kurds in northern Iraq as recently as 1997. Iraq is under UN trade sanctions, which will not be lifted until the country destroys its weapons of mass destruction. Iraq's government has impeded inspections meant to verify that the weapons arsenals are being destroyed. The trade embargo is causing great hardship for Iraqis. ■

IRELAND

Official name Ireland

PEOPLE
Population 3,555,000. **Density** 131/mi² (51/km²). **Urban** 58%. **Capital** Dublin, 478,389. **Ethnic groups** Irish (Celtic), English. **Languages** English, Irish Gaelic. **Religions** Roman Catholic 93%, Church of Ireland 3%. **Life expectancy** 79 female, 73 male. **Literacy** 98%.

POLITICS
Government Republic. **Parties** Fianna Fail, Fine Gael, Labor, others. **Suffrage** Universal, 18 and over. **Memberships** EU, OECD, UN. **Subdivisions** 26 counties.

ECONOMY
GDP $54,600,000,000. **Per capita** $15,350. **Monetary unit** Pound (punt). **Trade partners** Exports: U.K., Germany, France. Imports: U.K., U.S., Germany. **Exports** Chemicals, data processing equipment, machinery, livestock, animal products. **Imports** Food, feed grain, petroleum, petroleum products, machines, textiles, clothing.

LAND
Description Northwestern European island (five-sixths of island of Ireland). **Area** 27,137 mi² (70,285 km²). **Highest point** Carrauntoohil, 3,406 ft (1,038 m). **Lowest point** Sea level.

People. Most of Ireland's population is descended from the Celts, a people who flourished in Europe and Great Britain in ancient times. Irish Gaelic, a form of ancient Celtic, and English are official languages. Most people are Roman Catholic. Protestants mainly belong to the Church of Ireland, a member of the Anglican Communion. With a long literary tradition, the country has contributed greatly to world literature.

Economy and the Land. Ireland's economy was agricultural until the 1950s, when a program of rapid industrialization began. This expansion resulted in significant foreign investment, especially by the United States. Most of the Irish labor force is unionized. Agriculture continues to play an important role, however, and food is produced for domestic and foreign consumption. The country of Ireland occupies most of the island but excludes Northern Ireland, which is part of the United Kingdom. The fertile central region features green, rolling hills, suitable for farming and pastureland, and is surrounded by coastal highlands. The climate is temperate maritime, with mild summers and winters and plentiful rainfall.

History and Politics. Around the 4th century B.C., Ireland's indigenous population was conquered by Gaels, a Celtic tribe, from continental Europe and Great Britain. Christianity was introduced by St. Patrick in A.D. 432, and periodic Viking raids began near the end of the 8th century. In the 12th century the pope made Henry II the Norman king of England, overlord of the island; the English intervened in a dispute between Irish kings; and centuries of British influence began. As British control grew, so did Irish Catholic hostility, arising from seizure of land by English settlers, the Protestant Reformation, and the elimination of political and religious freedoms. The Protestant majority of present-day Northern Ireland was established in the 1600s, when land taken from the Irish was distributed to English and Scottish Protestants. In 1801 the British Act of Union established the United Kingdom of Great Britain, and Northern Ireland. Religious freedom was regained in 1829, but the struggle for independence continued. Most of the Irish depended upon potatoes as a staple food, and hundreds of thousands died or emigrated in the 1840s when the crop failed because of a plant disease. Following an armed rebellion, the Irish Free State, a dominion of Great Britain, was created in 1921, with the predominantly Protestant counties in the north remaining under British rule. The country became a republic in 1949. The explosive issue of reunification with Northern Ireland continues to dominate Irish politics. ■

ISLE OF MAN

See UNITED KINGDOM.

ISRAEL

Official name State of Israel

PEOPLE
Population 5,765,000. **Density** 719/mi² (278/km²). **Urban** 91%. **Capital** Jerusalem, 567,100. **Ethnic groups** Jewish 82%, Arab and others 18%. **Languages** Hebrew, Arabic. **Religions** Jewish 82%, Muslim 14%, Christian 2%, Druze 2%. **Life expectancy** 79 female, 75 male. **Literacy** 96%.

POLITICS
Government Republic. **Parties** Labor, Likud, MERETZ, SHAS, others. **Suffrage** Universal, 18 and over. **Memberships** UN. **Subdivisions** 6 districts.

ECONOMY
GDP $80,100,000,000. **Per capita** $15,638. **Monetary unit** Shekel. **Trade partners** Exports: U.S., Japan, U.K. Imports: U.S., Belgium, Germany. **Exports** Machinery, equipment, cut diamonds, chemicals, textiles, clothing, metals. **Imports** military equipment, investment goods, rough diamonds, oil, raw materials.

LAND
Description Southwestern Asia. **Area** 8,019 mi² (20,770 km²). **Highest point** Mt. Meron, 3,963 ft (1,208 m). **Lowest point** Dead Sea, -1,339 ft (-408 m).

People. Most Israelis are Jewish immigrants or descendants of Jews who settled in the region in the late 1800s. The two main ethnic groups are the Ashkenazim of central and eastern European origin and the Sephardim of the Mediterranean and Middle East. The non-Jewish population is predominantly Arab and Muslim, and many Palestinians inhabit the Israeli-occupied West Bank, the status of which is still in dispute. Hebrew and Arabic are the official languages, and both are used on documents and currency. Conflict between conservative and liberal Jewish groups has spilled over into the country's political life.

Economy and the Land. Despite drastic levels of inflation and a constant trade deficit, Israel has experienced continuous economic growth. Skilled labor supports the market economy based on services, manufacturing, and commerce. Tourism and grants and loans from other countries are other major sources of income. The country is poor in natural resources, but through improved irrigation and soil conservation Israel now produces much of its own food. Because of its limited natural resources, Israel must import most of the raw materials it needs for industry. The region's varied terrain includes coastal plains, central mountains, the Jordan Rift Valley, and the desert region of the Negev. Except in the Negev, the climate is temperate.

History and Politics. Israel comprises much of the historic region of Palestine, known in ancient times as Canaan and the site of most biblical history. Hebrews arrived in this region around 1900 B.C. The area experienced subsequent immigration and invasion by diverse peoples, including Assyrians, Babylonians, and Persians. In 63 B.C. it became part of the Roman Empire, was renamed Judaea and finally, Palestine. In the A.D. 600s invading Arabs brought Islam to the area, and Muslims comprised a majority by the early 1500s when Ottoman Turks conquered the region. During the late 1800s, as a result of oppression in eastern Europe, many Jews immigrated to Palestine, hoping to establish a Jewish state. This movement, called Zionism, and the increasing Jewish population led to Arab-Jewish tensions. Turkey sided with Germany in World War I, and after the war the Ottoman Empire collapsed. Palestine became a mandated territory of Britain in 1920. Jewish immigration and Arab-Jewish hostility increased during the years of Nazi Germany. Additional unrest arose from conflicting interpretations of British promises and the terms of the mandate. In 1947, Britain turned to the United Nations for help, and in 1948 the country of Israel was established. Neighboring Arab countries invaded immediately, and war ensued, during which Israel gained some land. A truce was signed in 1949, but Arab-Israeli wars broke out periodically throughout the 1950s, 1960s, and 1970s. Israel signed a peace treaty with Egypt in 1979, annexed the Golan Heights in 1981, and returned the Sinai to Egypt the following year. The years since have seen continual conflict over the occupation of the Gaza Strip and West Bank. In 1993, an historic accord between Israel and the Palestinians was reached. Limited autonomy over the Gaza Strip and Jericho were granted first, followed by expanded autonomy throughout the West Bank. Israelis remain divided about the future of the accord, however, and its ability to bring about lasting peace. In 1995 Israel's Prime Minister, Itzhak Rabin, was assassinated. The following year, Binyamin Netanyahu, a conservative, was elected Prime Minister. Although the Netanyahu government has continued to negotiate with the Palestinians, it also has encouraged the construction of Israeli housing in occupied areas. ∎

ITALY

Official name Italian Republic

PEOPLE
Population 57,570,000. **Density** 495/mi² (191/km²). **Urban** 67%. **Capital** Rome, 2,649,765. **Ethnic groups** Italian (Latin). **Languages** Italian, German, French, Slovene. **Religions** Roman Catholic 98%. **Life expectancy** 79 female, 75 male. **Literacy** 98%.

POLITICS
Government Republic. **Parties** Democratic Party of the Left, Forza Italia, National Alliance, Northern League, others. **Suffrage** Universal, 18 and over. **Memberships** EU, NATO, OECD, UN. **Subdivisions** 20 regions.

ECONOMY
GDP $1,088,600,000,000. **Per capita** $18,666. **Monetary unit** Lira. **Trade partners** Exports: Germany, France, U.S. Imports: Germany, France, Netherlands. **Exports** Textiles, clothing, metals, transportation

equipment, chemicals, machinery. **Imports** Petroleum, machines, chemicals, metals, food, agricultural products.

LAND
Description Southern Europe. **Area** 116,336 mi² (301,309 km²). **Highest point** Mont Blanc (Monte Bianco), 15,774 ft (4,808 m). **Lowest point** Sea level.

People. Italy is populated mainly by Italian Roman Catholics. Most speak Italian, although dialects often differ from region to region. Despite an ethnic homogeneity, the people exhibit diversity in terms of politics and culture. The country has about 12 political parties, and northern inhabitants are relatively prosperous, employed primarily in industry, whereas southerners are generally farmers and often poor. The birthplace of the Renaissance, Italy has made substantial contributions to world culture.

Economy and the Land. The Italian economy is based on private enterprise, although the government is involved in some industrial and commercial activities. Industry and commercial agriculture are centered in the north, which produces steel, textiles, and chemicals. A hilly terrain makes parts of the south unsuited for crop raising, and livestock grazing is a main activity. Tourism is also important; visitors are drawn by the northern Alps, the sunny south, and the Italian cultural tradition. The island of Sicily, off Italy's southwest coast, produces fruits, olives, and grapes. Sardinia, a western island, engages in some sheep and wheat raising. Except for the northern Po Valley, narrow areas along the coast, and a small section of the southern peninsula, Italy's terrain is mainly rugged and mountainous. The climate varies from cold in the Alps to mild and Mediterranean in other regions.

History and Politics. Early influences in Italy included Greeks, Etruscans, and Celts. From the 5th century B.C. to the 5th century A.D., the dominant people were Romans descended from Sabines and neighboring Latins, who inhabited the Latium coast. Following the demise of the Roman Empire, rulers and influences included Byzantines; Lombards, an invading Germanic tribe; and the Frankish King Charlemagne, whom the pope crowned emperor of the Romans in 800. During the 11th century Italy became a region of city-states, and its cultural life led to the Renaissance, which started in the 1300s. As the city-states weakened, Italy was invaded and ruled by France, Spain, and Austria, with these countries controlling various regions at different times. In 1861 Victor Emmanuel II, the king of Sardinia, proclaimed Italy a kingdom, and by 1871 the country included the entire peninsula, with Rome as the capital and Victor Emmanuel as king. In 1922 Benito Mussolini, the leader of Italy's Fascist movement, came to power and ruled as dictator until his death at the hands of Italian partisans in 1945. The country allied itself with Germany in World War II, and a popular resistance movement evolved. Recent politics have been marked by a volatility that has produced frequent changes in government. In 1996 a movement in northern Italy began to campaign for secession, claiming north-south inequities in government taxation and spending. ■

IVORY COAST see COTE D'IVOIRE

JAMAICA

Official name Jamaica

PEOPLE
Population 2,626,000. **Density** 619/mi² (239/km²). **Urban** 54%. **Capital** Kingston, 552,931. **Ethnic groups** Black 76%, mulatto 15%. **Languages** English, Creole. **Religions** Church of God 18%, Baptist 10%, Anglican 7%, Seventh-Day Adventist 7%. **Life expectancy** 77 female, 72 male. **Literacy** 85%.

POLITICS
Government Parliamentary state. **Parties** Labor, People's National, National Democratic Movement. **Suffrage** Universal, 18 and over. **Memberships** CW, OAS, UN. **Subdivisions** 14 parishes.

ECONOMY
GDP $8,200,000,000. **Per capita** $3,173. **Monetary unit** Dollar. **Trade partners** Exports: U.S., U.K., Canada. Imports: U.S., U.K., Venezuela. **Exports** Bauxite, alumina, sugar, rum, bananas. **Imports** Machines, transportation equipment, food, fuel, manufactures, building materials.

LAND
Description Caribbean island. **Area** 4,244 mi² (10,991 km²). **Highest point** Blue Mountain Pk., 7,402 ft (2,256 m). **Lowest point** Sea level.

People. Most Jamaicans are of African or Afro-European descent, and the majority are Christian. English is the official language, but many Jamaicans also speak Creole. Population is concentrated on the coastal plains, where the main commercial crops are also grown.

Economy and the Land. Agriculture is the traditional mainstay, and more than one-third of the population is engaged in farming. Sugar cane and bananas are principal crops. Mining is also important, and Jamaica is a leading producer of bauxite. The tropical climate, tempered by ocean breezes, makes the island a popular tourist destination. A mountainous inland region is surrounded by coastal plains and beaches.

History and Politics. Christopher Columbus claimed the island for Spain in 1494. As the enslaved native population died out, blacks were brought from Africa to work plantations. Britain invaded and gained control of Jamaica in the 17th century, and for a time the island was one of the most important sugar and slave centers of the New World. In 1838 the British abolished slavery, the plantation economy broke down, and most slaves became independent farmers. Local political control began in the 1930s, and the country became fully independent in 1962. Since then it has faced unemployment, inflation, and poverty, with periodic social unrest. ■

JAPAN

Official name Japan

PEOPLE
Population 125,850,000. **Density** 863/mi² (333/km²). **Urban** 78%. **Capital** Tōkyō, Honshū I., 8,163,573. **Ethnic groups** Japanese 99.4%. **Languages** Japanese. **Religions** Buddhist and Shinto 84%. **Life expectancy** 83 female, 77 male. **Literacy** 99%.

POLITICS
Government Constitutional monarchy. **Parties** Democratic, Liberal Democratic, Shinshinto, others. **Suffrage** Universal, 20 and over. **Memberships** OECD, UN. **Subdivisions** 47 prefectures.

ECONOMY
GDP $2,679,200,000,000. **Per capita** $21,304. **Monetary unit** Yen. **Trade partners** Exports: U.S., Germany, Korea. Imports: U.S., Indonesia, Korea. **Exports** Machinery, motor vehicles, consumer

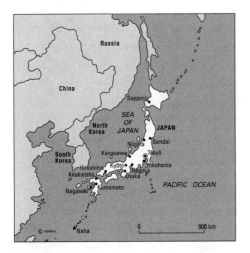

Russia

China

Sapporo

SEA
OF
JAPAN

North
Korea

JAPAN

Niigata Sendai

South
Korea

Kanazawa Tokyō

Hiroshima Kyōto Yokohama
Kitakyūshū Nagoya
Osaka

Nagasaki Kumamoto

PACIFIC OCEAN

Naha

0   900 km

electronics. **Imports** Manufactures, fuel, food and raw materials.

LAND

Description Eastern Asian islands. **Area** 145,850 mi² (377,750 km²). **Highest point** Mt. Fuji, 12,388 ft (3,776 m). **Lowest point** Hachiro-gata reclamation area, Honshū I., -13 ft (-4 m).

People. The Japanese constitute Japan's major ethnic group; there is a small Korean minority. Shintoism and Buddhism are the principal religions. Almost all the population lives on the coastal plains. Japan's culture blends East and West, with karate, tea ceremonies, and kimonos balanced by baseball, fast food, and business suits. Although its arts have been greatly influenced by China, Japan has developed distinctive music, literature, and painting.

Economy and the Land. One of the world's leading industrial powers, Japan is remarkable for its economic growth rate since World War II, considering that it has few natural resources. It has also become famous for its innovative technology. Manufacturing is the basis of the economy, and Japan is a leading producer of ships, machinery, cars, and electronic equipment. Its chemical, iron, and steel industries are extremely profitable. Agriculture's part in the economy is small, since little of the rugged island terrain is arable. Fishing still plays a significant role in Japan's economy as Japan maintains one of the world's largest fishing fleets. Overseas trade has expanded rapidly since the 1960s because Japan requires raw materials for its many industries. Trade barriers and the competitiveness of Japanese products overseas have led to trade deficits with many Western countries. Japan's mountainous terrain includes both active and dormant volcanoes; earthquakes occur occasionally. The climate ranges from subtropical to temperate.

History and Politics. Legend states that Japan's first emperor was descended from the sun goddess and came to power around 600 B.C. The arrival of Buddhism, Confucianism, and new technologies from China in the 5th and 6th centuries A.D. revolutionized society. Feuding nobles controlled Japan between 1192 and 1867 and ruled as *shoguns*, or generals, in the name of the emperor. The warrior class, or *samurai*, developed early in this period. The arrival of Europeans in the 16th century caused fear of an invasion among the *shoguns*, and in the 1630s they dissolved all foreign contacts. Japan's isolation lasted until 1854 when United States Commodore Matthew Perry opened the country to the West with a show of force. The subsequent Meiji Restoration modernized Japan by adopting Western technologies and legal systems, and by stressing industrialization and education. Japan embarked on military expansion in the late 19th century, annexing Korea in 1910 and adding to its holdings after participating in World War I as a British ally. It occupied Manchuria in 1931 and invaded China in 1937. As part of the Axis powers in World War II, Japan attacked U.S. military bases in Pearl Harbor, Hawaii, in 1941. After the U.S. dropped atomic bombs on Hiroshima and Nagasaki in 1945, Japan surrendered. Allied forces occupied the country until 1952, by which time the Japanese had approved a constitution that shifted power from the emperor to the people and abolished the military. With the help of U.S. aid, Japan experienced a rapid economic recovery. In the 1970s and 1980s Japan's uniquely organized economy, with close cooperation between the government and private industry, fostered its tremendous growth into one of the world's largest economies. This resulted in a large trade imbalance with the U.S. that still exists today. Foreign trade issues and an economic slump dominated the early 1990s, and presently Japan is fighting off a recession. ∎

JERSEY See UNITED KINGDOM.

JORDAN

Official name Hashemite Kingdom of Jordan

PEOPLE

Population 4,380,000. **Density** 125/mi² (48/km²). **Urban** 72%. **Capital** 'Ammān, 963,490. **Ethnic groups** Arab 98%, Circassian 1%, Armenian 1%. **Languages** Arabic. **Religions** Sunni Muslim 92%, Christian 8%. **Life expectancy** 72 female, 68 male. **Literacy** 87%.

POLITICS

Government Constitutional monarchy. **Parties** Islamic Action Front, others. **Suffrage** Universal, 20 and over. **Memberships** AL, UN. **Subdivisions** 8 governorates.

ECONOMY

GDP $19,300,000,000. **Per capita** $4,646. **Monetary unit** Dinar. **Trade partners** Exports: India, Iraq, Saudi Arabia. Imports: U.S., Iraq, France. **Exports** Phosphates, fertilizer, potash, agricultural products, manufactures. **Imports** Petroleum, machinery, transportation equipment, food, livestock, manufactures.

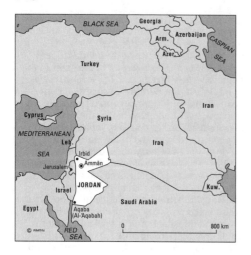

LAND
Description Southwestern Asia. **Area** 35,135 mi² (91,000 km²). **Highest point** Mt. Ramm, 5,755 ft (1,754 m). **Lowest point** Dead Sea, -1,339 ft (-408 m).

People. Most Jordanians are Arabs, but there are Circassian, Armenian, and Kurdish minorities, as well as a small nomadic population, the Bedouins, in desert areas. About one-third of all Jordanians are Palestinian refugees, displaced by Arab-Israeli wars. Jordan is the only Arab country that has granted citizenship to the Palestinians. Arabic is the official language, and most people are Sunni Muslim, legacies of the Muslim conquest in A.D. 600s.

Economy and the Land. A country with few natural resources, limited rainfall, and little arable land, Jordan has suffered further economic damage from an influx of refugees and the chronic political instability of the Middle East. In a 1967 war with Israel, Jordan lost control of Jerusalem and the West Bank, which made up about half the country's farmland. Agriculture remains the most important activity, and tourism has helped bolster a weak economy that relies heavily on foreign aid and investment from the United States and Arab countries. There is some light industry and mining. The Jordan River forms the country's westernmost boundary, and the terrain is marked by deserts, mountains, and rolling plains. The climate ranges from Mediterranean in the West to desert in the East.

History and Politics. Jordan is the site of one of the world's oldest settlements, dating back to about 8000 B.C. The area came under the rule of the Hebrews, Assyrians, Egyptians, Persians, Greeks, and Romans, and around A.D. 636, Arab Muslims. Rule by the Ottoman Turks began in the 16th century, and in World War I Arab armies helped the British defeat Turkey. At the end of the war, present-day Israel and Jordan became the British mandate of Palestine, which in 1922 was divided into the mandates of Transjordan,

lying east of the Jordan River, and Palestine, lying to the West. Transjordan gained full independence in 1946. In 1948 the Palestine mandate created Israel, and Arab-Israeli fighting ensued. After capturing the West Bank, Transjordan was renamed Jordan in 1949. During the Arab-Israeli Six-Day War in 1967, this region and the Jordanian section of Jerusalem fell to Israel. After each war, Jordan's Palestinian refugee population grew. A 1970 civil war pitted the Jordanian monarchy against Palestinian guerrillas who sought to overthrow the government. The guerrillas were expelled following the war, but subsequent Arab-Israeli hostilities led to Jordan's recognition of the Palestine Liberation Organization. Although Jordan relinquished all claims to the Israeli-held West Bank area in 1988, the country continues to be involved in discussions on the fate of the Palestinians who live there. Jordan is a constitutional monarchy and has been headed by King Hussein since 1953. In the 1990s King Hussein's moderate policies were increasingly criticized, not only by Palestinian radicals but also by a growing number of Muslim fundamentalists. Parliamentary elections in 1993 were won by moderates, however, endorsing peace efforts that resulted in an historic 1994 peace treaty with Israel. ∎

KAZAKHSTAN

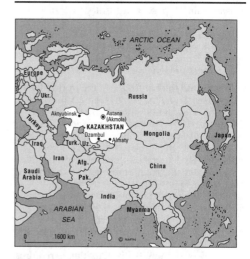

Official name Republic of Kazakhstan

PEOPLE
Population 16,875,000. **Density** 16/mi² (6.2/km²). **Urban** 60%. **Capital** Astana (Akmola), 286,000. **Ethnic groups** Kazakh 40%, Russian 38%, German 6%, Ukrainian 5%. **Languages** Kazakh, Russian. **Religions** Muslim 47%, Russian Orthodox 44%. **Life expectancy** 75 female, 67 male. **Literacy** 98%.

POLITICS
Government Republic. **Parties** Democratic, People's Congress, People's Unity, Socialist, others. **Suffrage**

Universal, 18 and over. **Memberships** UN. **Subdivisions** 19 oblasts.

ECONOMY
GDP $46,900,000,000. **Per capita** $2,730. **Monetary unit** Tenge. **Trade partners** Exports: Russia, Ukraine, Uzbekistan. Imports: Russia and other former Soviet republics. **Exports** Petroleum, metals, chemicals, grain, wool, meat, coal. **Imports** Machinery and parts, industrial materials, oil, gas.

LAND
Description Central Asia, landlocked. **Area** 1,049,156 mi² (2,717,300 km²). **Highest point** Khan-Tengri Pk., 22,949 ft (6,995 m). **Lowest point** Karagiye Basin, -433 ft (-132 m).

People. Kazakhstan is the traditional homeland of the Kazakh people, Turkic-speaking descendants of the Mongols. Prior to Soviet control, most Kazakhs were Muslim and nomadic. Immigration into Kazakhstan from other republics has left the Kazakhs with only 42 percent of the population. Russians are the next largest group, with more than one-third of the population.

Economy and the Land. The world's ninth-largest country in land area, Kazakhstan is generally a vast tableland. The climate is harsh and dry, with hot summers and cold winters. Agriculture is concentrated in the north and the irrigated areas of the southeast. Industry, based mainly on the country's vast mineral resources, makes the largest contributions to the economy. Kazakhstan produces large amounts of coal and boasts tremendous undeveloped oil resources.

History and Politics. Two important trade routes brought early travelers through Kazakhstan on their way to China. The people known as the Kazakhs have inhabited the region since the 16th century. Russian expansion into the region began in the mid-1700s, and one of the area's most powerful states joined the Russian empire in the mid-1800s. After the Russian revolution, the region was organized into the Kirghiz Autonomous Republic, but then enlarged in 1925 to form the Kazak Autonomous Republic. Kazakhstan became a Soviet Republic in 1936. As the heartland of the Soviet Union, Kazakhstan was home to the country's space program and held much of the country's nuclear arsenal. Since the break-up of the Soviet Union in late 1991, Kazakhstan has emerged as the leader of the newly independent central Asian states, and has taken a lead in modernizing its economy. In 1993 Kazakhstan voted to dismantle its nuclear weapons. A large Russian minority threatens the stability of the government. ■

KENYA

Official name Republic of Kenya

PEOPLE
Population 29,140,000. **Density** 130/mi² (50/km²). **Urban** 30%. **Capital** Nairobi, 1,505,000. **Ethnic groups** Kikuyu 21%, Luhya 14%, Luo 13%, Kamba 11%,

Kalenjin 11%, Kisii 6%, Meru 5%. **Languages** English, Swahili, indigenous. **Religions** Tribal religionist 54%, Anglican and other Protestant 40%, Muslim 6%. **Life expectancy** 55 female, 53 male. **Literacy** 78%.

POLITICS
Government Republic. **Parties** African National Union, Democratic, Forum for the Restoration of Democracy, others. **Suffrage** Universal, 18 and over. **Memberships** CW, OAU, UN. **Subdivisions** 7 provinces, 1 capital district.

ECONOMY
GDP $36,800,000,000. **Per capita** $1,271. **Monetary unit** Shilling. **Trade partners** Exports: U.K., Germany, Uganda. Imports: U.K., Japan, United Arab Emirates. **Exports** Tea, coffee, petroleum products. **Imports** Machinery, transportation equipment, oil, petroleum products, iron and steel.

LAND
Description Eastern Africa. **Area** 224,961 mi² (582,646 km²). **Highest point** Kirinyaga (Mt. Kenya), 17,057 ft (5,199 m). **Lowest point** Sea level.

People. Nearly all Kenyans are black Africans belonging to one of more than 40 different groups, each with its own language and culture. Some groups are nomadic, like the Masai. Arab and European minorities—found mostly along the coast—reflect Kenya's history of foreign rule. Most Kenyans live in the southwestern highlands, raising crops or livestock. Most citizens practice either tribal religions or a Protestant faith, while a minority follow Islam. Swahili, a blend of Bantu and Arabic, is an official language; it serves as a communication link among Kenya's many ethnic groups. English is also an official language. The national slogan of *harambee*, or "pull together," illustrates the need for cooperation among Kenya's diverse groups. The government promotes such national unity.

Economy and the Land. Scenic terrain, tropical beaches, and abundant wildlife have given Kenya a thriving tourist industry, and land has been set aside for national parks and game preserves. Agriculture is the primary activity, even though the northern three-fifths of the country is semi-arid. The most productive soils are found in the southwestern highlands where tea and coffee are the main export crops. Much of the land is also used for raising livestock, another leading economic contributor. Oil from other countries is refined in Kenya, and food processing and cement production are also significant activities. Kenya's climate varies from arid in the north to temperate in the highlands and tropical along the coast.

History and Politics. Remains of early humans dating back more than two million years have been found in Kenya. Settlers from other parts of Africa arrived about 1000 B.C. A thousand years later Arab traders reached the coast and controlled the area by the 8th century A.D. The Portuguese ruled the coast between 1498 and the late 1600s. Kenya came under British control in 1895 and was known as the East African Protectorate. Opposition to British rule began to mount in the 1940s as Kenyans demanded a voice in government. The Mau Mau rebellion of the 1950s, an armed revolt, was an outgrowth of this discontent. Kenya gained independence from Britain in 1963 and became a republic in 1964. Its first president was Jomo Kenyatta, a Kikuyu who had been an active leader in the previous revolt. Recent administrations have pursued a policy of Africanization, under which land and other holdings have been transferred from European to African hands. The first multiparty elections in 26 years were held in December 1992. The incumbent, Daniel arap Moi, won reelection as president despite widespread allegations of voting fraud. Tribal fighting has become a serious problem in recent years. ∎

KERGUELEN ISLANDS
See FRANCE.

KIRIBATI

Official name Republic of Kiribati

PEOPLE
Population 83,000. **Density** 265/mi² (102/km²). **Urban** 36%. **Capital** Bairiki, Tarawa Atoll, 2,226. **Ethnic groups** Kiribatian (Micronesian) 98%. **Languages** English, I-Kiribati. **Religions** Roman Catholic 53%, Congregationalist 39%, Bahai 2%. **Life expectancy** 56 female, 53 male.

POLITICS
Government Republic. **Parties** Maneaban Te Mauri, National Progressive, others. **Suffrage** Universal, 18 and over. **Memberships** CW. **Subdivisions** 6 districts.

ECONOMY
GDP $68,000,000. **Per capita** $850. **Monetary unit** Australian dollar. **Trade partners** Exports: Netherlands, Denmark, Fiji. Imports: Australia, Japan, Fiji. **Exports** Fish, copra, seaweed. **Imports** Food, fuel, manufactures, machinery and equipment.

LAND
Description Central Pacific islands. **Area** 313 mi² (811 km²). **Highest point** 246 ft (75 m). **Lowest point** Sea level.

People. The people of Kiribati, a country of 33 islands in the central Pacific, are mostly Micronesian. Almost all the population lives on the Gilbert Islands in small villages and practices Roman Catholicism or Protestantism. English, the official language, and I-Kiribati are spoken.

Economy and the Land. A small, unskilled work force combined with small land area and few natural resources have given Kiribati a subsistence economy. Tourism is of increasing importance. Copra and fish are the main exports. Kiribati depends on economic aid from Australia, New Zealand, and Great Britain. The islands of Kiribati are almost all coral reefs, composed of hard sand and little soil; many surround a lagoon. The climate is tropical.

History and Politics. Samoa invaded Kiribati in the 1400s. The islands were declared a British protectorate in 1892 and, from 1916 until 1975, they were administered as part of the Gilbert and Ellice Islands. Fighting between the United States and Japan took place during World War II on Tarawa Island. The Ellice Islands became independent in 1978 and renamed the country Tuvalu, and the Gilbert Islands gained independence as part of the Republic of Kiribati one year later. ∎

KOREA, NORTH

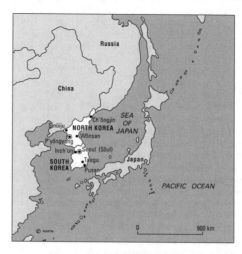

Official name Democratic People's Republic of Korea

PEOPLE
Population 24,530,000. **Density** 527/mi² (204/km²). **Urban** 62%. **Capital** P'yŏngyang, 2,355,000. **Ethnic groups** Korean 100%. **Languages** Korean. **Religions** Buddhist, Chondoist, Christian, Confucian. **Life expectancy** 75 female, 69 male. **Literacy** 99%.

POLITICS

Government Socialist republic. **Parties** Chondoist Chongu, Social Democratic, Workers'. **Suffrage** Universal, 17 and over. **Memberships** UN. **Subdivisions** 9 provinces, 3 special cities.

ECONOMY

GDP $21,500,000,000. **Per capita** $907. **Monetary unit** Won. **Trade partners** Former Soviet republics, Japan, China. **Exports** Minerals, metal products, agricultural and fishery products, manufactures. **Imports** Petroleum, machinery and equipment, coal, grain, manufactures.

LAND

Description Eastern Asia. **Area** 46,540 mi^2 (120,538 km^2). **Highest point** Paektu Mtn., 9,003 ft (2,744 m). **Lowest point** Sea level.

People. Despite a history of invasions, North Korea has a homogeneous population with virtually no minorities. Several dialects of Korean are spoken. Korean religions include Confucianism, Buddhism, Chondoism, and Christianity, though the government discourages religious activity. Urban population has grown rapidly since 1953, due to an emphasis on manufacturing. The country remains more sparsely populated than South Korea.

Economy and the Land. The division of the Korean peninsula after World War II left North Korea with most of the industry and natural resources but little agricultural land and few skilled workers. The country has succeeded in becoming one of the most industrialized countries in Asia and in overcoming its agricultural problems. Most industry is government-owned, and mines produce a variety of minerals. Farming is collectivized, and output has been aided by irrigation and other modern practices. The Soviet Union and China aided North Korea's development, but the theory of self-reliance was the government's guiding principle. A central mountainous region is bounded by coastal plains, and the climate is temperate.

History and Politics. History of North and South Korea follows SOUTH KOREA. ∎

KOREA, SOUTH

Official name Republic of Korea

PEOPLE

Population 46,980,000. **Density** 1,229/mi^2 (474/km^2). **Urban** 83%. **Capital** Seoul, 10,627,790. **Ethnic groups** Korean. **Languages** Korean. **Religions** Christian 49%, Buddhist 47%, Confucian 3%. **Life expectancy** 76 female, 69 male. **Literacy** 98%.

POLITICS

Government Republic. **Parties** Democratic, New Korea, National Congress for New Politics, United Liberal Democratic, others. **Suffrage** Universal, 20 and over. **Memberships** OECD, UN. **Subdivisions** 9 provinces, 6 special cities.

ECONOMY

GDP $590,700,000,000. **Per capita** $13,115. **Monetary unit** Won. **Trade partners** Exports: U.S., Japan, China.

Imports: Japan, U.S., Germany. **Exports** Electronic and electrical equipment, machinery, steel, automobiles, ships. **Imports** Machinery, electronics, oil, steel, transportation equipment, textiles, grain.

LAND

Description Eastern Asia. **Area** 38,230 mi^2 (99,016 km^2). **Highest point** Halla Mtn., 6,398 ft (1,950 m). **Lowest point** Sea level.

People. The homogeneous quality of South Korea's population is similar to that of North Korea. Population density, however, is much greater in South Korea, where two million Koreans migrated following World War II. The major language is Korean. Christianity is practiced by most South Koreans, although Buddhism and Confucianism have influenced much of life.

Economy and the Land. South Korea was traditionally the peninsula's agricultural zone, and following the 1945 partition of the country the south was left with little industry and few resources but abundant manpower. The economy has advanced rapidly since 1953, and today agriculture and industry are of almost equal importance. Rice, barley, and beans are principal crops; electronics and textiles are significant manufactured products. Central mountains give way to plains in the south and west, and the climate is temperate.

History and Politics. Korea's strategic location between Russia, China, and Japan has made it prey to foreign powers. China conquered the northern part of the peninsula in 108 B.C., influencing culture, religion, and government. Mongols controlled Korea for most of the 13th and 14th centuries. The rule of the Yi dynasty lasted from 1392 to 1910, when Japan annexed Korea. In 1945, following Japan's defeat in World War II, Soviet troops occupied northern Korea while the United States military occupied the south. The Soviet Union, the U.S., and Great Britain tried to aid unification of the country but failed. The Soviets opposed a subsequent plan for United Nations-supervised elections. Separate governments were formed in 1948: the northern Democratic People's Republic of Korea and the southern Republic of Korea. Both governments claimed the peninsula, and relations became strained. After several border clashes, North Korea invaded South Korea in 1950. Chinese Communists fought on the side of North Korea, and U.S./UN forces aided the south. An armistice ended the war in 1953, but a permanent peace treaty has never been signed.

North Korea. The Democratic People's Republic of Korea was established in 1948, several months after the formation of South Korea. The country incurred about three million casualties during the war with South Korea. Following the war, the government moved quickly to modernize industry and the military; North Korea maintains one of the world's largest armies. North Korea's reported development of nuclear facilities has raised serious concerns worldwide. After Kim Il Sung's death in 1994, the new leadership agreed to dismantle North Korea's nuclear weapons program in return for energy-related concessions. By 1997, North Korea was experiencing an economic crisis and a severe shortage of food due to economic stagnation and recurrent floods. The resulting hardship induced the government to obtain foreign food aid. In 1997 a severe drought began, and by 1998 thousands migrated to China in search of food. It is believed that more than one million have died of starvation. The UN is attempting to provide food aid to one-half of the population.

South Korea. The Republic of Korea was established on August 15, 1948. The country has since experienced a presidential overthrow, military rule, and a presidential assassination. In 1980 it adopted its fifth constitution since 1948, which initiated the Fifth Republic. The first non-military president in more than 30 years was elected in December 1992. When the Thailand currency crisis struck in 1997, South Korea's currency also declined, and the government solicited help from the International Monetary Fund (IMF). The IMF gave South Korea a record $57 billion in loans and aid, in return for which the government agreed to restructure the economy. As the economy stabilized, prices increased and unemployment rose dramatically. In December 1997 a reform candidate won the presidential election. In 1998 the government passed an economic reform plan. ∎

KUWAIT

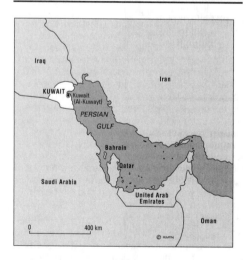

Official name State of Kuwait

PEOPLE
Population 2,145,000. **Density** 312/mi² (120/km²). **Urban** 97%. **Capital** Kuwait, 28,859. **Ethnic groups** Kuwaiti 45%, other Arab 35%, South Asian 9%, Iranian

4%. **Languages** Arabic, English. **Religions** Sunni Muslim 45%, Shiite Muslim 30%. **Life expectancy** 78 female, 74 male. **Literacy** 79%.

POLITICS
Government Constitutional monarchy. **Parties** None. **Suffrage** Limited adult male. **Memberships** AL, OPEC, UN. **Subdivisions** 5 governorates.

ECONOMY
GDP $30,800,000,000. **Per capita** $17,092. **Monetary unit** Dinar. **Trade partners** Exports: Iraq, Saudi Arabia, China. Imports: U.S., Japan, Germany. **Exports** Petroleum. **Imports** Food, construction materials, motor vehicles and parts, clothing.

LAND
Description Southwestern Asia. **Area** 6,880 mi² (17,818 km²). **Highest point** 922 ft (281 m). **Lowest point** Sea level.

People. Kuwait's recent prosperity has drawn emigrants from the Persian Gulf and beyond, giving it a diverse population with Palestinian, Iranian, and Pakistani minorities. The population has risen dramatically since the 1930s, when the oil industry began. Arabic is the official language; English is also taught and widely spoken. Almost all residents of Kuwait observe Islam, the state religion. Most belong to the Sunni branch, but there is a sizable Shiite community.

Economy and the Land. The economy centers on the largely government-controlled petroleum industry. Kuwait is one of the world's largest oil producers, and its oil reserves are among the world's most extensive. The petroleum fields that were heavily damaged in Iraq's 1990 invasion have been repaired, and production has returned to normal. Since there is very little water and virtually no arable land, all food other than fish must be imported. Kuwait occupies a desert plain on the northwestern coast of the Persian Gulf.

History and Politics. Arab nomads settled Kuwait Bay around A.D. 1700. The Al Sabah dynasty has ruled the country since the mid-1700s. Alarmed by Turk and Arabic expansion, Kuwait signed an agreement with Britain in 1899 to guarantee Kuwait's defense. Drilling for oil began in 1936, and by 1945 Kuwait had become a major exporter. Independence came in 1961. Iraq immediately made a claim to the state but was discouraged from attacking by the arrival of British troops. Official border agreements have never been made between Kuwait and Iraq. Kuwait briefly cut off oil shipments to Western countries in retaliation for their support of Israel in the 1967 and 1973 Arab-Israeli wars. Kuwait's remarkable oil wealth, which transformed it from a poor country into an affluent one, has enabled it to offer its citizens a wide range of benefits and to aid other Arab states. Kuwait allied itself with Iraq in the 1980-1988 Iran/Iraq war. This did not, however, prevent Iraq from invading Kuwait in August 1990. International outrage resulted in allied military action against Iraq in January 1991. Less than two months later Iraq was forced to withdraw. The constitution, which was suspended in 1976, was revived after the war. In 1992 elections, a number of opposition candidates won seats in the National Assembly, and the process of democratization had begun. ■

KYRGYZSTAN

Official name Kyrgyz Republic

PEOPLE
Population 4,535,000. **Density** 59/mi² (23/km²) **Urban** 39%. **Capital** Bishkek (Frunze), 631,300. **Ethnic groups** Kirghiz 52%, Russian 22%, Uzbek 13%. **Languages** Kirghiz, Russian. **Religions** Muslim 75%, Russian Orthodox 20%. **Life expectancy** 74 female, 67 male. **Literacy** 97%.

POLITICS
Government Republic. **Parties** Democratic Movement, Republican Popular, Social Democratic, others. **Suffrage** Universal, 18 and over. **Memberships** UN. **Subdivisions** 6 oblasts.

ECONOMY
GDP $5,400,000,000. **Per capita** $1,189. **Monetary unit** Som. **Trade partners** Russia, Ukraine, Uzbekistan, Kazakhstan. **Exports** Wool, meat, chemicals, cotton, metals, footwear, machinery, tobacco. **Imports** Grain, wood, industrial products, metals, fuel, machinery, shoes, electricity.

LAND
Description Central Asia, landlocked. **Area** 76,641 mi² (198,500 km²). **Highest point** Pobeda Pk., 24,406 ft (7,439 m). **Lowest point** Along Chu River, 1,804 ft (550 m).

People. About one-half of the people are Kirghiz, Turkic-speaking descendants of the region's original nomadic herdsmen. Russians are the next largest ethnic group, followed by the Uzbeks. Ethnic tension exists between the Kirghiz and the Uzbeks, and fighting between the two groups claimed hundreds of lives in 1990. Most people live in the countryside and are engaged in agriculture, although the Russians tend to live in the cities.

Economy and the Land. High, snow-capped mountains dominate the landscape of Kyrgyzstan. Most of the economic activity takes place in the Fergana and Chu Valleys. Temperature and precipitation vary widely with elevation but, in general, the climate is harsh. The land is rich in minerals, including gold, coal, petroleum, natural gas, uranium, lead, zinc, and mercury. Although the Kirghiz were forced to give up their nomadic lifestyle, the livestock raising of goats, sheep, and horses remains important. The Kyrgyz government is in the process of implementing a market-based economy.

History and Politics. The Kirghiz people have lived in the mountains and valleys of Kyrgyzstan since at least the second millennium B.C. Kirghiz warlords controlled the region when it was used as a trade route to China. One of the Kirghiz warlords first turned to Russia for protection in the mid-1800s. By 1870 central Kyrgyzstan had been conquered by Russia, and control was consolidated after the 1917 revolution. It became the Kirghiz Soviet Socialist Republic within the Soviet Union in 1936. The Republic of Kyrgyzstan declared itself independent in December 1990 and elected its first President in October 1991. Its independence was internationally recognized in December 1991, after the collapse of the Soviet Union. Kyrgyzstan stands today as an example of a developing democracy. ■

LAOS

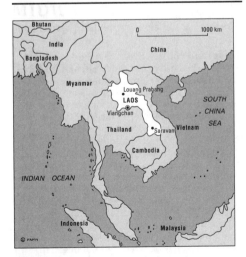

Official name Lao People's Democratic Republic

PEOPLE
Population 5,185,000. **Density** 57/mi² (22/km²). **Urban** 21%. **Capital** Viangchan (Vientiane), 464,000. **Ethnic groups** Lao 50%, Phoutai 12%, Khmu 11%, Hmong 6%, Lu 3%. **Languages** Lao, French, English. **Religions** Buddhist 60%, Animist and others 40%. **Life expectancy** 55 female, 52 male. **Literacy** 57%.

POLITICS
Government Socialist republic. **Parties** People's Revolutionary. **Suffrage** Universal, 18 and over. **Memberships** ASEAN, UN. **Subdivisions** 16 provinces, 1 municipality.

ECONOMY
GDP $5,200,000,000. **Per capita** $1,060. **Monetary unit** Kip. **Trade partners** Exports: Thailand, Malaysia, Vietnam. Imports: Thailand, former Soviet republics, Japan, France. **Exports** Electricity, wood, coffee, tin, clothing. **Imports** Food, petroleum products, manufactures.

LAND
Description Southeastern Asia, landlocked. **Area** 91,429 mi² (236,800 km²). **Highest point** Mt. Bia, 9,252 ft (2,820 m). **Lowest point** Along Mekong River, 230 ft (70 m).

People. Laos is populated by various ethnic groups, each with its own customs, religion, and language. Its history of culturally diverse communities is mirrored in the political divisions of recent years. The Lao are numerically and politically dominant, and Lao is the official language. Small Vietnamese and Chinese minorities exist. Most Laotians are rice farmers.

Economy and the Land. Years of warfare, a landlocked position, and a poor transportation system have hindered the development of Laos's economy. Although agriculture is the basis of the economy, very little of the fertile land is cultivated. Substantial mineral deposits and large timber reserves also have not been exploited to their potential. Manufacturing is limited, partly because of an unskilled work force. Situated in a mountainous, densely-forested region, Laos has a tropical climate and experiences seasonal monsoons.

History and Politics. By A.D. 900 the forerunners of the Lao had arrived from southern China. The first united Lao kingdom was founded in 1353 and included much of modern Thailand. It dissolved into three rival states by the early 1700s, setting the stage for interference by Myanmar (Burma), Vietnam, and Siam, present-day Thailand. In 1899, France made Laos part of French Indochina. Laos gained some autonomy in 1949, but this period saw the growth of Communist and anti-Communist factions whose rivalry would prevent any unified government until 1975. Although Geneva peace agreements declared Laos neutral in 1954 and 1962, the country became increasingly embroiled in the Vietnam War as both sides in that conflict entered Laos. A protracted civil war began in 1960 between the Pathet Lao, a Communist faction aided by the North Vietnamese, and government forces backed by the Thai and South Vietnamese. A cease-fire was signed in 1973 and a new coalition government was formed a year later. Following Communist victories in Vietnam and Cambodia, the Pathet Lao gained control in 1975 and established the Lao People's Democratic Republic. Laos began permitting private enterprise in 1986, but has allowed only limited contact with the outside world. Relief agencies were called upon after a drought in 1993 decimated the rice harvest. In 1996, Laos applied for membership in the Association of Southeast Asian Nations (ASEAN). ∎

LATVIA

Official name Republic of Latvia

PEOPLE
Population 2,417,000. **Density** 98/mi² (38/km²). **Urban** 73%. **Capital** Rīga, 874,200. **Ethnic groups** Latvian 52%, Russian 34%, Belorussian 5%, Ukrainian 3%, Polish 2%. **Languages** Lettish, Lithuanian, Russian, other. **Religions** Lutheran, Roman Catholic, Russian Orthodox. **Life expectancy** 75 female, 63 male. **Literacy** 100%.

POLITICS
Government Republic. **Parties** Democratic (Saimnieks), Latvia's Way, For Latvia, Fatherland and Freedom, others. **Suffrage** Universal, 18 and over. **Memberships** UN. **Subdivisions** 26 counties, 7 municipalities.

ECONOMY
GDP $14,700,000,000. **Per capita** $5,829. **Monetary unit** Lat. **Trade partners** Russia, Ukraine, other former Soviet republics. **Exports** Timber, textiles, dairy products. **Imports** Fuel, cars, chemicals.

LAND
Description Eastern Europe. **Area** 24,595 mi² (63,700 km²). **Highest point** Gaizina Hill, 1,020 ft (311 m). **Lowest point** Sea level.

People. The Latvians are closely related to the neighboring Lithuanians, and the Latvian language is one of the oldest in Europe. Many Latvians were killed or deported during World War II and the subsequent Soviet invasion. Today, more than one-third of the people are Russian. Most Latvians are Lutheran or Roman Catholic.

Economy and the Land. Despite its lack of energy resources, Latvia has a rapidly growing market economy. Industrial production is highly diversi-fied. Latvia's farms are efficient, and food is plen-tiful. Most of the land is low plains, and much is forested. The capital city of Rīga is one of the Baltic region's busiest ports.

History and Politics. Latvian history was pro-foundly affected by the Teutonic Knights, who ruled the country for more than 200 years start-ing in the mid-1300s. They established them-selves as landowners and forced the Latvians into serfdom. Latvia was subsequently captured by Poland, Sweden, and Russia. After 100 years of Russian rule, serfdom in Latvia was eliminated in the early 1700s. An independent Latvian state was established in 1918. Political instability fol-lowed, and the country descended into fascism. In 1940, the Soviet Union invaded Latvia, ending 22 years of Latvian independence. The Latvians resisted Soviet domination and regained their independence in 1991. They have begun a transi-tion to a free market economy. ∎

LEBANON

Official name Republic of Lebanon

Subdivisions 6 governorates.

PEOPLE
Population 3,898,000. **Density** 971/mi² (375/km²). **Urban** 88%. **Capital** Beirut, 509,000. **Ethnic groups** Arab 95%, Armenian 4%. **Languages** Arabic, French, Armenian, English. **Religions** Muslim 70%, Christian 30%. **Life expectancy** 72 female, 68 male. **Literacy** 92%.

POLITICS
Government Republic. **Parties** Amal, Baath, Phalangist, others. **Suffrage** 21 and over, Females with elementary education. **Memberships** AL, UN.

ECONOMY
GDP $18,300,000,000. **Per capita** $4,897. **Monetary unit** Pound. **Trade partners** Exports: Saudi Arabia, Switzerland, Jordan. Imports: Italy, France, U.S., Turkey. **Exports** Agricultural products, chemicals, textiles, jewelry, metals, metal products. **Imports** Manufactures, machinery, transportation equipment, metals, petroleum products.

LAND
Description Southwestern Asia. **Area** 4,015 mi² (10,400 km²). **Highest point** Mt. Sawda, 10,115 ft (3,083 m). **Lowest point** Sea level.

People. Traditionally home to many diverse groups, Lebanon has recently been shaken by the conflicting demands of its population. Almost all

Lebanese are of Arab stock, and Arabic and French are the official languages. Palestinian refugees have settled here since the creation of Israel in 1948, many of them living in refugee camps. Lebanon's religious makeup is notable for its variety, encompassing 17 recognized sects. Islam is now the majority religion, although Christianity continues to be a strong presence. Muslims are divided among the majority Shiite, minority Sunni, and Druze sects, while most Christians are Maronites.

Economy and the Land. Situated strategically between the West and the Middle East, Lebanon has long been a center of commerce. Its economy is fueled by the service sector, particularly bank-ing. Prolonged fighting, beginning with the 1975 civil war, has greatly damaged all economic activity. Much of the work force is engaged in agriculture, and various crops are grown. The coastal area consists of a plain, behind which lie mountain ranges separated by a fertile valley. The climate is Mediterranean.

History and Politics. The Phoenicians settled parts of Lebanon about 3000 B.C. and were fol-lowed by Egyptian, Assyrian, Persian, Greek, and Roman rulers. Christianity came to the area dur-ing the Byzantine Empire, around A.D. 325, and Islam followed in the 7th century. In 1516, Lebanon was incorporated into the Ottoman Empire. Between the end of World War I, when the Ottoman Empire collapsed, and 1943, when Lebanon became independent, the country was a French mandate. After independence, Muslims and Christians shared government power. Opposition to Lebanon's close ties to the West led to a 1958 insurrection, which United States marines put down at the government's request. The Palestine Liberation Organization (PLO), a group working to establish a Palestinian state, began operating from bases in Lebanon. This led to clashes with Israel in the late 1970s and early 1980s. The presence of the PLO divided Muslims, who generally supported it, and Christians, who opposed it. Civil war between Muslims and Christians broke out in 1975, and fighting slowed the next year with the requested aid of Syrian deterrent forces. Internal instability continued, however, along with Israeli-Palestinian hostili-ties. In 1982 Israel invaded Lebanon, driving the PLO from Beirut and the south. Hundreds of Palestinian refugees were killed by the Christian Lebanese forces. A multinational peacekeeping force left the country after falling victim to terror-ist attacks. Israel began a gradual withdrawal from Lebanon in 1985, but maintains a buffer zone in southern Lebanon, where occasional fighting and casualties continue to occur. An uneasy peace has returned in Lebanon, but negotiations with Israel for a complete withdraw-al of its troops have been unsuccessful. ∎

LESOTHO

Official name Kingdom of Lesotho

PEOPLE
Population 2,027,000. **Density** 173/mi² (67/km²).
Urban 25%. **Capital** Maseru, 98,017. **Ethnic groups**
Sotho 99%. **Languages** English, Sesotho. **Religions**
Roman Catholic and other Christian 80%, tribal
religionist 20%. **Life expectancy** 66 female, 61 male.
Literacy 71%.

POLITICS
Government Constitutional monarchy under military
rule. **Parties** Basotho Congress, others. **Suffrage**
Universal, 21 and over. **Memberships** CW, OAU, UN.
Subdivisions 10 districts.

ECONOMY
GDP $2,800,000,000. **Per capita** $1,388. **Monetary
unit** Loti. **Trade partners** South Africa, Western
European countries. **Exports** Clothing, furniture,
footwear, wool. **Imports** Corn, building materials,
clothing, vehicles, machinery, pharmaceuticals.

LAND
Description Southern Africa, landlocked. **Area**
11,720 mi² (30,355 km²). **Highest point** Mt. Ntlenyana,
11,425 ft (3,482 m). **Lowest point** Along Orange River,
5,000 ft (1,524 m).

People. The Sotho, a black African group, comprise almost all of Lesotho's population. Most
Sotho live in the lowlands and raise livestock and
crops. The official languages are Sesotho, a Bantu
tongue, and English. The traditional religion is
based on ancestor worship, though most Sotho
are Roman Catholic. A system of tribal chieftain-
cy is followed locally.

Economy and the Land. Surrounded by South
Africa and having few resources, Lesotho is
almost entirely dependent on South Africa for
economic survival. Much of the male population
must seek employment there, usually spending
several months a year in South African mines or
industries. Agriculture remains at the subsistence
level, and soil erosion threatens production.

Livestock raising represents a significant part of
Lesotho's economy. Wool and mohair are among
the chief exports. Diamond mining, one of the
few industries, employs a small portion of the
population. Most of the terrain is mountainous;
the fairly high elevations give Lesotho a temperate climate.

History and Politics. Refugees from tribal wars in
southern Africa arrived in what is now Lesotho
between the 16th and 19th centuries A.D. Chief
Moshoeshoe united the Sotho tribes in 1818 and
led them in war against the Boers, settlers of
Dutch or Huguenot descent. At Moshoeshoe's
request, Basutoland came under British protection in 1868. It resisted attempts at absorption by
the Union of South Africa and became the independent kingdom of Lesotho in 1966. The country was governed by a Council of Ministers until
1986, when the military took over. In 1990 King
Moshoeshoe was deposed, but he was returned
to the throne in 1995 in an attempt by the government to restore political stability. When King
Moeshoeshoe died in 1996, he was succeeded by
his son. ■

LIBERIA

Official name Republic of Liberia

PEOPLE
Population 2,177,000. **Density** 57/mi² (22/km²). **Urban**
46%. **Capital** Monrovia, 465,000. **Ethnic groups**
Indigenous African 95%, descendants of freed
American slaves 5%. **Languages** English, indigenous.
Religions Animist 70%, Muslim 20%, Christian 10%.
Life expectancy 59 female, 56 male. **Literacy** 38%.

POLITICS
Government Republic. **Parties** Action, National
Democratic, others. **Suffrage** Universal, 18 and over.
Memberships OAU, UN. **Subdivisions** 11 counties,
2 territories.

ECONOMY
GDP $2,300,000,000. **Per capita** $830. **Monetary unit**

Dollar. **Trade partners** Exports: Germany, U.S., Italy. Imports: U.S., Germany, Netherlands. **Exports** Iron ore, rubber, timber, coffee. **Imports** Rice, food, fuel, chemicals, machines, transportation equipment, manufactures.

LAND
Description Western Africa. **Area** 38,250 mi² (99,067 km²). **Highest point** Mt. Wuteve, 4,528 ft (1,380 m). **Lowest point** Sea level.

People. Most Liberians belong to one of about 20 indigenous black groups. Few of them are descended from the freed American slaves who founded modern Liberia, but this relatively small group—known as Americo-Liberians—has traditionally been politically dominant. The official language is English, but more than 20 other tongues are also spoken. Most people are farmers and practice traditional religious beliefs, although Islam and Christianity also have adherents. Liberia is the only black African state to have escaped colonialism.

Economy and the Land. Before the recent war, Liberia owed its healthy economy largely to an open-door policy, which had made its extensive resources attractive to foreign counties. Two of the most important activities—iron-ore mining and rubber production—were developed by western firms. Large timber reserves have not yet been fully exploited. Liberia also profits from the vast merchant fleet registered under its flag. The land is characterized by a coastal plain, plateaus, and low mountains, while the hot, humid climate is marked by distinct wet and dry seasons.

History and Politics. Early settlers are thought to have migrated from the north and east between the 12th and 17th centuries A.D. Trade between Europeans and coastal groups developed after the Portuguese visited the area in the late 1400s. The American Colonization Society, a private United States organization devoted to resettling freed slaves, purchased land in Liberia, and in 1822 the first settlers landed at the site of Monrovia. The settlers declared their independence in 1847, setting up a government based on the U.S. model and creating Africa's first independent republic. For the next century, the Liberian government endured attempts at colonization by France and Britain, as well as internal tribal opposition. The string of Americo-Liberian rulers was broken in 1980, when a small group of soldiers of African descent toppled the government and imposed martial law. A series of splinter groups have since ruled the country, but peace and stability have been elusive and there have been a series of failed peace agreements. West African peacekeeping forces have been in Liberia since 1990 but have not been successful in stabilizing the country. In 1996 President Roosevelt Johnson fled to Ghana, and Ruth Perry was chosen as interim head of the government. In the presence of a regional peacekeeping force and international observers, elections were held in 1997 without incident. ■

LIBYA

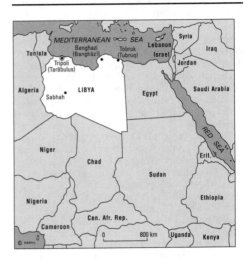

Official name Socialist People's Libyan Arab Jamahiriya

PEOPLE
Population 5,745,000. **Density** 8.5/mi² (3.3/km²). **Urban** 86%. **Capital** Tripoli, 591,062. **Ethnic groups** Arab-Berber 97%. **Languages** Arabic. **Religions** Sunni Muslim 97%. **Life expectancy** 68 female, 64 male. **Literacy** 76%.

POLITICS
Government Socialist republic. **Parties** None. **Suffrage** Universal, 18 and over. **Memberships** AL, OAU, OPEC, UN. **Subdivisions** 13 municipalities.

ECONOMY
GDP $32,900,000,000. **Per capita** $6,391. **Monetary unit** Dinar. **Trade partners** Exports: Italy, France, Greece. Imports: Italy, Japan, Germany. **Exports** Petroleum, petroleum products, natural gas. **Imports** Machinery, transportation equipment, food, manufactures.

LAND
Description Northern Africa. **Area** 679,362 mi² (1,759,540 km²). **Highest point** Bīkkū Bīttī, 7,438 ft (2,267 m). **Lowest point** Sabkhat Ghuzayyil, -154 ft (-47 m).

People. Libya, originally settled by Berbers, is largely a mix of Arab and Berber today. Almost all Libyans live along the coast, with some nomadic groups in desert areas. Large migrations from rural areas to the cities have accompanied Libya's oil-based prosperity. Islam is the majority religion, and nearly all Libyans speak Arabic. Traditional social orders still exist, despite centuries of foreign rule.

Economy and the Land. The discovery of oil in 1959 propelled Libya from the ranks of the world's poorest countries to one of its leading oil producers. It has used these revenues to develop industry and agriculture to diversify its economy. Most of Libya is covered by the Sahara Desert, and the limited agriculture has been further hurt by Libyan farmers migrating to the cities. The climate is desert except for the coast, which has moderate temperatures.

History and Politics. For much of its history, Libya was dominated by Mediterranean empires: Phoenician, Carthaginian, Greek, and Roman. In the 7th century A.D. the area was taken by Muslim Arabs, whose language and religion transformed Libyan culture. Although the Ottoman Turks conquered the region in the 16th century, local rulers remained virtually autonomous. Italy invaded Libya in 1911, and the country became an Italian colony in 1912. Following World War II, British and French forces occupied the area until a United Nations resolution made Libya an independent country in 1951. A monarchy ruled until 1969, when a military coup established a republic headed by Colonel Mu'ammar al-Qadhafi. Under his leadership, Libya has backed Arab unity and the Palestinian cause, opposed foreign influences, and created a welfare system. Libya's support of terrorist activities resulted in a controversial United States air strike against the country in 1986. Libya's refusal to turn over accused terrorists has led to UN sanctions. ∎

LIECHTENSTEIN

Official name Principality of Liechtenstein

PEOPLE
Population 32,000. **Density** 516/mi² (200/km²). **Urban** 21%. **Capital** Vaduz, 5,085. **Ethnic groups** Liechtensteiner (Alemannic) 95%. **Languages** German. **Religions** Roman Catholic 81%, Protestant 7%. **Life expectancy** 81 female, 74 male. **Literacy** 100%.

POLITICS
Government Constitutional monarchy. **Parties** Fatherland Union, Progressive Citizens', Free List. **Suffrage** Universal, 20 and over. **Memberships** UN. **Subdivisions** 11 communes.

ECONOMY
GDP $630,000,000. **Per capita** $20,323. **Monetary unit**

Swiss franc. **Trade partners** Switzerland and other European countries. **Exports** Machinery, dental products, stamps, hardware, pottery. **Imports** Machinery, metal goods, textiles, food, motor vehicles.

LAND
Description Central Europe, landlocked. **Area** 62 mi² (160 km²). **Highest point** Vorder Grauspitz, 8,527 ft (2,599 m). **Lowest point** Ruggleller Riet, 1,411 ft (430 m).

People. In spite of its location at the crossroads of Europe, Liechtenstein has retained a largely homogeneous ethnicity. Almost all Liechtensteiners are descended from Germanic tribes, and German is the official language. Roman Catholicism is the most widely practiced religion, but a Protestant minority also exists. Most of the country is mountainous, and population is concentrated on the fertile plains adjacent to the Rhine River, which forms the country's western boundary. Most Liechtensteiners work in factories or in trades.

Economy and the Land. The last few decades have seen the economy shift from agricultural to highly industrialized. An economic alliance with Switzerland dating from 1923 has been profoundly beneficial to Liechtenstein: the two countries form a customs union and use the same currency. Other important sources of revenue are tourism, the sale of postage stamps, and taxation of foreign businesses headquartered here. Most of Liechtenstein, one of the world's smallest countries, is covered by the Alps; nonetheless, its climate is mild.

History and Politics. Early inhabitants of what is now Liechtenstein included the Celts, Romans, and Alemanni, who arrived about A.D. 500. The area became part of the empire of the Frankish King Charlemagne in the late 700s, and following Charlemagne's death it was divided into the lordships of Vaduz and Schellenberg. By 1719, when the state became part of the Holy Roman Empire, the Austrian House of Liechtenstein had purchased both lordships, uniting them as the Imperial Principality of Liechtenstein. The country's independence dates from the abolition of the empire by France's Napoleon Bonaparte in 1806. Liechtenstein was neutral in both world wars and has remained unaffected by European conflicts. The government is a hereditary constitutional monarchy; the prince is the head of the House of Liechtenstein, thus chief of state, and the prime minister is the head of government. Women gained the right to vote in 1984. ∎

LITHUANIA

Official name Republic of Lithuania

PEOPLE
Population 3,627,000. **Density** 144/mi² (56/km²). **Urban** 73%. **Capital** Vilnius, 584,400. **Ethnic groups** Lithuanian 80%, Russian 9%, Polish 8%, Byelorussian 2%. **Languages** Lithuanian, Polish, Russian. **Religions** Roman Catholic, Lutheran. **Life expectancy** 76 female, 65 male. **Literacy** 98%.

POLITICS

Government Republic. **Parties** Center Union, Christian Democratic, Conservative, Democratic Labor, others. **Suffrage** Universal, 18 and over. **Memberships** UN. **Subdivisions** 44 regions, 11 municipalities.

ECONOMY

GDP $13,300,000,000. **Per capita** $3,315. **Monetary unit** Litas. **Trade partners** Russia, Ukraine, other former Soviet republics. **Exports** Electronics, petroleum products, food, chemicals. **Imports** Petroleum, machinery, chemicals, grain.

LAND

Description Eastern Europe. **Area** 25,212 mi² (65,300 km²). **Highest point** Juozapines Hill, 965 ft (294 m). **Lowest point** Sea level.

People. Lithuanians are a Baltic people related to the Latvians. Although about 80 percent of the people are ethnic Lithuanians, Russian immigrants held many key positions in Lithuania under Soviet rule. Lithuanians also chafed under Soviet rules restricting religion because most are devoutly Roman Catholic. Lithuanians are known for their fine singing and splendid choral festivals.

Economy and the Land. Prior to Soviet rule, Lithuania was predominately rural with an agricultural economy based on meat and dairy products. Today the Lithuanian economy is dependent on industrial production, although it lacks significant mineral fuel deposits. The country has suffered from a severe oil shortage since independence when the Russians ceased to supply subsidized oil. The land is generally flat. There are fine white-sand beaches along the coastline of the Baltic Sea.

History and Politics. Unlike the neighboring Soviet republics of Latvia and Estonia, Lithuania has had a long tradition of independence. By the mid-1300s, Lithuania extended from the Baltic to the Black seas, and was a major regional power. Close political association with Poland led to a merger in 1569 and eventual annexation by Russia in the late 19th century. In 1918, Lithuania

again claimed its independence, which it enjoyed until 1940 when it was overtaken by the Soviets. Stalin killed or deported about one-third of the Lithuanian population. Friction between Lithuania and the Soviet Union increased after the introduction of *glasnost* fueled Lithuanian aspirations for independence. A Soviet invasion in early 1991 was followed by international recognition of Lithuania as an independent state later in the year. The Lithuanians' disillusionment with their lagging economy led to a surprise victory by the ex-Communist Democratic Labor Party in October 1992. ■

LUXEMBOURG

Official name Grand Duchy of Luxembourg

PEOPLE

Population 426,000. **Density** 427/mi² (165/km²). **Urban** 90%. **Capital** Luxembourg, 75,377. **Ethnic groups** Luxembourger (mixed Celtic, French, and German). **Languages** French, Luxembourgish, German. **Religions** Roman Catholic 97%, Jewish and Protestant 3%. **Life expectancy** 80 female, 73 male. **Literacy** 100%.

POLITICS

Government Constitutional monarchy. **Parties** Christian Socialist, Democratic, Socialist Workers, others. **Suffrage** Universal, 18 and over. **Memberships** EU, NATO, OECD, UN. **Subdivisions** 3 districts.

ECONOMY

GDP $10,000,000,000. **Per capita** $25,253. **Monetary unit** Franc. **Trade partners** Exports: Western European countries, U.S. Imports: Belgium, Germany, France. **Exports** Aluminum, industrial products, steel goods, chemicals, rubber products, glass. **Imports** minerals, metals, food, consumer goods.

LAND

Description Western Europe, landlocked. **Area** 998 mi² (2,586 km²). **Highest point** Buurgplaatz, 1,834 ft (559 m). **Lowest point** Confluence of Moselle and Sûre Rivers, 427 ft (130 m).

People. Luxembourg's population bears the imprint of foreign influences, yet retains an individual character. Most Luxembourgers are a blend of Celtic, French, and German stock. French is an official language, as is Luxembourgish, an indigenous German dialect. Roman Catholicism is observed by virtually all the population. There are significant communities of guest workers from several European countries.

Economy and the Land. Luxembourg's industrial sector, previously dominated by steelmaking, has been diversified toward high technology, plastics and chemicals to compensate for the decline in demand for steel. Tourism and financial services, including banking, also have become more important. Luxembourg's trade benefits from the country's membership in the European Community and the Benelux union. Luxembourg has two distinct regions: the mountainous, wooded north and the open, rolling south, known as Bon Pays. The climate is temperate.

History and Politics. The present city of Luxembourg developed from a castle built in A.D. 963 by Count Siegfried of Ardennes. Several heavily fortified towns grew up around the castle, and the area became known as the "Gibraltar of the North" because of those fortifications. The duchy remained semiautonomous until the Burgundians conquered the area in 1443. Various Euro-pean powers ruled Luxembourg for most of the next four centuries, and in 1815 the duchy was elevated to a grand duchy. It became autonomous in 1839 and was recognized in 1867 as an independent state. Despite Luxembourg's declaration of neutrality, Germany occupied the country in both world wars. ∎

MACAU

Official name Macau

PEOPLE
Population 425,000. **Density** 64,394/mi² (25,000/km²). **Urban** 99%. **Capital** Macau, Macau I., 425,000. **Ethnic groups** Chinese 95%, Portuguese 3%. **Languages** Portuguese, Chinese (Cantonese). **Religions** Buddhist 45%, Roman Catholic 7%. **Life expectancy** 82 female, 77 male. **Literacy** 90%.

POLITICS
Government Overseas territory (Portugal). **Parties** Association to Defend the Interests of Macau, Democratic Center, others. **Suffrage** Universal, 18 and over. **Memberships** None. **Subdivisions** 2 districts.

ECONOMY
GDP $6,400,000,000. **Per capita** $15,764. **Monetary unit** Pataca. **Trade partners** Exports: U.S., China, Germany. Imports: China, Japan. **Exports** Textiles, clothing, toys. **Imports** Raw materials, food, machinery.

LAND
Description Eastern Asia (islands and peninsula on China's southeastern coast). **Area** 6.6 mi² (17 km²). **Highest point** Coloane Alto, 571 ft (174 m). **Lowest point** Sea level.

People. Situated on the southeastern China coast, 17 miles (27.4 km) west of Hong Kong, Macau is populated almost entirely by Chinese. A former overseas province of Portugal, the island also includes people of Portuguese and mixed Chinese-Portuguese descent. Several Chinese dialects are widely spoken, and Portuguese is the official language. Buddhism is Macau's principal religion; a small percentage of its population are Roman Catholics.

Economy and the Land. Tourism, gambling, and light industry help make up Macau's economy; however, its leading industries are textiles and light manufacturing, which employ the majority of the labor force. Macau has been likened to Hong Kong because of its textile exports, yet it remains a heavy importer, relying on China for drinking water and much of its food supply. The province consists of the city of Macau, located on a peninsula, and the nearby islands of Taipa and Coloane. The climate is maritime tropical, with cool winters and warm summers.

History and Politics. Macau became a Portuguese trading post in 1557. It flourished as the midpoint for trade between China and Japan but declined when Hong Kong became a trading power in the mid-1800s. Macau remained a neutral port during World War II and was economically prosperous. Although the government is nominally directed by Portugal, any policies relating to Macau are subject to China's approval. Macau is the oldest European settlement in the Far East. It will be returned to China in 1999 under a negotiated agreement whereby the present capitalist system will be maintained for 50 years. ∎

MACEDONIA

Official name Republic of Macedonia

PEOPLE
Population 2,119,000. **Density** 213/mi² (82/km²).
Urban 60%. **Capital** Skopje, 440,577. **Ethnic groups**
Macedonian 65%, Albanian 22%, Turkish 4%, Serb
2%. **Languages** Macedonian, Albanian. **Religions**
Eastern Orthodox 67%, Muslim 30%. **Life expectancy**
76 female, 70 male.

POLITICS
Government Republic. **Parties** Democratic Prosperity,
Liberal, Social Democratic Alliance, others. **Suffrage**
Universal, 18 and over. **Memberships** UN.
Subdivisions 34 counties.

ECONOMY
GDP $1,900,000,000. **Per capita** $876. **Monetary unit**
Denar. **Trade partners** Exports: Former Yugoslavian
republics, Germany, Greece. Imports: Former
Yugoslavia republics, Greece, Albania. **Exports**
Manufactures, machinery, transportation equipment,
raw materials, food, drink. **Imports** Fuels, lubricants,
manufactures, machinery, transportation equipment,
food.

LAND
Description Eastern Europe, landlocked. **Area**
9,928 mi² (25,713 km²). **Highest point** Korab, 9,035 ft
(2,754 m). **Lowest point** Along Vardar River, 164 ft
(50 m).

People. Most Macedonians are of mixed Serbian
and Bulgarian descent, reflected in the country's
Slavic dialect. Albanians are the most significant
minority. Many Macedonians practice the Orthodox religion, although there is a significant
Muslim minority in the western part of the country. Macedonians are proud of their folklore and
traditional music.

Economy and the Land. Landlocked Macedonia
is predominately mountainous, and most of the
people are involved in agriculture and herding.
Agricultural products include cereal grains,
tobacco, and cotton. The country has deposits of
coal, iron ore, lead, zinc, nickel, and chromium.
Macedonia is the poorest and least developed of
the former Yugoslavian republics.

History and Politics. The country of Macedonia
is part of a larger historical region of the same
name. Macedonia reached its zenith under the
rule of Alexander the Great, who created a vast
Macedonian empire in the 4th century B.C. that
extended from Egypt to northern India. The
empire fell apart after Alexander's death, and
Rome then conquered the region. The Slavic people, who were the ancestors of today's Macedonians, migrated to the area in the 6th century A.D.
The region suffered numerous invasions over the
centuries. After 500 years of Turkish rule, it was
finally split between Serbia, Greece, and Bulgaria
in 1913, after serving as a battleground for two
Balkan wars. In 1945, the Serbian portion of
Macedonia became a full republic of Yugoslavia.
It remained part of Yugoslavia until 1991, when it
followed the lead of neighboring Yugoslavian
republics and declared its independence. International peacekeeping forces in Macedonia
are attempting to prevent a spillover of ethnic
strife. ∎

MADAGASCAR

Official name Republic of Madagascar

PEOPLE
Population 14,250,000. **Density** 63/mi² (24/km²).
Urban 27%. **Capital** Antananarivo, 1,250,000. **Ethnic
groups** Merina, Betsimisaraka, Betsileo, Tsimihety,
Antaisaka, other tribes. **Languages** Malagasy, French.
Religions Animist 52%, Christian 41%, Muslim 7%.
Life expectancy 61 female, 58 male. **Literacy** 46%.

POLITICS
Government Republic. **Parties** Committee of Living
Forces, Militant Party for the Development of
Madagascar, others. **Suffrage** Universal, 18 and over.
Memberships OAU, UN. **Subdivisions** 6 provinces.

ECONOMY
GDP $11,400,000,000. **Per capita** $804. **Monetary unit**
Franc. **Trade partners** Exports: France, U.S., Japan.
Imports: France, U.S., former Soviet republics. **Exports**
Coffee, vanilla, cloves, shellfish, sugar, petroleum.
Imports Manufactures, machinery, petroleum, food.

LAND
Description Southeastern African island. **Area**
226,658 mi² (587,041 km²). **Highest point**
Maromokotro, 9,436 ft (2,876 m). **Lowest point**
Sea level.

People. Most of the population is of mixed African and Indonesian descent. Those who live
on the coast, the *cotiers*, are of predominantly
African origin, while those on the inland plateau
have Asian roots. There is a long-standing rivalry
between the *cotiers* and the inland groups, most
of whom belong to the Merina people. The official language is Malagasy. Sizable Christian communities exist, but most Malagasy practice
indigenous Animist beliefs.

Economy and the Land. Madagascar is chiefly an
agricultural country, with the majority of the
work force engaged in farming or herding.
Overpopulation and outmoded cultivation have
recently cut into yields of rice, an important crop,
and other products. Varied mineral resources,

including oil, point to possible expansion. The climate is tropical on the coastal plains and moderate in the inland highlands.

History and Politics. Madagascar's first settlers are thought to be Indonesians, who brought African wives and slaves around 2,000 years ago. Arab traders established themselves on the coast in the 7th century. The Portuguese first sighted the island in the 1500s, and other Europeans followed. The Merina kingdom, based in the central plateau, gained control over most of the island in the 1790s. French influence grew throughout the 19th century, and in 1896 France made the island a colony after subduing the Merina. Resentment of French rule continued, culminating in an armed revolt in 1947. Full independence came in 1960. After 12 years of rule by the same president, a coup placed the military in power. A new constitution was adopted in 1975 that established the Democratic Republic of Madagascar. By 1991 there were major protests against the government, and a late 1992 election was won by the opposition. A new constitution was approved after much dissension; the highland people favoring a unitary form of government won over the coastal people who wanted a federal system with stronger regional control. ∎

MADEIRA ISLANDS
See PORTUGAL.

MALAWI

Official name Republic of Malawi

PEOPLE
Population 9,695,000. **Density** 212/mi² (82/km²). **Urban** 14%. **Capital** Lilongwe, 223,318. **Ethnic groups** Chewa, Nyanja, Tumbuko, Yao, Lomwe, others.

Languages Chichewa, English. **Religions** Protestant 55%, Roman Catholic 20%, Muslim 20%. **Life expectancy** 45 female, 44 male. **Literacy** 56%.

POLITICS
Government Republic. **Parties** Alliance for Democracy, Congress, United Democratic Front, others. **Suffrage** Universal, 21 and over. **Memberships** CW, OAU, UN. **Subdivisions** 3 regions.

ECONOMY
GDP $6,900,000,000. **Per capita** $694. **Monetary unit** Kwacha. **Trade partners** Exports: U.K., Germany, South Africa. Imports: South African countries, U.K., Japan. **Exports** Tobacco, tea, sugar, coffee, peanuts, wood products. **Imports** Food, petroleum products, manufactures, transportation equipment.

LAND
Description Southern Africa, landlocked. **Area** 45,747 mi² (118,484 km²). **Highest point** Sapitwa, 9,849 ft (3,002 m). **Lowest point** Along Shire River, 120 ft (37 m).

People. Almost all Malawians are black Africans descended from Bantu peoples. The Chewa constitute the majority in the central area, while the Nyanja are dominant in the south and the Tumbuko in the north. Chichewa and English are official languages. The majority of the population is rural, and traditional village customs are prevalent. For the most part, the society is matriarchal. Many Malawians combine Christian or Muslim beliefs with traditional religious practices.

Economy and the Land. A landlocked country with limited resources and a largely unskilled work force, Malawi relies almost entirely on agriculture. A recent series of poor harvests, combined with a tripling of the population between 1950 and 1989, has contributed to the decline in agricultural output and consequent food shortages. Among the main exports are tea and tobacco. Many Malawians work part of the year as miners in South Africa, Zambia, and Zimbabwe. Malawi, situated along the Great Rift Valley, has a varied terrain with highlands, plateaus, and lakes. The climate is subtropical, and rainfall varies greatly from north to south.

History and Politics. Archeological findings indicate that Malawi has been inhabited for at least 50,000 years. Bantu-speaking peoples, ancestors of the Malawians, immigrated from the north around A.D. 1400 and soon formed centralized kingdoms. In the 1830s, other Bantu groups, involved in the slave trade, invaded the region. The arrival of Scottish missionary David Livingstone in 1859 began a period of British influence; in 1891 the territory became the British protectorate of Nyasaland. Beginning in 1953, Nyasaland was part of the larger Federation of Rhodesia and Nyasaland. Malawi attained independence in 1964 and became a republic in 1966, with nationalist leader Dr. Hastings Banda as its first president. The Malawi Congress party appointed Banda as president-for-life in 1970, but a 1993 referendum strongly favored the creation of a multiparty system. In May 1994, President Banda, who was the oldest head of state in the world and Africa's longest-ruling dictator, was ousted from office and then charged with the murder of political foes. ■

MALAYSIA

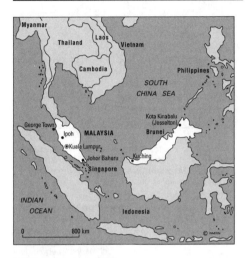

Official name Malaysia

PEOPLE
Population 20,585,000. **Density** 162/mi² (62/km²).
Urban 54%. **Capital** Kuala Lumpur, 1,145,075. **Ethnic groups** Malay 58%, Chinese 26%, Indian 7%.
Languages Malay, Chinese dialects, English, Tamil.
Religions Muslim, Hindi, Buddhist, Taoist, Christian.
Life expectancy 74 female, 70 male. **Literacy** 84%.

POLITICS
Government Federal constitutional monarchy. **Parties** Democratic Action, Islamic, National Front, others.
Suffrage Universal, 21 and over. **Memberships** ASEAN, CW, UN. **Subdivisions** 13 states, 2 federal territories.

ECONOMY
GDP $193,600,000,000. **Per capita** $9,709. **Monetary unit** Ringgit. **Trade partners** Exports: Singapore, U.S., Japan. Imports: Japan, U.S., Singapore. **Exports** Electronics, petroleum, petroleum products, wood, rubber, palm oil, textiles. **Imports** Food, petroleum products, machinery and equipment, chemicals.

LAND
Description Southeastern Asia (includes part of the island of Borneo). **Area** 127,320 mi² (329,758 km²).
Highest point Mt. Kinabalu, 13,455 ft (4,101 m).
Lowest point Sea level.

People. Malaysia's location at one of Southeast Asia's maritime crossroads has left it with a diverse population, including Malays, Chinese, Indians, and native non-Malay groups. The mostly rural Malays dominate politically, while the predominantly urban Chinese are very active in economic life. Considerable tension exists between the two groups. Although most Malays speak Malay and practice Islam, Malaysia's eth-

nic groups have resisted assimilation; Chinese, Indian, and Western languages and beliefs are also part of the culture. Most Malaysians live in Peninsular Malaysia.

Economy and the Land. The economy is one of the healthiest in the region, supported by multiple strengths in agriculture, mining, forestry, and fishing. The country is one of the world's leading producers of rubber, palm oil, and tin, and one of the Far East's largest petroleum exporters. Manufacturing is also being developed. Malaysia consists of the southern portion of the Malay Penin-sula and the states of Sarawak and Sabah on northern Borneo. The land features swampy areas, mountains, and rain forests. The climate is tropical and very humid.

History and Politics. The Malay Peninsula has been inhabited since the late Stone Age. Hindu and Buddhist influences were widespread from the 9th through the 14th centuries A.D., after which Islam was introduced. In 1511 the Portuguese seized Melaka, a trading center, but were soon replaced, first by the Dutch in 1641 and then by the British in 1795. By the early 1900s, Britain was in control of present-day Malaysia and Singapore: the areas that were occupied by Japan during World War II. Following the war, the Federation of Malaya was created as a semi-autonomous state under British authority. A guerrilla war ensued, waged by Chinese Communists and others who opposed the British. The country gained full independence in 1963 with the unification of Malaysia. Singapore seceded in 1965. Government attempts in 1993 to curb the powers of hereditary rulers threaten peace in the country. When Thailand's economy descended into its 1997 currency crisis, it strongly affected Malaysia. Since the Malaysian government resisted asking the International Monetary Fund (IMF) for help, it is expected that Malaysia's economic recovery will take longer than that of other Southeast Asian countries. ■

MALDIVES

Official name Republic of Maldives

PEOPLE
Population 285,000. **Density** 2,478/mi² (956/km²).
Urban 27%. **Capital** Male', Male I., 55,130. **Ethnic groups** Maldivian (mixed Sinhalese, Dravidian, Arab, and black). **Languages** Divehi. **Religions** Sunni Muslim. **Life expectancy** 63 female, 66 male.
Literacy 93%.

POLITICS
Government Republic. **Parties** None. **Suffrage** Universal, 21 and over. **Memberships** CW, UN. **Subdivisions** 19 districts, 1 capital city.

ECONOMY
GDP $390,000,000,000. **Per capita** $1,554. **Monetary unit** Rufiyaa. **Trade partners** Exports: U.S., U.K., Sri Lanka. Imports: Singapore, Germany, Sri Lanka. **Exports** Fish, clothing. **Imports** Manufactures, petroleum products.

LAND

Description Indian Ocean islands. **Area** 115 mi² (298 km²). **Highest point** 10 ft (3 m). **Lowest point** Sea level.

People. Most Maldivians are descended from Sinhalese peoples from Sri Lanka; southern Indians, or Dravidians; and Arabs. Nearly all Maldivians are Sunni Muslims and speak Divehi. The population is concentrated on Male, the capital island.

Economy and the Land. The country draws on its advantages as a union of 1,100 islands to fuel its economy: Tourism, shipping, and fishing are the mainstays. With limited arable land and infertile soil, agriculture is marginal. The Maldives, flat coral islands, form a chain of nineteen atolls. Seasonal monsoons mark the tropical climate.

History and Politics. The Maldives are believed to have been originally settled by southern Indian peoples. Arab sailors brought Islam to the islands in the 12th century A.D. Although a Muslim sultanate remained in power with only two interruptions from 1153 until 1968, the Portuguese and Dutch controlled the islands intermittently between the 1500s and the 1700s. The Maldives were a British protectorate from 1887 until 1965, when they achieved independence. The country was declared a republic three years later. ∎

MALI

Official name Republic of Mali

PEOPLE

Population 10,080,000. **Density** 21/mi² (8.1/km²). **Urban** 28%. **Capital** Bamako, 658,275. **Ethnic groups** Mande 50%, Fulani 17%, Voltaic 12%, Songhai 6%. **Languages** French, Bambara, indigenous. **Religions** Sunni Muslim 90%, Animist 9%, Christian 1%. **Life expectancy** 50 female, 46 male. **Literacy** 31%.

POLITICS

Government Republic. **Parties** Alliance for Democracy, National Congress for Democratic Initiative, Sudanese Union/African Democratic, others. **Suffrage** Universal, 21 and over. **Memberships** OAU, UN. **Subdivisions** 8 regions, 1 capital district.

ECONOMY

GDP $5,400,000,000. **Per capita** $563. **Monetary unit** CFA franc. **Trade partners** Exports: Cote d'Ivoire, Senegal, former Soviet republics. Imports: France, Cote d'Ivoire, Senegal. **Exports** Livestock, cotton, gold. **Imports** Textiles, petroleum, machinery and equipment, construction materials, food.

LAND

Description Western Africa, landlocked. **Area** 482,077 mi² (1,248,574 km²). **Highest point** Hombori Mtn., 3,789 ft (1,155 m). **Lowest point** Along Senegal River, 75 ft (23 m).

People. The majority of Malians belong to one of several black groups, although there is a small non-black nomadic population that includes the Tuareg, who launched a rebellion in 1990. The Tuareg continue to resist the government's efforts to encourage them to settle and farm. Most Malians are farmers who live in small villages. The official language is French, but most people communicate in Bambara, a market language. The population is concentrated in the basins of the Niger and Senegal Rivers in the south. Heirs of three ancient empires, Malians have produced a distinct culture.

Economy and the Land. One of the world's poorest countries, Mali depends primarily on agriculture but is limited by a climate that produces drought and a terrain that is almost half desert. Mineral reserves have not been exploited because of poor transportation and power facilities. Food processing and textiles account for most industry. A landlocked country, Mali faces a growing national debt due to its dependence on foreign goods. The climate is hot and dry, with alternating dry and wet seasons.

History and Politics. Parts of present-day Mali once belonged to the Ghana, Mali, and Songhai empires. These wealthy empires, which ruled from about A.D. 300 to 1600, traded with the Mediterranean world and were centers of Islamic learning. Fierce native resistance delayed colonization by the French until 1904, when French Sudan, as the area was called, was made part of French West Africa. In 1959 it joined Senegal to form the Federation of Mali. Senegal soon withdrew from the union, and French Sudan declared itself the Republic of Mali in 1960. A military coup overthrew the republic, a socialist state, in 1968. This government, in turn, was overthrown and the country has since moved haltingly toward democracy. ■

MALTA

Official name Republic of Malta

PEOPLE
Population 382,000. **Density** 3,131/mi² (1,209/km²). **Urban** 90%. **Capital** Valletta, 9,144. **Ethnic groups** Maltese (mixed Arab, Sicilian, Norman, Spanish, Italian, and English). **Languages** English, Maltese, Italian. **Religions** Roman Catholic 98%. **Life expectancy** 79 female, 75 male. **Literacy** 84%.

POLITICS
Government Republic. **Parties** Labor, Nationalist. **Suffrage** Universal, 18 and over. **Memberships** CW, UN. **Subdivisions** 6 regions.

ECONOMY
GDP $4,400,000,000. **Per capita** $11,860. **Monetary unit** Lira. **Trade partners** Exports: Italy, Germany, U.K. Imports: Italy, U.K., Germany. **Exports** Machinery and transportation equipment, clothing, footwear, printed matter. **Imports** Food, petroleum, machinery, semimanufactured goods.

LAND
Description Mediterranean island. **Area** 122 mi² (316 km²). **Highest point** 829 ft (253 m). **Lowest point** Sea level.

People. Malta's diverse population reflects centuries of rule by Arabs, Normans, and British. The official languages are English and Maltese, the latter a blend of Arabic and a Sicilian dialect of

Italian. Roman Catholicism is practiced by the majority of residents. Malta is one of the world's most densely populated countries.

Economy and the Land. Situated strategically between Europe and Africa, Malta became an important military site for foreign powers with the opening of the Suez Canal in 1869. Its economy, shaped by the patterns of war and peace in the Mediterranean, has recently turned toward commercial shipbuilding, construction, manufacturing, and tourism. Its soil is poor, and most food is imported. Although there are many natural harbors and hundreds of miles of coastline, fishing is not a major source of income. Malta, with its hilly terrain, is subtropical in summer and temperate the rest of the year.

History and Politics. The Phoenicians and Carthaginians first colonized the island of Malta between 1000 and 600 B.C. After becoming part of the Roman and Byzantine empires, Malta was ruled successively by Arabs, Normans, and various feudal lords. In the 1500s, the Holy Roman Emperor Charles V ceded Malta to the Knights of St. John of Jerusalem, an order of the Roman Catholic church. The Knights' reign, marked by cultural and architectural achievements, ended with surrender to France's Napoleon Bonaparte in 1798. The Maltese resisted French rule, however, and offered control to Britain, becoming part of the United Kingdom in 1814. Throughout both world wars, Malta was a vital naval base for the Allied forces. It achieved independence from Britain in 1964 and became a republic ten years later. In 1979, the last British and North Atlantic Treaty Organization (NATO) military forces departed, and Malta declared its neutrality. ■

MARSHALL ISLANDS

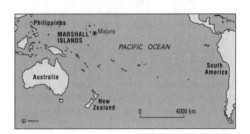

Official name Republic of the Marshall Islands

PEOPLE
Population 61,000. **Density** 871/mi² (337/km²). **Urban** 70%. **Capital** Majuro (island). **Ethnic groups** Micronesian. **Languages** English, indigenous, Japanese. **Religions** Protestant, Roman Catholic. **Life expectancy** 65 female, 62 male. **Literacy** 93%.

POLITICS
Government Republic (U.S. protection). **Parties** Our Islands, Ralik Ratak Democratic. **Suffrage** Universal, 18 and over. **Memberships** UN. **Subdivisions** None.

ECONOMY

GDP $94,000,000. **Per capita** $1,709. **Monetary unit** U.S. dollar. **Trade partners** U.S., Japan. **Exports** Coconut oil, fish, livestock, shells. **Imports** Food, machinery, beverages, tobacco, fuel.

LAND

Description North Pacific islands. **Area** 70 mi^2 (181 km^2). **Highest point** 80 ft (24 m). **Lowest point** Sea level.

People. Most Marshall Islanders are Micronesian, although there is a Polynesian minority. Both English and Malay-Polynesian languages are spoken on the islands.

Economy and the Land. The main industry of the Marshall Islands is coconuts, and many islanders continue to practice subsistence farming and fishing. The islands remain dependent on economic aid from the United States. Part of the area of the Pacific Ocean known as Micronesia, the two major island groups are the eastern Ratak Chain and the western Ralik Chain. The coral islands are mostly flat and low-lying, and the climate is hot and rainy.

History and Politics. The history of the Marshall Islands prior to the arrival of Europeans is largely unknown, but it is likely that the earliest settlers came from Southeast Asia. The islands received their name from Captain John Marshall, a Briton who reached the Marshalls in 1788. In the 1880s the Marshall Islands became a German protectorate, and in 1914, during World War I, Japan seized the islands. During World War II, the U.S. captured the islands from Japan, and in 1947, the Marshall Islands were incorporated into the Trust Territory of the Pacific Islands established by the United Nations, and placed under U.S. protection. In the late 1940s and early 1950s, the U.S. conducted dozens of nuclear test explosions throughout the Marshall Islands. The U.S. continues to provide compensation to those victimized by radiation-related illnesses and destruction of property, but the displaced inhabitants of Bikini Atoll insist that the U.S. should restore their island's environment. In 1986, the Marshall Islands became self-governing when a compact of free association with the U.S. was finalized. Official recognition of the new republic did not come until 1991, when the UN removed the Marshall Islands from the trusteeship. ■

MARTINIQUE

Official name Department of Martinique

PEOPLE

Population 406,000. **Density** 931/mi^2 (360/km^2). **Urban** 94%. **Capital** Fort-de-France, 100,080. **Ethnic groups** Black or mulatto 90%, white 5%. **Languages** French, Creole. **Religions** Roman Catholic 95%. **Life expectancy** 80 female, 74 male. **Literacy** 93%.

POLITICS

Government Overseas department (France). **Parties** Martinique Independence Movement, Progressive, Rally for the Republic, Union for French Democracy, others.

Suffrage Universal, 18 and over. **Memberships** None. **Subdivisions** 3 arrondissements.

ECONOMY

GDP $3,950,000,000. **Per capita** $10,286. **Monetary unit** French franc. **Trade partners** Exports: France, Guadeloupe, French Guiana. Imports: France, United Arab Emirates, U.K. **Exports** Petroleum products, bananas, rum, pineapples. **Imports** Petroleum products, petroleum, food, building materials, vehicles, clothing.

LAND

Description Caribbean island. **Area** 436 mi^2 (1,128 km^2). **Highest point** Pelée, Montagne, 4,583 ft (1,397 m). **Lowest point** Sea level.

People. Blacks and people of mixed black-and-French ancestry compose the majority group on Martinique. The culture is a unique blend of French and West Indian lifestyles.

Economy and the Land. Martinique's tropical climate and beautiful scenery attract many visitors each year. Agriculture provides additional income, and major products include bananas, sugar, and rum. Forested mountains cover much of the island.

History and Politics. Caribs inhabited the island when Christopher Columbus first sighted it in 1493. Columbus did not come ashore until his 1502 voyage, and Carib hostility discouraged colonization. French settlement began in 1635, and except for short periods of British rule, the island has remained in French hands. In 1946 Martinique became an overseas department of France. ■

MAURITANIA

Official name Islamic Republic of Mauritania

PEOPLE

Population 2,447,000. **Density** 6.1/mi^2 (2.4/km^2). **Urban** 53%. **Capital** Nouakchott, 393,325. **Ethnic groups** Mixed Moor and black 40%, Moor 30%, black 30%. **Languages** Arabic, Pular, Soninke, Wolof.

Religions Sunni Muslim 100%. **Life expectancy**
55 female, 52 male. **Literacy** 38%.

POLITICS
Government Republic. **Parties** Democratic and Social
Republican, others. **Suffrage** Universal, 18 and over.
Memberships AL, OAU, UN. **Subdivisions** 12 regions,
1 capital district.

ECONOMY
GDP $2,800,000,000. **Per capita** $1,257. **Monetary
unit** Ouguiya. **Trade partners** Exports: Japan, France,
Spain. Imports: France, Spain, Senegal. **Exports** Iron
ore, fish, fish products. **Imports** Food, manufactures,
petroleum products.

LAND
Description Western Africa. **Area** 397,956 mi²
(1,030,700 km²). **Highest point** Mt. Jill, 3,002 ft
(915 m). **Lowest point** Sebkha Te-n-Dgâmcha,
-10 ft (-3 m).

People. Most Mauritanians are Moors, descendants of Arabs and Berbers, or of mixed Arab,
Berber, and black descent. The Moors, who speak
Arabic, are mostly nomadic herdsmen. The
remainder of the population is composed of
black Africans, who speak several languages and
farm in the Senegal River valley. Virtually all
Mauritanians are Muslim. Proportionally, the
nomadic population has declined recently
because of long periods of drought, although
overall population is increasing.

Economy and the Land. Mauritania's economy
is based on agriculture, with many farmers producing only subsistence-level outputs. Crop production, confined chiefly to the Senegal River
valley, has recently fallen because of drought and
outmoded cultivation methods. Mining of high-
grade iron ore deposits is the main industrial
activity, although fishing and fish processing are
also important. Inadequate transportation and
communication systems have crippled the economy. In addition to the river valley, land regions
include a northern desert and southeastern
grasslands. Mauritania has a hot, dry climate.

History and Politics. Berbers began settling in
parts of the area around A.D. 300 and established
a network of caravan trading routes. From this
time until the late 1500s, sections of the south
were dominated by the Ghana, the Mali, and
finally the Songhai empires. Contact with
Europeans grew between the 1600s and 1800s,
and in 1920 France made Mauritania a colony.
Mauritania attained independence in 1960,
although Morocco claimed the area and did not
recognize the state until 1970. During the late
1970s, Mauritania became embroiled in a war
with Morocco and the Polisario Front, a Western
Saharan nationalist group, for control of Western
Sahara. Mauritania withdrew its claim to the area
in 1979. A new constitution providing for universal suffrage was approved in 1991, and multiparty elections have been held. There are reports of
slavery and discrimination against the black
population. ∎

MAURITIUS

Official name Republic of Mauritius

PEOPLE
Population 1,161,000. **Density** 1,473/mi² (569/km²).
Urban 41%. **Capital** Port Louis, Mauritius I., 132,460.
Ethnic groups Indo-Mauritian 68%, Creole 27%,
Sino-Mauritian 3%, Franco-Mauritian 2%. **Languages**
English, Creole, Bhojpuri, French, Hindi, Tamil, others.
Religions Hindu 52%, Roman Catholic 28%, Muslim
17%. **Life expectancy** 75 female, 68 male. **Literacy**
83%.

POLITICS
Government Republic. **Parties** Labor, Militant
Movement, Militant Renaissance, Militant Socialist
Movement, others. **Suffrage** Universal, 18 and over.
Memberships CW, OAU, UN. **Subdivisions** 9 districts.

ECONOMY
GDP $10,900,000,000. **Per capita** $9,629. **Monetary
unit** Rupee. **Trade partners** Exports: U.K., France, U.S.
Imports: France, China, U.S., South Africa. **Exports**
Textiles, sugar, manufactures. **Imports** Manufactures,
equipment, food, petroleum products, chemicals.

LAND
Description Indian Ocean island. **Area** 788 mi²
(2,040 km²). **Highest point** Piton de la Petite Rivière
Noire, 2,717 ft (828 m). **Lowest point** Sea level.
The above information includes dependencies.

People. Mauritius's diverse ethnicity is largely
the product of its past as a sugar-producing
colony. Creoles are descendants of African slaves
and European plantation owners, while the
Indian community traces its roots to laborers
who replaced the Africans after slavery was abolished. There are also people of Chinese and
French descent. Franco-Mauritians now compose most of the nation's elite. English is the official tongue, although a French creole and many
other languages are also spoken. Religious activity is similarly varied and includes Hinduism,
Christianity and Islam.

Economy and the Land. Once heavily dependent
on sugar production, Mauritius diversified its

economy as the price of sugar fell. Tourism has become important, as well as international finance and light industry, earning it the reputation as Africa's Hong Kong. The country includes the island of Mauritius, Rodrigues Island, Agalega Islands, and Cargados Carajos Shoals. The climate is tropical.

History and Politics. Although visited by Arab, Malay, and Portuguese sailors between the 10th and 16th centuries A.D., Mauritius was uninhabited until 1598 when the Dutch claimed it. They abandoned the island in 1710, and five years later the French made it their colony. During the 1700s the French used Mauritius, which they called île de France, as a naval base and established plantations worked by imported slaves. The British ousted the French in 1810 and outlawed slavery soon afterward. In the 19th century indentured workers from India replaced the slaves. Mauritius began its history as an independent state in 1968 with a system of parliamentary democracy, and became a republic in 1992. ■

MAYOTTE See FRANCE.

MEXICO

Official name United Mexican States

PEOPLE
Population 98,460,000. **Density** 130/mi² (50/km²). **Urban** 74%. **Capital** Mexico City, 8,489,007. **Ethnic groups** Mestizo 60%, Amerindian 30%, white 9%. **Languages** Spanish, indigenous. **Religions** Roman Catholic 89%, Protestant 6%. **Life expectancy** 75 female, 69 male. **Literacy** 90%.

POLITICS
Government Federal republic. **Parties** Democratic Revolutionary, Institutional Revolutionary, National Action, others. **Suffrage** Universal, 18 and over. **Memberships** OAS, OECD, UN. **Subdivisions** 31 states, 1 federal district.

ECONOMY
GDP $721,400,000,000. **Per capita** $7,607. **Monetary unit** Peso. **Trade partners** Exports: U.S., Japan, Spain. Imports: U.S., Germany, Japan. **Exports** Petroleum, petroleum products, coffee, silver, engines, vehicles, cotton. **Imports** Machinery, electrical equipment, transportation parts and equipment.

LAND
Description Southern North America. **Area** 759,534 mi² (1,967,183 km²). **Highest point** Volcán Pico de Orizaba, 18,406 ft (5,610 m). **Lowest point** Laguna Salada, -26 ft (-8 m).

People. Most Mexicans are mestizos, descended from the indigenous peoples and the Spaniards who conquered the region in the 1500s. Spanish is spoken by most inhabitants, and Roman Catholicism is the predominant religion. Another major ethnic group is comprised of Amerindians, some of whom speak only indigenous languages and hold traditional religious beliefs. Mexico's rapid population growth has contributed to poverty among rural dwellers, spurring a migration to the cities. Due to its mild climate and fertile soils, Mexico's central plateau is home to most of the population.

Economy and the Land. Mexico is a leading producer of petroleum and silver, a growing manufacturer of iron, steel, and chemicals, and an exporter of coffee and cotton. Foreign visitors—drawn by archeological sites and warm, sunny weather—make tourism an important industry as well. Despite economic gains made since the mid-1900s in agriculture and industry, Mexico has been troubled recently by inflation, declining oil prices, rising unemployment, and a trade deficit that has grown with the need for imported materials. In recent years the peso has been significantly devalued, and banks have been nationalized to help reduce a massive international debt. Austerity plans and foreign aid are helping to revitalize the economy. Terrain and climate are greatly varied, ranging from tropical jungles along the coast to desert plains in the north. A temperate central plateau is bounded by rugged mountains in the south, east, and west.

History and Politics. Farm settlements grew in the Valley of Mexico between 6500 and 1500 B.C., and during the subsequent 3,000 years Mexico gave birth to the great civilizations of the Olmec, Maya, Toltec, and Aztec peoples. The Aztec Empire was overthrown by the Spanish in 1521, and Mexico became the viceroyalty of New Spain. Although there was much dissatisfaction with Spanish rule, rebellion did not begin until 1810. Formal independence came in 1821. Mexico lost considerable territory, including Texas, to the United States during the Mexican War, from 1846 to 1848. During subsequent years, power changed hands frequently as liberals demanding social and economic reforms battled conservatives. A brief span of French imperial rule, from 1864 to 1867, interrupted the struggle. Following a revolution that started in

1910, a new socialist constitution was adopted in 1917, and progress toward reform began, culminating in the separation of church and state and the redistribution of land. Mexico joined the U.S. and Canada in approving the North American Free Trade Agreement (NAFTA) in 1992. Momentum for political change developed after the January 1994 peasant rebellion in the state of Chiapas. Another signal for change was the 1997 election defeat of Mexico's ruling political party that broke its 70-year hold on the government. In December more civilians were slaughtered in Chiapas, and the Governor and Interior Minister of the state were forced to resign. Rebel demands for the government to give Chiapas greater autonomy could threaten Mexico's unity. ■

MICRONESIA, FEDERATED STATES OF

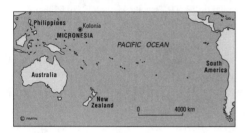

Official name Federated States of Micronesia

PEOPLE
Population 118,000. **Density** 435/mi² (168/km²). **Urban** 28%. **Capital** Kolonia, 6,306 (de facto); Paliker (future). **Ethnic groups** Micronesian, Polynesian. **Languages** English, indigenous. **Religions** Protestant, Roman Catholic. **Life expectancy** 70 female, 66 male. **Literacy** 89%.

POLITICS
Government Republic (U.S. protection). **Parties** None. **Suffrage** Universal, 18 and over. **Memberships** UN. **Subdivisions** 4 states.

ECONOMY
GDP $205,000,000. **Per capita** $1,752. **Monetary unit** U.S. dollar. **Trade partners** U.S., Japan. **Exports** Fish, garments, bananas, black pepper. **Imports** Food, manufactures, machinery and equipment, beverages.

LAND
Description North Pacific islands. **Area** 271 mi² (702 km²). **Highest point** Ngihneni, 2,566 ft (782 m). **Lowest point** Sea level.

People. Most inhabitants of Chuuk, Yap, Kosrae, and Pohnpei—the four states of the Federated States of Micronesia—are Micronesian, a group of mixed Melanesian, Polynesian, and Malaysian origin. Eight native languages are spoken, and English is the unifying language.

Economy and the Land. Subsistence farming and fishing are the primary activities for most islanders. Coconuts are the main cash crop. The states are heavily dependent on economic assistance from the United States. Each of the four states comprises a number of islands and, together with the territory of Palau, form the Caroline Islands, made up of volcanic and coral islands. The climate is tropical.

History and Politics. The ancestors of today's population probably arrived in the region more than 2,500 years ago. Spanish and German competition for the islands came to an end in 1899, when Germany purchased the Caroline Islands and most of the Mariana Islands from Spain. Japan controlled the islands from World War I until 1947, when the islands became part of the Trust Territory of the Pacific Islands. The trust territory was established by the United Nations and placed under U.S. administration. In 1978, Chuuk, Yap, Kosrae, and Pohnpei, along with the Marshall Islands and Palau, voted on a constitution that would have united all of Micronesia into a single entity. The Marshall Islands and Palau rejected the proposal, but Chuuk, Yap, Kosrae, and Pohnpei elected to become the Federated States of Micronesia. The U.S. recognized the Micronesian constitution in 1979, and in 1982 a compact of free association was signed. The compact received final approval in 1986 and the country became self-governing. However, full independence was not achieved until 1991, when the UN officially removed the Federated States of Micronesia from trusteeship status. A new capital is planned at Palikir on the island of Pohnpei. ■

MIDWAY ISLANDS
See UNITED STATES.

MOLDOVA

Official name Republic of Moldova

PEOPLE
Population 4,476,000. **Density** 344/mi^2 (133/km^2).
Urban 52%. **Capital** Chişinău (Kishinev), 676,700.
Ethnic groups Moldovan 65%, Ukrainian 14%, Russian
13%, Gagauz 4%, Jews 2%. **Languages** Romanian
(Moldovan), Russian, Gagauz. **Religions** Eastern
Orthodox 99%. **Life expectancy** 72 female,
64 male. **Literacy** 96%.

POLITICS
Government Republic. **Parties** Agrarian Democratic,
Christian Democratic Popular Front, Peasants and
Intellectuals Bloc, Socialist, others. **Suffrage** Universal,
18 and over. **Memberships** UN. **Subdivisions** None.

ECONOMY
GDP $10,400,000,000. **Per capita** $2,255. **Monetary
unit** Leu. **Trade partners** Former Soviet republics.
Exports Food, wine, tobacco, textiles and footwear,
machinery, chemicals. **Imports** Oil, gas, coal, steel,
machinery, food, automobiles, manufactures.

LAND
Description Eastern Europe, landlocked. **Area**
13,012 mi^2 (33,700 km^2). **Highest point** 1,407 ft
(429 m). **Lowest point** Along Dnestr River, 3 ft (1 m)

People. After the Soviet Union wrested Moldova
from Romanian control, it claimed that the
Moldovans were a distinct ethnic group with
their own language. In fact, Moldovans claim
Romanian ancestry, and their language is virtual-
ly the same as Romanian. Most people also speak
Russian, and there are substantial Russian and
Ukrainian minorities.

Economy and the Land. Most of Moldova is gen-
tly rolling plains, rising to wooded hills in the
central part of the country. Much of the land is
suitable for agriculture, and wheat, grapes, and
other fruits are important crops. Although agriculture and food processing dominate the economy, Moldova also has some light manufacturing.
The country has no significant energy resources.

History and Politics. Formerly known as
Bessarabia, this region was ruled by Romanian-
speaking Moldovan princes beginning in the
1300s. Bessarabia fell under the control of the
Ottoman Turks from the 1600s until 1812, when
the Turks were defeated by Russia. In 1918 control went to Romania and the territory was subsequently shifted back and forth between the two
countries. In 1944 the Soviet Union defeated
Romania and the Moldavian Soviet Socialist
Republic was established. Moldovans began agitating for greater autonomy within the Soviet
Union as early as 1989. They gained their independence in December 1991 after the demise of
the Soviet Union. A new 1994 constitution established Moldova as a neutral republic. Romania
has pressed for reunification with Moldova, but
Moldovans have rejected the offer. The government is in conflict with the secessionist
Transdneister region. ■

MONACO

Official name Principality of Monaco

PEOPLE
Population 32,000. **Density** 45,714/mi^2 (16,842/km^2).
Urban 100%. **Capital** Monaco, 32,000. **Ethnic groups**
French 47%, Monegasque 16%, Italian 16%.
Languages French, English, Italian, Monegasque.
Religions Roman Catholic 95%. **Life expectancy**
82 female, 74 male.

POLITICS
Government Constitutional monarchy. **Parties** National
and Democratic Union. **Suffrage** Universal,
21 and over. **Memberships** UN. **Subdivisions**
3 communes.

ECONOMY
GDP $788,000,000. **Per capita** $24,625. **Monetary unit**
French franc.

LAND
Description Southern Europe (on the southeastern
coast of France). **Area** 0.7 mi^2 (1.9 km^2). **Highest point**
459 ft (140 m). **Lowest point** Sea level.

People. Monaco is inhabited mostly by French
citizens, while Monegasques—citizens of indigenous descent—and various Europeans form the
rest of the population. Many foreigners have
taken up residence, drawn by the country's tax
benefits. French is the official language. Monegasque, a blend of French and Italian, is also spoken, as are Italian and English. Most residents are
Roman Catholic.

Economy and the Land. Monaco's scenic seaside
location, mild Mediterranean climate, and
renowned gambling casino in Monte Carlo make
it a popular tourist haven. Consequently, tourism
forms the backbone of the economy. Production
of chemicals, food products, and perfumes,
among other light industries, are additional
sources of income. Monaco also profits from
many foreign businesses, which are attracted by
the favorable tax climate and headquartered in
the principality. France and Monaco form a customs union for a mutually beneficial trade system; the French franc is Monaco's official currency. The world's second-smallest independent
state in area—after Vatican City—Monaco has

four regions: the old city of Monaco-Ville, site of the royal palace; Monte Carlo, the resort and major tourist center; La Condamine, the port area; and Fontvieille, the rapidly growing industrial section.

History and Politics. Known to the Phoenicians, Greeks, and Romans, the region became a Genoese colony in the 12th century A.D. Around the turn of the 14th century, the area was granted to the Grimaldi family of Genoa. France, Spain, and Sardinia had intermittent control of Monaco from 1400 until 1861, when its autonomy was recognized by the Franco-Monegasque Treaty. Another treaty, providing for French protection of Monaco, was signed in 1918. The absolute rule of Monaco's princes ended with the 1911 constitution. Monaco joined the United Nations in 1993. ∎

MONGOLIA

Official name Mongolia

PEOPLE
Population 2,560,000. **Density** 4.2/mi² (1.6/km²). **Urban** 61%. **Capital** Ulan Bator, 575,000. **Ethnic groups** Mongol 90%, Kazakh 4%, Chinese 2%, Russian 2%. **Languages** Khalkha Mongol, Turkish, Russian, Chinese. **Religions** Tibetan Buddhist, Muslim. **Life expectancy** 67 female, 64 male. **Literacy** 83%.

POLITICS
Government Republic. **Parties** National Democratic, People's Revolutionary, Social Democratic, others. **Suffrage** Universal, 18 and over. **Memberships** UN. **Subdivisions** 18 provinces, 3 municipalities.

ECONOMY
GDP $4,900,000,000. **Per capita** $1,940. **Monetary unit** Tughrik. **Trade partners** Exports: Former Soviet republics, China, Japan. Imports: Former Soviet republics, Austria, China. **Exports** Copper, livestock, animal products, cashmere, wool, hides, nonferrous metals. **Imports** Machinery, equipment, fuel, food, manufactures, chemicals, building materials.

LAND
Description Central Asia, landlocked. **Area** 604,829 mi² (1,566,500 km²). **Highest point** Kuyten-Uul, 14,350 ft (4,374 m). **Lowest point** Höh Lake, 1,837 ft (560 m).

People. Mongols, a central Asian people, make up the vast majority of Mongolia's population. Khalkha Mongol is the predominant language. Turkic-speaking Kazakhs, as well as Russians and Chinese, comprise minorities. Tibetan Buddhism was once the most common religion; however, during the years of Communist rule the government discouraged religious practice. The traditional nomadic way of life is becoming less common, as recent government policies have led to urbanization and settled agriculture.

Economy and the Land. Mongolia's economy, long based on the raising of livestock, has been shaped by the ideal grazing land found in most of the country. Livestock outnumber people in Mongolia by a ratio of 15 to one. Significant economic changes have taken place since the collapse of the Soviet economy because 90 percent of Mongolia's trade was with Russia and Eastern Europe. Market reforms have produced economic hardship. Mongolia's terrain varies from mountains in the north and west to steppe in the east and desert in the south. Located in the heart of Asia, remote from any moderating body of water, Mongolia has a rigorous continental climate with little precipitation.

History and Politics. Mongolian tribes were united under the warlord Genghis Khan around A.D. 1200, and he and his successors built one of history's largest land empires. In 1691 the Manchu dynasty of China subdued Outer Mongolia, as the area was then known, but allowed the Mongol rulers autonomy. Mongolia remained a Chinese province until the Mongols ousted the Chinese in 1911. In 1912 the state accepted Russian protection, but was unable to prevent another Chinese advance, and in 1919 Outer Mongolia again became a Chinese province. In 1921 a combined Soviet and Mongolian force defeated Chinese and Belorussian, or White Russian, troops, and the Mongolian People's Republic was declared in 1924. A mutual-assistance pact was signed by Mongolia and Russia in 1966. In 1989 the Soviets agreed to withdraw most of their troops from Mongolia. Increasing pressure for democratization led to the country's first free, multiparty elections in August 1990. A new constitution, describing Mongolia as a republic with parliamentary government, was adopted in 1992. In 1996 the Mongolians elected a non-Communist Parliament. ∎

MONTSERRAT
See UNITED KINGDOM.

MOROCCO

Official name Kingdom of Morocco

PEOPLE
Population 30,695,000. **Density** 178/mi² (69/km²).
Urban 53%. **Capital** Rabat, 717,000. **Ethnic groups**
Arab-Berber 99%. **Languages** Arabic, Berber dialects,
French. **Religions** Muslim 99%. **Life expectancy**
68 female, 64 male. **Literacy** 44%.

POLITICS
Government Constitutional monarchy. **Parties**
Constitutional Union, Democracy and Istiqlal, National
Rally of Independents, Popular Movement, others.
Suffrage Universal, 21 and over. **Memberships** AL,
UN. **Subdivisions** 36 provinces, 2 prefectures.

ECONOMY
GDP $87,400,000,000. **Per capita** $3,186. **Monetary
unit** Dirham. **Trade partners** Exports: France, Spain,
Italy. Imports: France, Spain, Iraq. **Exports** Food,
beverages, semiprocessed goods, manufactures,
phosphates. **Imports** Machinery, semimanufactures,
raw materials, fuel, lubricants, food, beverages.

LAND
Description Northwestern Africa. **Area** 172,414 mi²
(446,550 km²). **Highest point** Mt. Toubkal, 13,665 ft
(4,165 m). **Lowest point** Sebkha Tah, -180 ft (-55 m).
The above information excludes Western Sahara.

People. Moroccans, virtually homogeneous in
race and culture, are mostly a mix of Arab and
Berber stocks and speak Arabic. A few Berber
dialects are spoken in rural mountain areas, but
French and Spanish, the colonial tongues, are
common in business and government. The
majority of people are Sunni Muslim. The
population is concentrated west of the Atlas
Mountains, which border the Sahara Desert.
Rural people are migrating to cities, where the
standard of living is higher.

Economy and the Land. Although agriculture
employs much of the work force and is an important activity, the country depends on mining for
most of its income. Morocco is a leading exporter
of phosphates, and has other mineral reserves as

well. Fishing and tourism are growing sources of
revenue. Recently, severe drought, rising dependency on imported oil, and a costly war in Western Sahara have slowed productivity, while investments by Arab countries have bolstered the
economy. Morocco, with its varied terrain of
desert, forests, and mountains, has an equally
varied climate that is semitropical along the
coast, and desert beyond the Atlas Mountains.

History and Politics. In ancient times, Morocco
was a province of Carthage and Rome. Vandals
and Byzantine Greeks, the subsequent rulers,
were followed in the A.D.700s by Arabs, who
brought Islam. Morocco's strategic position
awakened the interest of colonial powers in the
1800s, and by 1912 the area was divided into
French and Spanish protectorates. A nationalist
movement began in the 1920s, occasionally
bringing violence, but not until 1956 did
Morocco become independent from France.
The last of Spain's holdings in Morocco were
returned in 1969. War broke out in 1976, when
Morocco claimed the northern part of Western
Sahara and was challenged by the Saharan
nationalist Polisario Front. In 1979 Mauritania
surrendered its claim, and Morocco established
claim to the entire territory. Negotiations over
the final disposition of Western Sahara have been
sporadic. King Hassan shares power with directly
elected groups under a complex formula. ■

MOZAMBIQUE

Official name Republic of Mozambique

PEOPLE
Population 18,590,000. **Density** 60/mi² (23/km²).
Urban 35%. **Capital** Maputo, 1,069,727. **Ethnic
groups** Chopi, Makua, Lomwe, Makonde, Shona,
Thonga, Tonga. **Languages** Portuguese, indigenous.
Religions Tribal religionist 50%, Roman Catholic and
other Christian 30%, Musli. **Life expectancy** 48 female,
45 male. **Literacy** 40%.

POLITICS
Government Republic. **Parties** Democratic Union, Front for the Liberation of Mozambique, National Resistance. **Suffrage** Universal, 18 and over. **Memberships** CW, OAU, UN. **Subdivisions** 10 provinces, 1 independent city.

ECONOMY
GDP $12,200,000,000. **Per capita** $683. **Monetary unit** Metical. **Trade partners** Exports: U.S., Germany, Japan. Imports: Former Soviet republics, South African countries, Portugal. **Exports** Shrimp, cashews, cotton, sugar, copra, fruit. **Imports** Food, clothing, farm equipment, petroleum.

LAND
Description Southern Africa. **Area** 308,642 mi² (799,380 km²). **Highest point** Monte Binga, 7,995 ft (2,437 m). **Lowest point** Sea level.

People. Black Africans belonging to about ten groups compose the vast majority of the population. Most black Mozambicans live in rural areas, while small European and Asian minorities live primarily in urban centers. Traditional African religions are followed by a majority, while others practice Islam and Christianity. Although Portuguese is the official language, most blacks speak Bantu tongues.

Economy and the Land. Mozambique's underdeveloped economy is largely the product of its colonial past, during which its human and natural resources were neglected. Recent political developments in southern Africa have created more economic woes, as lucrative trade agreements with racially divided neighbors have ceased. While the mainstays of the economy are agriculture and transport services, fishing and mining are also being developed. The Marxist government allowed some private enterprise, and foreign aid is important. The climate is tropical or subtropical along the coastal plain that covers nearly half of the country, with cooler conditions in the western high plateaus and mountains.

History and Politics. Bantu-speaking peoples settled in present-day Mozambique around the first century A.D. Subsequent immigrants included Arab traders in the 800s and the Portuguese in the late 1400s. European economic interest in the area was hindered by lucrative trading with other colonies, and Mozambique wasn't recognized as a Portuguese colony until 1885. Policies instituted by the Portuguese benefited European settlers and Portugal, but overlooked the welfare of Mozambique and its native inhabitants. In the early 1960s the country made clear its opposition to foreign rule, with the formation of the Front for the Liberation of Mozambique, a Marxist nationalist group that initiated an armed campaign against the Portuguese. In 1975 Mozambique became an independent state, but fighting between the socialist government and opposition forces continued. A new constitution passed in 1990 marked the end of single-party rule in Mozambique. The civil war, resulting in a million casualties and nearly two million refugees, ended in October 1992. A fragile peace and the return of more than one million refugees was complicated by the worst drought of the century. The country's first multiparty elections were held in October 1994. ∎

MYANMAR

Official name Union of Myanmar

PEOPLE
Population 47,245,000. **Density** 181/mi² (70/km²). **Urban** 26%. **Capital** Yangon (Rangoon), 2,705,039. **Ethnic groups** Burman 68%, Karen 7%, Rakhine 4%. **Languages** Burmese, indigenous. **Religions** Buddhist 89%, Muslim 4%, Christian 4%. **Life expectancy** 62 female, 59 male. **Literacy** 83%.

POLITICS
Government Provisional military government. **Parties** National League for Democracy, National Unity Party, others. **Suffrage** Universal, 18 and over. **Memberships** ASEAN, UN. **Subdivisions** 7 divisions, 7 states.

ECONOMY
GDP $47,000,000,000. **Per capita** $1,033. **Monetary unit** Kyat. **Trade partners** Exports: Southeast Asian countries, India, Japan. Imports: Japan, Western European countries, China. **Exports** Pulses, beans, teak, rice, hardwood. **Imports** Machinery, food, transportation equipment, building materials, manufactures.

LAND
Description Southeastern Asia. **Area** 261,228 mi² (676,577 km²). **Highest point** Hkakabo Razi, 19,296 ft (5,881 m). **Lowest point** Sea level.

People. The population of Myanmar is highly diverse, with many ethnic groups including Tibetan-related Burman, who compose the majority; Karen, who inhabit mainly the south and east; and Thai-related Shan, found on the eastern plateaus. Diversity results in many languages, although Burmese predominates. Buddhist monasteries and pagodas dot the landscape, and minority religions include Christianity, indigenous beliefs, and Islam. The primarily rural population is concentrated in the fertile valleys and on the delta of the Irrawaddy River.

Economy and the Land. Fertile soils, dense woodlands, and mineral deposits provide a resource base for agriculture, forestry, and mining. Myanmar has been beset with economic problems, however, caused mainly by the destruction of World War II, as well as post-independence instability. Today agriculture continues as the economic mainstay. The hot, wet climate is ideal for rice production. In addition, dense forests provide for a timber industry, and resource deposits include petroleum and various minerals. Myanmar's economic future depends on exploitation of natural resources and political stability. The terrain is marked by mountains, rivers, and forests, and the climate is tropical.

History and Politics. Myanmar's Chinese and Tibetan settlers were first united in the 11th century. Independence ended with the invasion of Mongols led by Kublai Khan, followed by national unification in the 15th and 18th centuries. Annexation to British India in the 19th century ended Myanmar's monarchy. During World War II, Japanese occupation and subsequent Allied-Japanese conflicts caused much economic and physical damage. Myanmar officially became independent in 1948. After initial stability, the government was unable to withstand separatist and political revolts, and military rule has alternated with civilian governments. The latest attempts to reestablish democracy were thwarted when the results of elections in 1990 were contested by 93 opposition parties. The military government refused to relinquish control or hold new elections. The 1991 Nobel Peace Prize award to the country's main opposition leader, Aung San Suu Kyi, focused world attention on human rights abuses. Released in 1995 after six years of house arrest, Suu Kyi continues to work to establish democracy and the rule of law. ■

NAMIBIA

Official name Republic of Namibia

PEOPLE
Population 1,751,000. **Density** 5.5/mi² (2.1/km²). **Urban** 37%. **Capital** Windhoek, 147,056. **Ethnic groups** Ovambo 49%, Kavango 9%, Damara 8%, Herero 7%, white 7%, mixed 7%. **Languages** English, Afrikaans, German, indigenous. **Religions** Lutheran and other Protestant, Roman Catholic, Animist. **Life expectancy** 63 female, 60 male. **Literacy** 38%.

POLITICS
Government Republic. **Parties** Democratic Turnhalle Alliance, South West Africa People's Organization, others. **Suffrage** Universal, 18 and over. **Memberships** CW, OAU, UN. **Subdivisions** 13 regions.

ECONOMY
GDP $5,800,000,000. **Per capita** $3,452. **Monetary**

unit South African Rand. **Trade partners** Exports: Switzerland, South Africa, Germany. Imports: South Africa, Germany, U.S. **Exports** Uranium, diamonds, zinc, copper, lead, gold, cattle, processed fish, hides. **Imports** Food, petroleum products, fuel, machinery and equipment.

LAND
Description Southern Africa. **Area** 317,818 mi² (823,144 km²). **Highest point** Brandberg, 8,461 ft (2,579 m). **Lowest point** Sea level.

People. The largest ethnic group is black African, composed of many indigenous peoples. South Africans, Britons, and Germans constitute the white minority. Black Namibians speak various native dialects, while the majority of whites speak Afrikaans. Blacks still follow traditional customs and religions, but a considerable number have converted to Christianity.

Economy and the Land. Namibia's economy is based on the mining of diamonds, copper, lead, and other minerals. Agriculture makes a marginal contribution, but livestock raising is important. Manufacturing remains undeveloped because of an unskilled work force, and Namibia imports most of its finished goods from South Africa, its partner in a customs union. A variety of factors, including continuing drought and political instability, have held back economic growth. Namibia consists of a high plateau that encompasses the Namib Desert and part of the Kalahari Desert. The climate is subtropical with marginal rainfall.

History and Politics. Bushmen were probably the area's first inhabitants, followed by other African peoples. European exploration of the coast began in the A.D. 1500s, but the coastal desert prevented foreign penetration. In 1884 Germany annexed all of the territory except for the coastal enclave of Walvis Bay, which had been claimed by Britain in 1878. After South African troops ousted the Germans from the area during World War I, the League of Nations mandated Namibia, then known as South West Africa, to South Africa. Following World War II, the United Nations requested that the territory become a trusteeship. South Africa refused to cooperate. In 1966 the UN revoked South Africa's mandate, yet South Africa kept control of Namibia. Beginning in the 1960s, the South West Africa People's Organization (SWAPO), a Namibian nationalist group with Communist support, made guerrilla raids on South African forces from bases in Zambia and later from Angola. In 1989, after years of continued pressure, an assembly was elected to draft a constitution. Independence was achieved in 1990. In 1994, Namibia's first post-independence election resulted in a major victory by SWAPO. ■

NAURU

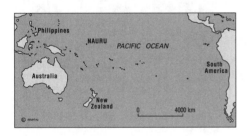

Official name Republic of Nauru

PEOPLE
Population 11,000. **Density** 1,358/mi² (524/km²). **Urban** 100%. **Capital** Yaren District. **Ethnic groups** Nauruan 58%, other Pacific Islander 26%, Chinese 8%, European 8%. **Languages** Nauruan, English. **Religions** Congregationalist and other Protestant 67%, Roman Catholic 33%. **Life expectancy** 69 female, 64 male.

POLITICS
Government Republic. **Parties** None. **Suffrage** Universal and Compulsory, 20 and over. **Memberships** CW. **Subdivisions** 14 districts.

ECONOMY
GDP $100,000,000. **Per capita** $10,000. **Monetary unit** Australian dollar. **Trade partners** Exports: Australia, New Zealand. Imports: Australia, U.K., New Zealand, Japan. **Exports** Phosphates. **Imports** Food, fuel, manufactures, building materials, machinery.

LAND
Description South Pacific island. **Area** 8.1 mi² (21 km²). **Highest point** 236 ft (72 m). **Lowest point** Sea level.

People. Indigenous Nauruans are a mix of Polynesian, Micronesian, and Melanesian stock, and many residents are from other Pacific islands. Nauruan is the language of most inhabitants, but English is widely spoken. Nearly all Nauruans are Christian.

Economy and the Land. The economy depends primarily on its sole resource, phosphates; the government is establishing trust funds to support islanders when the resource is depleted. Mining has destroyed 80 percent of the island and, with limited agriculture, nearly all food and water must be imported. Nauru is one of the smallest countries in the world. Most of the coral island is a plateau, and the climate is tropical.

History and Politics. Nauru was most likely settled by castaways from nearby islands. Noted by a British explorer in 1798, Nauru remained autonomous until it came under German control in 1881. In 1914 Germany surrendered the island, and it was subsequently mandated to Australia, Britain, and New Zealand. World War II brought occupation by Japan. Nauru reverted to Australian rule in 1947 as a trusteeship. It became independent in 1968 and nationalized the phosphate industry in 1970. The country is preparing for the near future when phosphate is gone and the people must either restore the land or move. Mismanagement of Nauru's trust fund has compromised its future, but ambitious plans to redevelop the island are underway. ■

NEPAL

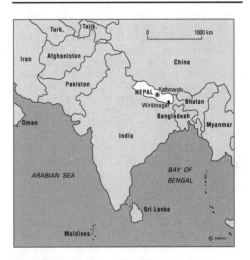

Official name Kingdom of Nepal

PEOPLE
Population 22,905,000. **Density** 403/mi² (156/km²). **Urban** 11%. **Capital** Kathmandu, 421,258. **Ethnic groups** Newar, Indian, Tibetan, Gurung, Magar, Tamang, Bhotia, Sherpa, others. **Languages** Nepali, Maithali, Bhojpuri, other indigenous. **Religions** Hindu 90%, Buddhist 5%, Muslim 3%. **Life expectancy** 57 female, 57 male. **Literacy** 28%.

POLITICS
Government Constitutional monarchy. **Parties** Communist/United Marxist and Leninist, Congress, National Democratic, others. **Suffrage** Universal, 18 and over. **Memberships** UN. **Subdivisions** 14 zones.

ECONOMY
GDP $25,200,000,000. **Per capita** $1,155. **Monetary unit** Rupee. **Trade partners** Exports: U.S., Germany, India. Imports: India, Singapore, Japan. **Exports** Clothing, carpets, leather goods, jute goods, grain. **Imports** Petroleum products, fertilizer, machinery.

LAND
Description Southern Asia, landlocked. **Area** 56,827 mi² (147,181 km²). **Highest point** Mt. Everest, 29,028 ft (8,848 m). **Lowest point** Unnamed, 197 ft (60 m).

People. Nepal's mixed population results from migrations over the centuries from India, Tibet, and central Asia. Most of Nepal's ruling families have been of Indian descent, and Nepali, the official language, is derived from Sanskrit, an ancient Indian language. Although the majority of the population practices Hinduism, Nepal is the birthplace of Buddha and has been greatly influenced by Buddhism as well. The importance of both religions is reflected in the more than 2,700 shrines in the Kathmandu Valley. Most Nepalese are rural farmers.

Economy and the Land. Because of geographic remoteness and a political policy of isolation lasting until the 1950s, Nepal's economy is one of the least developed in the world. Agriculture, concentrated chiefly in the south, is the most significant activity, even though most of Nepal is covered by the Himalayas, the world's highest mountains. This range—which includes Mount Everest, the world's highest peak—has made tourism increasingly lucrative. Nepal has potential in hydroelectricity and forestry, but inadequate transportation routes, overpopulation, and deforestation present obstacles to development. Nepal has received financial aid from many countries, partly because of its strategic location between India and China. The climate varies from subtropical in the flat, fertile south to temperate in the central hill country. Himalayan summers are cool and winters severe.

History and Politics. Several small Hindu-Buddhist kingdoms had emerged in the Kathmandu Valley by about A.D. 300. These states were unified in the late 1700s by the founder of the Shah dynasty. The Rana family wrested control from the Shahs in 1846 and pursued an isolationist course, which thwarted foreign influence but stunted economic growth. Opposition to the Ranas mounted during the 1930s and 1940s, and in 1951 the Shah monarchy was restored by a revolution. In 1962 the king established a government that gave the crown dominance and abolished political parties. A 1980 referendum narrowly upheld this system. In November 1990, a pro-democracy movement forced the king to approve a new constitution providing for a multiparty structure and the country's new status as a constitutional monarchy. The first democratic election took place in 1991. Elections since have resulted in a coalition government. ∎

NETHERLANDS

Official name Kingdom of the Netherlands

PEOPLE
Population 15,700,000. **Density** 971/mi² (375/km²). **Urban** 89%. **Capital** Amsterdam (designated), 713,304; The Hague (seat of government), 441,561. **Ethnic groups** Dutch (mixed Scandinavian, French, and Celtic) 96%. **Languages** Dutch. **Religions** Roman Catholic 34%, Dutch Reformed and other Protestant 25%, Muslim 3%. **Life expectancy** 81 female, 75 male. **Literacy** 99%.

POLITICS
Government Constitutional monarchy. **Parties** Christian Democratic Appeal, Democrats 66, Labor, Liberal, others. **Suffrage** Universal, 18 and over. **Memberships** EU, NATO, OECD, UN. **Subdivisions** 12 provinces.

ECONOMY
GDP $301,900,000,000. **Per capita** $19,477. **Monetary unit** Guilder. **Trade partners** Exports: Germany, Belgium, France. Imports: Germany, Belgium, U.K. **Exports** Agricultural products, food, tobacco, natural gas, chemicals, metal products. **Imports** Raw materials, consumer goods, transportation equipment, petroleum, food.

LAND
Description Western Europe. **Area** 16,164 mi²

Places and Possessions of the NETHERLANDS

Entity	Status	Area	Population	Capital/Population
Aruba (Caribbean island)	Self-governing territory (Netherlands protection)	75 mi² (193 km²)	68,000	Oranjestad, 19,800
Curaçao (Caribbean island)	Division of Netherlands Antilles (Neth.)	171 mi² (444 km²)	154,000	Willemstad, 31,883
Netherlands Antilles (Caribbean islands)	Self-governing territory (Netherlands protection)	309 mi² (800 km²)	212,000	Willemstad, 31,883

(41,864 km²). **Highest point** Vaalserberg, 1,053 ft (321 m). **Lowest point** Prins Alexander polder, -23 ft (-7 m).

People. The major ethnic group is the Dutch, for the most part a mixture of French, Scandinavian, and Celtic peoples. There are small minorities from the former Dutch possessions of Indonesia and Suriname. Dutch is the official language, but many Netherlanders also speak English or German. Although most Dutch are Christian, the country has a history of religious tolerance that has drawn countless refugees of other faiths.

Economy and the Land. A variety of manufacturing strengths—notably the metal, chemical, and food-processing industries—fuels the prosperous economy. Tourism and the production of natural gas are also important. Due to a lack of natural resources, the Netherlands must import many goods. The country benefits from its strategic position and has enjoyed success in shipping and trade. Much of the Netherlands, including most farmland, has been reclaimed from the sea through artificial drainage. The land is almost uniformly flat, and proximity to the sea produces a mild, damp climate. The Kingdom of the Netherlands includes the Netherlands Antilles, two groups of Caribbean islands, and Aruba.

History and Politics. The Germanic tribes of the area were conquered in 58 B.C. by the Romans, who were driven out in the A.D. 400s by the Franks. As part of the Low Countries with Belgium and Luxembourg, the Netherlands was dominated successively by Charlemagne, the dukes of Burgundy, the Hapsburgs, and rulers of Spain. Spanish persecution of Dutch Protestants led to a revolt that in 1581 created the Republic of the United Netherlands. In the 1600s the Netherlands became a maritime as well as a colonial power, and produced many masterpieces in painting. A series of wars with England and France ending in 1714 spelled the end of Dutch influence, and the country fell to France in 1795. With the defeat of Napoleon Bonaparte of France in 1815, the Netherlands was united with Belgium and became an independent kingdom. Belgium seceded in 1830. The Netherlands declared its neutrality in both world wars but was occupied by Germany from 1940 to 1945. World War II cost the country many lives and much of its economic strength, but membership in several international economic unions aided recovery. In recent years the Netherlands has been actively involved in the European Union. ∎

NETHERLANDS ANTILLES

Official name Netherlands Antilles

PEOPLE
Population 212,000. **Density** 686/mi² (265/km²). **Urban** 69%. **Capital** Willemstad, 31,883. **Ethnic groups** Mulatto 85%, West Indian, European. **Languages** Dutch, Papiamento, English. **Religions** Roman Catholic 74%, Methodist 12%. **Life expectancy** 76 female, 71 male. **Literacy** 95%.

POLITICS
Government Self-governing territory (Netherlands protection). **Parties** Antillean Restructuring, National People's, Patriotic Movement of Sint Maarten, others. **Suffrage** Universal, 18 and over. **Memberships** None. **Subdivisions** 5 island councils.

ECONOMY
GDP $1,920,000,000. **Per capita** $9,366. **Monetary unit** Guilder. **Trade partners** Exports: U.S., Italy, Japan. Imports: Venezuela, U.S., Netherlands. **Exports** Petroleum products. **Imports** Petroleum, food, manufactures.

LAND
Description Caribbean islands. **Area** 309 mi² (800 km²). **Highest point** 2,828 ft (862 m). **Lowest point** Sea level.

People. The people of the Netherlands Antilles are of mixed African, Carib, and European descent. Most people are multilingual, and languages include Dutch, English, and Papiamento, which combines Spanish, Dutch, Portuguese, English, and West Indian elements.

Economy and the Land. The bases of the islands' economy are financial services, petroleum refining, and tourism. Tax incentives have drawn some industry. Poor soils and aridity limit agriculture. The mainly volcanic St. Martin, Saba, and St. Eustatius make up the northern island group; the coral islands of Curaçao and Bonaire constitute the southern islands. The climate is tropical.

History and Politics. The Caribs were the original inhabitants of the northern islands, and the Caiquetio people resided on the islands to the south. Christopher Columbus reached the northern islands in 1493, and the Spanish arrived at the southern islands in 1499. In the 1630s, both island groups came under Dutch rule. Some of the islands were ruled briefly by the French and British, but since 1816 all have been under Dutch control. The Netherlands Antilles are a self-governing territory of the Netherlands. Aruba was part of the territory until 1986. Hurricane Luis hit the Netherlands Antilles in 1995, killing nine people on St. Martin. ∎

NEW CALEDONIA

Official name Territory of New Caledonia and Dependencies

PEOPLE
Population 193,000. **Density** 27/mi² (10/km²). **Urban** 62%. **Capital** Nouméa, New Caledonia I., 65,110. **Ethnic groups** Melanesian (Kanak) 45%, French 34%, Wallisian 9%, Indonesian 3%, Tahitian 3%. **Languages** French, indigenous. **Religions** Roman Catholic 60%, Protestant 30%. **Life expectancy** 76 female, 71 male. **Literacy** 93%.

POLITICS
Government Overseas territory (France). **Parties** Kanaka Socialist National Liberation Front,

Rassemblement pou la Caledonie dans la Republique, others. **Suffrage** Universal, 18 and over. **Memberships** None. **Subdivisions** 3 provinces.

ECONOMY
GDP $1,500,000,000. **Per capita** $8,197. **Monetary unit** CFP franc. **Trade partners** Exports: France, Japan, U.S. Imports: France, Australia, Japan, U.S. **Exports** Nickel. **Imports** Food, fuel, minerals, machinery, electrical equipment.

LAND
Description South Pacific islands. **Area** 7,172 mi^2 (18,575 km^2). **Highest point** Mont Panié, 5,344 ft (1,629 m). **Lowest point** Sea level.

People. The Melanesian, or Kanak, comprise the largest ethnic group in New Caledonia, a group of Pacific islands northeast of Australia. People of French descent make up the second largest group, with Asians and Polynesians composing significant minorities. New Caledonia's status as an overseas French territory is reflected in its languages, which include French as well as regional dialects, and in a population that is largely Christian.

Economy and the Land. The principal economic activity in New Caledonia, the mining and smelting of nickel, has fallen off in recent years. Small amounts of coffee and copra are exported, and tourism is important in Nouméa, the capital. Possessing few resources, New Caledonia imports almost all finished products from France. The main island, also called New Caledonia, is mountainous and accounts for almost 90 percent of the territory's land area. Smaller islands include the Isle of Pines, Loyalty and Bélep islands. The climate is tropical.

History and Politics. New Caledonia was settled by Melanesian people about 2000 B.C. Europeans first reached the main island in 1774, when Captain James Cook of Britain gave it its present name. In 1853 France annexed New Caledonia and used the main island as a penal colony for prisoners until the turn of the century. During World War II the islands served as a base for the United States military. Officially a French overseas territory since 1946, New Caledonia experienced violence in the 1980s, stemming from the desire of the Kanak population for independence. A referendum on independence is planned for 1998, although the Kanaks may gain some form of autonomy earlier. ■

NEW ZEALAND

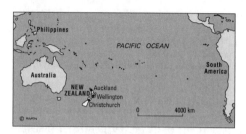

Official name New Zealand

PEOPLE
Population 3,608,000. **Density** 35/mi^2 (13/km^2). **Urban** 86%. **Capital** Wellington, North I., 150,301. **Ethnic groups** European origin 79%, Maori 13%, Samoan and other Pacific islander 5%. **Languages** English, Maori. **Religions** Anglican 22%, Presbyterian 16%, Roman Catholic 15%, Methodist 4%. **Life expectancy** 79 female, 73 male. **Literacy** 99%.

POLITICS
Government Parliamentary state. **Parties** Alliance, Labor, National, New Zealand First, others. **Suffrage** Universal, 18 and over. **Memberships** CW, OECD, UN. **Subdivisions** 14 regions.

ECONOMY
GDP $62,300,000,000. **Per capita** $17,267. **Monetary unit** Dollar. **Trade partners** Exports: Australia, Japan, U.S. Imports: Australia, U.S., Japan. **Exports** Wool, lamb, mutton, beef, fruit, fish, cheese, manufactures, chemicals. **Imports** Petroleum, manufactures, motor vehicles, aircraft, machinery.

LAND
Description South Pacific islands. **Area** 104,454 mi^2 (270,534 km^2). **Highest point** Mt. Cook, 12,316 ft (3,754 m). **Lowest point** Sea level.

People. The majority of New Zealanders are descended from Europeans, mostly Britons, who arrived in the 1800s. The indigenous Maori, of Polynesian descent, form the largest minority. After a period of decline following the arrival of the Europeans, the Maori population has been increasing. The major languages are English and Maori. Most New Zealanders live on North Island. Christian religions are observed by many residents, and the Maori have incorporated some Christian elements into their beliefs.

Economy and the Land. Success in agriculture and trade has allowed New Zealand to overcome

Places and Possessions of NEW ZEALAND

Entity	Status	Area	Population	Capital/Population
Cook Islands (South Pacific)	Self-governing state (New Zealand protection)	91 mi^2 (236 km^2)	20,000	Avarua, 10,886
Niue (South Pacific island)	Self-governing state (New Zealand protection)	100 mi^2 (259 km^2)	2,200	Alofi, 682
Tokelau (South Pacific islands)	Island territory (New Zealand)	4.6 mi^2 (12 km^2)	1,500	None

its small work force, remoteness from major markets, and a relative lack of natural resources. A terrain with much ideal grazing land and a climate that is temperate year-round have encouraged cattle and sheep farming. Manufacturing, including the food-processing and paper industries, is expanding, as is tourism. New Zealand consists of two large islands—North Island and South Island—and many smaller islands scattered throughout the South Pacific. The country administers several island territories.

History and Politics. The Maori, the original settlers, are thought to have arrived around A.D. 1000. In 1642 they fought off the Dutch, the first Europeans to reach the area. Captain James Cook of Britain charted the islands in the late 1700s. Soon after, European hunters and traders, drawn by the area's whales, seals, and forests, began to arrive. Maori chiefs signed the 1840 Treaty of Waitangi, establishing British sovereignty, and British companies began to send settlers to New Zealand. Subsequent battles between settlers and Maori ended with the Maori's defeat in 1872. In 1907 New Zealand became a self-governing dominion of Britain; formal independence came 40 years later. New Zealand supported Britain in both world wars, but foreign policy has recently focused on Southeast Asia and the South Pacific. The country has banned vessels carrying nuclear weapons through its waters. Compensation to Maori groups for land claims going back to 1840 has begun. In 1996 New Zealand gave the island territory of Tokelau more legislative authority, but did not make it a self-governing territory. ■

NICARAGUA

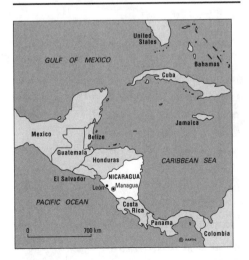

Official name Republic of Nicaragua

PEOPLE
Population 4,443,000. **Density** 89/mi² (34/km²). **Urban** 63%. **Capital** Managua, 864,201. **Ethnic groups** Mestizo 69%, white 17%, black 9%, Amerindian 5%.

Languages Spanish, English, indigenous. **Religions** Roman Catholic 95%. **Life expectancy** 70 female, 67 male. **Literacy** 66%.

POLITICS
Government Republic. **Parties** Liberal Alliance, Sandinista National Liberation Front, others. **Suffrage** Universal, 16 and over. **Memberships** OAS, UN. **Subdivisions** 16 departments.

ECONOMY
GDP $7,100,000,000. **Per capita** $1,553. **Monetary unit** Cordoba. **Trade partners** Exports: Belgium, Cuba, Germany. Imports: Former Soviet republics, Mexico. **Exports** Coffee, cotton, sugar, bananas, seafood, meat, gold. **Imports** Petroleum, food, chemicals, machinery, manufactures.

LAND
Description Central America. **Area** 50,054 mi² (129,640 km²). **Highest point** Mogotón, 6,913 ft (2,107 m). **Lowest point** Sea level.

People. Nicaraguan society closely reflects the country's history as a Spanish colony: most of its inhabitants are Spanish-speaking, Roman Catholic, and mestizo, a mix of Amerindian and European stocks. Amerindian and black communities are found mostly in the Caribbean region. The educational level has improved in the past decade.

Economy and the Land. Nicaragua is chiefly an agricultural country, relying on the production of textiles, coffee, and sugar. A large foreign debt inherited from the previous regime, and continuing political instability, have severely hindered economic prosperity. The country also relies heavily on imported goods. The terrain includes a low-lying Pacific region, central highlands, and a flat Caribbean area. The climate is tropical.

History and Politics. Spanish conquistadores, who came via Panama in 1522 to what is now Nicaragua, found a number of independent indigenous states. Nicaragua was ruled by Spain as part of Guatemala until it became independent in 1821. In 1823 the former Spanish colonies of the region formed the Federation of Central America, a union which collapsed in 1838, resulting in the independent Republic of Nicaragua. For the next century, Nicaragua was the stage both for conflict between the Liberal and Conservative parties and for United States military and economic involvement. Members of the Somoza family, who had close ties to America, directed a repressive regime from 1936 to 1979, when the widely supported Sandinistas overthrew the government. The Sandinistas, led by Daniel Ortega, were opposed by rival political parties and the Contras, rebels linked to the former Somoza administration and backed by the U.S. Five Central American countries reached an agreement in 1987 on a plan to dismantle Contra forces. In 1990 elections, Ortega was defeated by Violeta Chamorro of the National Opposition Union. Despite the disbanding of the Contras in 1990, the situation remained unstable as Chamorro tried to placate the still powerful Sandinistas and revive the moribund economy.

In 1996, the presidential term limit barred Chamorro from running for re-election. Ortega once again ran for president, and he was again defeated. The new government has pledged to build closer ties to the U.S. and to open more markets. The conservative right has ruled Nicaragua since 1990. Nicaragua's biggest domestic problems are poverty and crime. ■

NIGER

Official name Republic of Niger

PEOPLE
Population 9,522,000. **Density** 19/mi² (7.5/km²). **Urban** 19%. **Capital** Niamey, 392,165. **Ethnic groups** Hausa 56%, Djerma 22%, Fulani 9%, Taureg 8%, Beriberi 4%. **Languages** French, Hausa, Djerma, indigenous. **Religions** Muslim 80%, Animist and Christian 20%. **Life expectancy** 50 female, 47 male. **Literacy** 14%.

POLITICS
Government Republic. **Parties** Alliance for Democracy and Social Progress, National Union of Independents for Democratic Renewal, others. **Suffrage** Universal, 18 and over. **Memberships** OAU, UN. **Subdivisions** 7 departments.

ECONOMY
GDP $5,500,000,000. **Per capita** $583. **Monetary unit** CFA franc. **Trade partners** Exports: France, Nigeria. Imports: France, U.S., Cote d'Ivoire, Nigeria. **Exports** Uranium, livestock products, cowpeas, onions. **Imports** Petroleum, raw materials, machinery, transportation equipment, manufactures.

LAND
Description Western Africa, landlocked. **Area** 489,191 mi² (1,267,000 km²). **Highest point** Idoûkâl-en-Taghés, 6,634 ft (2,022 m). **Lowest point** Along Niger River, 528 ft (161 m).

People. Nearly all residents of Niger are black Africans belonging to culturally diverse groups. The Hausa and the Djerma, farmers who live mostly in the south, constitute the two largest groups. The remaining inhabitants are nomadic herders who inhabit the northern desert regions.

Although the official language is French, most inhabitants speak indigenous tongues. Islam is the most commonly observed religion, but some people hold indigenous and Christian beliefs.

Economy and the Land. Niger's economy is chiefly agricultural, although arable land is scarce and drought common. The raising of livestock, grain, beans, and peanuts accounts for most farming activity. Uranium mining, a growing industry, has become less productive recently due to a slump in the world uranium market. Mountains and the Sahara Desert cover most of northern Niger, while the south is savanna. The climate is hot and dry.

History and Politics. Because of its central location in northern Africa, Niger was a crossroads for many peoples during its early history and was dominated by several African empires before European explorers arrived in the 1800s. The area was placed within the French sphere of influence in 1885, but not until 1922 did France make Niger a colony of French West Africa. Gradual moves toward autonomy were made during the 1940s and 1950s, and Niger became fully independent in 1960. Unrest caused in part by a prolonged drought led to a coup in 1974 and the establishment of a military government. Frequent clashes with the Tuareg in the north have abated since a peace agreement was reached in 1995. A democratic constitution was passed in 1992, but the elected government was overthrown in a 1996 military coup. ■

NIGERIA

Official name Federal Republic of Nigeria

PEOPLE
Population 108,660,000. **Density** 305/mi² (118/km²). **Urban** 41%. **Capital** Lagos (de facto), 1,213,000; Abuja (designated), 250,000. **Ethnic groups** Hausa, Fulani, Yoruba, Ibo, others. **Languages** English, Hausa, Fulani, Yorbua, Ibo, indigenous. **Religions** Muslim 50%,

Christian 40%, Animist 10%. **Life expectancy** 54 female, 51 male. **Literacy** 57%.

POLITICS
Government Provisional military government. **Parties** Center, Congress, Democratic, Grassroots Democratic Movement, Committee for National Consensus. **Suffrage** Universal, 21 and over. **Memberships** CW, OAU, OPEC, UN. **Subdivisions** 30 states, 1 capital territory.

ECONOMY
GDP $135,900,000,000. **Per capita** $1,321. **Monetary unit** Naira. **Trade partners** Exports: U.S., France, Netherlands. Imports: U.K., Germany, U.S., France. **Exports** Petroleum, cocoa, rubber. **Imports** Manufactures, machinery, chemicals, food, livestock, transportation equipment.

LAND
Description Western Africa. **Area** 356,669 mi^2 (923,768 km^2). **Highest point** Mt. Waddi, 7,936 ft (2,419 m). **Lowest point** Sea level.

People. Nigeria, Africa's most populous country, contains more than 250 distinct African groups. The largest groups are the Hausa and the Fulani, who dominate the north; the Yoruba, found primarily in the southwest; and the Ibo, who live in the southeast and have historically been active in government and trade. Most Hausa and Fulani are Muslim, but a sizable Christian community is found mainly in the south. Nigerians commonly combine traditional beliefs with Islam or Christianity. Indigenous tongues are more widely spoken than English, the official language. Competition among Nigeria's many ethnic groups has threatened national unity.

Economy and the Land. Nigeria's economy is based on mining and agriculture. Petroleum is very important to the Nigerian economy, but a number of factors—including unskilled labor, poor power facilities, and the worldwide dip in oil prices—have silenced the oil boom of the 1970s and slowed development in other areas. In 1983 and 1985, the government expelled millions of illegal aliens in an effort to revive the economy. The terrain is diverse, encompassing tropical forest, savanna, and semidesert. The climate is predominantly tropical.

History and Politics. From about 500 B.C. to A.D. 200 the region was home to the sophisticated Nok civilization. Later cultures that dominated parts of the area included the Hausa, Fulani, and Yoruba. The Portuguese arrived in the 1400s, but the British gained control over the following centuries, uniting the region in 1914 as the Colony and Protectorate of Nigeria. Nigerian calls for self-rule culminated in independence in 1960. Internal tensions began to wrack the new country, and in 1966 two military coups took place. After subsequent massacres of Ibo, that group declared eastern Nigeria the autonomous republic of Biafra. A three-year civil war followed, ending in 1970 with Biafra's surrender. Nigeria prospered during the 1970s as it developed its oil reserves. A succession of mainly military governments has struggled unsuccessfully to contain ethnic and religious conflicts. In 1993 the military refused to relinquish power to an elected civilian president, and has become increasingly repressive despite international condemnation. ∎

NIUE See NEW ZEALAND.

NORFOLK ISLAND
See AUSTRALIA.

NORTHERN MARIANA ISLANDS See UNITED STATES.

NORWAY

Official name Kingdom of Norway

PEOPLE
Population 4,416,000. **Density** 30/mi^2 (11/km^2). **Urban** 73%. **Capital** Oslo, 470,204. **Ethnic groups** Norwegian (Scandinavian), Lapp (Sami). **Languages** Norwegian, Lapp, Finnish. **Religions** Lutheran 88%, other Protestant and Roman Catholic 4%. **Life expectancy** 81 female, 74 male. **Literacy** 99%.

POLITICS
Government Constitutional monarchy. **Parties** Center, Conservative, Labor, others. **Suffrage** Universal, 18 and over. **Memberships** NATO, OECD, UN. **Subdivisions** 19 counties.

ECONOMY
GDP $106,200,000,000. **Per capita** $24,470. **Monetary unit** Krone. **Trade partners** Exports: U.K., Sweden, Germany. Imports: Sweden, Germany, U.K., U.S. **Exports** Petroleum, natural gas, fish, ships and boats, aluminum, wood pulp, paper. **Imports** Machinery, fuels and lubricants, chemicals, manufactures, raw materials, food.

LAND
Description Northern Europe. **Area** 149,405 mi^2

(386,958 km²). **Highest point** Galdhøpiggen, 8,100 ft (2,469 m). **Lowest point** Sea level.
The above information includes Svalbard and Jan Mayen.

People. Because of its relatively remote location in far northern Europe, Norway has seen few population migrations and possesses a virtually homogeneous population, which is predominantly Germanic, Norwegian speaking, and Lutheran. Small communities of Lapps and Finns live in the far north, while most Norwegians live in the south and along the coast. The people enjoy many government-provided social services and programs.

Economy and the Land. Norway's economy—based on shipping, trade, and the mining of offshore oil and natural gas—takes its shape from the country's proximity to several seas. Shipbuilding, fishing, and forestry are also important activities. Norway is a leading producer of hydroelectricity. Combined with some government control of the economy, these lucrative activities have given the country a high standard of living and fairly low unemployment. Most of Norway is a high plateau covered with mountains. The Gulf Stream gives the country a much milder climate than other places at the same latitude.

History and Politics. Parts of present-day Norway were inhabited by about 9000 B.C. Germanic tribes began immigrating to the area about 2000 B.C. Between A.D. 800 and 1100, Viking ships from Norway raided coastal towns throughout Western Europe and also colonized Greenland and Iceland. Unified around 900, Norway was subsequently shaken by civil war, plague, and the end of its royal line. It entered a union with Denmark in 1380, becoming a Danish province in 1536. Around the end of the Napoleonic Wars, in 1814, Norway became part of Sweden. A long struggle against Swedish rule ended in 1905 as Sweden recognized Norwegian independence, and a Danish prince was made king. Norway was neutral in World War I but endured German occupation during World War II. In 1967 the government initiated a wide-ranging social welfare system. ■

OMAN

Official name Sultanate of Oman

PEOPLE
Population 2,496,000. **Density** 30/mi² (12/km²). **Urban** 78%. **Capital** Muscat, 34,683. **Ethnic groups** Arab, Baluchi, South Asian, African. **Languages** Arabic, English, Baluchi, Urdu, Indian dialects. **Religions** Ibadite Muslim 75%, Sunni Muslim, Shiite Muslim, Hindu. **Life expectancy** 73 female, 69 male.

POLITICS
Government Monarchy. **Parties** None. **Suffrage** None. **Memberships** AL, UN. **Subdivisions** 7 regions.

ECONOMY
GDP $19,100,000,000. **Per capita** $8,830. **Monetary unit** Rial. **Trade partners** Exports: United Arab

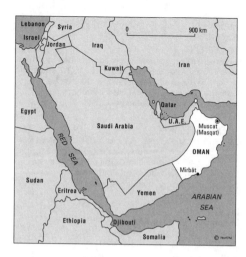

Emirates, Saudi Arabia, U.K. Imports: United Arab Emirates, Japan, U.K. **Exports** Petroleum, fish, copper, textiles. **Imports** Machinery, transportation equipment, manufactures, food, livestock, lubricant.

LAND
Description Southwestern Asia. **Area** 82,030 mi² (212,457 km²). **Highest point** Mt. Sham, 9,957 ft (3,035 m). **Lowest point** Sea level.

People. Most of Oman's population is Arab, Arabic-speaking, and belongs to the Ibadite sect of Islam. Other forms of Islam are also practiced. There is a significant foreign community that includes Indians, Baluchis from Pakistan, and East African blacks. Many of them are guest workers in the oil industry.

Economy and the Land. Once a mainstay of Oman's economy, oil revenues declined as prices fell throughout the 1980s. The mining of natural gas and copper is being developed, as are agriculture and fishing. A central position in the politically volatile Persian Gulf and revolutionary internal strife have led Oman to devote a considerable portion of its budget to defense. Land regions include a coastal plain and interior mountains and desert. Oman's land borders are undefined and in dispute. A desert climate prevails over most areas except the coast, which has humid conditions.

History and Politics. Islam came to Muscat and Oman, as the country was known before 1970, in the 7th century A.D. The Portuguese gained control of parts of the coast in 1508 but were driven out in 1650 by the Arabs. At about this time the hereditary sultanate—which absorbed the political power formerly held by the Ibadite religious leaders, or imams—was founded. Close relations with Britain, cemented in a 1798 agreement and subsequent treaties, have continued to the present. Conflicts between the sultan and Omanis, who wanted to be ruled exclusively by their imam, erupted intermittently after 1900, and in 1959 the sultan defeated the rebels with British help and outlawed the office of imam. Marxist insurgency was put down in 1975. Sultan Qaboos bin Said, who overthrew his father's regime in 1970, has liberalized some policies and worked to modernize the country. Oman is still somewhat isolated and discourages foreign contacts. ∎

ORKNEY ISLANDS

See UNITED KINGDOM.

PAKISTAN

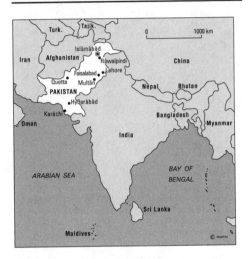

Official name Islamic Republic of Pakistan

PEOPLE
Population 133,620,000. **Density** 393/mi² (152/km²). **Urban** 35%. **Capital** Islāmābād, 204,364. **Ethnic groups** Punjabi, Sindhi, Pathan, Baluchi, others. **Languages** English, Urdu, Punjabi, Sindhi, Pashto. **Religions** Sunni Muslim 77%, Shiite Muslim 20%. **Life expectancy** 65 female, 63 male. **Literacy** 38%.

POLITICS
Government Federal Islamic republic. **Parties** Muslim League (Nawaz), People's, others. **Suffrage** Universal, 21 and over. **Memberships** CW, UN. **Subdivisions** 4 provinces, 1 tribal area, 1 capital territory, 2 areas.

ECONOMY
GDP $274,200,000,000. **Per capita** $2,072. **Monetary unit** Rupee. **Trade partners** Exports: U.S., Japan, Germany. Imports: U.S., Japan, Kuwait. **Exports** Cotton, textiles, clothing, rice, leather, carpets. **Imports** Petroleum, machinery, transportation equipment, oils, fats, chemicals.

LAND
Description Southern Asia. **Area** 339,732 mi² (879,902 km²). **Highest point** K2, 28,250 ft (8,611 m). **Lowest point** Sea level.
The above information includes part of Jammu and Kashmir.

People. Pakistan's varied ethnicity is the product of centuries of incursions by different races. Today each ethnic group is concentrated in a different region and speaks its own language;

English and Urdu, the official languages, are not widely spoken. The Punjabis compose the largest ethnic group and traditionally have been influential in government and commerce. Virtually all of Pakistan, which was created as a Muslim homeland, follows Islam. Spurred by poor living conditions and a lack of jobs, many Pakistanis work abroad.

Economy and the Land. Despite recent progress in manufacturing, agriculture remains the economic mainstay. Improvement in farming techniques has increased productivity. Government planning and foreign assistance have aided all sectors, but Pakistan remains troubled by population growth, unskilled labor, a trade deficit, and an influx of refugees fleeing the war in Afghanistan. Pakistan's terrain includes mountains, fertile plains, and desert. The climate is continental, with extremes in temperature.

History and Politics. Around 2500 B.C., the Indus Valley civilization flourished in the area of modern Pakistan. Various empires and immigrants followed, including Aryans, Persians, and Greeks. Invading Arabs introduced Islam to the region in the A.D. 700s. In the 1500s the Mogul Empire of Afghanistan came to include nearly all of present-day Pakistan, India, and Bangladesh, and as that empire declined, various peoples ruled the area. Through wars and treaties, the British presence in Asia expanded, and by the early 20th century British India included all of modern Pakistan. Because of hostilities between British India's Muslims and Hindus, the separate Muslim state of Pakistan was created when British India gained independence in 1947. With its boundaries drawn around the Muslim population centers, Pakistan was formed from the northeastern and northwestern parts of India, and its eastern region was separated from the west by more than 1,000 miles (1,600 kilometers). East Pakistanis felt that power was unfairly concentrated in the west, and a civil war erupted in 1971. Aided by India, East Pakistan won the war and became the independent country of Bangladesh. Since Pakistan's independence in 1947, it has been at war with India three times. As a result of their animosity toward each other, both India and Pakistan have developed nuclear capabilities. In 1998 India conducted underground nuclear tests. Pakistan responded with its own tests, increasing the risk of nuclear proliferation in the region. ∎

PALAU

Official name Republic of Palau

PEOPLE
Population 17,000. **Density** 87/mi² (33/km²). **Urban** 72%. **Capital** Koror (de facto), 9,018; Melekeok (future), 42. **Ethnic groups** Palauan (Mixed Polynesian, Malayan, and Melanesian). **Languages** Angaur, English, Japanese, Palauan, Sonsorolese, Tobi. **Religions** Roman Catholic, Protestant, tribal religionist. **Life expectancy** 73 female, 69 male. **Literacy** 92%.

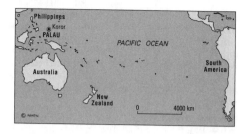

Palau's original constitution banned all nuclear materials from the islands, but controversy ensued when the U.S. offered financial enticements in exchange for the elimination of the clause. After 13 years and eight inconclusive votes, the nuclear-free provision was abandoned. Palau gained independence in 1994. ∎

PANAMA

Official name Republic of Panama

POLITICS
Government Republic. **Parties** Nationalist. **Suffrage** Universal, 18 and over. **Memberships** UN. **Subdivisions** 16 states.

ECONOMY
GDP $81,800,000. **Per capita** $5,113. **Monetary unit** U.S. dollar. **Trade partners** U.S., Japan. **Exports** Fish, copra, handicrafts. **Imports** Food, consumer goods.

LAND
Description North Pacific islands. **Area** 196 mi^2 (508 km^2). **Highest point** Keramadoo, 699 ft (213 m). **Lowest point** Sea level.

People. Also known as Belau, Palau was originally settled by Micronesians, a group of mixed Melanesian, Polynesian, and Malaysian origin. Each island has its own Malay-Polynesian dialect. English and Japanese languages are legacies of occupation by foreign powers.

Economy and the Land. Most people are involved in subsistence agriculture and fishing, and the government is the largest employer of those who have jobs. The country is trying to develop a tourism industry by enticing visitors from Taiwan, Korea, and other east Asian countries. The United States supplies Palau with massive economic assistance in exchange for military access to the islands. Palau is made up of about 200 islands in the Caroline Islands chain, less than ten of which are permanently populated. The northern islands in the group are volcanic, and the southern islands are coral. The climate is tropical.

History and Politics. In 1543, the Spanish seafarer Ruy Lopez de Vilalobos was the first to sight the Palau Islands. Spaniards controlled the islands until 1899 when Spain sold Palau to Germany. Following World War I, Palau came under Japan's jurisdiction as a League of Nations mandate. Some of World War II's bloodiest battles between the U.S. and Japan took place in 1944 at a Japanese naval base on the island of Beliliou (Peleliu). War memorials for both Japanese and American soldiers stand on the island today. After the war Palau, the Northern Mariana Islands, the islands of the Federated States of Micronesia, and the Marshall Islands, were combined into a United Nations trust territory under U.S. administration. Palau adopted a constitution in 1980, declaring itself the Republic of Palau, and a constitutional government was installed in 1981. Palau was the last territory in the U.N. trusteeship to achieve independence.

PEOPLE
Population 2,720,000. **Density** 93/mi^2 (36/km^2). **Urban** 56%. **Capital** Panamá, 411,549. **Ethnic groups** Mestizo 70%, West Indian 14%, white 10%, Amerindian 6%. **Languages** Spanish, English. **Religions** Roman Catholic 85%, Protestant 15%. **Life expectancy** 76 female, 72 male. **Literacy** 91%.

POLITICS
Government Republic. **Parties** Arnulfista, Democratic Revolutionary, others. **Suffrage** Universal, 18 and over. **Memberships** OAS, UN. **Subdivisions** 9 provinces, 1 intendency.

ECONOMY
GDP $13,600,000,000. **Per capita** $5,028. **Monetary unit** Balboa. **Trade partners** Exports: U.S., Germany, Costa Rica. Imports: U.S., Ecuador, Japan. **Exports** Bananas, shrimp, sugar, clothing, coffee. **Imports** Machinery, petroleum, food, manufactures, chemicals.

LAND
Description Central America. **Area** 29,157 mi^2 (75,517 km^2). **Highest point** Volcán Barú, 11,401 ft (3,475 m). **Lowest point** Sea level.

People. Most Panamanians are mestizos, a mixture of Spanish and Amerindian heritage. Indigenous peoples, blacks from the West Indies, and whites form the remaining population. A Spanish legacy is reflected by the official language, Spanish, and the predominance of Roman Catholicism. Most people live near the Panama Canal. A wealthy elite has traditionally directed the government and economy.

Economy and the Land. Because of its location, Panama has been a strategic center for trade and transportation. The 1914 opening of the Panama Canal, connecting the Atlantic and Pacific oceans, accentuated these strengths and has provided additional revenue and jobs; the canal area is now Panama's most economically developed region. Agriculture is an important activity; and oil refining, food processing, fishing, and financial services all contribute to the economy as well. Panama will have to adjust to the economic and technical losses that will accompany the end of United States operation of the canal in 1999. The country has a mountainous interior and a tropical climate.

History and Politics. Originally inhabited by indigenous peoples, Panama became a Spanish colony in the early 1500s and served as a vital transportation center. In 1821 it overcame Spanish rule and entered the Republic of Greater Colombia. After Colombia vetoed a U.S. plan to build a canal across the narrow isthmus, Panama, encouraged by the U.S., seceded from the republic and became independent in 1903. Eleven years later, America completed the canal and established control over it and the Panama Canal Zone. Dissatisfaction with this arrangement resulted in several anti-American riots in the 1950s and 1960s. A 1968 coup placed the Panamanian National Guard in power, and the movement to end American control of the Canal Zone gained momentum. A 1977 treaty arranged for Panamanian sovereignty of the Canal and gradual withdrawal of the U.S. by 1999. There is a tentative agreement for American troops to remain beyond 1999 as part of a regional anti-drug effort. The country has been wracked by corruption and political instability. ■

PAPUA NEW GUINEA

Official name Independent State of Papua New Guinea

PEOPLE
Population 4,546,000. **Density** 25/mi² (9.8/km²). **Urban** 16%. **Capital** Port Moresby, New Guinea I., 193,242. **Ethnic groups** Melanesian, Papuan, Negrito, micronesian, Polynesian. **Languages** English, Motu, Pidgin, indigenous. **Religions** Animist 34%, Roman Catholic 22%, Lutheran 16%, United Church 8%. **Life expectancy** 59 female, 57 male. **Literacy** 72%.

POLITICS
Government Parliamentary state. **Parties** Pangu (United), People's Action, People's Democratic Movement, People's Progress, others. **Suffrage** Universal, 18 and over. **Memberships** CW, UN. **Subdivisions** 19 provinces, 1 capital district.

ECONOMY
GDP $10,200,000,000. **Per capita** $2,349. **Monetary unit** Kina. **Trade partners** Exports: Japan, Germany, Korea. Imports: Australia, Japan, U.S. **Exports** Copper, gold, coffee, lumber, palm oil, cocoa, lobster. **Imports** Machinery and transportation equipment, food, fuel, manufactures, chemicals.

LAND
Description South Pacific islands. **Area** 178,704 mi² (462,840 km²). **Highest point** Mt. Wilhelm, 14,793 ft (4,509 m). **Lowest point** Sea level.

People. Almost all inhabitants are Melanesians belonging to several thousand culturally diverse and geographically isolated communities. More than 700 languages are spoken, but most people also speak Motu or a dialect of English. European missionaries brought Christianity, but Animist faiths remain common. The traditions of village life remain strong.

Economy and the Land. The main economic activities are agriculture, copper and gold mining, and oil production. Papua New Guinea has other mineral resources, as well as potential for forestry. The country consists of the eastern half of the island of New Guinea, plus New Britain, New Ireland, Bougainville, and 600 smaller islands. Terrain includes mountains, volcanoes, broad valleys, and swamps; the climate is tropical.

History and Politics. Settlers from Southeast Asia are thought to have arrived as long as 50,000 years ago. Isolated villages were found by the Spanish and Portuguese in the early 1500s. In 1884 Germany annexed the northeastern part of the island of New Guinea and its offshore islands, and Britain took control of the southeastern section and its islands. Australia assumed administration of the British territory, known as Papua, in 1906 and seized the German regions, or German New Guinea, during World War I. The League of Nations granted Australia a mandate to New Guinea in 1920. After being occupied by Japan in World War II, Papua and New Guinea were united as an Australian territory from 1945 to 1946. Papua New Guinea gained independence in 1975. A separatist movement on the island of Bougainville continues to pressure the government for reparation for land damaged by mining. In 1991 a peace accord was signed, but sporadic fighting continued. Despite a major military offensive in 1996, the government was unable to gain control of the island. Another agreement was reached in early 1998, but the island's future status is uncertain.■

PARAGUAY

Official name Republic of Paraguay

PEOPLE
Population 5,148,000. **Density** 33/mi² (13/km²). **Urban** 53%. **Capital** Asunción, 502,426. **Ethnic groups** Mestizo 95%, white and Amerindian 5%. **Languages** Spanish, Guarani. **Religions** Roman Catholic 90%, Mennonite and other Protestant. **Life expectancy** 73 female, 69 male. **Literacy** 92%.

POLITICS
Government Republic. **Parties** Authentic Radical Liberal, Colorado, National Encounter, others. **Suffrage** Universal, 18 and over. **Memberships** OAS, UN. **Subdivisions** 19 departments, 1 city.

ECONOMY
GDP $17,000,000,000. **Per capita** $3,476. **Monetary unit** Guarani. **Trade partners** Exports: Brazil, Netherlands. Imports: Brazil, Argentina, Algeria, U.S. **Exports** Cotton, soybeans, wood, vegetable oil, coffee, tung oil, meat. **Imports** Machinery, manufactures, petroleum, fuel, raw materials, food.

LAND
Description Central South America, landlocked. **Area** 157,048 mi² (406,752 km²). **Highest point** 2,625 ft (800 m). **Lowest point** Confluence of Paraná and Paraguay Rivers, 151 ft (46 m).

People. Paraguay's population displays a homogeneity unusual in South America; most people are a mix of Spanish and Guarani ancestry, are Roman Catholic, and speak both Spanish and Guarani. The small number of unassimilated Guarani live mostly in western Paraguay, known as the Gran Chaco. There are some foreign communities, mostly German, Japanese, and Brazilian. The culture combines Spanish and native traditions.

Economy and the Land. Agriculture—based on cotton, soybeans, and cattle—forms the keystone of the economy. Forestry also contributes significantly to Paraguay's exports. Unskilled labor, a history of war, lack of direct access to the sea, and instability have resulted in an underdeveloped economy; manufacturing, in particular, has suffered. The world's largest hydroelectric project, the Itaipu Dam, was completed in 1988. Paraguay has two distinct regions, divided by the Paraguay River: the semiarid Gran Chaco plains in the west, and the temperate, fertile east, where most farming takes place.

History and Politics. The indigenous Guarani formed an agricultural society centered around what is now Asunción. Portuguese and Spanish explorers arrived in the early 1500s, and the region gained importance as the center of Spanish holdings in southern South America. During the 1700s Jesuit missionaries converted thousands of Amerindians to Roman Catholicism. After gaining independence in 1811, Paraguay was ruled by a succession of dictators. A disastrous war against Argentina, Brazil, and Uruguay from 1865 to 1870 cost the country half its population. Another war against Bolivia from 1932 to 1935 increased Paraguay's territory but further weakened its stability. A military coup in 1989 ended the 35-year regime of General Stroessner, but the 1993 election of a civilian leader brought little change. The country is still controlled by the military. ■

PERU

Official name Republic of Peru

PEOPLE
Population 24,520,000. **Density** 49/mi² (19/km²). **Urban** 71%. **Capital** Lima, 371,122. **Ethnic groups** Amerindian 45%, mestizo 37%, white 15%. **Languages** Quechua, Spanish, Aymara. **Religions** Roman Catholic. **Life expectancy** 69 female, 66 male. **Literacy** 89%.

POLITICS
Government Republic. **Parties** American Popular Revolutionary Alliance, Change 90-New Majority, Union for Peru, others. **Suffrage** Universal, 18 and over. **Memberships** OAS, UN. **Subdivisions** 24 departments, 1 constitutional province.

ECONOMY
GDP $87,000,000,000. **Per capita** $3,580. **Monetary unit** Sol. **Trade partners** Exports: U.S., Japan, U.K. Imports: U.S., Panama, Germany, Argentina. **Exports** Copper, fishmeal, zinc, petroleum, lead, silver,

coffee, cotton. **Imports** Food, machinery, transportation equipment, petroleum, iron, steel, chemicals.

LAND
Description Western South America. **Area** 496,225 mi^2 (1,285,216 km^2). **Highest point** Nevado Huascarán, 22,133 ft (6,746 m). **Lowest point** Sea level.

People. Peru's indigenous population constitutes the country's largest ethnic group and the largest Amerindian concentration in North or South America. Although whites make up the third largest group after Amerindians and mestizos, they have historically controlled much of the wealth. The Amerindians are often geographically and culturally remote from the ruling classes and generally live in poverty. Most Peruvians practice Roman Catholicism.

Economy and the Land. Considerable natural resources have made Peru a leader in the production of minerals—notably copper, lead, and silver—and in fishing. Other major industries are food processing, textile production, and oil refining. Productivity has been slowed by a mountainous terrain that impedes transport and communication; earthquakes and other natural disasters; a largely unskilled work force; and years of stringent military rule. Climate varies from arid to mild in the coastal desert, to temperate but cool in the Andean highlands, to hot and humid in the eastern jungles and plains.

History and Politics. Several Native American cultures arose in the region between 900 B.C. and A.D. 1200, the last of which was the Incan. In 1987 the excavation began of the richest pre-Hispanic ruins ever discovered, revealing further evidence of the sophistication of these cultures. Builders of an empire stretching from Colombia to Chile, the Inca were conquered by the Spanish in 1533. For almost the next 300 years, Peru was a harshly ruled Spanish colony and center for colonial administration. Peru achieved independence from Spain in 1821, largely through the efforts of José de San Martín of Argentina and Simón Bolívar of Venezuela. Spain, however, did not formally recognize Peruvian independence until 1879. Military officers ruled the country through the rest of the century. In 1883, Chile and Bolivia defeated Peru in the War of the Pacific, and the country lost its valuable southern nitrite region. Fernando Belaúnde Terry, a moderate reformer, was elected in 1963. A military junta ousted him in 1968, nationalized some industries, and instituted land reform. Inflation and unemployment caused dissatisfaction and a 1975 coup. Elections in 1980 and 1985 restored democratic leadership. Economic chaos has since destabilized the government, however, and allowed the growth of the Shining Path, a terrorist guerrilla movement. Alberto Fujimori, first elected in 1990, assumed dictatorial power to bring the Shining Path terrorists under control. In 1996, Tupac Amaru guerrillas seized the Japanese ambassador's residence, taking hostage all the guests at a social event. The guerrillas were still holding 72 hostages when the Peruvian military ended the crisis in 1997. ■

PHILIPPINES

Official name Republic of the Philippines

PEOPLE
Population 77,080,000. **Density** 665/mi^2 (257/km^2). **Urban** 55%. **Capital** Manila, Luzon I., 1,601,234. **Ethnic groups** Christian Malay 92%, Muslim Malay 4%, Chinese 2%. **Languages** English, Pilipino, Tagalog. **Religions** Roman Catholic 83%, Protestant 9%, Muslim 5%, Buddhist and others 3%. **Life expectancy** 70 female, 67 male. **Literacy** 95%.

POLITICS
Government Republic. **Parties** Democratic Filipino Struggle, National People's Coalition, others. **Suffrage** Universal, 18 and over. **Memberships** ASEAN, UN. **Subdivisions** 73 provinces.

ECONOMY
GDP $179,700,000,000. **Per capita** $2,426. **Monetary unit** Peso. **Trade partners** Exports: U.S., Japan. Imports: U.S., Japan, China. **Exports** Electrical equipment, textiles, minerals, agriculture products, coconut, fish. **Imports** Raw materials, machinery, petroleum.

LAND
Description Southeastern Asian islands. **Area** 115,831 mi^2 (300,000 km^2). **Highest point** Mt. Apo, 9,692 ft (2,954 m). **Lowest point** Sea level.

People. Nearly all Filipinos are descended from Malay peoples. The majority are Roman Catholic, a reflection of centuries of Spanish rule. A Muslim minority has begun agitating for autonomy. Although nearly 90 native languages and dialects are spoken, Pilipino and English are the official languages. The wide gap between rich and poor, inherited from a plantation economy, has concentrated wealth in the hands of the landowners.

Economy and the Land. Philippines is a primarily agricultural country, relying on rice, sugar, coconuts, and wood. Fishing is a significant part of the economy. Considerable reserves of copper, nickel, and chromite make mining important. Manufacturing is developing through government incentives. A dependence on imported goods, and inadequate but growing power and transport systems have hampered growth. The archipelago of more than 7,000 islands includes mountains, volcanoes, forests, and inland plains. The climate is tropical and includes a typhoon season.

History and Politics. The islands are thought to have been settled by Negritos about 30,000 years ago. Malay immigrants began to arrive around 3000 B.C, but by 1565 the area was under Spanish control. The Roman Catholic church had considerable influence throughout the Spanish period. In the late 1800s, a movement for independence developed but was put down first by the Spanish and then by the United States, which acquired the islands in 1898 after defeating Spain in the Spanish-American War. Japan occupied the Philippines during World War II. Independence came in 1946 and was followed by a Communist rebellion demanding land reform; the rebels were defeated in 1954. Ferdinand Marcos was elected president in 1965 and, in the face of opposition from many quarters, declared martial law in 1972. Marcos lifted martial law in 1981 but was defeated in a 1986 presidential election by Corazon Aquino, wife of assassinated opposition leader Benigno Aquino. Marcos eventually fled the island, and Aquino stayed in power until 1992. The closing of Clark Air Force Base and Subic Bay Naval Base in 1992 ended an era of U.S. military presence in the Philippines. There is increasing conflict between Muslim and Christian factions, particularly in the Muslim-majority southern islands. In 1996, a peace agreement granted some autonomy to a Muslim secessionist group in the southern Philippines, but some casualties still occur in the ongoing conflict. ∎

PITCAIRN

Official name Pitcairn, Henderson, Ducie and Oeno Islands

PEOPLE
Population 100. **Density** 5.3/mi² (2.0/km²). **Urban** 0%. **Capital** Adamstown, 59. **Ethnic groups** Mixed European and Tahitian. **Languages** English, Tahitian. **Religions** Seventh Day Adventist 100%.

POLITICS
Government Dependent territory (U.K.). **Parties** None. **Suffrage** Universal, 18 and over. **Memberships** None. **Subdivisions** None.

ECONOMY
Monetary unit New Zealand dollar. **Exports** Fruits, vegetables, curios. **Imports** Fuel oil, machinery, building materials, flour, sugar, food.

LAND
Description South Pacific islands. **Area** 19 mi² (49 km²). **Highest point** 1,445 ft (440 m). **Lowest point** Sea level.
The above information includes dependencies.

People. The population of Pitcairn is of mixed European and Tahitian ancestry, most descendants of British sailor Fletcher Christian and his fellow mutineers from H.M.S. *Bounty*. Uninhabited for about three years in the late 1850s, Pitcairn has been permanently occupied since 1859. In the past decades emigration to New Zealand has been an ongoing trend.

Economy and the Land. Fertile soil provides for subsistence farming as well as some export crops. Many islanders engage in fishing and sell handicrafts to the passengers of ships that dock here. Pitcairn is a rugged, volcanic island, and its shores are nearly inaccessible. The colony includes the uninhabited islands of Henderson, Dulcie, and Oeno. The climate is mild.

History and Politics. More than 600 years ago, Polynesians likely lived on Pitcairn intermittently, but the island was uninhabited when the British admiral Philip Carteret arrived in 1767, naming the island after the midshipman who first sighted it. In 1789, crew members of the H.M.S. *Bounty*, led by Fletcher Christian, carried out a mutiny in the South Pacific, and the following year Christian, eight other mutineers, six Tahitian women, and 12 Tahitian men left Tahiti and sailed to Pitcairn. Violence marked the community's early days; by 1800, John Adams was the only surviving adult male. In 1808, a U.S. ship inadvertently arrived at the island, yet Pitcairn remained largely unheard of until 1814 when the British ships *Briton* and *Tagus* reached its shores. Between 1814 and 1831 the population grew from 40 to 86, and concern about drought and dwindling resources caused the Pitcairners to leave for Tahiti. Unable to adjust to the lifestyle of the island, they returned to Pitcairn six months later. In 1838 the islanders obtained a constitution and universal adult suffrage, and most Pitcairners trace the island's colonial status back to this time. Pitcairn was evacuated again when the United Kingdom arranged for resettlement on Norfolk Island in 1856, but 43 Pitcairners returned to the island between 1859 and 1864. Pitcairn was officially made a British colony under the Settlements Act of 1887, and the island continues as a colony of the United Kingdom. ∎

POLAND

Official name Republic of Poland

PEOPLE
Population 38,725,000. **Density** 320/mi² (123/km²). **Urban** 64%. **Capital** Warsaw, 1,644,500. **Ethnic groups** Polish (mixed Slavic and Teutonic) 98%, German 1%. **Languages** Polish. **Religions** Roman Catholic 95%. **Life expectancy** 76 female, 67 male. **Literacy** 99%.

POLITICS
Government Republic. **Parties** Democratic Left Alliance, Freedom Union, Solidarity Electoral Action, others. **Suffrage** Universal, 18 and over. **Memberships** OECD, UN. **Subdivisions** 49 provinces.

ECONOMY

GDP $226,700,000,000. **Per capita** $5,832. **Monetary unit** Zloty. **Trade partners** Exports: Former Soviet republics, Germany, U.K. Imports: Former Soviet republics, Germany, Austria. **Exports** Machinery, metals, fuel, transportation equipment, food. **Imports** Machinery, fuel, chemicals, manufactures, transportation equipment.

LAND

Description Eastern Europe. **Area** 121,196 mi² (313,895 km²). **Highest point** Rysy, 8,199 ft (2,499 m). **Lowest point** Raczki Elbląskie, -7 ft (-2 m).

People. Poland's homogeneous population is partially a result of Nazi persecution during World War II, which virtually obliterated the Jewish community and led to the emigration of most minorities. Roman Catholicism, practiced by almost all Poles, remains a unifying force. The urban population has risen in the postwar period because of government emphasis on industrialization.

Economy and the Land. Government policies since the war transformed Poland from an agricultural country into an industrial one. Machinery and textiles are important products. Since the collapse of Communism in Eastern Europe, an entrepreneurial spirit has taken hold. Privatization is proceeding slowly in the hope of controlling inflation and unemployment. Poland has a mostly flat terrain—except for mountains in the south—and a temperate climate.

History and Politics. Slavic tribes inhabited the region of modern Poland several thousand years ago. The Piast dynasty began in the A.D. 900s and established Roman Catholicism as the official religion. In the 16th century, the Jagiellonian dynasty guided the empire to its height of expansion. A subsequent series of upheavals and wars weakened Poland, and from the 1770s to the 1790s it was partitioned three times, finally disappearing as an independent state. In 1918, following the Allies' World War I victory, Poland regained its independence and, through the 1919 Treaty of Versailles, much of its former territory. World War II began with Germany's invasion of Poland in 1939. With the end of the war, Poland came under Communist control and Soviet domination. Antigovernment strikes and riots, some spurred by rising food prices, erupted periodically. In the first free election since Communist control, the trade union Solidarity, led by Lech Walesa, won an overwhelming victory in 1989. Overall, the economy is improving as it continues its transition to free market conditions. Poland is expected to join NATO in 1999. ■

PORTUGAL

Official name Portuguese Republic

PEOPLE

Population 9,868,000. **Density** 278/mi² (107/km²). **Urban** 36%. **Capital** Lisbon, 663,394. **Ethnic groups** Portuguese (Mediterranean) 99%, black 1%.

Places and Possessions of PORTUGAL

Entity	Status	Area	Population	Capital/Population
Azores (North Atlantic islands)	Autonomous region (Portugal)	868 mi² (2,247 km²)	242,000	Ponta Delgada, 20,807
Macau (Eastern Asia; islands and peninsula on China's southeastern coast)	Overseas territory	6.6 mi² (17 km²)	425,000	Macau, 342,548
Madeira Islands (North Atlantic islands; northwest of Africa)	Autonomous region (Portugal)	307 mi² (794 km²)	260,000	Funchal, 39,753

Languages Portuguese. **Religions** Roman Catholic 97%, Protestant 1%. **Life expectancy** 79 female, 72 male. **Literacy** 85%.

POLITICS

Government Republic. **Parties** Social Democratic, Socialist, others. **Suffrage** Universal, 18 and over. **Memberships** EU, NATO, OECD, UN. **Subdivisions** 18 districts, 2 autonomous regions.

ECONOMY

GDP $116,200,000,000. **Per capita** $11,750. **Monetary unit** Escudo. **Trade partners** Exports: Germany, France, Spain. Imports: Spain, Germany, France. **Exports** Clothing, footwear, machinery, cork and paper products, hides. **Imports** Machines, transportation equipment, agriculture products, chemicals, petroleum.

LAND

Description Southwestern Europe. **Area** 35,516 mi² (91,985 km²). **Highest point** Ponta do Pico, 7,713 ft (2,351 m). **Lowest point** Sea level.

People. Although many foreign invaders have been drawn by Portugal's long coastline, the country's population is relatively homogeneous. One group of invaders, the Romans, laid the basis for the chief language, Portuguese, which developed from Latin. The only significant minority is composed of black Africans from former colonies. Most Portuguese are rural and belong to the Roman Catholic church, which has had a strong influence on society.

Economy and the Land. The mainstays of agriculture and fishing were joined in the mid-1900s by manufacturing, chiefly of textiles, clothing, cork products, metals, and machinery. A variety of social and political ills contribute to Portugal's status as one of Europe's poorest countries: They include past wars with African colonies, an influx of colonial refugees, and intraparty violence. Tourism is increasingly important, but agriculture has suffered from outdated techniques and a rural-to-urban population shift. The terrain is mostly plains and lowlands, with some mountains; the climate is mild and sunny.

History and Politics. Inhabited by an Iberian people about 5,000 years ago, the area was later visited by Phoenicians, Celts, and Greeks before falling to the Romans around the first century B.C. The Romans were followed by Germanic Visigoths and in A.D. 711 by North African Muslims, who greatly influenced Portuguese art and architecture. Spain absorbed Portugal in 1094, and Portugal declared its independence in 1143. About 100 years later, the last of the Muslims were expelled. Portugal's golden age—during which its navigators explored the globe and founded colonies in South America, Africa, and the Far East—lasted from 1385 to the late 1500s. Rival European powers soon began to seize Portuguese holdings. In 1580 Spain invaded Portugal, ruling until 1640, when the Spanish were driven out and independence reestablished. After the 1822 loss of Brazil, Portugal's most valuable colony, and decades of opposition, a weakened monarchy was overthrown in 1910. The

hardships of World War I battered the newly established republic, and in 1926 its parliamentary democracy fell to a military coup. Antonio Salazar became prime minister in 1932, ruling as a virtual dictator until 1968. Salazar's favored treatment of the rich and his refusal to relinquish Portugal's colonies aggravated the economic situation. A 1974 coup toppled Salazar's successor and set up a military government—events that sparked violence among political parties. Almost all Portuguese colonies gained independence during the next two years. A democratic government was adopted in 1976; varying coalitions have since ruled the country. ■

PUERTO RICO

Official name Commonwealth of Puerto Rico

PEOPLE

Population 3,829,000. **Density** 1,089/mi² (421/km²). **Urban** 74%. **Capital** San Juan, 426,832. **Ethnic groups** Hispanic. **Languages** Spanish, English. **Religions** Roman Catholic 85%, Protestant and other 15%. **Life expectancy** 80 female, 72 male. **Literacy** 88%.

POLITICS

Government Commonwealth (U.S. protection). **Parties** New Progressive, Popular Democratic, others. **Suffrage** Universal, 18 and over. **Memberships** None. **Subdivisions** 78 municipalities.

ECONOMY

GDP $29,700,000,000. **Per capita** $7,781. **Monetary unit** U.S. dollar. **Trade partners** U.S. **Exports** Pharmaceuticals, electronics, clothing, beverages, manufactures, tuna, rum. **Imports** Chemicals, clothing, food, fish, petroleum.

LAND

Description Caribbean island. **Area** 3,515 mi² (9,104 km²). **Highest point** Cerro de Punta, 4,390 ft (1,338 m). **Lowest point** Sea level.

People. Puerto Rico's chief language, Spanish, and religion, Roman Catholicism, reflect this

American commonwealth's past under Spanish rule. Most of the population is descended from Spaniards and black African slaves. A rising population has caused housing shortages and unemployment. Many Puerto Ricans live in the United States, mostly in New York City.

Economy and the Land. Once dependent on such plantation crops as sugar and coffee, Puerto Rico is now a manufacturing center, specializing in food processing and electrical equipment. Commonwealth incentives for foreign investors aided this transformation, also known as Operation Bootstrap, after World War II. Foreign visitors, attracted by the tropical climate, make tourism another important activity. Puerto Rico lacks natural resources. The island's terrain is marked by mountains, lowlands, and valleys.

History and Politics. The original inhabitants, the Arawaks, were wiped out by Spanish colonists, who first settled the island in 1508. Despite successive attacks by the French, English, and Dutch, Puerto Rico remained under Spanish control until 1898, when the U.S. took possession after the Spanish-American War. A civil government under a U.S. governor was set up in 1900; 17 years later Puerto Ricans were made U.S. citizens. In 1952 the island became a self-governing commonwealth. This status was upheld in a referendum in 1967, and again in 1993 after fierce internal debate. ■

QATAR

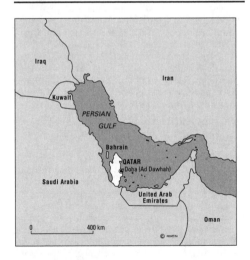

Official name State of Qatar

PEOPLE
Population 568,000. **Density** 129/mi² (50/km²). **Urban** 92%. **Capital** Doha, 361,540. **Ethnic groups** Arab 40%, Pakistani 18%, Indian 18%, Iranian 10%. **Languages** Arabic, English. **Religions** Muslim 95%. **Life expectancy** 75 female, 70 male. **Literacy** 79%.

POLITICS
Government Monarchy. **Parties** None. **Suffrage** None. **Memberships** AL, OPEC, UN. **Subdivisions** 9 municipalities.

ECONOMY
GDP $10,700,000,000. **Per capita** $19,039. **Monetary unit** Riyal. **Trade partners** Exports: Japan, Brazil, United Arab Emirates. Imports: U.K., Japan, U.S., Italy. **Exports** Petroleum, steel, fertilizer. **Imports** Food, beverages, chemicals, machinery.

LAND
Description Southwestern Asia. **Area** 4,412 mi² (11,427 km²). **Highest point** Aba al Bawl Hill, 344 ft (105 m). **Lowest point** Sea level.

People. Qatar's population is distinguished by a relatively high proportion of Iranians, Pakistanis, and Indians who began arriving during the oil boom of the 1950s. Most Qataris are Sunni Muslims and live in or near Doha, the capital. In recent years the government has encouraged the nomadic Bedouins to take up settled lifestyles. Despite a political trend toward a modern welfare state, Qatar retains many elements of a traditional Islamic society.

Economy and the Land. Oil provides the great majority of Qatar's income, while extensive reserves of natural gas await exploitation. The government has made moves toward economic diversification, investing in agriculture and industry; fertilizer and cement are important new products. Most of Qatar is stony desert, and the climate is hot and arid.

History and Politics. No strong central government existed in Qatar before Saudi Muslims gained control in the late 18th century. Ottoman Turks occupied the region from 1872 to 1916, when Qatar became a British protectorate. Although oil was discovered in 1940 on the western side of Qatar's peninsula, the outbreak of World War II postponed exploitation for another nine years. Qatar became independent in 1971 after failing to agree on the terms of a union with eight Persian Gulf sheikdoms—today the United Arab Emirates and Bahrain. Oil revenues have been used to improve housing, transportation, and public health. ■

REUNION

Official name Department of Reunion

PEOPLE
Population 699,000. **Density** 723/mi² (279/km²). **Urban** 68%. **Capital** Saint-Denis, 121,999. **Ethnic groups** Reunionese (mixed French, African, Malagasy, Chinese, Pakistani, and Indian). **Languages** French, Creole. **Religions** Roman Catholic 94%. **Life expectancy** 79 female, 71 male. **Literacy** 79%.

POLITICS
Government Overseas department (France). **Parties** Communist, Socialist, Rally for the Republic, Union for French Democracy, others. **Suffrage** Universal, 18 and over. **Memberships** None. **Subdivisions** 4 arrondissements.

ECONOMY
GDP $2,900,000,000. **Per capita** $4,394. **Monetary unit** French franc. **Trade partners** Exports: France, Comoros, Madagascar, Japan. Imports: France, Bahrain, Germany, Italy. **Exports** Sugar, rum and molasses, perfume essence, lobster, vanilla and tea. **Imports** Manufactures, food, beverages, tobacco, machinery, transportation equipment.

LAND
Description Indian Ocean island. **Area** 967 mi^2 (2,504 km^2). **Highest point** Piton des Neiges, 10,072 ft (3,070 m). **Lowest point** Sea level.

People. Reunion has a racially mixed population, mainly descended from French settlers, African slaves, and Asian laborers. French is the official language, but most inhabitants speak a Creole dialect. The mainly Roman Catholic population is densely concentrated in the lowland areas along the coast. Social stratification is rigid.

Economy and the Land. Reunion's traditional coffee crop was replaced by sugar early on, and sugar continues as an economic mainstay today. Industry is based on the production of sugar by-products, such as rum and molasses. Unemployment is a problem, and the island remains dependent upon French aid. The mountainous terrain is marked by one active and several extinct volcanoes. The tropical climate is subject to occasional cyclones and trade winds that bring high rainfall to the south and southeast.

History and Politics. Although known to the Arabs and Portuguese, Reunion was uninhabited when French settlement began in the 1660s. First called Bourbon, the island originally served as a stopover on the French shipping route to India. The French soon developed coffee and sugar plantations, bringing slaves from Africa to work them. British-French rivalry for control of the area led to brief British rule during the early 1800s. After several name changes, from Bourbon to Reunion to Bonaparte and back to Bourbon again, the French settled on the name Reunion in 1848. After slavery was abolished, indentured laborers were brought from Indochina, India, and eastern Africa. Reunion was a French colony until 1946, when it became an overseas department.■

ROMANIA

Official name Romania

PEOPLE
Population 22,305,000. **Density** 243/mi^2 (94/km^2). **Urban** 56%. **Capital** Bucharest, 2,066,723. **Ethnic groups** Romanian (mixed Latin, Thracian, Slavic, and Celtic) 89%, Hungarian 9%. **Languages** Romanian, Hungarian, German. **Religions** Romanian Orthodox 70%, Roman Catholic 6%, Protestant 6%. **Life expectancy** 73 female, 67 male. **Literacy** 97%.

POLITICS
Government Republic. **Parties** Democratic Convention, Democratic, Social Democratic, others. **Suffrage** Universal, 18 and over. **Memberships** UN. **Subdivisions** 40 counties, 1 municipality.

ECONOMY
GDP $105,700,000,000. **Per capita** $4,653. **Monetary unit** Leu. **Trade partners** Exports: Former Soviet republics, Italy, Germany. Imports: Former Soviet republics, Iran, Egypt. **Exports** Machinery, transportation equipment, fuel, minerals, metals, chemicals, food. **Imports** Fuel, minerals, metals, machinery, transportation equipment, chemicals, food.

LAND
Description Eastern Europe. **Area** 91,699 mi^2 (237,500 km^2). **Highest point** Moldoveanu, 8,346 ft (2,544 m). **Lowest point** Sea level.

People. The majority population of Romania belongs to the Romanian Orthodox church and traces its roots to Latin-speaking Romans, Thracians, Slavs, and Celts. Minorities, concentrated in Transylvania and areas north and west of Bucharest, are mainly Roman Catholic Hungarians and Germans. Other minorities include Gypsies, Serbs, Croats, Ukrainians, Greeks, Turks, and Armenians. Almost all inhabitants speak Romanian, although minority groups often speak other languages.

Economy and the Land. When Romania became a Communist country in the 1940s, the government began to refocus the country's economy from agriculture to industry. Romania's economy is now based on such major products as iron and steel. Most agriculture is still collectivized, and corn and wheat are major crops. The transition to a market economy has been slow and troubled. The terrain is marked by a south-to-northeast plateau that curves around several mountain ranges, including the Carpathians, located in the northern and central regions. The climate is continental, with cold, snowy winters and warm summers.

History and Politics. First colonized by the Dacians, a Thracian tribe, around the 4th century B.C., the area became the Roman province of Romania in the 2nd century A.D. Invading Bulgars, Goths, Huns, Magyars, Slavs, and Tartars followed the Romans. Between 1250 and 1350, the independent Romanian principalities of Walachia and Moldavia emerged. In the 15th and 16th centuries, Ottoman Turks conquered the principalities and, following a Russian-Turkish war, Russians occupied the states. In 1861 Walachia and Moldavia were united as Romania. In 1878 they gained independence, and in 1881 Romania was proclaimed a kingdom. Oppression and a concentration of land and wealth among the aristocracy marked the country's government, and in 1907 its army quelled a rebellion. In 1919, after a World War I alliance with the Allies, Romania gained Transylvania and other territories. Instability and dissatisfaction, spurred by worldwide economic depression, continued through the 1930s. With the cooperation of Romanian leadership, Germany occupied the country in World War II. In 1944 Soviet troops entered Romania, and the country joined the Allies. A Communist government was established in 1945, and in 1947 the king was forced to abdicate as Romania officially became a Communist country. Initially Romania's policies were closely tied to those of the Soviet Union, but renewed nationalism in the 1960s led to several independent policy decisions. Nicolae Ceausescu's 24 years of harsh, repressive leadership led to a popular revolt and his execution in 1989. Elections held in 1990 by an interim government were won by the National Salvation Front (former Communists). The country approved a new constitution in December 1991 that allowed multiparty representation. There have been periodic riots over continued government failure to improve economic conditions. ■

RUSSIA

Official name Russian Federation

PEOPLE
Population 150,500,000. **Density** 23/mi² (8.8/km²). **Urban** 76%. **Capital** Moscow, 8,747,000. **Ethnic** groups Russian 82%, Tatar 4%, Ukrainian 3%, Chuvash 1%. **Languages** Russian, Tatar, Ukrainian. **Religions** Russian Orthodox, Muslim. **Life expectancy** 74 female, 62 male. **Literacy** 98%.

POLITICS
Government Federal republic. **Parties** Communist, Liberal Democratic, Our Home is Russia, Yabloko, others. **Suffrage** Universal, 18 and over. **Memberships** UN. **Subdivisions** 21 republics, 1 autonomous oblast, 49 oblasts, 6 krays, 10 autonomous okrugs, 2 cities.

ECONOMY
GDP $796,000,000,000. **Per capita** $5,289. **Monetary unit** Ruble. **Trade partners** Western and eastern European countries, Japan. **Exports** Petroleum, natural gas, lumber, nonferrous metals, chemicals, manufactures. **Imports** Machinery and equipment, manufactures, pharmaceuticals, food.

LAND
Description Eastern Europe and Northern Asia. **Area** 6,592,849 mi² (17,075,400 km²). **Highest point** Mt. Elbrus, 18,510 ft (5,642 m). **Lowest point** Caspian Sea, -92 ft (-28 m).

People. The Russians are a Slavic people who have occupied the land between the Baltic and Black Seas for at least 1,500 years. Russia is also home to many other ethnic groups, including the Tatars, Yakuts, Ossetians, and Buryats. Many of the minority ethnic groups reside in their own autonomous regions. The Russian church is the largest of the Eastern Orthodox churches, and dates back to A.D. 988. Once discouraged under Communist rule, religion is now experiencing a revival. Russians are known for their many great contributions to the arts and sciences.

Economy and the Land. Before the fall of Communism and subsequent breakup of the Soviet Union, the national government controlled the economy. Despite its strength as one of the world's industrial powers, the Soviet economy was plagued with low productivity, chronic shortages, and technological stagnation. The Soviet Union traded primarily with other Communist countries until the late 1980s, when economic reform led to greater trade with the West. Geographically, Russia is the largest country in the world. Its terrain is widely varied and richly endowed with minerals. Though the country contains some of the world's most fertile land, long winters and hot, dry summers make agriculture difficult and risky.

History and Politics. Inhabited as early as the Stone Age, what is now Russia was much later invaded by the Scythians, Sarmatians, Goths, Huns, Bulgars, Slavs, and others. By A.D. 989, Byzantine cultural influence had become predominant. Various groups and regions were slowly incorporated into a single state. In 1547, Ivan the Terrible was crowned czar of all Russia, beginning a tradition of czarist rule and expansionism. The borders of all the Russian empire in the mid-1800s roughly approximated those of the former Soviet Union. Czarist rule continued until the 1917 Russian Revolution, when the

Bolsheviks came to power and named Vladimir Lenin as head of the first Soviet government. The Bolsheviks established a new, experimental Communist state based on the works of economist Karl Marx. A bitter civil war ensued as all private property was seized by the government. Many areas that had been part of Czarist Russia were briefly independent until Joseph Stalin succeeded Lenin, reclaimed the lost territories, and began a series of political purges that lasted through the 1930s. The Soviet Union became embroiled in World War II, siding with the Allies, losing more than 20 million people, and suffering widespread destruction of its cities and countryside. It emerged from the war with extended influence, however, having annexed part of Finland and occupying many Eastern European nations. In the years following World War II, the Soviet Union and the United States and their allies were engaged in a "Cold War," which was characterized by escalating production of nuclear weapons and severe restrictions on travel and communications between the two sides. Mikhail Gorbachev took office in 1985 and introduced a new era of reform and government restructuring. The new political climate resulted in the end of the Cold War and the ultimate breakup of the Soviet Union. Russia emerged as an independent state in late 1991. Russian president Boris Yeltsin rose to prominence as the leader of Russia and emphasized economic reform and closer ties with all Western countries. In response to the expansion of NATO in Europe, Russia instituted a union with several other former Soviet Republics called the Commonwealth of Independent States. A recent peace accord with Chechnya—a part of Russia that has been battling for independence—defers the decision on Chechen independence until 2001. Chechnya is already functioning as if it were independent, however. The Chechens now call their country the Republic of Ichkeriya, and they have adopted Islamic law. Russia continues to be politically and economically unstable. ∎

RWANDA

Official name Republic of Rwanda

PEOPLE
Population 8,548,000. **Density** 841/mi² (325/km²). **Urban** 6%. **Capital** Kigali, 232,733. **Ethnic groups** Hutu 80%, Tutsi 19%, Twa (Pygmy) 1%. **Languages** English, French, Kinyarwanda, Swahili. **Religions** Roman Catholic 65%, Animist 25%, Protestant 9%. **Life expectancy** 48 female, 45 male. **Literacy** 61%.

POLITICS
Government Republic. **Parties** Democratic and Socialist, Democratic Republican, Liberal, Patriotic Front, others. **Suffrage** Universal adult. **Memberships** OAU, UN. **Subdivisions** 10 prefectures.

ECONOMY
GDP $3,800,000,000. **Per capita** $518. **Monetary unit** Franc. **Trade partners** Exports: Italy, Belgium, France. Imports: Belgium, Japan, Kenya. **Exports** Coffee, tea,

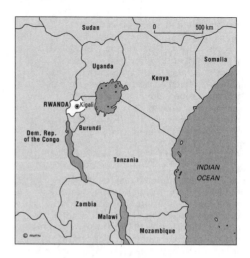

cassiterite, wolframite, pyrethrum. **Imports** Textiles, food, machinery, steel, petroleum, cement, construction materials.

LAND
Description Eastern Africa, landlocked. **Area** 10,169 mi² (26,338 km²). **Highest point** Volcan Karisimbi, 14,787 ft (4,507 m). **Lowest point** Along Ruzizi River, 3,117 ft (950 m).

People. Most Rwandans are Hutu, mainly farmers of Bantu stock. Minorities include the Tutsi, a pastoral people that dominated politically until a Hutu rebellion in 1959; and the Twa, Pygmies descended from the original population. English, French, and Kinyarwanda are official languages, but most people speak Kinyarwanda, a Bantu tongue. Roman Catholicism is the major religion, and minority groups practice indigenous beliefs as well as Protestantism and Islam. A high population density and a high birthrate characterize Rwanda.

Economy and the Land. Agriculture is the major activity, although plagued by the erosion and overpopulation of arable land. Many Rwandans practice subsistence farming, while coffee and tea are major export crops. The production and export of minerals, partly fueled by foreign investment, is also important. The country's landlocked position and underdeveloped transportation system hinder economic growth. The terrain consists mainly of grassy uplands and hills, with volcanic mountains in the west and northwest, while the climate is mild.

History and Politics. The Twa, the region's original inhabitants, were followed by the Hutu. The Tutsi most likely arrived about the 14th century, subjugated the weaker Hutu, and dominated the region. The areas of present-day Rwanda and Burundi became part of German East Africa in the 1890s. In 1919, following World War I, the region was mandated to Belgium as Ruanda-Urundi, and following World War II, Ruanda-Urundi was made a United Nations trust territory under Belgian administration. In 1959 a Hutu revolt against Tutsi domination resulted in the death of many Tutsi and the flight of many more. After gaining independence in 1962, the former territory split into the countries of Rwanda and Burundi. The military overthrew the country's first president in 1973. Ethnic violence erupted after the death in April 1994 of President Habyarimana in a plane crash. In 1997 the government began to arrest and prosecute Hutus who were involved in the 1994 genocidal murder of nearly one million Tutsi. Widespread violence and massacres continue. Since Rwanda's independence, it has generated what is thought to be the largest stream of refugees in the history of Africa. ∎

ST. HELENA See UNITED KINGDOM.

ST. KITTS AND NEVIS

Official name Federation of St. Kitts and Nevis

PEOPLE
Population 42,000. **Density** 404/mi² (156/km²). **Urban** 34%. **Capital** Basseterre, St. Christopher I., 14,725. **Ethnic groups** Black 94%, mixed 3%, white 1%. **Languages** English. **Religions** Anglican, Methodist, Moravian, Roman Catholic. **Life expectancy** 70 female, 64 male. **Literacy** 97%.

POLITICS
Government Parliamentary state. **Parties** Concerned Citizens Movement, Labor, Nevis Reformation, People's Action Movement. **Suffrage** Universal, 18 and over. **Memberships** CW, OAS, UN. **Subdivisions** 14 parishes.

ECONOMY
GDP $220,000,000. **Per capita** $5,366. **Monetary unit** East Caribbean dollar. **Trade partners** U.S., U.K., Trinidad and Tobago. **Exports** Sugar, clothing, electronics, machinery, food, beverages, tobacco. **Imports** Food, manufactures, machinery, fuel.

LAND
Description Caribbean islands. **Area** 104 mi² (269 km²). **Highest point** Mt. Liamuiga, 3,793 ft (1,156 m). **Lowest point** Sea level.

People. Most of the inhabitants of the islands of St. Kitts, often called St. Christopher, and Nevis are of black African descent. The primarily rural population is concentrated along the coast. English is spoken throughout the islands, and most people are Protestant, evidence of former British rule.

Economy and the Land. Agriculture and tourism are the economic mainstays of St. Kitts and Nevis. Sugarcane is a major crop, cultivated mainly on St. Kitts Island, while Nevis Island produces cotton, fruits, and vegetables. Agriculture also provides for sugar processing, the major industrial activity. A tropical climate, beaches, and a scenic mountainous terrain provide an ideal setting for tourism.

History and Politics. The islands were first inhabited by the Arawaks, who were displaced by the warlike Caribs. In 1493 Christopher Columbus sighted the islands, and in the 1600s British settlement of both islands began, along with French settlement on St. Christopher. Sugar plantations were soon established, and slaves were imported from Africa. Britain's control of the islands was recognized by the 1783 Treaty of Paris, and for a time St. Kitts, Nevis, and Anguilla were ruled as a single colony. Anguilla became a separate dependency of Britain in 1980, and St. Kitts and Nevis gained independence in 1983. The Nevis legislature has recently voted for their island to secede from the country of St. Kitts and Nevis. The secession will be put to a referendum for Nevis voters in 1998. ∎

ST. LUCIA

Official name St. Lucia

PEOPLE
Population 158,000. **Density** 664/mi² (256/km²). **Urban** 37%. **Capital** Castries, 11,147. **Ethnic groups** Black 90%, mixed 6%, East Indian 3%. **Languages** English, French. **Religions** Roman Catholic 90%, Protestant 7%, Anglican 3%. **Life expectancy** 74 female, 66 male. **Literacy** 67%.

POLITICS
Government Parliamentary state. **Parties** Labor, United Workers', others. **Suffrage** Universal, 18 and over. **Memberships** CW, OAS, UN. **Subdivisions** 11 quarters.

ECONOMY
GDP $640,000,000. **Per capita** $4,076. **Monetary unit** East Caribbean dollar. **Trade partners** Exports: U.K., U.S., Dominica. Imports: U.S., U.K., Trinidad and Tobago. **Exports** Bananas, clothing, cocoa, vegetables, fruit, coconut oil. **Imports** Manufactures, machinery, transportation equipment, food, chemicals, fuel.

LAND
Description Caribbean island. **Area** 238 mi² (616 km²). **Highest point** Mt. Gimie, 3,117 ft (950 m). **Lowest point** Sea level.

People. St. Lucia's population is composed mainly of descendants of black African slaves, and minority groups include people of African-European descent, whites, and East Indians. During the colonial period, the island frequently shifted between British and French control, and its culture reflects both British and French elements. Although English is widely spoken, many St. Lucians speak a French dialect. Roman Catholicism is the main religion, and the Protestant minority includes Anglicans.

Economy and the Land. Agriculture remains important, and principal crops include bananas and cocoa. Tax incentives and relative political stability have caused an increase in industrial development and foreign investment, mainly from the United States. Tourism is becoming increasingly important, with visitors drawn by the tropical climate, scenic mountainous terrain, and excellent beaches.

History and Politics. The Arawaks arrived between the A.D. 200s and 400s and were conquered by the Caribs between the 9th and 11th centuries. Dutch, French, and British rivalry for control began in the 17th century, but the Europeans were unable to subdue the Caribs. The first successful settlement was established by the French in 1651. After many years of alternating French and British control, St. Lucia came under British rule through the 1814 Treaty of Paris. The island gained full independence in 1979. ■

ST. PIERRE AND MIQUELON See FRANCE.

ST. VINCENT AND THE GRENADINES

Official name St. Vincent and the Grenadines

PEOPLE
Population 119,000. **Density** 793/mi² (307/km²). **Urban** 50%. **Capital** Kingstown, St. Vincent I., 15,466. **Ethnic groups** Black 82%, mixed 14%, East Indian 2%, white 1%. **Languages** English, French. **Religions** Anglican, Methodist, Roman Catholic, Baptist. **Life expectancy** 74 female, 71 male. **Literacy** 96%.

POLITICS
Government Parliamentary state. **Parties** New Democratic, Unity Labor, others. **Suffrage** Universal, 18 and over. **Memberships** CW, OAS, UN. **Subdivisions** 5 parishes.

ECONOMY
GDP $240,000,000. **Per capita** $2,051. **Monetary unit** East Caribbean dollar. **Trade partners** Exports: U.K., Trinidad and Tobago, U.S. Imports: U.S., U.K. **Exports** Bananas, eddoes and taro, arrowroot starch, tennis racquets, flour. **Imports** Food, machinery, chemicals, fuel, fertilizer, minerals.

LAND
Description Caribbean islands. **Area** 150 mi² (388 km²). **Highest point** Soufrière, 4,049 ft (1,234 m). **Lowest point** Sea level.

People. The people of St. Vincent are mainly descended from black African slaves. The colonial influences of Britain and France are evident in the languages and religions. English is the official language, though a French patois is also spoken. Most people are Anglican, Methodist, or Roman Catholic.

Economy and the Land. St. Vincent's economy is based on agriculture, especially banana production. Tourism also plays a role, both on the main island of St. Vincent and in the Grenadines. St. Vincent is the largest island, and about 100 smaller islands make up the Grenadines. The terrain is mountainous, with coastlines marked by sandy beaches, and the climate is tropical.

History and Politics. The indigenous Arawaks were conquered by the Caribs about 1300. Christopher Columbus probably reached the area in 1498. Although the Caribs fought the Europeans, the British began settling St. Vincent in the 1760s. A period of French control began in 1779, and the islands were returned to the British in 1783. St. Vincent and the Grenadines remained under British rule until they gained independence in 1979. ■

SAMOA

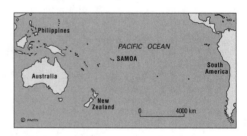

Official name Samoa

PEOPLE
Population 222,000. **Density** 203/mi² (78/km²). **Urban** 21%. **Capital** Apia, Upolu I., 34,126. **Ethnic groups** Samoan (Polynesian) 93%, mixed European and Polynesian 7%. **Languages** English, Samoan. **Religions** Congregational, Roman Catholic, Methodist, Mormon. **Life expectancy** 71 female, 68 male. **Literacy** 97%.

POLITICS
Government Constitutional monarchy. **Parties** Human Rights Protection, National Development, others. **Suffrage** Universal, 21 and over. **Memberships** CW, UN. **Subdivisions** 11 districts.

ECONOMY
GDP $415,000,000. **Per capita** $2,412. **Monetary unit** Tala. **Trade partners** Exports: New Zealand, American Samoa, Germany. Imports: New Zealand, Australia, Japan. **Exports** Coconut products, taro, copra, cocoa. **Imports** Manufactures, food, machinery.

LAND
Description South Pacific Islands. **Area** 1,093 mi² (2,831 km²). **Highest point** Mt. Silisili, 6,096 ft (1,858 m). **Lowest point** Sea level.

People. Most Samoans are of Polynesian descent, and a significant minority are of mixed Samoan and European heritage. Most of the population is Christian and practices a variety of faiths introduced by European missionaries and traders. Samoan and English are the principal languages.

Economy and the Land. The tropical climate of Samoa, which is composed of volcanic islands, is suited for agriculture—the country's chief economic support. Bananas, coconuts, and tropical fruits are the most important crops.

History and Politics. Polynesians settled the Samoan islands more than 2,000 years ago. Dutch explorers visited the islands in the early 1700s, and English missionaries arrived in 1830. Rivalry between the islands' royal families increased, along with competition among the United Kingdom, the United States, and Germany. In 1900 the islands were divided between the U.S., which called its portion Eastern Samoa, and Germany, which called its portion Western Samoa. By the end of World War I, New Zealand had gained control of Western Samoa. Growing demand for independence led to United Nations intervention and gradual steps toward self-government. The islands became fully independent in 1962. The country maintains friendly relations with New Zealand and neighboring Pacific islands. In 1997 the government officially changed the name from Western Samoa to Samoa. ■

SAN MARINO

Official name Republic of San Marino

PEOPLE
Population 25,000. **Density** 1,042/mi² (410/km²). **Urban** 95%. **Capital** San Marino, 2,794. **Ethnic groups** Sanmarinese (mixed Latin, Adriatic, and Teutonic), Italian. **Languages** Italian. **Religions** Roman Catholic. **Life expectancy** 85 female, 77 male. **Literacy** 96%.

POLITICS
Government Republic. **Parties** Christian Democratic, Progressive Democratic, Socialist, others. **Suffrage** Universal, 18 and over. **Memberships** UN. **Subdivisions** 9 municipalities.

ECONOMY
GDP $380,000,000. **Per capita** $15,833. **Monetary unit** Italian lira. **Trade partners** Italy. **Exports** Building materials, lime, wood, chestnuts, wheat, wine. **Imports** Consumer goods, food.

LAND
Description Southern Europe, landlocked. **Area** 24 mi²

(61 km²). **Highest point** Monte Titano, 2,425 ft (739 m). **Lowest point** Unnamed, 164 ft (50 m).

People. San Marino, completely surrounded by Italy, has strong ethnic ties to the Italians, combining Latin, Adriatic, and Teutonic roots. Italian is the main language, and Roman Catholicism the major religion in San Marino. Despite San Marino's similarities to Italy, its tradition of independence has given its citizens a strong national identity.

Economy and the Land. Close economic ties between San Marino and surrounding Italy have produced a mutually beneficial customs union: Italians have no customs restrictions at San Marino's borders, and San Marino receives annual budget subsidiary payments from Italy. Most San Marinese are employed in agriculture; livestock raising is a main activity, and crops include wheat and grapes. In addition, tourism and the sale of postage stamps are major economic contributors, as is industry, which produces construction materials for export. Located in the Apennine Mountains of central Italy, San Marino has a rugged terrain and a generally moderate climate.

History and Politics. San Marino is considered the world's oldest republic. Tradition has it that Marinus, a Christian stonecutter seeking religious freedom in a time of repressive Roman rule, founded the state in the 4th century A.D. Partly because of the natural geographic protection afforded by its mountainous terrain, San Marino has been able to maintain continuous independence despite attempted invasions by outsiders. In the 1300s the country became a republic, and the pope recognized its independent status in 1631. San Marino signed its first treaty of friendship with Italy in 1862. In its foreign relations, the country maintains a distinct identity and status. ■

SAO TOME AND PRINCIPE

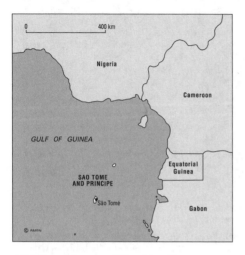

Official name Democratic Republic of Sao Tome and Principe

PEOPLE
Population 148,000. **Density** 398/mi² (154/km²). **Urban** 44%. **Capital** São Tomé, São Tomé I., 5,245. **Ethnic groups** Mestico, Angolares, Forros, Servicais, Tongas, European descent. **Languages** Portuguese, Fang and other indigenous. **Religions** Roman Catholic, Evangelical Protestant, Seventh Day Adventist. **Life expectancy** 66 female, 62 male. **Literacy** 73%.

POLITICS
Government Republic. **Parties** Democratic Convergence-Reflection Group, Independent Democratic Action, Movement for the Liberation, others. **Suffrage** Universal, 18 and over. **Memberships** OAU, UN. **Subdivisions** 7 districts.

ECONOMY
GDP $138,000,000. **Per capita** $1,087. **Monetary unit** Dobra. **Trade partners** Exports: Germany, Netherlands, China. Imports: Portugal, Germany, Angola, China. **Exports** Cocoa, copra, coffee, palm oil. **Imports** Machinery, electrical equipment, food.

LAND
Description Western African islands. **Area** 372 mi² (964 km²). **Highest point** Pico de São Tomé, 6,640 ft (2,024 m). **Lowest point** Sea level.

People. Descendants of African slaves and people of Portuguese-African heritage compose most of Sao Tome and Principe's population. Colonial rule by Portugal is evidenced by the predominance of the Portuguese language and Roman Catholicism. Most people live on São Tomé.

Economy and the Land. Cocoa dominates Sao Tome and Principe's economy. Copra and palm-oil production are also important, and fishing plays an economic role. Through the development of vegetable crops, the government hopes to diversify agricultural output; food must now be imported. Part of an extinct volcanic mountain range, Sao Tome and Principe have a mostly mountainous terrain. The climate is tropical.

History and Politics. When Portuguese explorers arrived in the 1400s, Sao Tome and Principe were uninhabited. Early settlers included Portuguese convicts and exiles. Cultivation of the land and importation of slaves led to a thriving sugar economy by the mid-1500s. In the 1800s, following slave revolts and the decline of sugar production, coffee and cocoa became the islands' mainstays, and soon large Portuguese plantations, called *rocas*, were established. Slavery was abolished by Portugal in 1876, but an international controversy arose in the early 1900s when Angolan contract workers were allegedly treated as virtual slaves. Decades of unrest led to the 1953 Batepa Massacre, in which Portuguese rulers killed several hundred rioting African workers. A movement for independence began in the late 1950s, and Sao Tome and Principe became independent in 1975. The country has established ties with other former Portuguese colonies in northern Africa since gaining independence. The first presidential elections were held in March 1990. ■

SAUDI ARABIA

Official name Kingdom of Saudi Arabia

PEOPLE
Population 20,415,000. **Density** 25/mi² (9.5/km²). **Urban** 84%. **Capital** Riyadh, 1,250,000. **Ethnic groups** Arab 90%, Afro-Asian 10%. **Languages** Arabic. **Religions** Muslim 100%. **Life expectancy** 73 female, 70 male. **Literacy** 63%.

POLITICS
Government Monarchy. **Parties** None. **Suffrage** None. **Memberships** AL, OPEC, UN. **Subdivisions** 14 emirates.

ECONOMY
GDP $189,300,000,000. **Per capita** $9,929. **Monetary unit** Riyal. **Trade partners** Exports: Japan, U.S., Singapore. Imports: U.S., Japan, U.K.

Exports Petroleum. **Imports** Manufactures, transportation equipment, food.

LAND

Description Southwestern Asia. **Area** 830,000 mi² (2,149,690 km²). **Highest point** Mt. Sawda, 10,522 ft (3,207 m). **Lowest point** Sea level.

People. Saudi Arabia is inhabited primarily by Arab Muslims descended from Semitic peoples who settled in the region several thousand years ago. The petroleum industry has attracted a sizable minority of Arabs from other countries, Europeans, and non-Arab Muslims from Africa and Asia. The country's official language is Arabic, although English is used among educated Saudis in business and international affairs. Islam dominates Saudi life, and nearly all the people belong to the religion's Sunni branch. Various forms of Christianity and traditional religions are practiced among foreign workers and indigenous minority groups. Most live in urban areas, but some Bedouin tribes preserve their nomadic way of life.

Economy and the Land. The economy of Saudi Arabia has been shaped by its vast deserts and huge petroleum and natural gas reserves. The hot, mostly arid climate has prevented agricultural abundance and stability: The country must import nearly all its food. Oil was discovered in the 1930s, but the country did not begin rapid economic development until the reserves were aggressively exploited following World War II. Saudi Arabia is one of the world's leading exporters of petroleum, possessing the largest concentration of known oil reserves in the world. The government is seeking to diversify the economy, improve transportation and communication lines, and build agricultural output. Private enterprise and foreign investment are encouraged. Saudi Arabia is divided into the western highlands bordering the Red Sea, a central plateau, northern deserts, the huge Rub' al-Khālī desert in the south, and the eastern lowlands. Only the coastal regions receive appreciable rainfall, and some inland desert areas may go without rain for several years.

History and Politics. Even though Saudi Arabia established prosperous trade routes thousands of years ago, its history began with the founding of Islam by Muhammad in the early 600s A.D. By the end of that century, Mecca and Medina were established as the political and religious centers of Islam that they remain today. The territory split into numerous states that warred among themselves for more than 1,000 years. The Ottoman Turks gained control over the coastal region of Hejaz in the early 1500s, while Britain set up protectorates along the southern and eastern coasts of Arabia during the 1800s. The Saud family dynasty, founded in the 1400s, managed to remain a dominant religious and political force. Members of the dynasty fought to establish the supremacy of Islamic law and unite the various clans into one country. In 1932 Ibn Saud pro-

claimed the Kingdom of Saudi Arabia and established a Saud monarchy that has continued despite dissension within the royal family. Since the 1960s Saudi Arabia has aggressively sought to upgrade local governments, industry, education, the status of women, and the standard of living while maintaining Islamic values and traditions. Saudi Arabia is a dominant member of the Organization of Petroleum Exporting Countries (OPEC). Despite disagreements with the West and continuing conflicts with Israel, the country maintains strong diplomatic and economic ties with Western countries. During the Gulf War, Saudi Arabia received help from a coalition of countries to protect its borders from Iraqi invasion. The ruling family continues to resist both democratic and extreme fundamentalist influences. ∎

SENEGAL

Official name Republic of Senegal

PEOPLE

Population 9,552,000. **Density** 126/mi² (49/km²). **Urban** 44%. **Capital** Dakar, 1,490,450. **Ethnic groups** Wolof 36%, Serer 17%, Fulani 17%, Toucouleur 9%, Diola 9%. **Languages** French, Wolof, Fulani, Serer, indigenous. **Religions** Muslim 92%, Tribal religionist 6%. **Life expectancy** 52 female, 50 male. **Literacy** 33%.

POLITICS

Government Republic. **Parties** Democratic, Socialist, others. **Suffrage** Universal, 18 and over. **Memberships** OAU, UN. **Subdivisions** 10 regions.

ECONOMY

GDP $14,500,000,000. **Per capita** $1,586. **Monetary unit** CFA franc. **Trade partners** Exports: France, India, Mali, Italy. Imports: France, Nigeria, Italy. **Exports** Fish, peanuts, petroleum products, phosphates. **Imports** Manufactures, food, petroleum.

LAND

Description Western Africa. **Area** 75,951 mi² (196,712 km²). **Highest point** 1,906 ft (581 m). **Lowest point** Sea level.

People. Most Senegalese are black Africans from many ethnic groups, each with its own customs and language. The country has many immigrants from other African countries. While French is the official language, Wolof is widely spoken. Islam is the religion of the vast majority. Senegal is mainly a rural country of subsistence farmers.

Economy and the Land. The mainstays of the economy are petroleum, agriculture, fishing, and mining. Tourism is a rapidly growing new industry. Manufactured goods, fish, peanuts, and petroleum products rank as Senegal's primary exports. Agricultural output is often hurt by irregular weather patterns, and the country must import nearly all its energy. Senegal has one of the finest transportation systems in Africa. Small plateaus, low massifs, marshy swamps, and a sandy coast highlight the terrain, which is mainly flat. The climate is marked by dry and rainy seasons, with differing precipitation patterns in the south and the more arid north.

History and Politics. The area that is now Senegal has been inhabited by black Africans since prehistoric times. When Europeans first established trade ties with the Senegalese in the mid-1400s, the country had been divided into several independent kingdoms. By the early 1800s, France had gained control of the region and in 1895 made Senegal part of French West Africa. In 1959 Senegal joined with French Sudan, or present-day Mali, to form the Federation of Mali, which became independent in 1960. Senegal withdrew from the federation later in the year, however, to found the independent Republic of Senegal. The new government was plagued by coup attempts and an economy crippled by the severe droughts of the late 1960s and early 1970s. Although there is political pluralism, the Socialist Party has controlled the government since 1960. The people of the southern region of Cassamance are fighting for independence. ■

SEYCHELLES

Official name Republic of Seychelles

PEOPLE
Population 79,000. **Density** 451/mi² (174/km²). **Urban** 55%. **Capital** Victoria, Mahé I., 23,000. **Ethnic groups** Seychellois (mixed Asian, African, and European). **Languages** English, French, Creole. **Religions** Roman Catholic 90%, Anglican 8%. **Life expectancy** 74 female, 66 male. **Literacy** 84%.

POLITICS
Government Republic. **Parties** Democratic, People's Progressive Front, others. **Suffrage** Universal, 17 and over. **Memberships** CW, OAU, UN. **Subdivisions** 21 districts.

ECONOMY
GDP $430,000,000. **Per capita** $5,733. **Monetary unit** Rupee. **Trade partners** Exports: France, Kuwait, Reunion. Imports: South Africa, U.K., Kuwait. **Exports** Fish, copra, cinnamon bark. **Imports** Manufactures,

food, tobacco, beverages, machinery, transportation equipment

LAND
Description Indian Ocean islands. **Area** 175 mi² (453 km²). **Highest point** Morne Seychellois, 2,969 ft (905 m). **Lowest point** Sea level.

People. The majority of Seychellois are of mixed African, European, and Asian ancestry. The islands' culture combines French and African elements, and although the official languages of French and English are widely spoken, most also speak a Creole dialect of French. Many of the more than 100 islands are coral atolls, unable to support human life. The population is concentrated on Mahé, the largest island, while the remainder live mainly on Praslin and La Digue islands.

Economy and the Land. The basis of the economy is tourism, with foreign visitors attracted by the tropical climate, white-sand beaches, and exotic flora and wildlife found on the granite islands. Mountainous granite islands, which contain fertile soils for growing cinnamon and coconuts, and flat coral islands comprise Seychelles.

History and Politics. The Portuguese reached the uninhabited islands in the early 1500s. For more than 200 years, the islands served as little more than pirates' havens: France claimed them in 1756. By the 1770s white planters and African slaves had begun to settle Mahé. After a French-English war, France ceded the islands to Britain in 1814. Seychelles achieved independence in 1976. Opposition parties were legalized in 1991 and a new constitution was approved in 1993. ■

SHETLAND ISLANDS
See UNITED KINGDOM.

SIERRA LEONE

Official name Republic of Sierra Leone

PEOPLE
Population 5,091,000. **Density** 182/mi² (70/km²).
Urban 34%. **Capital** Freetown, 469,776. **Ethnic groups** Temne 30%, Mende 30%, other African.
Languages English, Krio, Mende, Temne, indigenous.
Religions Muslim 60%, Animist 30%, Christian 10%.
Life expectancy 43 female, 39 male. **Literacy** 31%.

POLITICS
Government Republic. **Parties** People's, People's Democratic, United National People's, others. **Suffrage** Universal, 18 and over. **Memberships** CW, OAU, UN.
Subdivisions 3 provinces, 1 area.

ECONOMY
GDP $4,400,000,000. **Per capita** $914. **Monetary unit** Leone. **Trade partners** Exports: U.S., U.K., Netherlands. Imports: U.K., U.S., Germany. **Exports** Rutile, bauxite, cocoa, diamonds, coffee. **Imports** Machinery, food, manufactures, fuel, lubricants.

LAND
Description Western Africa. **Area** 27,925 mi² (72,325 km²). **Highest point** Bintimani, 6,381 ft (1,945 m). **Lowest point** Sea level.

People. The population of Sierra Leone is divided into nearly 20 main ethnic groups. The two major groups are the Temne in the north and west and the Mende in the south. Descendants of freed American slaves, who settled in Freetown on the coast, make up a sizable Creole minority. English is the official language, but most of the people speak local African tongues. The Creoles speak Krio, a dialect of English. Most people practice Islam or various local religions, and a small number are Christian.

Economy and the Land. Sierra Leone is one of the world's largest producers of industrial and commercial diamonds. The country also mines bauxite and rutile. Poor soil, a fluctuating tropical climate, and traditional farming methods keep crop yields low. Sierra Leone is one of Africa's poorest countries. Rice, coffee, and cocoa are important crops. To improve agricultural production, the government is clearing some of the coastal mangrove swamplands. The interior of Sierra Leone is marked by a broad coastal plain in the north and by mountains and plateaus that rise along the country's northern and eastern borders. During the wet season Sierra Leone receives heavy rainfall in the Freetown area and significantly less in the north.

History and Politics. When the Portuguese reached the region in 1460, they found the area inhabited by the Temne. The British followed the Portuguese in the 1500s. Europeans took slaves from the area for the New World until Britain abolished the slave trade. In 1787, Englishman Granville Sharp settled nearly 400 freed black American slaves in what is now Freetown. Britain declared the peninsula a colony in 1808 and a protectorate in 1896. In 1961 Sierra Leone became an independent country with a constitution and parliamentary form of government. A military takeover in 1967 was short-lived, and the constitution was rewritten in 1971 to make the country a republic. Government corruption has resulted in ongoing guerrilla warfare which has caused enormous hardship for civilians since 1991. In 1997 the recently elected government was overthrown in a military coup. Nigerian troops entered the country and restored the elected president in 1998. ∎

SINGAPORE

Official name Republic of Singapore

PEOPLE
Population 3,494,000. **Density** 14,203/mi² (5,494/km²).
Urban 100%. **Capital** Singapore, 3,494,000. **Ethnic groups** Chinese 78%, Malay 14%, Indian 7%.
Languages Chinese (Mandarin), English, Malay, Tamil.
Religions Taoist, Buddhist, Muslim, Christian, Hindu.
Life expectancy 79 female, 74 male. **Literacy** 91%.

POLITICS
Government Republic. **Parties** Democratic, People's Action, Workers', others. **Suffrage** Universal, 20 and over. **Memberships** ASEAN, CW, UN. **Subdivisions** None.

ECONOMY
GDP $66,100,000,000. **Per capita** $22,762. **Monetary unit** Dollar. **Trade partners** Exports: U.S., Malaysia, Japan. Imports: Japan, U.S., Malaysia. **Exports** Petroleum products, rubber, electronics, manufactures. **Imports** Machinery, petroleum, chemicals, food, aircraft.

LAND
Description Southeastern Asian island. **Area** 246 mi² (636 km²). **Highest point** Timah Hill, 531 ft (162 m). **Lowest point** Sea level.

People. Singapore is one of the most densely populated countries in the world. Most of the population is Chinese. A significant minority is Malay, and the remainder is European or Indian. Singapore's languages include Chinese, English, Malay, and Tamil. The main religions—Taoism, Buddhism, Islam, Christianity, and Hinduism—reflect the cultural diversity of the country. A mixture of Western and traditional customs and dress characterize Singapore's society. Nearly all the population lives in the city of Singapore on Singapore Island.

Economy and the Land. Singapore is a leading Asian economic power. The city of Singapore is well known throughout the world as a financial center and major harbor for trade. The country's factories produce a variety of goods, such as chemicals, electronic equipment, and machinery, and are among the world leaders in petroleum refining. Singapore has few natural resources, however, and little arable land. Most agricultural output is consumed domestically; the country must import much of its raw materials and food. The country consists of one main island, which is characterized by wet lowlands and many small offshore islets. Cool sea breezes and a tropical climate make Singapore an attractive spot for tourists.

History and Politics. Present-day Singapore has been inhabited since prehistoric times. From the 1100s to the 1800s, Singapore served mainly as a trading center. It also served as refuge for pirates. The British East India Company, the major colonial force in India, realized Singapore's strategic importance to British trade and gained possession of the harbor in 1819. Singapore became a crown colony of Great Britain in 1826. As the port prospered as a trading center, the island's population grew rapidly. Following World War II, the people of Singapore moved from internal self-government to achieve independence in 1965. The government continues to work in partnership with the business community to further Singapore's economic growth. Singapore's standard of living is one of the highest in eastern Asia. The country's first presidential elections were held in August 1993. ∎

SLOVAKIA

Official name Slovak Republic

PEOPLE
Population 5,401,000. **Density** 285/mi² (110/km²). **Urban** 59%. **Capital** Bratislava, 441,453. **Ethnic groups** Slovak 86%, Hungarian 11%, Gypsy 2%. **Languages** Slovak, Hungarian. **Religions** Roman Catholic 60%, Protestant 8%, Orthodox 4%. **Life expectancy** 75 female, 67 male.

POLITICS
Government Republic. **Parties** Christian Democratic Movement, Democratic Left, Movement for a Democratic Slovakia, others. **Suffrage** Universal, 18 and over. **Memberships** UN. **Subdivisions** 4 regions.

ECONOMY
GDP $39,000,000,000. **Per capita** $7,159. **Monetary unit** Koruna. **Trade partners** Czech Republic, former Soviet republics, Germany, Poland. **Exports** Machinery and transportation equipment; chemicals; fuels, minerals, and metals. **Imports** Machinery, transportation equipment, fuels, lubricants, manufactures, raw inputs.

LAND
Description Eastern Europe, landlocked. **Area** 18,933 mi² (49,035 km²). **Highest point** Gerlachovka, 8,711 ft (2,655 m). **Lowest point** Along Bodrog River, 308 ft (94 m).

People. The people of Slovakia are related to the Czechs, but they are culturally linked to the Hungarians rather than the Germans. The Slovak language is similar to Czech and has the same roots. Slovakia has a large Hungarian minority, and Hungarians complain that the Slovaks are trying to eliminate their language and culture. Roman Catholicism is the main religion. The Slovaks are proud of their literary heritage and artistic achievements.

Economy and the Land. Slovakia suffers from both high inflation and unemployment as it struggles to create a new economy in the aftermath of eastern European Communism. Although some industrialization took place under Communist rule, agriculture remains the most important economic activity. Most agriculture takes place in the fertile Hungarian Plain in the south. The country has important mineral deposits, but lacks any significant energy resources. Slovakia is bounded on the north and east by the Carpathian Mountains.

History and Politics. Slavic people settled Slovakia in the 5th century, and were incorporated into the Moravian state that was established in the 9th century. Slovakia fell under Hungarian rule in the early 10th century, and little economic or social development took place for 300 years, until Hungary's grasp on the region weakened and the Slovaks began to make contact with the outside world. Slovakia remained under Hungarian rule despite a growing nationalist movement that gained momentum throughout the 19th century. After Austria-Hungary was defeated in World War I, the Slovaks and the Czechs were united to form the independent country of Czechoslovakia in 1918. The Slovaks, who had envisioned a federal state, were angered by the centrist government that was established, and extremists began demanding separation less than ten years after the country was formed. The Slovak separatist movement remained active until it was obliterated by the Communists who took over Czechoslovakia after World War II. In 1968 Czechoslovakia adopted a liberal reform plan that called for greater autonomy for Slovakia, but the invasion of the Warsaw Pact countries prevented the plan from being implemented. Communist rule ended in 1989, and Slovakia gained full independence in 1993. With its authoritarian leadership and lack of economic development, Slovakia is lagging behind other Eastern European countries. ∎

SLOVENIA

Official name Republic of Slovenia

PEOPLE
Population 1,943,000. **Density** 248/mi² (96/km²). **Urban** 52%. **Capital** Ljubljana, 292,589. **Ethnic groups** Slovene 88%, Croat 3%, Serb 2%, Muslim 1%. **Languages** Slovenian, Serbo-Croatian. **Religions** Roman Catholic 73%, Orthodox 2%, Muslim 2%. **Life expectancy** 78 female, 69 male. **Literacy** 99%.

POLITICS
Government Republic. **Parties** Christian Democrats, Liberal Democratic, People's, Social Democratic, others. **Suffrage** Universal, 18 and over. **Memberships** UN. **Subdivisions** None.

ECONOMY
GDP $22,600,000,000. **Per capita** $11,008. **Monetary unit** Tolar. **Trade partners** Exports: Former Yugoslav republics, Austria, Italy. Imports: Former Yugoslav republics, Germany. **Exports** Machinery, transportation equipment, manufactures, chemicals, food. **Imports** Machines, transportation equipment, manufactures, chemicals, fuel, lubricants.

LAND
Description Eastern Europe. **Area** 7,820 mi² (20,253 km²). **Highest point** Triglav, 9,396 ft (2,864 m). **Lowest point** Sea level.

People. The Slovenes managed to keep their own language and traditions only by resisting centuries of unrelenting pressure to adopt German culture. Most people are Roman Catholic, and their religion is an important part of their national identity. Slovenia is also home to small Croatian and Serbian minorities.

Economy and the Land. Slovenia has had a well-developed industrial sector since the mid-1800s. Most people are engaged in industry. Before it achieved independence in 1991, prosperity in Slovenia was greater than in the other Yugoslav republics. Slovenia's economy is very well-rounded, and despite the mountainous terrain, agriculture is also an important activity. Major crops are potatoes, hops, hemp, and flax. Dairy farming is also an important agricultural activity. Coal and timber are produced in abundance.

History and Politics. Until the 1990s, Slovenia had never been an independent country in modern times. Ancestors of the modern Slovenes are believed to have arrived in the region around A.D. 600. By the 8th century, they had been conquered by the Franks and were converted to Roman Catholicism by the emperor Charlemagne. The Slovenes were serfs under German feudal lords until the region came under the control of the Austro-Hungarian Hapsburg empire in the late 1200s. The Hapsburgs maintained control for 700 years, although the area was subjected to occasional Turkish raids. The German-speaking Hapsburg empire attempted to impose its language on the Slovenian people, who resisted and continued to speak their own Slavic language. Slovenia became part of Yugoslavia in 1918. During World War II, Slovenia was divided among Germany, Italy, and Hungary. Once again, the Germans attempted to eliminate Slovenian culture by killing the Slovenes in concentration camps or forcing them to migrate to other parts of Yugoslavia. Slovenia gained considerable autonomy after Yugoslavia was reconstituted as a federal Communist republic following the war. Under Communist rule, many Slovenians resented their obligation to support Serbia and the other poorer Yugoslav republics. Without massive demonstrations or public unrest, the country slowly moved towards a more peaceful separation from the rest of Yugoslavia. In June 1991 Slovenia, along with neighboring Croatia, declared its independence from Yugoslavia. Shortly after the announcement, the Yugoslav army made a brief attempt to thwart the will of the people before ordering its troops out of Slovenia. Slovenia received international recognition in January 1992. A lack of public-sector reform has slowed economic development. In 1997 Eastern Slovenia was contested by the Croats and the Serbs. ■

SOLOMON ISLANDS

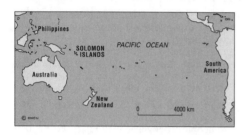

Official name Solomon Islands

PEOPLE
Population 434,000. **Density** 40/mi² (15/km²). **Urban** 18%. **Capital** Honiara, Guadalcanal I., 30,413. **Ethnic groups** Melanesian 93%, Polynesian 4%. **Languages** English, Pidgin. **Religions** Anglican 34%, Roman Catholic 19%, Baptist 17%, United Church 11%. **Life expectancy** 74 female, 70 male.

POLITICS
Government Parliamentary state. **Parties** National Unity and Reconciliation, People's Alliance, others. **Suffrage** Universal, 21 and over. **Memberships** CW, UN. **Subdivisions** 7 provinces, 1 town.

ECONOMY
GDP $1,000,000,000. **Per capita** $2,463. **Monetary unit** Dollar. **Trade partners** Exports: Japan, U.K., Thailand. Imports: Australia, Japan. **Exports** Fish, wood, copra, cocoa, palm oil. **Imports** Machinery, manufactures, fuel, food.

LAND
Description South Pacific islands. **Area** 10,954 mi² (28,370 km²). **Highest point** Mt. Makarakomburu, 8,028 ft (2,447 m). **Lowest point** Sea level.

People. More than 90 percent of the people are Melanesian, and the remainder are Polynesian, European, Chinese, and Micronesian. English is the official language, but some 90 local languages are also spoken. Most people are Anglican, Roman Catholic, Baptist, or other Protestants. The population is primarily rural, and much of its

social structure is patterned on traditional village life.

Economy and the Land. The economy is based on subsistence farming and exports of fish, wood, copra, spices, and palm oil. Tourism is of growing importance. Food, machinery, gasoline, and manufactured goods are imported. Terrain ranges from forested mountains to low-lying coral atolls. The climate is warm and moist, with heavy annual rainfall.

History and Politics. Hunter-gatherers lived on the islands as early as 1000 B.C. Because of disease and native resistance, early attempts at colonization failed, and Europeans did not firmly establish themselves until the mid-1800s. Britain declared the islands a protectorate in 1893. The area was the site of fierce battles between the Japanese and Allied forces during World War II, and following the war, moves were made toward independence. In 1978 the Solomon Islands adopted a constitution and became a sovereign country. ■

SOMALIA

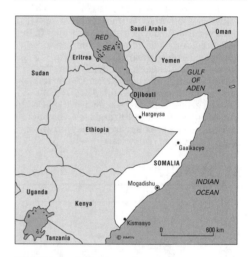

Official name Somalia

PEOPLE
Population 10,085,000. **Density** 41/mi² (16/km²). **Urban** 26%. **Capital** Mogadishu, 600,000. **Ethnic groups** Somali 85%, Bantu. **Languages** Arabic, Somali, English, Italian. **Religions** Sunni Muslim. **Life expectancy** 51 female, 47 male. **Literacy** 24%.

POLITICS
Government None. **Parties** United Somali Congress. **Suffrage** Universal, 18 and over. **Memberships** AL, OAU, UN. **Subdivisions** 18 regions.

ECONOMY
GDP $3,600,000,000. **Per capita** $501. **Monetary unit** Shilling. **Trade partners** Exports: Saudi Arabia, United Arab Emirates. Imports: Italy, Bahrain, U.K. **Exports** Bananas, livestock, fish, hides and skins. **Imports** Petroleum, food, construction materials.

LAND
Description Eastern Africa. **Area** 246,201 mi² (637,657 km²). **Highest point** Shimbiris, 7,897 ft (2,407 m). **Lowest point** Sea level.

People. Unlike the population in many African countries, the people of Somalia are remarkably homogeneous in their language, culture, and identity. Most of the Somalis are nomadic or seminomadic herders; only a quarter of the people have settled in permanent communities in southern Somalia. While Arabic and Somali are official languages, English and Italian are spoken by many. Nearly all the Somali people practice the Sunni Muslim religion.

Economy and the Land. Somalia is a developing country that has not exploited its rich deposits of iron ore and gypsum. There is little manufacturing in Somalia. The economy is agricultural, though activity is restricted to the vicinity of the rivers and certain coastal areas. A hot climate with recurring droughts, as well as a lack of transportation infrastructure such as railroads and paved highways, hamper economic development. The terrain ranges from central and southern flatlands to northern hills.

History and Politics. In the A.D. 800s or 900s, Arabs converted the ancestors of the Somalis who settled the region to Islam. They fought many religious wars with the Christian kingdom of Ethiopia between the 1300s and 1500s. The British, Italians, and French arrived in the region in the latter half of the 1800s and divided the Somali territory among themselves, with Ethiopia seizing Ogaden in the west. After World War II, Italy was made administrator of its former colony to prepare it for independence. In 1960 British Somaliland and Italian Somalia joined to form an independent republic. Since that time, Somalia has had many border clashes with Kenya and Ethiopia over the rights of Somalis living in these countries to determine their own destiny. Military leaders staged a successful coup in 1969, subsequently changed the country's name to Somali Democratic Republic, and abolished all political parties. Military activity has since resulted in a civil war, famine, and the killing of thousands of civilians. In 1991 rebel forces overcame the government, and northern Somalia seceded from the rest of the country. Clan-based fighting led to mass starvation and the deaths of hundreds of thousands of people. In late 1992 the United States military intervened in an attempt to enable worldwide relief efforts to proceed safely. The United Nations took over in 1993 but withdrew in 1995, having failed to find a solution to Somalia's political and economic instability. In October 1997 the country was hit with a disastrous flood. In December, 26 of Somalia's 29 factions signed a peace treaty. If the agreement succeeds, it will create the first centralized government since 1991. ■

SOUTH AFRICA

Official name Republic of South Africa

PEOPLE
Population 42,845,000. **Density** 91/mi² (35/km²). **Urban** 50%. **Capital** Pretoria (administrative), 525,583; Cape Town (legislative), 854,616; Bloemfontein (judicial), 126,867. **Ethnic groups** Black 77%, white 13%, mulatto (coloured) 9%, Asian 2%. **Languages** Afrikaans, English, Sotho, Tswana, Zulu, others. **Religions** Black Independent 17%, Dutch Reformed 10%, Roman Catholic 8%. **Life expectancy** 68 female, 62 male. **Literacy** 82%.

POLITICS
Government Republic. **Parties** African National Congress, Inkatha Freedom, National, others. **Suffrage** Universal, 18 and over. **Memberships** CW, OAU, UN. **Subdivisions** 9 provinces.

ECONOMY
GDP $215,000,000,000. **Per capita** $5,091. **Monetary unit** Rand. **Trade partners** Exports: Italy, Japan, U.S. Imports: Germany, Japan, U.K. **Exports** Gold, minerals and metals, food, chemicals. **Imports** Machinery, transportation equipment, chemicals, oil, textiles.

LAND
Description Southern Africa. **Area** 471,010 mi² (1,219,909 km²). **Highest point** eNjesuthi, 11,306 ft (3,446 m). **Lowest point** Sea level.

People. South Africa's population is classified into four main groups: black, white, coloured, and Indian. The black population, which is of African heritage, makes up the majority. The white minority are either British or Afrikaner (who are of Dutch, German, and French descent). The coloured population has a mixed black, white, and Indian ancestry. The remainder of the population are of Indian descent. Afrikaans and English are the official languages, although the blacks, coloureds, and East Indians speak their own languages as well. The dominant religions are Christian; however, many groups follow traditional practices. For decades the South African government enforced apartheid, a policy of racial segregation widely criticized for violating the rights of blacks, coloureds, and Indians.

Economy and the Land. The discovery of gold and diamonds in South Africa in the late 1800s shaped the country's prosperous economy. Revenue from mining promoted industry, and today South Africa is one of the richest and most highly developed countries in Africa. Mining remains a mainstay, as does agriculture; the country is almost self-sufficient in food production. Many effects of apartheid, including discriminatory systems of education and job reservation, kept the majority population from the benefits of national prosperity. The varied landscape features coastal beaches, plateaus, mountains, and deep valleys. The climate is temperate.

History and Politics. Southern Africa has been inhabited for many thousands of years. Ancestors of the area's present African population had settled there by the time Portuguese explorers reached the Cape of Good Hope in the late 1400s. The first white settlers, ancestors of today's Afrikaners, established colonies in the 17th century. Britain gained control of the area in the late 18th century, and relations between Afrikaners and the British soon became strained. To escape British rule, many Afrikaners migrated northward to lands occupied by black Africans. The discovery of gold and diamonds in the late 1800s brought an influx of Europeans and further strained relations between Afrikaners and the British, with both groups striving for control of valuable mineral deposits. Two wars broke out, and in 1902 the British defeated the Afrikaners, or Boers, and incorporated the Boer territories into the British Empire. The British also subdued black Africans, and in 1910 they formed the white-controlled Union of South Africa. Afrikaner nationalism grew in the early 20th century and led to the formation of the National party, which gained control in 1924 and again in 1948. The party began the apartheid system of separation of the races in the late 1940s, and subsequent decades saw increasing apartheid legislation and racial tension. In 1951 South Africa embarked on a program to create a white majority by setting up "independent" black republics, or homelands, within its borders. During the 1980s, the government began to force blacks to move into the homelands and to renounce their citizenship, thereby sparking international outcry. Foreign and internal pressure forced the government to respond with reforms and to dismantle apart-

heid. The 1990 release of Nelson Mandela, leader of the African National Congress (ANC), after 27 years in prison, paved the way for a new South Africa. Under the leadership of Mandela and President F.W. de Klerk, the country was led to relatively peaceful elections in April 1994. Mandela was elected president and an interim constitution abolishing the homelands was established. In 1996 a new constitution was approved, and de Klerk resigned from the coalition government. There is ongoing political violence in the KwaZulu province, and from an Afrikaner terrorist group that seeks to create a separate Afrikaner state within South Africa. ■

SOUTH GEORGIA AND THE SOUTH SANDWICH ISLANDS See UNITED KINGDOM.

SPAIN

Official name Kingdom of Spain

PEOPLE
Population 39,285,000. **Density** 202/mi² (78/km²).
Urban 77%. **Capital** Madrid, 3,102,846. **Ethnic groups** Spanish (mixed Mediterranean and Nordic). **Languages** Spanish (Castilian), Catalan, Galician, Basque.
Religions Roman Catholic 99%. **Life expectancy** 81 female, 75 male. **Literacy** 97%.

Places and Possessions of SPAIN

Entity	Status	Area	Population	Capital/Population
Balearic Islands (Mediterranean Sea)	Province	1,936 mi² (5,014 km²)	848,000	Palma, 249,000
Canary Islands (North Atlantic; northwest of Africa)	Part of Spain (2 provinces)	2,808 mi² (7,273 km²)	1,734,000	None
Spanish North Africa (Cities on northern coast of Morocco)	Five possessions	12 mi² (32 km²)	142,000	None

POLITICS

Government Constitutional monarchy. **Parties** Communist, Popular, Socialist Workers, United Left, others. **Suffrage** Universal, 18 and over. **Memberships** EU, NATO, OECD, UN. **Subdivisions** 17 autonomous communities.

ECONOMY

GDP $565,000,000,000. **Per capita** $14,309. **Monetary unit** Peseta. **Trade partners** Exports: U.S., Japan, U.K. Imports: Germany, U.S., U.K. **Exports** Transportation equipment, manufactures, food, machinery. **Imports** Machinery, transportation equipment, fuel, food, manufactures.

LAND

Description Southwestern Europe. **Area** 194,885 mi² (504,750 km²). **Highest point** Pico de Teide, 12,198 ft (3,718 m). **Lowest point** Sea level.

People. The population of Spain is a mixture of ethnic groups from northern Europe and the area surrounding the Mediterranean Sea. Spanish is the official language; however, several regional dialects of Spanish are commonly spoken. The Basque minority, one of the oldest surviving ethnic groups in Europe, lives mainly in the Pyrenees in northern Spain, preserving its own language and traditions. Since the 1978 constitution was approved, Spain has not had an official religion, yet nearly all its people are Roman Catholic. Spain has a rich artistic tradition, blending Moorish and Western cultures.

Economy and the Land. Spain has benefited greatly from an economic restructuring program that began in the 1950s. The country has concentrated on developing industry, which now employs more than 30 percent of the population. The chemical industry, high technology, electronics, and tourism are important sources of revenue. The agricultural contribution to the economy has declined to about half of peak production. Spain's terrain is mainly composed of a dry plateau area; mountains cover the northern section, and plains extend down the country's eastern coast. The climate in the eastern and southern regions is Mediterranean, while the northwest has more rainfall and less sunshine throughout the year.

History and Politics. Spain is among the oldest inhabited regions in Europe. A Roman province for centuries, Spain was conquered by the Visigoths in the A.D. 500s, only to change hands again in the 700s when the Arab-Berbers, or Moors, seized control of all but a narrow strip of northern Spain. Christian kings reclaimed the country from the 11th to the 14th centuries. Controlled by the three kingdoms of Navarre, Aragon, and Castile, Spain was united in the late 1400s under King Ferdinand and Queen Isabella. At the height of its empire, Spain claimed territory in North and South America, northern Africa, Italy, and the Canary Islands. A series of wars burdened Spain financially, however, and in the 1500s the country entered a period of decline under King Philip II. Throughout the 1700s and 1800s, the country lost most of its colonial possessions through either treaty or revolution. In 1936, a bitter civil war erupted between an insurgent fascist group and supporters of the republic. General Francisco Franco, leader of the successful insurgent army, ruled as dictator of Spain from the end of the war until his death in 1975. Spain has prospered but has had to grapple with separatist movements in Catalonia and the Basque region. Since Franco's death, King Juan Carlos has led the country toward a more democratic form of government. ■

SRI LANKA

Official name Democratic Socialist Republic of Sri Lanka

PEOPLE

Population 18,865,000. **Density** 756/mi² (292/km²). **Urban** 22%. **Capital** Colombo (designated), 612,000; Sri Jayawardenapura (seat of government), 108,000. **Ethnic groups** Sinhalese 74%, Sri Lankan Tamil 10%, Moor 7%, Indian Tamil 5%. **Languages** English, Sinhala, Tamil. **Religions** Buddhist 70%, Hindu 16%, Muslim 8%, Christian 7%. **Life expectancy** 75 female, 71 male. **Literacy** 91%.

POLITICS

Government Socialist republic. **Parties** Eelam People's Democratic, People's Alliance, Tamil United Liberation, United National, others. **Suffrage** Universal, 18 and over. **Memberships** CW, UN. **Subdivisions** 8 provinces.

ECONOMY

GDP $65,600,000,000. **Per capita** $3,607. **Monetary unit** Rupee. **Trade partners** Exports: U.S., Germany, U.K. Imports: Japan, Iran, U.S. **Exports** Textiles, clothing, tea, petroleum, gems, coconut, rubber. **Imports** Food, textiles, petroleum, machinery, building materials.

LAND

Description Southern Asian island. **Area** 24,962 mi² (64,652 km²). **Highest point** Pidurutalagala, 8,281 ft (2,524 m). **Lowest point** Sea level.

People. The two principal groups in Sri Lanka are the majority Sinhalese and the minority Tamils. Other minorities include the Moors; Burghers, who are descendants of Dutch, Portuguese, and British colonists; Malays; and Veddah aborigines. Sinhala, Tamil, and English are official languages. Most Sinhalese are Buddhist, most Tamils are Hindu, and the majority of the Moors and Malays are Muslims.

Economy and the Land. Sri Lanka's economy is based on agriculture, which employs nearly half the people in producing tea, rubber, and coconuts. Industrial production has increased, and major exports include rubber and textile products. The country also sponsors several internal development programs. Continuing high government subsidy and welfare policies threaten economic growth, however. A low coastal plain, mountainous and forested southern interior, and tropical climate characterize Sri Lanka.

History and Politics. The Sinhalese dynasty was founded by a northern Indian prince in about 500 B.C. Later, the Tamils from southern India settled in the north of Sri Lanka. European control began in the 1500s, when the Portuguese and Dutch ruled the island. It became a British possession in 1796 and the independent country of Ceylon in 1948. In 1972 it changed its name to Sri Lanka. Tensions between the ruling Sinhalese and the minority Tamils resulted in violence. The country has been in the grip of a civil war since 1983, when Tamils in northern Sri Lanka began a secessionist rebellion. ■

SUDAN

Official name Republic of the Sudan

PEOPLE
Population 33,195,000. **Density** 34/mi² (13/km²).
Urban 32%. **Capital** Khartoum, 473,597. **Ethnic groups** Black 52%, Arab 39%, Beja 6%. **Languages** Arabic, Nubian and other indigenous, English.

Religions Sunni Muslim 70%, Animist 25%, Christian 5%. **Life expectancy** 56 female, 54 male. **Literacy** 46%.

POLITICS
Government Republic. **Parties** None. **Suffrage** Universal. **Memberships** AL, OAU, UN. **Subdivisions** 9 states.

ECONOMY
GDP $25,000,000,000. **Per capita** $820. **Monetary unit** Pound. **Trade partners** Exports: Saudi Arabia, Thailand, Egypt. Imports: Saudi Arabia, U.K., Germany. **Exports** Cotton, livestock, meat, gum arabic. **Imports** Food, petroleum, manufactures, machinery, medicine, chemicals, textiles.

LAND
Description Eastern Africa. **Area** 967,500 mi² (2,505,813 km²). **Highest point** Kinyeti, 10,456 ft (3,187 m). **Lowest point** Sea level.

People. Sudan's population is composed of two distinct cultures—black African and Arab. African blacks of diverse ethnicity are a majority and are concentrated in the south, where they practice traditional lifestyles and beliefs and speak indigenous languages. Arabic-speaking Muslims, belonging to several ethnic groups, live mainly in northern and central regions.

Economy and the Land. The economy is based on agriculture; and irrigation has made arid Sudan a leading producer of cotton, although the land is vulnerable to drought. Forests provide for production of gum Arabic, used in making candy and perfumes, while other crops include peanuts and sesame seeds. Economic activity is concentrated near the Nile River and its branches, as well as near water holes and wells. The mostly flat terrain is marked by eastern and western mountains; southern forests and savanna give way to swampland, scrubland, and northern desert. The climate varies from desert in the north to tropical in the south.

History and Politics. Egypt mounted repeated invasions of what is now northern Sudan beginning about 300 B.C. Sudan remained a collection of small independent states until 1821, when Egypt conquered and unified the northern portion. Egypt was unable to establish control over the south, which was often raided by slave traders. In 1881 a Muslim leader began uniting various groups in a revolt against Egyptian rule, and success came four years later. His successor ruled until 1898, when British and Egyptian forces reconquered the land. Renamed the Anglo-Egyptian Sudan, the region was ruled jointly by Egypt and Britain, with British administration dominating. Since gaining independence in 1956, a series of military coups, a continuing civil war, and severe famine have burdened Sudan with political and economic instability. Sudan's government supports international terrorism, abuses human rights, and has been accused of producing a famine in southern Sudan by destroying agricultural resources and blocking food relief. The UN Human Rights Commission denounced the government in 1996. ■

SURINAME

Official name Republic of Suriname

PEOPLE
Population 446,000. **Density** 7.1/mi² (2.7/km²).
Urban 50%. **Capital** Paramaribo, 241,000. **Ethnic
groups** East Indian 37%, Creole 31%, Javanese 15%,
black 10%, Amerindian 3%, Chinese 2%. **Languages**
Dutch, Sranan Tongo, English, Hindustani, Javanese.
Religions Hindu 27%, Protestant 25%, Roman
Catholic 23%, Muslim 20%. **Life expectancy**
74 female, 69 male. **Literacy** 93%.

POLITICS
Government Republic. **Parties** Democratic Alternative
'91, National Democratic, New Front, others. **Suffrage**
Universal, 18 and over. **Memberships** OAS, UN.
Subdivisions 10 districts.

ECONOMY
GDP $1,300,000,000. **Per capita** $3,002. **Monetary
unit** Guilder. **Trade partners** Exports: Norway,
Netherlands, U.S. Imports: U.S., Netherlands Antilles,
Trinidad and Tobago. **Exports** Alumina, bauxite,
aluminum, rice, seafood, bananas, wood. **Imports**
Machinery, petroleum, food, cotton, manufactures.

LAND
Description Northeastern South America. **Area**
63,251 mi² (163,820 km²). **Highest point** Juliana Mtn.,
4,035 ft (1,230 m). **Lowest point** Sea level.

People. Descendants of East Indians and
Creoles—of mixed European-black African heritage—compose Suriname's two major groups.
Black African slaves and contract laborers,
imported from the east, resulted in various ethnic populations. Minority groups include the
Javanese; Bush Negroes, a black group; Amerindians, descendants of Arawak and Caribs;
Chinese; and Europeans. Dutch is the official language, but most groups have preserved their distinct language, culture, and religion.

Economy and the Land. The economy is based
on mining and metal processing, and bauxite
and alumina are the major exports. Agriculture

plays an economic role as well and, together with
fishing and forestry, offers potential for expansion. A narrow coastal swamp, central forests and
savanna, and southern jungle-covered hills mark
the country's terrain. The climate is tropical.

History and Politics. Prior to the arrival of
Europeans, present-day Suriname was inhabited by indigenous Amerindians. Christopher
Columbus sighted the coast in 1498, but the
area's lack of gold slowed Spanish and Portuguese exploration. The British established the
first settlement in 1651, and in 1665 Jews from
Brazil erected the first synagogue in the Western
Hemisphere. In 1667 the British traded the area
to the Netherlands for the Dutch colony of New
Amsterdam—present-day Manhattan, New York.
Subsequent wars and treaties shifted ownership
of Suriname among the British, French, and
Dutch until 1815, when the Netherlands regained
control. In 1954 Suriname became an autonomous part of the Netherlands, with status
equal to that of the Netherlands Antilles.
Suriname gained independence in 1975. In
1980, the military seized power and soon established a military-civilian government. The military has retained considerable control, however.
A general election in May 1991 resulted in a
degree of democratic representation. ∎

SWAZILAND

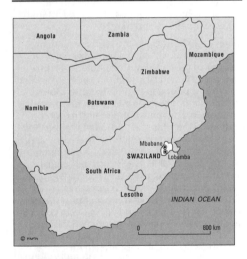

Official name Kingdom of Swaziland

PEOPLE
Population 1,031,000. **Density** 154/mi² (59/km²).
Urban 32%. **Capital** Mbabane (administrative),
38,290; Lobamba (legislative). **Ethnic groups** Swazi
90%. **Languages** English, siSwati. **Religions** African
Protestant and other Christian 77%, tribal religionist
21%. **Life expectancy** 62 female, 58 male.
Literacy 77%.

POLITICS
Government Monarchy. **Parties** None. **Suffrage**

Restricted, 21 and over. **Memberships** CW, OAU, UN. **Subdivisions** 4 districts.

ECONOMY

GDP $3,600,000,000. **Per capita** $3,666. **Monetary unit** Lilangeni. **Trade partners** Exports: South Africa, Western European countries, Canada. Imports: South Africa, Japan, Belgium. **Exports** Soft drink concentrates, sugar, wood, fruit. **Imports** Transportation equipment, machinery, petroleum, food, chemicals.

LAND

Description Southern Africa, landlocked. **Area** 6,704 mi² (17,364 km²). **Highest point** Emlembe, 6,109 ft (1,862 m). **Lowest point** Along Usutu River, 70 ft (21 m).

People. About 90 percent of the people of Swaziland are black Africans called Swazi, though small minorities of white Europeans and Zulus also live in the country. The two official languages are English and siSwati. Government and official business is conducted primarily in English. Most of the Swazi belong to Christian churches, while others practice traditional African religions.

Economy and the Land. Most Swazi are subsistence farmers. Cattle are highly prized for their own sake but are being used increasingly for milk, meat, and profit. Europeans own nearly half the land in Swaziland and raise most of the cash crops, including fruits, sugar, tobacco, cotton, and wood. Although mining has declined in recent years, Swaziland has deposits of coal, pottery clay, gold, and tin. The country's mountains and forests have brought a growing tourist industry. The climate is temperate.

History and Politics. According to legend, the Swazi originally came from the area near Maputo, in present-day Mozambique. British traders and Dutch farmers from South Africa first reached Swaziland in the 1830s; more whites arrived in the 1880s when gold was discovered. Swazi leaders unknowingly granted many concessions to the whites at this time. After the Boer War, Britain assumed administration of Swaziland and ruled until 1967. Swaziland became independent in 1968. The British designed a constitution, but many Swazi thought it disregarded their traditions and interests. In 1973 King Sobhuza abolished this constitution, suspended the legislature, and appointed a commission to produce a new constitution. Sobhuza ruled until his death in 1982. King Mswati III, the last surviving absolute monarch in Africa, has ruled the country since 1986. His benign rule is being challenged by citizens who want to form political parties and move toward democracy. ■

SWEDEN

Official name Kingdom of Sweden

PEOPLE

Population 8,976,000. **Density** 52/mi² (20/km²). **Urban** 83%. **Capital** Stockholm, 674,452. **Ethnic groups**

Swedish (Scandinavian) 94%. **Languages** Swedish, Lapp, Finnish. **Religions** Lutheran (Church of Sweden) 94%, Roman Catholic 2%. **Life expectancy** 82 female, 76 male. **Literacy** 99%.

POLITICS

Government Constitutional monarchy. **Parties** Center, Liberal People's, Moderate, Social Democratic, others. **Suffrage** Universal, 18 and over. **Memberships** EU, OECD, UN. **Subdivisions** 24 counties.

ECONOMY

GDP $177,300,000,000. **Per capita** $20,038. **Monetary unit** Krona. **Trade partners** Exports: Germany, U.K., U.S. Imports: Germany, U.S., U.K. **Exports** Machinery, transportation equipment, paper, pulp and wood, iron and steel. **Imports** Machinery, petroleum, chemicals, transportation equipment, food.

LAND

Description Northern Europe. **Area** 173,732 mi² (449,964 km²). **Highest point** Kebnekaise, 6,926 ft (2,111 m). **Lowest point** Sea level.

People. The most significant minorities in the largely urban Swedish population are Swedes of Finnish origin and a small number of Lapps. Sweden is also the home of immigrants from other Nordic countries, Yugoslavia, Greece, and Turkey. Swedish is the main language, although Finns and Lapps often speak their own tongues. English is the leading foreign language, especially among students and younger people.

Economy and the Land. Sweden has one of the highest standards of living in the world. Taxes are also high, but the government provides exceptional benefits for most citizens, including free education and medical care, pension payments, four-week vacations, and payments for child care. The country is industrial and bases its economy on its three most important natural resources: timber, iron ore, and water power. The iron and steel industry produces high-quality steel used in ball bearings, precision tools, agricultural machinery, aircraft, automobiles, and ships. Swedish farmers rely heavily on dairy products and livestock, and most farms are part of Sweden's agricultural-cooperative movement. Sweden's varied terrain includes mountains, forests, plains, and sandy beaches. The climate is temperate overall, but winters in the north are cold.

History and Politics. Inhabitants of what is now Sweden began to trade with the Roman Empire about 50 B.C. Sailing expeditions by Swedish Vikings began about A.D. 800. In the 14th century the kingdom came under Danish rule, but declared its independence in 1523. The Swedish king offered protection to the followers of Martin Luther, and Lutheranism was soon declared the state religion. By the late 1660s, Sweden had become one of the great powers of Europe; it suffered a military defeat by Russia in 1709, however, and gradually lost most of its European possessions. An 1809 constitution gave most of the executive power of the government to the king. Despite this, the power of the Parliament gradually increased, and parliamentary rule was adopted in 1917. A 1975 constitution reduced the king's role to a ceremonial one. Sweden remained neutral during both world wars. Except for 1976-82, when Sweden was run by a conservative coalition, the country had a Socialist government. In February 1990, the socialists failed to carry Parliament in an economic reform bill. By 1994 the Socialist Party was back in power. ■

SWITZERLAND

Official name Swiss Confederation

PEOPLE
Population 7,271,000. **Density** 456/mi² (176/km²). **Urban** 61%. **Capital** Bern, 136,338. **Ethnic groups** German 65%, French 18%, Italian 10%, Romansch 1%. **Languages** German, French, Italian, Romansch. **Religions** Roman Catholic 48%, Protestant 40%. **Life expectancy** 82 female, 75 male. **Literacy** 99%.

POLITICS
Government Federal republic. **Parties** Christian Democratic People's, Free Democratic, People's, Social Democratic, others. **Suffrage** Universal, 18 and over. **Memberships** OECD. **Subdivisions** 26 cantons.

ECONOMY
GDP $158,500,000,000. **Per capita** $22,438. **Monetary unit** Franc. **Trade partners** Exports: Germany, France, Italy. Imports: Germany, France, Italy. **Exports** Machinery, precision instruments, metals, food, clothing and textiles. **Imports** Agricultural products, machines, transportation equipment, chemicals, textiles.

LAND
Description Central Europe, landlocked. **Area** 15,943 mi² (41,293 km²). **Highest point** Dufourspitze, 15,203 ft (4,634 m). **Lowest point** Lago Maggiore, 633 ft (193 m).

People. About 700 years ago, separate Swiss cultural and ethnic groups began joining together for mutual defense, but preserved their regional differences in language and customs. The country has four official languages: German, French, Italian, and Romansch, which is spoken by a minority. Dialects often differ from community to community, even within the same region. The population is concentrated on a central plain located between mountain ranges.

Economy and the Land. The Alps and Jura Mountains cover nearly 70 percent of Switzerland, making much of the land unsuited for agriculture but provide a good basis for a thriving tourist industry. The central plain contains rich cropland and holds Switzerland's major cities and manufacturing facilities, many specializing in high-quality precision products. Switzerland is also an international banking and finance center. Straddling the ranges of Europe's central Alps, Switzerland features mountains, hills, and plateaus. The climate is temperate, but weather and temperatures vary with altitude.

History and Politics. Helvetic Celts inhabited the area of present-day Switzerland when Julius Caesar conquered the region, annexing it to the Roman Empire. As the Roman Empire declined, northern and western Germanic tribes began a series of invasions, and in the 800s the region became part of the empire of the Frankish king Charlemagne. In 1291 leaders of the three Swiss cantons, or regions, signed an agreement declaring their freedom and promising mutual aid against any foreign ruler. The confederation was the beginning of modern Switzerland. Over the next few centuries Switzerland became a military power, expanding its territories until 1515, when it was defeated by France. Soon after, Switzerland adopted a policy of permanent neutrality. The country was again conquered by France during the French Revolution; however, after Napoleon's final defeat in 1815, the Congress of Vienna guaranteed Switzerland's neutrality, a guarantee that has never been broken. ■

SYRIA

Official name Syrian Arab Republic

PEOPLE
Population 16,430,000. **Density** 230/mi² (89/km²).
Urban 53%. **Capital** Damascus, 1,549,932. **Ethnic groups** Arab 90%, Kurdish, Armenian, and others 10%.
Languages Arabic, Kurdish, Armenian, Aramaic, Circassian. **Religions** Sunni Muslim 74%, other Muslim 16%, Christian 10%. **Life expectancy** 71 female, 67 male. **Literacy** 79%.

POLITICS
Government Socialist republic. **Parties** Arab Socialist, Arab Socialist Renaissance (Ba'th), Communist, others. **Suffrage** Universal, 18 and over. **Memberships** AL, UN. **Subdivisions** 14 districts.

ECONOMY
GDP $91,200,000,000. **Per capita** $6,242. **Monetary unit** Pound. **Trade partners** Exports: Former Soviet republics, Italy, France. Imports: France, Germany, U.S. **Exports** Petroleum, agricultural products, textiles, industrial goods, animal products. **Imports** Food, metals, machinery, textiles, petroleum, transportation equipment.

LAND
Description Southwestern Asia. **Area** 71,498 mi² (185,180 km²). **Highest point** Mt. Hermon, 9,232 ft (2,814 m). **Lowest point** Near Sea of Galilee, -656 ft (-200 m).

People. Most Syrians are Arabic-speaking descendants of Semites, who settled the region in ancient times. The majority are Sunni Muslim, and Islam is a powerful cultural force. Non-Arab Syrians include Kurds and Armenians, who maintain their own languages and customs. French is widely understood, and English is spoken in larger cities. The population is evenly divided between urban and rural settlements.

Economy and the Land. Syria is a developing country with great potential for economic growth. Textile manufacturing is a major industry, and oil, the main natural resource, provides for expanding activity in oil refining. The plains

and river valleys are fertile, but irregular rainfall makes irrigation necessary to sustain agriculture. The terrain is marked by mountains, the Euphrates River valley, and a semiarid plateau. The climate is hot and dry, with relatively cold winters.

History and Politics. Syria was the site of one of the world's most ancient civilizations, and Damascus and other Syrian cities were centers of world trade as early as 2500 B.C. Greater Syria, as the area was called until the end of World War I, originally included much of modern Israel, Jordan, Lebanon, and parts of Turkey. The region was occupied and ruled by the Phoenicians, Assyrians, Babylonians, Persians, and Greeks, before coming under Roman rule in 64 B.C. During subsequent years, Christianity arose in the part of Greater Syria called Palestine. In 636 the region fell to Arab Muslims, who governed until 1260, when Egypt gained control. Syria became part of the Turkish Ottoman Empire in 1516. During World War I, Syria aided Britain in defeating the Turks and Germans in return for independence. After the war, however, the League of Nations divided Greater Syria into four mandates—Syria, Lebanon, Palestine, and Transjordan—and placed Syria under French control. When Syria gained independence in 1946, many nationals wanted to reunite Greater Syria, but the United Nations made part of Palestine into the Jewish state of Israel. Tensions between Israel and Syria erupted in war in 1967 and 1973 and remain unresolved. In the 1980s Syria began to maintain a military presence in Lebanon. ■

TAIWAN

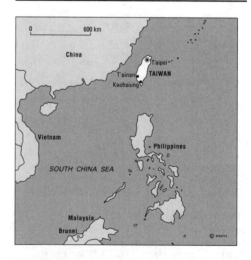

Official name Republic of China

PEOPLE
Population 21,755,000. **Density** 1,565/mi² (604/km²).
Urban 71%. **Capital** T'aipei, 2,706,453. **Ethnic groups** Taiwanese 84%, Chinese 14%, aborigine 2%.

Languages Chinese (Mandarin), Taiwanese (Min), Hakka. **Religions** Buddhist, Confucian, and Taoist 93%, Christian 5%. **Life expectancy** 79 female, 72 male. **Literacy** 86%.

POLITICS
Government Republic. **Parties** Chinese New, Democratic Progressive, Kuomintang (Nationalist), others. **Suffrage** Universal, 20 and over. **Memberships** None. **Subdivisions** 16 counties, 7 municipalities.

ECONOMY
GDP $290,500,000,000. **Per capita** $13,458. **Monetary unit** Dollar. **Trade partners** Exports: U.S., Japan. Imports: Japan, U.S., Germany. **Exports** Machinery, textiles, food, wood, electronics, footwear. **Imports** Machinery, metals, chemicals, petroleum, food, electronics.

LAND
Description Eastern Asian island. **Area** 13,900 mi² (36,002 km²). **Highest point** Yu Mtn., 13,114 ft (3,997 m). **Lowest point** Sea level.

People. Most of Taiwan's inhabitants are descendants of Chinese who migrated from China in the 18th and 19th centuries. In 1949, when the Communists came to power in mainland China, many educated Chinese fled to Taiwan. Native Islanders, a small group living in the mountains of central Taiwan, are most likely of Malay-Polynesian origin. Taiwan's languages are mainly dialects of Chinese, a Fujian dialect, and a dialect known as "Hakka." Most religious practices combine Buddhist and Taoist beliefs with the Confucian ethical code.

Economy and the Land. Since World War II, Taiwan's economy has changed from agriculture to industry. A past emphasis on light industry, producing mainly consumer goods, has shifted to technology and heavy industry. Although only one-quarter of the island is arable, farmland is intensely cultivated, with some areas producing two and three crops a year. Though rice, sugarcane, fruits, tea, and fishing are important, much food is imported. The island's terrain is marked by steep eastern mountains sloping to a fertile western region. The capital of T'aipei administers the Penghu Islands and about 20 offshore islands as well as the island of Taiwan. The climate is maritime subtropical.

History and Politics. Chinese migration to Taiwan began as early as A.D. 500. Dutch traders claimed the island in 1624 as a base for trade with China and Japan. It was ruled by China's Manchu dynasty from 1683 until 1895, when China ceded Taiwan to Japan after the first Sino-Japanese war. Following World War II, China regained possession of Taiwan. A civil war in mainland China between Nationalist and Communist forces ended with the victory of the Communists in 1949. Nationalist leader Chiang Kai-shek fled to Taiwan, proclaiming T'aipei the provisional capital of Nationalist China. In 1971, the People's Republic of China replaced Taiwan in the United Nations. Since 1990, new Taiwanese leadership has given up its claim to be the legitimate ruler of all China, but mainland China remains firm in its claim to Taiwan. Although the two countries continue to hold unofficial talks regarding reunification, there is a growing consensus in Taiwan that the island should remain independent of the mainland. China has threatened to invade Taiwan if the island tries formally to declare its independence. ■

TAJIKISTAN

Official name Republic of Tajikistan

PEOPLE
Population 6,053,000. **Density** 110/mi² (42/km²). **Urban** 32%. **Capital** Dushanbe, 582,400. **Ethnic groups** Tajik 65%, Uzbek 25%, Russian 4%. **Languages** Tajik, Russian. **Religions** Sunni Muslim 80%, Shiite Musilm 5%. **Life expectancy** 74 female, 69 male. **Literacy** 98%.

POLITICS
Government Republic. **Parties** Communist, People's, others. **Suffrage** Universal, 18 and over. **Memberships** UN. **Subdivisions** 1 autonomous region, 3 regions.

ECONOMY
GDP $6,400,000,000. **Per capita** $1,071. **Monetary unit** Ruble. **Trade partners** Russia, Kazakhstan, Ukraine, Uzbekistan. **Exports** Aluminum, cotton, fruit, vegetable oil, textiles. **Imports** Chemicals, machinery and transportation equipment, textiles, food, fuel.

LAND
Description Central Asia, landlocked. **Area** 55,251 mi² (143,100 km²). **Highest point** Communism Peak, 24,590 ft (7,495 m). **Lowest point** Along Syr Darya River, 984 ft (300 m).

People. The Tajik people are indistinguishable from the neighboring Uzbeks, although the country also includes many minority groups indigenous to the Pamir Mountains in the west. The Tajik language is closely related to Farsi, the principal language of Iran. The country is home to many people who were born in Uzbekistan, as well as many Russians. Islam has always been widely practiced in Tajikistan, even when the country was under Soviet rule. Most people live in small towns throughout the mountains. Folklore is important to the Tajiks, who are known for their colorful legends and poetry.

Economy and the Land. Cotton is among the country's principal crops, and irrigation allows production of fruits and grains. Cattle breeding is also an important agricultural activity. Tajikistan has many minerals, including coal, petroleum, uranium, lead, and zinc. Despite these significant resources, Tajikistan has the lowest standard of living of all of the former Soviet republics. The elevation of more than one-half of the country lies above 10,000 feet. The climate is harsh and precipitation is low. Earthquakes are common.

History and Politics. Iranian people are known to have lived in the region of Tajikistan since the first century B.C. Arabs brought Islam to the region between the 7th and 8th centuries A.D. Tajikistan came under Russian control in 1895 as part of a region known as Turkestan. There was substantial local resistance to the implementation of Communism following the Russian Revolution, and several years of armed struggle ensued. The country became an Autonomous Republic within the Soviet Union in 1924, and a Soviet Socialist Republic in 1929. It declared its sovereignty in September 1991 and achieved full independence after the breakup of the Soviet Union the following December. Communists and Islamic fundamentalists have been fighting for control of the country since 1992. In 1996 the latest of a series of short-lived peace treaties was signed, and in 1997 formal talks between Islamic groups and the government were attempted, but failed. Most of the country remains under the control of minor rebel groups. Sporadic violence continues. ■

TANZANIA

Official name United Republic of Tanzania

PEOPLE
Population 29,550,000. **Density** 81/mi² (31/km²). **Urban** 25%. **Capital** Dar es Salaam (de facto), 1,096,000; Dodoma (legislative), 85,000. **Ethnic groups** African (Sukuma, Masai, Haya, other). **Languages** English, Swahili, indigenous. **Religions** Christian 45%, Muslim 35%, Animist 20%. **Life expectancy** 53 female, 50 male. **Literacy** 68%.

POLITICS
Government Republic. **Parties** Civic United Front, Revolutionary, others. **Suffrage** Universal, 18 and over. **Memberships** CW, OAU, UN. **Subdivisions** 25 regions.

ECONOMY
GDP $23,100,000,000. **Per capita** $815. **Monetary unit** Shilling. **Trade partners** Exports: Germany, U.K. Imports: U.K., Japan, Germany. **Exports** Coffee, cotton, sisal, tea, cashews, tobacco, diamonds, gold. **Imports** Manufactures, machinery, transportation equipment, cotton goods, petroleum, food.

LAND
Description Eastern Africa. **Area** 364,900 mi² (945,087 km²). **Highest point** Kilimanjaro, 19,341 ft (5,895 m). **Lowest point** Sea level.

People. The largely rural African population of Tanzania consists of more than 130 ethnic groups; most speak a distinct language. Religious beliefs include Christian, Muslim, and traditional religions.

Economy and the Land. Agriculture accounts for the most export earnings and employs 80 percent of the work force. Yet two-thirds of the land cannot be cultivated because of tsetse-fly infestation and lack of water. Mainland farmers grow cassava, corn, and beans, while other cash crops include coffee and cashews. The islands of Zanzibar and Pemba are famous sources of cloves. Diamonds, salt, and iron are important mineral resources. Hot, humid coastal plains; an arid central plateau; and temperate lake and highland areas characterize mainland Tanzania. The climate is equatorial and the country experiences monsoons.

History and Politics. The northern mainland has fossil remains of some of humanity's earliest ancestors. Subsequent early inhabitants were gradually displaced by Bantu farmers and Nilotes. Arabs were trading with coastal groups as early as the 8th century, and by the early 1500s the Portuguese had claimed the coastal region. They were displaced in the 1700s by Arabs, who established a lucrative slave trade. Germans began colonizing the coast in 1884 and six years later signed an agreement with Great Britain, which secured German dominance along the coast and made Zanzibar a British protectorate. After World War I, Britain received part of German East Africa from the League of Nations as a mandate and renamed it Tanganyika. The area became a trust territory under the United Nations following World War II. The country achieved independence in 1961, and two years later Zanzibar received its independence as a constitutional monarchy under the sultan. A 1964 revolt by the African majority overthrew the sultan, and Zanzibar and Tanganyika subsequently united and became known as Tanzania. Tanzania developed a special African brand of Socialism in the 1960s, which served as a model throughout the continent. In 1996, the first multiparty election results were voided due to irregularities. ∎

TASMANIA See AUSTRALIA.

THAILAND

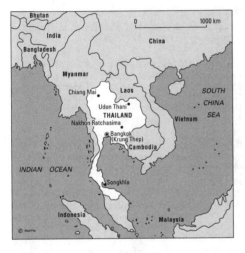

Official name Kingdom of Thailand

PEOPLE
Population 59,760,000. **Density** 302/mi² (116/km²). **Urban** 20%. **Capital** Bangkok, 5,620,591. **Ethnic groups** Thai 75%, Chinese 14%. **Languages** Thai, indigenous. **Religions** Buddhist 95%, Muslim 4%. **Life expectancy** 72 female, 65 male. **Literacy** 94%.

POLITICS
Government Constitutional monarchy. **Parties** Democrat, National Development, New Aspiration, Thai Nation, others. **Suffrage** Universal, 21 and over. **Memberships** ASEAN, UN. **Subdivisions** 73 provinces.

ECONOMY
GDP $416,700,000,000. **Per capita** $6,873. **Monetary unit** Baht. **Trade partners** Exports: U.S., Japan, Singapore. Imports: Japan, U.S., Singapore. **Exports** Machinery, manufactures, fuel, food, raw materials. **Imports** Machinery and manufactures, chemicals, fuel, raw materials, food.

LAND
Description Southeastern Asia. **Area** 198,115 mi² (513,115 km²). **Highest point** Mt. Inthanon, 8,530 ft (2,600 m). **Lowest point** Sea level.

People. Thailand's society is relatively homogeneous. More than 80 percent of its people speak varying dialects of Thai and share a common culture and common religion, Buddhism. Chinese immigrants are a substantial minority. Thai society is rural, with most people living in the rice-growing regions. The government has sponsored a successful family-planning program, which has greatly reduced the annual birth rate.

Economy and the Land. With an economy based on agriculture, Thailand exports large quantities of rice each year. Forests produce teak and rattan, and tin is another valuable natural resource. Tourism is the largest source of foreign income. Future industrialization may hinge on deposits of coal and natural gas. Thailand is experiencing a period of prosperity and economic growth which provides an ideal climate for foreign investment. A mountainous and heavily forested country, Thailand has a tropical climate, dominated by monsoons, high temperatures, and humidity.

History and Politics. Thai communities were established as early as 4000 B.C., although a Thai kingdom founded in the 13th century A.D. began the history of modern Thailand. In the late 1700s Burmese armies overwhelmed the kingdom. Rama I, founder of the present dynasty, helped to drive the invaders from the country in 1782. He subsequently renamed the country Siam and established a capital at Bangkok. Siam allowed Europeans to live within its borders during the period of colonial expansion, but the country never succumbed to foreign rule. As a result, Siam was the only South and Southeast Asian country never colonized by a European power. In 1932 a revolt changed the government from an absolute monarchy to a constitutional monarchy. Military officers assumed control in 1938, and the country reverted to its former name, Thailand, in 1939. The country was invaded by Japan in World War II. Following the war, Thailand was ruled by military officers until 1973, when civilians seized control and instigated a period of democracy that ended in 1976, when the military again took control. In May 1992, soldiers opened fire on anti-government demonstrators, killing at least 50 people. Ensuing outrage led to the formation of a new, more democratic government. In July 1997 Thailand placed its currency on the international open market. Its value quickly dropped, causing an economic crisis. The International Monetary Fund (IMF) provided $17 billion in aid to Thailand in August, and the government made aggressive economic reforms. The value of most other southeast Asian currencies dropped as well, causing economic crisis and social unrest throughout the region. ∎

TOGO

Official name Republic of Togo

PEOPLE
Population 4,815,000. **Density** 220/mi² (85/km²). **Urban** 31%. **Capital** Lomé, 500,000. **Ethnic groups** Black (Ewa, mina, Kabye, others) 99%. **Languages** French, Ewe, mina, Kabye, Dagomba. **Religions**

Animist 70%, Christian 20%, Muslim 10%. **Life expectancy** 59 female, 55 male. **Literacy** 52%.

POLITICS

Government Republic. **Parties** Action Committee for Renewal, Rally of the People, others. **Suffrage** Universal adult. **Memberships** OAU, UN. **Subdivisions** 21 prefectures.

ECONOMY

GDP $4,100,000,000. **Per capita** $913. **Monetary unit** CFA franc. **Trade partners** Exports: Canada, France, Spain, Italy. Imports: France, Netherlands, Germany. **Exports** Phosphates, cocoa, coffee, cotton, palm kernels. **Imports** Food, fuel, manufactures, machinery, chemicals.

LAND

Description Western Africa. **Area** 21,925 mi² (56,785 km²). **Highest point** Mont Agou, 3,235 ft (986 m). **Lowest point** Sea level.

People. Almost all the people of Togo are black Africans, coming primarily from the Ewe, Mina, and Kabye ethnic groups. Most of the population lives in the south and practices traditional religions. Significant Christian and Muslim minorities exist.

Economy and the Land. Togo is an agricultural country, but productive land is scarce. Fishing is a major industry in the coastal areas. Togo has one of the world's largest phosphate reserves. Much of Togo is mountainous, with a sandy coastal plain. The climate is hot and humid.

History and Politics. Togo's original inhabitants were probably the ancestors of the present-day central mountain people. Ewes entered the south in the 1300s, and refugees from war-torn northern countries settled in the north between the 1500s and 1800s. For 200 years, European ships raided the coastal region in search of slaves. In 1884 Germany claimed the territory. After World War I Togoland became a League of Nations mandate governed by Britain and France. The mandate was made a United Nations trust territory following World War II and remained under British and French administration. British Togo-

land voted to join the Gold Coast and nearby British-administered territories in 1957 and became the independent country of Ghana. French Togoland voted to become a republic in 1956 with internal self-government within the French Union, although the UN did not accept this method of ending the trusteeship. Togo peacefully severed its ties with France in 1960 and gained independence the same year. Internal political strife and military dominance of the government have characterized Togo's years of independence. ∎

TOKELAU See NEW ZEALAND.

TONGA

Official name Kingdom of Tonga

PEOPLE

Population 107,000. **Density** 372/mi² (143/km²). **Urban** 42%. **Capital** Nuku'alofa, Tongatapu I., 21,265. **Ethnic groups** Tongan (Polynesian). **Languages** Tongan, English. **Religions** Methodist 43%, Roman Catholic 16%, Mormon 12%. **Life expectancy** 71 female, 66 male. **Literacy** 100%.

POLITICS

Government Constitutional monarchy. **Parties** People's. **Suffrage** Universal, 21 and over. **Memberships** CW. **Subdivisions** 3 island groups.

ECONOMY

GDP $228,000,000. **Per capita** $2,073. **Monetary unit** Pa'anga. **Trade partners** Exports: New Zealand, U.S., Australia. Imports: New Zealand, Australia, Fiji. **Exports** Coconut oil, fish, vanilla beans, fruits, vegetables. **Imports** Food, machinery, transportation equipment, manufactures, fuel, chemicals.

LAND

Description South Pacific islands. **Area** 288 mi² (747 km²). **Highest point** 3,432 ft (1,046 m). **Lowest point** Sea level.

People. Almost all Tongans are Polynesian and follow Methodist and other Christian religions. About two-thirds of the population lives on the main island of Tongatapu.

Economy and the Land. Tonga's economy is dominated by both subsistence and plantation agriculture, while manufacturing is almost nonexistent. Most of the islands are coral reefs, and many have fertile soil. The climate is subtropical.

History and Politics. Tonga has been settled since at least 500 B.C. In the late 1700s, a civil war broke out among three lines of kings who sought to establish rulership. In 1822 Wesleyan Methodist missionaries converted one of the warring kings to Christianity. His faction prevailed, and he ruled as George Tupou I, founder of the present dynasty. Tonga came under British protection in 1900 but retained its autonomy in internal matters. The country became fully independent in 1970. Elections in 1993 highlighted the growth of two movements, the status quo as a constitutional monarchy vs. a pro-democracy faction. ∎

TRINIDAD AND TOBAGO

Official name Republic of Trinidad and Tobago

PEOPLE
Population 1,274,000. **Density** 643/mi^2 (248/km^2). **Urban** 72%. **Capital** Port of Spain, Trinidad I., 50,878. **Ethnic groups** Black 40%, East Indian 40%, mixed 14%, white 1%. **Languages** English, Hindi, French, Spanish. **Religions** Roman Catholic 34%, Hindu 26%, Anglican 15%, Muslim 6%. **Life expectancy** 75 female, 71 male. **Literacy** 98%.

POLITICS
Government Republic. **Parties** National Alliance for Reconstruction, People's National Movement, United Natioanl Congress. **Suffrage** Universal, 18 and over. **Memberships** CW, OAS, UN. **Subdivisions** 10 administrative areas.

ECONOMY
GDP $16,200,000,000. **Per capita** $12,736. **Monetary unit** Dollar. **Trade partners** Exports: U.S., Barbados, Netherlands Antilles. Imports: U.S., Venezuela, U.K. **Exports** Petroleum, steel, fertilizer, sugar, cocoa, coffee, fruit, chemicals. **Imports** Machinery, food, manufactures, livestock, transportation equipment.

LAND
Description Caribbean islands. **Area** 1,980 mi^2 (5,128 km^2). **Highest point** El Cerro Del Aripo, 3,084 ft (940 m). **Lowest point** Sea level.

People. The two islands of Trinidad and Tobago form a single country, but Trinidad has nearly all the land mass and population. About 80 percent of all Trinidadians are either black African or East Indian. Most Tobagonians are black African. The official language is English, and most people are Protestant.

Economy and the Land. Agriculture and tourism are important, but the economy is based on oil, which accounts for about 80 percent of the country's exports. Trinidad is also one of the world's chief sources of natural asphalt and possesses supplies of natural gas. Tropical rain forests, scenic beaches, and fertile farmland characterize the islands.

History and Politics. Trinidad was occupied by Arawaks when Christopher Columbus arrived and claimed the island for Spain in 1498. The island remained under Spanish rule until 1797, when the British captured it and ruled for more than 150 years. Tobago changed hands among the Dutch, French, and British until 1814, when Britain took control. In 1888 Trinidad and Tobago became a single British colony, and achieved independence in 1962. The racially diverse society is beginning to agitate for a more balanced representation in the government. In August 1990 Muslim militants kidnapped a large number of government officials in an unfocused and failed attempt to force the Prime Minister to resign. The militants, however, retain a hold on the country's politics. ■

TUNISIA

Official name Republic of Tunisia

PEOPLE
Population 9,265,000. **Density** 147/mi^2 (57/km^2). **Urban** 63%. **Capital** Tunis, 674,142. **Ethnic groups** Arab-Berber 98%, European 1%. **Languages** Arabic, French. **Religions** Muslim 98%, Christian 1%. **Life expectancy** 71 female, 68 male. **Literacy** 67%.

POLITICS
Government Republic. **Parties** Constitutional Democratic Rally, Movement of Democratic Socialists, others. **Suffrage** Universal, 20 and over. **Memberships** AL, OAU, UN. **Subdivisions** 23 governorates.

ECONOMY
GDP $37,100,000,000. **Per capita** $4,141. **Monetary unit** Dinar. **Trade partners** Exports: France, Italy, Germany. Imports: France, Italy, Germany. **Exports** Hydrocarbons, agricultural products, phosphates, chemicals. **Imports** Manufactures, petroleum, food, industrial equipment.

LAND
Description Northern Africa. **Area** 63,170 mi^2 (163,610 km^2). **Highest point** Mt. Chambi, 5,066 ft (1,544 m). **Lowest point** Chott el Gharsa, -56 ft (-17 m).

People. Tunisians are descended from a mix of Berber and Arab ethnic groups. Nearly all Tunisians are Muslim. Arabic is the official language, but French is widely spoken. Tunisia is a leader in the Arab world in promoting rights for women. A large middle class and equitable land distribution characterize its society.

Economy and the Land. Tunisia is an agricultural country; wheat, barley, citrus fruits, and olives are important crops. Oil from deposits discovered in the 1960s supplies domestic needs and serves as a major export, along with phosphates and other chemicals. Tourism is a growing industry, and despite an unemployment problem, Tunisia has a more balanced economy than many of its neighbors. Tunisia's terrain ranges from a well-watered and fertile northern area to more arid central and southern regions.

History and Politics. Phoenicians began the Carthaginian Empire in Tunisia about 1100 B.C. In 146 B.C. Romans conquered Carthage and ruled Tunisia for 600 years. Arab Muslims from the Middle East gained control of most of North Africa in the 7th century, influencing the religion and overall culture of the region. Tunisia became part of the Turkish Ottoman Empire in the late 1500s, and in 1881 France succeeded in establishing a protectorate in the area. Nationalistic calls for Tunisian independence began before World War I and gained momentum by the 1930s. When Tunisia gained independence in 1956, more than half of the European population emigrated, severely damaging the economy. A year later Tunisia abolished its monarchy and became a republic. The first multiparty parliament was elected in March 1994. Muslim fundamentalist parties are banned. ■

TURKEY

Official name Republic of Turkey

PEOPLE
Population 64,050,000. **Density** 213/mi² (82/km²). **Urban** 71%. **Capital** Ankara, 2,559,471. **Ethnic groups** Turkish 80%, Kurdish 20%. **Languages** Turkish, Kurdish, Arabic. **Religions** Muslim. **Life expectancy** 71 female, 67 male. **Literacy** 82%.

POLITICS
Government Republic. **Parties** Democratic Left, Motherland, Republican People's, True Path, Welfare, others. **Suffrage** Universal, 18 and over. **Memberships** NATO, OECD, UN. **Subdivisions** 74 provinces.

ECONOMY
GDP $345,700,000,000. **Per capita** $5,486. **Monetary unit** Lira. **Trade partners** Exports: Germany, Italy, U.S. Imports: Germany, U.S., Italy. **Exports** Steel, fruits, vegetables, textiles, apparel. **Imports** Fuel, machinery, raw materials, food.

LAND
Description Southeastern Europe and southwestern Asia. **Area** 300,948 mi² (779,452 km²). **Highest point** Mt. Ararat, 16,854 ft (5,137 m). **Lowest point** Sea level.

People. Most Turks are descended from an Asian people who migrated from Russia and Mongolia around A.D. 900. About half the Turkish population lives in cities and half in rural areas. Kurds, the largest minority, live in the country's mountainous regions. Arabs and whites compose smaller minorities. The population is mainly Sunni Muslim. The changing status of women and the influence of Islam on daily life are key issues in Turkish society.

Economy and the Land. More than half the workers in this developing country are farmers, but industrialization has increased greatly since 1950. The most productive lands are in the mild coastal regions, although wheat and barley are grown in the desert-like plateau area. The government owns or controls many important industries, transportation services, and utilities, while most small farms and manufacturing companies are privately owned. The climate is Mediterranean along the coast, but temperature extremes are typical in the inland plateau.

History and Politics. Hittites began to migrate to the area from Europe or central Asia around 2000 B.C. Successive dominant groups included Phrygians, Greeks, Persians, and Romans. Muslims and Christians battled in the area during the Crusades of the 11th and 12th centuries. In the 1300s Ottoman Turks began to build what would become a vast, 600-year empire. Mustafa Kemal founded the Republic of Turkey in 1923 after the collapse of the Ottoman Empire. In 1960, the Turkish government was overthrown by the military, which set up a provisional government, adopted a new constitution, and held free elections. In the 1960s and 1970s, disputes with Greece over Cyprus, which has majority Greek and minority Turkish populations, flared into violence. Radical groups committed terrorist acts against the Cypriot government. Turkey's generals assumed power in 1980 and restored order to the country. The government returned to civilian rule in 1984, and in 1993 elected its first female prime minister. A militant Kurdish insurrection and militant fundamentalist Muslims challenge Turkey's stability. In 1994 and 1995, Turkish troops drove thousands of Kurdish civilians into northern Iraqi refugee camps. Turkey continues to attack the Kurds as it establishes a buffer zone along the northern border of Iraq. ■

TURKMENISTAN

Official name Turkmenistan

PEOPLE
Population 4,657,000. **Density** 25/mi² (9.5/km²).
Urban 45%. **Capital** Ashgabat, 412,200. **Ethnic groups** Turkmen 77%, Uzbek 9%, Russian 7%, Kazakh 2%. **Languages** Turkmen, Russian, Uzbek. **Religions** Muslim 89%, Eastern Orthodox 9%. **Life expectancy** 70 female, 64 male. **Literacy** 98%.

POLITICS
Government Republic. **Parties** Democratic, others. **Suffrage** Universal, 18 and over. **Memberships** UN. **Subdivisions** 4 oblasts.

ECONOMY
GDP $11,500,000,000. **Per capita** $2,850. **Monetary unit** Manat. **Trade partners** Russia, Ukraine, Uzbekistan. **Exports** Natural gas, oil, cotton, textiles, carpets. **Imports** Machinery and parts, plastics, rubber, consumer durables, textiles, food.

LAND
Description Central Asia, landlocked. **Area** 188,456 mi² (488,100 km²). **Highest point** Mt. Ayrybaba, 10,292 ft (3,137 m). **Lowest point** Akdzhakaya Basin, -266 ft (-81 m).

People. Almost three-quarters of the people are Turkmen, although there are Russian and Uzbek minorities. Before the Russian Revolution, the Turkmen were nomads who were organized into tribes and clans. Under Communist rule, many people turned to agriculture. The Turkmen speak a Turkish dialect of the same name.

Economy and the Land. Most of Turkmenistan is a vast desert. Like most deserts, the climate is characterized by extreme variations in temperature. Agriculture takes place in the country's river valleys and oases, and cotton is the most significant crop. Grapes, melons, and vegetables are also grown. Animal husbandry is a traditional activity, and sheep, horses, and camels are raised. The sheep provide wool for the country's famous handmade Oriental carpets. Petroleum and natural gas are among Turkmenistan's most

important mineral resources. Only 10 percent of the people of Turkmenistan are engaged in industry.

History and Politics. In ancient times, Turkmenistan was part of the Persian Empire. Arabs invaded the region in the 8th century, bringing Islam. Turkic tribes conquered Turkmenistan in the 10th century, followed by the Mongols and the Uzbeks. The area was incorporated into Russian Turkestan in 1881. In 1925, Turkestan became a Soviet Socialist Republic within the Soviet Union. Turkmenistan was slow to make its claim to independence from the Soviet Union following the abortive coup against President Mikhail Gorbachev and the subsequent disbanding of the Soviet Communist party. The country gained full independence with the rest of the former Soviet republics in December 1991. Communists continue to dominate Turkmenistan's politics, and democratic institutions have not been established. With no opposition, the incumbent Turkmen Democratic Party was returned to power in 1994 and President Saparmurad Niyazov's term was extended to 2002. Turkmenistan is one of the few former Soviet republics that has not experienced ethnic strife, but there are signs of dissent over the autocratic rule and the austere economic circumstances that most people endure. ■

TURKS AND CAICOS ISLANDS See UNITED KINGDOM.

TUVALU

Official name Tuvalu

PEOPLE
Population 10,000. **Density** 1,000/mi² (385/km²). **Urban** 48%. **Capital** Funafuti, Funafuti I., 2,191. **Ethnic groups** Polynesian 96%. **Languages** Tuvaluan, English. **Religions** Congregationalist (Church of Tuvalu) 97%. **Life expectancy** 64 female, 62 male.

POLITICS
Government Parliamentary state. **Parties** None. **Suffrage** Universal, 18 and over. **Memberships** CW. **Subdivisions** 1 town council, 7 island councils.

ECONOMY
GDP $7,800,000. **Per capita** $780. **Monetary unit** Dollar, Australian dollar. **Trade partners** Exports: Fiji, Australia, New Zealand. Imports: Australia, New Zealand, U.K. **Exports** Copra. **Imports** Food, animals, fuel, machinery, manufactures.

LAND
Description South Pacific islands. **Area** 10 mi² (26 km²). **Highest point** 16 ft (5 m). **Lowest point** Sea level.

People. The small island country of Tuvalu has a mostly Polynesian population centered in rural villages. Tuvaluans speak the Tuvaluan language, derived from Polynesian, and many also speak English, reflecting ties with England.

Economy and the Land. The soil of the Tuvaluan coral reef islands is poor, and there are few natural resources other than coconut palms. Copra and developed film are the primary exports, and many Tuvaluans weave mats and baskets for export. Tuvalu has minimal manufacturing and no mining. The country consists of nine islands, most of them atolls surrounding lagoons. The climate is tropical.

History and Politics. Tuvalu's first inhabitants were probably Samoan immigrants. The islands were not seen by Europeans until 1568 and came under British control in the 1890s. Then called the Ellice Islands by Europeans, they were combined with the nearby Gilbert Islands in 1916 to form the Gilbert and Ellice Islands Colony. The island groups were separated in 1975. The Ellice Islands were renamed Tuvalu and gained independence in 1978. One year later, the Gilbert Islands became part of independent Kiribati. ■

UGANDA

Official name Republic of Uganda

PEOPLE
Population 20,835,000. **Density** 224/mi² (86/km²). **Urban** 13%. **Capital** Kampala, 773,463. **Ethnic groups** Ganda 17%, Karamojong 12%, Soga 8%, Iteso, 8%. **Languages** English, Luganda, Swahili, indigenous. **Religions** Roman Catholic 45%, Protestant 39%, Muslim 11%, Animist. **Life expectancy** 44 female, 42 male. **Literacy** 62%.

POLITICS
Government Republic. **Parties** National Resistance Movement; other parties exist but are not permitted to sponsor candidates. **Suffrage** Universal, 18 and over. **Memberships** CW, OAU, UN. **Subdivisions** 33 districts.

ECONOMY
GDP $16,800,000,000. **Per capita** $920. **Monetary unit** Shilling. **Trade partners** Exports: U.S., U.K., France. Imports: Kenya, U.K., Italy. **Exports** Coffee, cotton, tea. **Imports** Petroleum products, machinery, textiles, metals, transportation equipment, food.

LAND
Description Eastern Africa, landlocked. **Area** 93,104 mi² (241,139 km²). **Highest point** Margherita Pk., 16,762 ft (5,109 m). **Lowest point** Along Albert Nile River, 2,001 ft (610 m).

People. Primarily a rural country, Uganda has an African population, composed of various ethnic groups. Numerous differences divide Uganda's peoples and have traditionally inspired conflict. Though English is the official language, Luganda and Swahili are widely used, along with indigenous Bantu and Nilotic languages. Most Ugandans are Christian, but Muslims and followers of traditional beliefs compose significant minorities.

Economy and the Land. Despite attempts to diversify the economy, the country remains largely agricultural. Uganda meets most of its own food needs and grows coffee, cotton, and tea commercially. Copper deposits account for most mining activity. Though Uganda straddles the equator, temperatures are moderated by altitude. Most of the country is plateau, and Uganda benefits from its proximity to several major lakes.

History and Politics. Arab traders who traveled to the interior of Uganda in the 1830s found sophisticated kingdoms that had developed over several centuries. British explorers arrived in the 1860s while seeking the source of the Nile River, and European missionaries soon followed. Britain quickly became a dominant force in eastern Africa, and part of modern Uganda became a British protectorate in 1894. Subsequent border adjustments brought Uganda to its present boundaries in 1926. After increasing demands for independence, moves toward autonomy began in the mid-1950s. Independence came in 1962, followed by internal conflicts and power struggles. In 1971, Major General Idi Amin Dada led a successful coup against President Obote and declared himself president. His dictatorship was rife with corruption, economic decline, and disregard for human rights, and he was driven into exile in 1979. In July 1993, the ancient kingdom of Buganda was symbolically restored under King Ronald Mutebi. The country is actually run by President Yoweri Museveni, who gained power in a 1986 coup. In 1996, Uganda's first presidential election returned him to power. The country has suffered for 12 years from the brutal warfare of a northern rebel group. Thousands of children have been abducted and forced to fight for the rebels. ■

UKRAINE

Official name Ukraine

PEOPLE
Population 50,830,000. **Density** 218/mi² (84/km²). **Urban** 71%. **Capital** Kiev (Kyïv), 2,643,000. **Ethnic groups** Ukrainian 73%, Russian 22%. **Languages** Ukrainian, Russian, Romanian, Polish, Hungarian. **Religions** Ukrainian Orthodox, Ukrainian Catholic. **Life expectancy** 74 female, 64 male. **Literacy** 97%.

POLITICS

Government Republic. **Parties** Agrarian, Communist, Republican, Rukh, Socialist, others. **Suffrage** Universal, 18 and over. **Memberships** UN. **Subdivisions** 1 republic, 24 oblasts.

ECONOMY

GDP $174,600,000,000. **Per capita** $3,362. **Monetary unit** Hryvnia. **Trade partners** Russia, Belarus, Kazakhstan. **Exports** Coal, electricity, grain, metals, chemicals, machinery, transportation equipment **Imports** Machinery, transportation equipment, chemicals, textiles, energy.

LAND

Description Eastern Europe. **Area** 233,090 mi² (603,700 km²). **Highest point** Mt. Hoverla, 6,762 ft (2,061 m). **Lowest point** Sea level.

People. Ukraine's population is second only to Russia among the former Soviet republics. Although there are more than 100 minority groups, ethnic Ukrainians account for almost three-quarters of the population. Ukrainians are Slavs, and their language is closely related to Russian and Belorussian. The Ukrainians are proud of their traditional stories, music, and art.

Economy and the Land. The land is almost entirely flat plains. The topography and the extremely fertile soils combine to make Ukraine one of the world's most outstanding agricultural areas. Major products include grain, potatoes, meat, and milk. The country is also rich in mineral resources, including petroleum, coal, iron ore, and manganese. Industry is well developed in the eastern part of the country, and Ukraine boasts powerful steel and chemical industries. The coast of the Crimean Peninsula on the Black Sea is a famous resort area due to its warm Mediterranean climate. Unlike many former Soviet republics, Ukraine has a very well-developed transportation system.

History and Politics. Ukraine's first inhabitants were agricultural tribesmen who made their homes in the fertile river valleys. Slavic people found their way to the area around the 4th centu-ry A.D. In the 9th century, a dynasty centered at Kiev, called the Kievan Rus, was founded by the Scandinavian Varangians. This kingdom is considered the foundation of both the modern Ukrainian and Russian states. Kiev was destroyed during the Tatar-Mongol invasion in 1237. In the late 1300s, Ukraine was part of the Lithuanian empire and was later governed by Poland. The Ukrainians were made serfs under Polish rule, and religious rivalry between the Orthodox Ukrainians and the Roman Catholic Poles exacerbated the situation. Ukrainians who rebelled and fled from serfdom came to be known as Cossacks. The Cossacks established their own colonies and led several revolts against Polish rule and also against the Tatars. Eventually the Cossacks turned to the Russians for protection, and the first treaty was signed in 1654. By the late 1700s the Cossacks began to chafe under czarist rule, but the Russians managed to keep the territory under its control despite numerous revolts. Ukraine declared its independence after the Russian Revolution in 1917, but the new country was soon invaded by Germany. Bolshevik troops drove the Germans out and the country became a Soviet Socialist Republic in 1922. In the 1930s agricultural land was seized by the government and devastating political purges followed. Most of the farmers were killed, and millions of people died in the ensuing famine. Ukraine was again ravaged during the German invasion of the Soviet Union in World War II. The country prospered in the years after the war, but nationalist sentiments were revived during the upheaval accompanying Gorbachev's rule. The nuclear accident at the Chernobyl nuclear power plant in 1986 only added to the people's growing desire for greater control over their own territory. A referendum in Ukraine in early December 1991 called for complete independence from the Soviet Union and ultimately prompted the final collapse of the U.S.S.R. in late 1991. Anger over rampant inflation and general economic chaos resulted in a 1994 presidential election promising reform. In 1996, the last of Ukraine's nuclear warheads were sent to Russia. Crimea continues to press for independence. ■

UNITED ARAB EMIRATES

Official name United Arab Emirates

PEOPLE

Population 3,255,000. **Density** 101/mi² (39/km²). **Urban** 84%. **Capital** Abu Dhabi, 242,975. **Ethnic groups** South Asian 50%, Emiri 19%, other Arab 23%. **Languages** Arabic, Farsi, English, Hindi, Urdu. **Religions** Sunni Muslim 80%, Shiite Muslim 16%. **Life expectancy** 77 female, 74 male. **Literacy** 79%.

POLITICS

Government Federation of monarchs. **Parties** None. **Suffrage** None. **Memberships** AL, OPEC, UN. **Subdivisions** 7 emirates.

ECONOMY

GDP $70,100,000,000. **Per capita** $23,429. **Monetary**

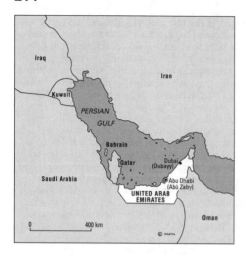

unit Dirham. **Trade partners** Exports: Japan, France, U.S. Imports: Japan, U.K., U.S. **Exports** Petroleum, natural gas, dried fish, dates. **Imports** Food, manufactures, machinery, transportation equipment.

LAND
Description Southwestern Asia. **Area** 32,278 mi² (83,600 km²). **Highest point** Mt. Yibir, 5,010 ft (1,527 m). **Lowest point** Sea level.

People. The United Arab Emirates (U.A.E.) is a predominantly urban federation of seven independent states, each with its own ruling emir. The indigenous population is mostly Arab and Muslim, but only a small percentage of residents are U.A.E. citizens. Other groups include foreigners attracted by jobs in industry, especially Asians and Western Europeans. Arabic is the official language, but Farsi and English are widely spoken. The country's population enjoys one of the highest per capita incomes in the world, as well as free medical and educational facilities.

Economy and the Land. Most of the U.A.E. is desert, which explains agriculture's small economic role. However, the federation is rich in oil, and major deposits—primarily in Abu Dhabi—account for nearly all of the Emirian national budget. The U.A.E. has tried to diversify its economy through production of natural gas, ammonia, and building materials. To attract tourists, airport expansion and hotel development are also on the rise.

History and Politics. Centuries ago, Arab rulers gained control of the region, formerly called the Trucial Coast, and Islam spread to the area in the A.D. 600s. In 1820, Arabian emirs signed the first of a number of treaties with the United Kingdom. Mutual self-interest led to an 1892 treaty that granted Britain exclusive rights to Trucial territory and government activity in return for military protection. Britain formally withdrew from Trucial affairs in 1971, and six of the Trucial emirates entered into a loose federation called the United Arab Emirates, which included Abu Dhabi, Dubai, Ash Shāriqah, ʻAjmān, Umm al

Qaywayn, and Al Fujayrah. The seventh, Ra's al Khaymah, joined in early 1972. Because each emirate has a great deal of control over its internal affairs and economic development, the growth of federal powers has been slow. Defense spending is on the increase, however, and growing Arab nationalism may lead to a more centralized government. ∎

UNITED KINGDOM

Official name United Kingdom of Great Britain and Northern Ireland

PEOPLE
Population 58,680,000. **Density** 623/mi² (240/km²). **Urban** 89%. **Capital** London, England, 7,650,944. **Ethnic groups** English 82%, Scottish 10%, Irish 2%, Welsh 2%. **Languages** English, Welsh, Scots Gaelic. **Religions** Anglican 47%, Roman Catholic 16%, Muslim 2%. **Life expectancy** 79 female, 75 male. **Literacy** 99%.

POLITICS
Government Parliamentary monarchy. **Parties** Conservative and Unionist, Labor, Liberal Democratic, others. **Suffrage** Universal, 18 and over. **Memberships** CW, EU, NATO, OECD, UN. **Subdivisions** 2 countries, 1 principality, 1 province.

ECONOMY
GDP $1,138,400,000,000. **Per capita** $19,490. **Monetary unit** Pound sterling. **Trade partners** Exports: U.S., Germany, France. Imports: Germany, U.S., France. **Exports** Manufactures, machinery, fuel, chemicals, transportation equipment. **Imports** Manufactures, machinery, food.

LAND
Description Northwestern European islands. **Area** 94,249 mi² (244,101 km²). **Highest point** Ben Nevis, 4,406 ft (1,343 m). **Lowest point** Holme Fen, England, -9 ft (-3 m).

People. The ancestry of modern Britons reflects many centuries of invasions and migrations from Scandinavia and the European continent. Today Britons are a mixture of Celtic, Roman, Anglo-

Places and Possessions of the UNITED KINGDOM

Entity	Status	Area	Population	Capital/Population
Anguilla (Caribbean island)	Dependent territory	35 mi² (91 km²)	11,000	The Valley, 1,462
Ascension (South Atlantic island)	Dependency (St. Helena)	34 mi² (88 km²)	1,100	Georgetown
Bermuda (North Atlantic islands; east of North Carolina)	Dependent territory	21 mi² (54 km²)	63,000	Hamilton, 1,100
British Indian Ocean Territory (Indian Ocean islands)	Dependent territory	23 mi² (60 km²)	None	None
Cayman Islands (Caribbean Sea)	Dependent territory	100 mi² (259 km²)	37,000	George Town, 12,921
Channel Islands (Northwestern Europe)	Two crown dependencies (U.K. protection)	75 mi² (194 km²)	153,000	None
Falkland Islands (South Atlantic; east of Argentina)	Dependent territory	4,700 mi² (12,173 km²)	2,000	Stanley, 1,557
Gibraltar (Southwestern Europe; peninsula on Spain's southern coast)	Dependent territory	2.3 mi² (6.0 km²)	29,000	Gibraltar, 28,074
Guernsey (Northwestern European islands)	Crown dependency (U.K. protection)	30 mi² (78 km²)	64,000	St. Peter Port, 16,648
Isle of Man (Northwestern European island)	Crown dependency (U.K. protection)	221 mi² (572 km²)	75,000	Douglas, 22,214
Jersey (Northwestern European island)	Crown dependency (U.K. protection)	45 mi² (116 km²)	89,000	St. Helier, 28,123
Montserrat (Caribbean island)	Dependent territory	39 mi² (102 km²)	13,000	Plymouth, 1,568
Orkney Islands (North Atlantic)	Part of Scotland	377 mi² (976 km²)	20,000	Kirkwall, 6,489
Pitcairn (South Pacific islands)	Dependent territory	19 mi² (49 km²)	100	Adamstown, 59
Shetland Islands (North Atlantic)	Part of Scotland	553 mi² (1,433 km²)	24,000	Lerwick, 7,336
South Georgia and the South Sandwich Islands (South Atlantic)	Dependent territory	1,450 mi² (3,755 km²)	None	None
St. Helena (South Atlantic islands)	Dependent territory	121 mi² (314 km²)	7,000	Jamestown, 1,413
Tristan da Cunha (South Atlantic islands)	Dependency (St. Helena)	40 mi² (104 km²)	300	Edinburgh, 401,910
Turks and Caicos Islands (Caribbean Sea)	Dependent territory	193 mi² (500 km²)	14,000	Grand Turk, 3,691
Virgin Islands, British (Caribbean Sea)	Dependent territory	59 mi² (153 km²)	14,000	Road Town, 2,479

Saxon, Norse, and Norman influences. English is the predominant language, although Celtic languages such as Welsh and Scottish Gaelic are also spoken. Anglican is the dominant religion in England, while many Scots practice Presbyterianism. A sizable minority is Roman Catholic. The population is primarily urban, with a significant percentage living in the southeastern corner of England.

Economy and the Land. A land of limited natural resources, the United Kingdom has relied on trading and, more recently, manufacturing to achieve economic strength. Easy access to the sea has helped the U.K. both economically and politically. The country maintains a large merchant fleet, which at one time dominated world trade. Great Britain is a leading producer of transportation equipment, metal products, and other manufactured goods. Although climate and limited acreage have hindered agricultural development, intensive, mechanized farming methods have allowed the country to produce half of its food supply. Livestock raising is especially important. Additional contributors to the country's industry are extensive deposits of coal and iron, which make mining important. London is well known as an international financial center. The United Kingdom includes Scotland, England, Wales, Northern Ireland, and several offshore islands. The varied terrain includes several mountain ranges, moors, rolling hills, and plains. The climate is tempered by the sea and is subject to frequent changes. Great Britain administers many overseas possessions.

History and Politics. Little is known of the earliest inhabitants of Britain, but evidence such as Stonehenge indicates the existence of a developed culture before the Roman invasion in the 50s B.C. Britain began to trade with the rest of Europe while under Roman rule. The Norman period after A.D. 1066 fostered the establishment of many cultural and political traditions that continue to be reflected in British life. Scotland came under the British Crown in 1603, and in 1707 England and Scotland agreed to unite as Great Britain. Ireland had been conquered by the early 17th century, and the 1801 British Act of Union established the United Kingdom of Great Britain and Ireland. Although colonial and economic expansion had taken Great Britain to the Far East, America, Africa, and India, the country's influence began to decrease at the end of the 19th century as the Industrial Revolution strengthened other countries. World War I significantly weakened the United Kingdom, and the period following World War II saw the demise of an empire as many colonies gained independence. In 1921, a rebellion prompted the partition of Ireland into the Irish Free State, an independent country, and Northern Ireland, part of the United Kingdom. Violence has continued, often including terrorist bombings in London. The Irish Republican Army has been the main antagonist, with Ireland's reunification as its goal. The issue of peace for Northern Ireland continues to dominate the U.K.'s political scene. ∎

UNITED STATES

Official name United States of America

PEOPLE
Population 270,130,000. **Density** 71/mi² (28/km²). **Urban** 76%. **Capital** Washington, D.C., 606,900. **Ethnic groups** White 83%, black 12%, Asian 3%, Amerindian 1%. **Languages** English, Spanish.

Religions Baptist and other Protestant 56%, Roman Catholic 28%, Jewish 2%. **Life expectancy** 80 female, 73 male. **Literacy** 97%.

POLITICS
Government Federal republic. **Parties** Democratic, Republican. **Suffrage** Universal, 18 and over. **Memberships** NATO, OECD, OAS, UN. **Subdivisions** 50 states, 1 district.

ECONOMY
GDP $7,247,700,000,000. **Per capita** $27,336. **Monetary unit** Dollar. **Trade partners** Exports: Canada, Japan, Mexico. Imports: Canada, Japan, Mexico. **Exports** Machinery, automobiles, raw materials, manufactures, agricultural products. **Imports** Petroleum, machinery, automobiles, manufactures, raw materials, food.

LAND
Description Central North America. **Area** 3,787,425 mi² (9,809,431 km²). **Highest point** Mt. McKinley, 20,322 ft (6,194 m). **Lowest point** Death Valley, California, -282 ft (-86 m).

Places and Possessions of the UNITED STATES

Entity	Status	Area	Population	Capital/Population
American Samoa (South Pacific islands)	Unincorporated territory	77 mi² (199 km²)	63,000	Pago Pago, 3,519
Guam (North Pacific island)	Unincorporated territory	209 mi² (541 km²)	163,000	Agana, 1,139
Johnston Atoll (North Pacific island)	Unincorporated territory	0.5 mi² (1.3 km²)	1,200	None
Midway Islands (North Pacific)	Unincorporated territory	2.0 mi² (5.2 km²)	500	None
Navassa Island (Caribbean Sea)	Unincorporated territory	1.9 mi² (4.9 km²)	None	None
Northern Mariana Islands (North Pacific)	Commonwealth (U.S. protection)	184 mi² (477 km²)	54,000	Saipan (island)
Puerto Rico (Caribbean island)	Commonwealth (U.S. protection)	3,515 mi² (9,104 km²)	3,829,000	San Juan, 426,832
Virgin Islands, United States (Caribbean Sea)	Unincorporated territory	133 mi² (344 km²)	97,000	Charlotte Amalie, 12,331
Wake Island (North Pacific)	Unincorporated territory	3.0 mi² (7.8 km²)	300	None

People. The diverse population of the United States is mostly composed of whites, many descended from 18th- and 19th-century immigrants; blacks, mainly descended from African slaves; peoples of Spanish and Asian origin; and indigenous Native Americans, Inuit, and Hawaiians. Religions encompass the world's major faiths, but Christianity predominates. English is the predominant language, though Spanish is spoken by many, and other languages are often found in ethnic enclaves.

Economy and the Land. The U.S. is an international economic power, and all sectors of the economy are highly developed. Fertile soils produce high crop yields, with considerable land under cultivation. Mineral output includes petroleum and natural gas, coal, copper, lead, and zinc; but high consumption makes the U.S. dependent on foreign oil. The country is a leading manufacturer, with a well-developed service sector. Mountains, prairies, woodlands, and deserts mark its vast terrain. The climate varies regionally, from mild year-round along the Pacific coast and in the South to temperate in the Northeast and Midwest. In addition to 48 contiguous states, the country includes the subarctic state of Alaska and the tropical state of Hawaii, an island group in the Pacific.

History and Politics. Thousands of years ago, Asiatic peoples, ancestors of the Native Americans, crossed the Bering Strait land bridge and migrated across North and South America. Vikings reached North America around A.D. 1000, and Christopher Columbus arrived in 1492. Following early explorations by Portugal and Spain, England established a colony at Jamestown, Virginia in 1607. Thirteen British colonies waged a successful war of independence against England from 1775 to 1783. U.S. expansion continued westward throughout the 19th century. Conflict over black slavery and states' rights led to the 1861-65 American Civil War, which pitted the North against the South. The war resulted in the end of slavery and a reunified country. Opportunities for prosperity accompanied the Industrial Revolution in the late 19th century and led to a large influx of immigrants. From 1917 to 1918 the country joined with the Allies in World War I. A severe economic depression began in 1929, and the U.S. did not really recover until World War II stimulated industry and the overall economy. In 1945 the use of the atomic bomb on Japan ended the war and changed the course of history. The 1964 Civil Rights Act and the 1961-75 Vietnam War brought an era of great social progress and turmoil. Technological advances were unparalleled with man's entry into space and the first landing on the moon in 1969. The 1980s saw increasing concern with a polluted environment and the nuclear arms race. In the 1990s, the U.S. entered its longest period of continual, gradual economic growth. However, companies often increased their profits through massive layoffs. After several terrorist bombings, there is increased concern over domestic and international terrorist activity. The public's increasing awareness of private militia groups has also fueled concern about possible violence. ■

URUGUAY

Official name Oriental Republic of Uruguay

PEOPLE
Population 3,273,000. **Density** 48/mi² (18/km²). **Urban** 91%. **Capital** Montevideo, 1,251,647. **Ethnic groups** White 88%, mestizo 8%, black 4%. **Languages** Spanish. **Religions** Roman Catholic 66%, Protestant 2%, Jewish 2%. **Life expectancy** 76 female, 70 male. **Literacy** 97%.

POLITICS
Government Republic. **Parties** Colorado, Encuentro Progresista, National (Blanco), others. **Suffrage** Universal, 18 and over. **Memberships** OAS, UN. **Subdivisions** 19 departments.

ECONOMY
GDP $24,400,000,000. **Per capita** $7,540. **Monetary unit** Peso. **Trade partners** Exports: Brazil, U.S., Germany. Imports: Brazil, Argentina, U.S. **Exports** Hides, leather goods, beef, wool, textiles, rice. **Imports** Machinery, transportation equipment, chemicals, minerals, plastics.

LAND
Description Eastern South America. **Area** 68,500 mi² (177,414 km²). **Highest point** Cerro Catedral, 1,686 ft (514 m). **Lowest point** Sea level.

People. Most Uruguayans are white descendants of 19th- and 20th-century immigrants from Spain, Italy, and other European countries. Mestizos of Spanish-Amerindian ancestry and blacks round out the population. Spanish is the dominant language, and Roman Catholicism is the major religion, with small Protestant and Jewish minorities. About one-third of all Uruguayans claim to follow no religion.

Economy and the Land. Uruguay's fertile soil, grassy plains, and temperate climate provide the basis for agriculture and are especially conducive to livestock raising. The country has virtually no mineral resources, and petroleum exploration has been unrewarding. Refinement of imported fuel is a major industry, however, and Uruguay has significant hydroelectric potential.

History and Politics. Uruguay's original inhabitants were Amerindians. In the 1680s the Portuguese established the first European settlement, followed by a Spanish settlement in the 1720s. By the 1770s Spain had gained control of the area, but in the 1820s Portugal once again came to power, annexing present-day Uruguay to Brazil. When nationalistic feelings in the early 19th century led to an 1828 war by Uruguayan patriots and Argentina against Brazil, the country achieved independence. Political unrest, caused in part by economic depression, resurfaced in the 1970s, leading to military intervention in the government and the jailing of thousands of political prisoners. The country restored its civilian government in 1985. The first democratic elections in 20 years were won by the centrist Colorado party, which is expected to introduce economic reforms. ■

UZBEKISTAN

Official name Republic of Uzbekistan

PEOPLE
Population 24,075,000. **Density** 139/mi² (54/km²). **Urban** 41%. **Capital** Tashkent, 2,113,300. **Ethnic groups** Uzbek 80%, Russian 5%, Tajik 5%, Kazakh 3%. **Languages** Uzbek, Russian. **Religions** Muslim 88%, Eastern Orthodox 9%. **Life expectancy** 73 female, 68 male. **Literacy** 97%.

POLITICS
Government Republic. **Parties** Fatherland Progress, People's Democratic, Social Democratic, others. **Suffrage** Universal, 18 and over. **Memberships** UN. **Subdivisions** 1 republic, 11 oblasts.

ECONOMY
GDP $54,700,000,000. **Per capita** $2,343. **Monetary unit** Som. **Trade partners** Russia, Ukraine, eastern European countries. **Exports** Cotton, gold, textiles, fertilizers, vegetable oil, natural gas, metals. **Imports** Machinery, manufactures, grain and other food.

LAND
Description Central Asia, landlocked. **Area** 172,742 mi² (447,400 km²). **Highest point** Mt. Khodza-Pir'yakh, 14,518 ft (4,425 m). **Lowest point** Mynbulak Basin, -39 ft (-12 m).

People. The third most populous of the former Soviet republics, Uzbekistan is a land of many ethnic groups. Ethnic Uzbeks account for 80 percent of the population. Other ethnic groups include Russians, Tajiks, Kazakhs, and Tatars. The Uzbeks speak a Turkish dialect and adhere to Islam.

Economy and the Land. Irrigation allows for the production of cotton, and Uzbekistan is one of the world's largest producers, although it hopes to diversify its economy and end its dependence on cotton. Fruit and silk are produced in the mountain valleys. Gold, uranium, natural gas, and other minerals are mined in abundance. Western Uzbekistan is a flat desert that rises to mountains in the eastern part of the country. Most of the population and economic activity is based in valleys that cross eastern Uzbekistan. Uzbekistan exports electricity to other former Soviet central Asian republics, and it is the region's largest machinery producer.

History and Politics. Uzbekistan was inhabited as far back as the Stone Age. Much later, the area was conquered by the Turks, the armies of Alexander the Great, the Arabs, and the Mongols. Uzbekistan was under the rule of the Mongol-Turk Tamerlane dynasty from the 13th to the 16th centuries. Various sovereign khanates ruled the land until Russia annexed Uzbekistan in 1885 as part of the region then known as Turkestan. After the Russian Revolution, Uzbekistan attempted to establish a western-style democracy, but the Soviets took over in 1924, and it was admitted to the Soviet Union the following year. Uzbekistan gained independence in 1991, following the dissolution of the Soviet Union. At first Uzbeks struggled to establish a new economy and form of government, but rising Islamic fundamentalism in neighboring Tajikistan has prompted a return to conservative government policies and a moratorium on reform. A new constitution, adopted December 1992, promised freedom and multiparty democracy. However, on the same day several opposition politicians were arrested. Elections in 1994 proved that power is still firmly in the hands of ex-Communists and a centralized economic system. Economic reform has been moderately effective. ■

VANUATU

Official name Republic of Vanuatu

PEOPLE
Population 184,000. **Density** 39/mi² (15/km²). **Urban** 19%. **Capital** Port Vila, Efate I., 19,311. **Ethnic groups** Ni-Vanuatu (Melanesian) 95%. **Languages** Bislama, English, French. **Religions** Presbyterian 35%, Anglican 14%, Roman Catholic 15%, other Protestant. **Life expectancy** 70 female, 66 male. **Literacy** 53%.

POLITICS
Government Republic. **Parties** Union of Moderate Parties, National United, Vanuatu, others. **Suffrage**

Universal, 18 and over. **Memberships** CW, UN.
Subdivisions 11 island councils.

ECONOMY
GDP $210,000,000. **Per capita** $1,304. **Monetary unit** Vatu. **Trade partners** Exports: Netherlands, Japan, France. Imports: Australia, New Zealand, Japan. **Exports** Copra, cocoa, meat, fish, timber. **Imports** Transportation equipment, food, manufactures, raw materials, chemicals.

LAND
Description South Pacific islands. **Area** 4,707 mi^2 (12,190 km^2). **Highest point** Mont Tabwémasana, 6,165 ft (1,879 m). **Lowest point** Sea level.

People. The majority of Vanuatuans are Melanesian. Europeans and Polynesians compose minorities. Languages include English and French, the languages of former rulers; and Bislama, a mixture of English and Melanesian. Most Vanuatuans are Christian, although indigenous religions are also practiced.

Economy and the Land. The economy is based on agriculture, and copra is the primary export crop. Fishing is also important, as is the growing tourist business. Narrow coastal plains, mountainous interiors, and a mostly hot, rainy climate characterize the more than 80 islands of Vanuatu.

History and Politics. In 1606, Portuguese explorers encountered indigenous Melanesian inhabitants on islands that now compose Vanuatu. Captain James Cook of Britain charted the islands in 1774 and named them the New Hebrides after the Hebrides islands of Scotland. British and French merchants and missionaries began to settle the islands in the early 1800s. To resolve conflicting interests, Great Britain and France formed a joint naval commission to oversee the area in 1887 and a condominium government in 1906. Demands for autonomy began in the 1960s, and the New Hebrides became the independent Republic of Vanuatu in 1980. The first national election since independence was held in 1991. ∎

VATICAN CITY

Official name State of the Vatican City

PEOPLE
Population 1,000. **Density** 5,000/mi^2 (2,500/km^2). **Urban** 100%. **Capital** Vatican City, 1,000. **Ethnic groups** Italian, Swiss. **Languages** Italian, Latin, other. **Religions** Roman Catholic. **Literacy** 100%.

POLITICS
Government Monarchical-sacerdotal state. **Parties** None. **Suffrage** Roman Catholic cardinals less than 80 years old. **Memberships** None. **Subdivisions** None.

ECONOMY
Monetary unit Lira.

LAND
Description Southern Europe, landlocked (within the city of Rome, Italy). **Area** 0.2 mi^2 (0.4 km^2). **Highest point** 249 ft (76 m). **Lowest point** Unnamed, 62 ft (19 m).

People. The Vatican City, the smallest independent state in the world, is the administrative and spiritual center of the Roman Catholic church and home to the pope, the church's head. The population is composed of administrative and diplomatic workers of more than a dozen nationalities; Italians and Swiss predominate. A military corps known as the Swiss Guard also resides here. Roman Catholicism is the only religion. The official language is Italian, although acts of the Holy See are drawn up in Latin.

Economy and the Land. The Vatican City does not engage in commerce per se; however, it does issue its own coins and postage stamps. In addition, it is the destination of thousands of tourists and pilgrims each year. Lying on a hill west of the Tiber River, the Vatican City is an urban enclave in northwestern Rome, Italy. The Vatican City enjoys a mild climate moderated by the Mediterranean Sea.

History and Politics. For centuries the popes of the Roman Catholic church ruled the Papal States, an area across central Italy which included Rome. The popes' temporal authority gradually was reduced to the city of Rome, which itself was eventually annexed by the Kingdom of Italy in 1870. Denying these rulings, the pope declared himself a prisoner in the Vatican, a status that lasted 59 years. The Vatican City has been an independent sovereign state since 1929, when Italy signed the Treaty of the Lateran in return for papal dissolution of the Papal States. The pope heads all branches of government, though day-to-day responsibilities are delegated to staff members. ∎

VENEZUELA

Official name Republic of Venezuela

PEOPLE
Population 22,605,000. **Density** 64/mi^2 (25/km^2). **Urban** 86%. **Capital** Caracas, 1,822,465. **Ethnic**

groups Mestizo 67%, white 21%, black 10%, Indian 2%. **Languages** Spanish, Amerindian. **Religions** Roman Catholic 96%, Protestant 2%. **Life expectancy** 76 female, 70 male. **Literacy** 91%.

POLITICS
Government Federal republic. **Parties** Democratic Action, Movement Toward Socialism, Social Christian, others. **Suffrage** Universal, 18 and over. **Memberships** OAS, OPEC, UN. **Subdivisions** 20 states, 2 territories, 1 dependency, 1 district.

ECONOMY
GDP $195,500,000,000. **Per capita** $8,949. **Monetary unit** Bolivar. **Trade partners** Exports: U.S., Japan, Colombia, Netherlands. Imports: U.S., Germany, Italy. **Exports** Petroleum, metals and ores, agricultural products, chemicals, manufactures. **Imports** Raw materials, construction materials, machinery, transportation equipment.

LAND
Description Northern South America. **Area** 352,145 mi² (912,050 km²). **Highest point** Pico Bolívar, 16,427 ft (5,007 m). **Lowest point** Sea level.

People. Spanish colonial rule of Venezuela is reflected in its predominantly mestizo population—people of Spanish-Amerindian blood— and its official language of Spanish. Minorities include Europeans, blacks, and Amerindians, who generally speak indigenous languages. Nearly all Venezuelans are Roman Catholic, further evidence of former Spanish domination. Protestants and lesser numbers of Jews and Muslims compose small minorities, and traditional religious practices continue among some Indians.

Economy and the Land. Since the expansion of the petroleum industry in the 1920s, Venezuela has experienced rapid economic growth, but unevenly distributed wealth, a high birthrate, and fluctuations in the price of oil have hampered the economy. Partly because of the emphasis on oil production, agriculture has declined; its contribution to the gross national product is minimal. Manufacturing and hydroelectric power are being developed. The varied Venezuelan landscape is dominated by the Andes Mountains, a coastal zone, high plateaus, and plains, or *llanos*. The climate is tropical, but temperatures vary with altitude. Most of the country experiences rainy and dry seasons.

History and Politics. The original inhabitants of modern Venezuela included the Arawak and Carib peoples. In 1498 Christopher Columbus was the first European to visit Venezuela. The area became a colony of Spain and was briefly under German rule. Independence was achieved in 1821 under the guidance of Simón Bolívar, Venezuela's national hero. Venezuela became a sovereign state in 1830. The 19th century saw political instability and revolutionary fervor, followed by a succession of dictators in the 20th century. Since 1958, Venezuela has tried to achieve a representational form of government and has held a number of democratic elections. The fall in oil prices, for a country heavily depen-

dent upon oil export, has been an economic hardship in recent years. Abortive coups and presidential corruption have underscored Venezuela's continuing political instability. ∎

VIETNAM

Official name Socialist Republic of Vietnam

PEOPLE
Population 75,720,000. **Density** 594/mi² (229/km²). **Urban** 19%. **Capital** Hanoi, 905,939. **Ethnic groups** Kinh 87%, Hao 2%, Thai 2%, Tay 2%. **Languages** Vietnamese, French, Chinese, English, Khmer, indigenous. **Religions** Buddhist, Taoist, Roman Catholic, Animist, Islamic. **Life expectancy** 70 female, 65 male. **Literacy** 94%.

POLITICS
Government Socialist republic. **Parties** Communist. **Suffrage** Universal, 18 and over. **Memberships** ASEAN, UN. **Subdivisions** 50 provinces, 3 municipalities.

ECONOMY
GDP $97,000,000,000. **Per capita** $1,304. **Monetary unit** Dong. **Trade partners** Japan, Singapore, Thailand, eastern European countries. **Exports** Agricultural products, petroleum, marine products, apparel. **Imports** Petroleum, steel, machinery, equipment, fertilizer, grain, cotton.

LAND
Description Southeastern Asia. **Area** 127,428 mi² (330,036 km²). **Highest point** Phan Si Pang, 10,312 ft (3,143 m). **Lowest point** Sea level.

People. Despite centuries of foreign invasion and domination, the people of Vietnam remain remarkably homogeneous; Vietnamese ethnic groups compose the majority of the population. Chinese influence is seen in the major religions of Buddhism and Taoism. Most people live along two rivers, the Red in the north and the Mekong in the south, separated by mountains. The official language is Vietnamese, but a history of foreign intervention is reflected in wide use of French, English, Chinese, and Russian.

Economy and the Land. The Vietnamese economy has struggled to overcome the effects of war and the difficulties inherent in unifying the once-divided country. Agriculture, centered in the fertile southern plains, continues to employ nearly 70 percent of the people. Vietnam intends to expand its war-damaged mining industry, which has been slowed by lack of skilled personnel and a poor transportation network. Vietnam's economic picture is not likely to improve until the country can resolve its political and social problems. The landscape of Vietnam ranges from mountains to plains, and the climate is tropical.

History and Politics. The first Vietnamese lived in what is now northern Vietnam. After centuries of Chinese rule, Vietnam finally became independent in the 1400s, but civil strife continued for nearly two centuries. French missionary activity began in the early 17th century, and by 1883 all of present-day Vietnam, Cambodia, and Laos were under French rule. When Germany occupied France during World War II, control of French Indochina passed to the Japanese until their defeat in 1945. The French presence continued until 1954, when Vietnamese Communists led by Ho Chi Minh gained control of North Vietnam. U.S. aid to South Vietnam began in 1961 and ended, after years of conflict, with a cease-fire in 1973. Communist victory and unification of the country as the Socialist Republic of Vietnam was achieved in 1975. Vietnamese military policy resulted in fighting with China and the occupation of Cambodia until 1989. A U.S. economic embargo was lifted in 1994. ■

VIRGIN ISLANDS,
BRITISH See UNITED KINGDOM.

VIRGIN ISLANDS, UNITED STATES
See UNITED STATES.

WAKE ISLAND See UNITED STATES.

WALLIS AND FUTUNA
See FRANCE.

WESTERN SAHARA

Official name Western Sahara

PEOPLE
Population 231,000. **Density** 2.2/mi² (0.9/km²).
Urban 94%. **Capital** None. **Ethnic groups** Arab, Berber. **Languages** Arabic. **Religions** Muslim.
Life expectancy 48 female, 45 male.

POLITICS
Government Occupied by Morocco. **Suffrage** none.
Memberships None.

ECONOMY
Monetary unit Moroccan dirham. **Trade partners** Morocco. **Exports** Phosphates. **Imports** Fuel, food.

LAND
Description Northwestern Africa. **Area** 102,703 mi² (266,000 km²). **Highest point** 2,640 ft (805 m). **Lowest point** Sea level.

People. Most Western Saharans are nomadic Arabs or Berbers. Because these nomads often cross national borders in their wanderings, the population of Western Sahara is in a constant state of flux. Islam is the principal religion, and Arabic is the dominant language.

Economy and the Land. Most of Western Sahara is desert, with a rocky, barren soil that severely limits agriculture. Mining of phosphate deposits began in 1972, and phosphates are now the primary export. Western Sahara is almost completely arid; rainfall is negligible, except along the coast.

History and Politics. By the 4th century B.C. Phoenicians and Romans had visited the area. Spain explored the region in the 16th century and gained control of the region in 1860, but Spanish Sahara was not designated a province of Spain until 1958. When Spanish control ceased in 1976, the area became known as Western Sahara. Mauritania and Morocco subsequently divided the territory, and Morocco gained control of valuable phosphate deposits. Fighting soon broke out between an independence movement, the Polisario Front, and troops from Morocco and Mauritania. In 1979 Mauritania gave up its claim to the area and withdrew. After years of conflict, Morocco and the Polisario Front agreed in 1988 to a cease-fire and a referendum to offer Western Saharans a choice between independence and integration with Morocco. The UN's attempts to organize a referendum have been consistently thwarted. ■

WESTERN SAMOA See SAMOA.

YEMEN

Official name Republic of Yemen

PEOPLE
Population 17,485,000. **Density** 86/mi² (33/km²).
Urban 34%. **Capital** Sana, 427,150. **Ethnic groups** Arab, Afro-Arab, south Asians. **Languages** Arabic.
Religions Muslim, Jewish, Christian, Hindu.
Life expectancy 52 female, 51 male. **Literacy** 38%.

POLITICS
Government Republic. **Parties** General People's Congress, Reform Grouping, others. **Suffrage** Universal, 18 and over. **Memberships** AL, UN.
Subdivisions 17 governorates.

ECONOMY
GDP $37,100,000,000. **Per capita** $2,469. **Monetary**

monarchy. The Imam Badr was overthrown in 1962, when the Yemeni army proclaimed creation of the Yemen Arab Republic. Meanwhile, Aden and the southeastern part of the country were under British domination since 1839, and became a protectorate in the 1930s. By the mid-1960s, Aden had become the focus of Arab nationalists, and in 1967 Britain granted independence to the People's Republic of South Yemen. After a coup by a Marxist faction in 1970, the country's name changed to the People's Democratic Republic of Yemen. Border clashes between the two Yemens were frequent during the 1970s but relations improved throughout the 1980s, and the two countries merged to form the Republic of Yemen in 1990. Four years later civil war broke out, fueled by dual military forces. It was won by the North, and unity was restored. ∎

unit Rial. **Trade partners** Exports: Italy, Saudi Arabia. Imports: Japan, Saudi Arabia, U.K. **Exports** Petroleum, cotton, coffee, hides, vegetables, fish. **Imports** Textiles, consumer goods, petroleum, food, cement, machinery, chemicals.

LAND
Description Southwestern Asia. **Area** 203,850 mi^2 (527,968 km^2). **Highest point** Mt. Nabi Shuayb, 12,008 ft (3,660 m). **Lowest point** Sea level.

People. Most inhabitants of Yemen are Arab, with small minorities of Indians, Pakistanis, and East Africans. Islam is the predominant religion, while Arabic is the primary language. The population includes both Sunni and Shiite Muslims. Small numbers of Christians, Hindus, and Jews also exist. Most of the population lives in the western part of the country.

Economy and the Land. Much of northwestern Yemen has a terrain suited for agriculture, the backbone of the country's economy. However, ineffective agricultural techniques combined with regional instability often hinder production. Industrial activity is growing slowly, with production based on domestic resources, but exploitation of oil, iron ore, and salt deposits is financially prohibitive at this time. Subsistence farming and nomadic herding characterize the drier, eastern part of the country. Yemen varies from arid lowlands to fertile, well-cultivated highlands. The climate is temperate in the highlands and hot and dry in the lowlands.

History and Politics. Between 1200 B.C. and A.D. 525, trade empires occupied the area of present-day Yemen, and it was part of the Kingdom of Sheba in the 900s B.C. Christian and Hebrew societies thrived before the 7th century, when Islam was introduced. The region's flourishing economy made it a focal point in the development of Islam. The country was divided in the early 16th century, when the Ottoman Empire conquered northwestern Yemen. The Turks stayed in power until 1918, when the Turkish military withdrew and gave control to the Zaidis, who established a

YUGOSLAVIA

Official name Socialist Federal Republic of Yugoslavia

PEOPLE
Population 10,675,000. **Density** 271/mi^2 (104/km^2). **Urban** 57%. **Capital** Belgrade, 1,136,786. **Ethnic groups** Serb 63%, Albanian 14%, Montenegrin 6%, Hungarian 4%. **Languages** Serbo-Croatian, Albanian. **Religions** Orthodox 65%, Muslim 19%, Roman Catholic 4%. **Life expectancy** 75 female, 70 male. **Literacy** 89%.

POLITICS
Government Republic. **Parties** Democratic Party of Socialists of Montenego, Serbian Radical, Serbian Socialist, Zajedno, others. **Suffrage** Universal, 18 and over; 16 if employed. **Memberships** None. **Subdivisions** 2 republics (2 autonomous provinces).

ECONOMY
GDP $20,600,000,000. **Per capita** $1,914. **Monetary unit** Dinar. **Trade partners** Exports: Former Yugoslav republics, former Soviet republics. **Exports** Machines, transportation equipment, manufactures, chemicals, food, raw inputs. **Imports** Machinery, fuels, lubricants, manufactures, chemicals, food, raw materials.

LAND
Description Eastern Europe. **Area** 39,449 mi² (102,173 km²). **Highest point** Đaravica, 8,714 ft (2,656 m). **Lowest point** Sea level.

People. The population of Yugoslavia is mainly Serb, although there are important Montenegrin, Albanian, and Hungarian minorities. Relations between the Orthodox Serbs and the Muslim Albanians are particularly tense in Kosovo province, where the Albanians form the majority.

Economy and the Land. Before the breakup of Yugoslavia in 1991, most industry was located in the republics of Croatia and Slovenia. As a result, the new Yugoslavia is struggling to improve its industrial base and move away from an agricultural economy. Economic conditions, which improved rapidly after World War II, are now poor as a result of political instability and failed economic restructuring. The country has many mineral resources, including coal. Much of the land is hilly or mountainous, although there are broad, fertile river valleys.

History and Politics. The area now known as Yugoslavia was originally inhabited by the Thracians and the Illyrians, who were eventually conquered by the Roman Empire. The Romans were, in turn, overtaken by Slavs who migrated to the area from Poland and Russia in the 7th century. Orthodox Christianity came to the area in the 10th century. In the 13th century, Serbia was established as an independent kingdom, and gained control over Montenegro. The Ottoman Turks conquered the region in the mid-1300s, and Turkey held the area for almost 500 years. The nation gained its independence in 1878, but was politically and economically dominated by Austria. Calls for Slavic unity began in the early 1800s. In 1914, a Slavic patriot assassinated Archduke Ferdinand of Austria-Hungary and triggered World War I. The Kingdom of Serbs, Croats, and Slovenes was formed in 1918. Fighting among the various groups encouraged King Alexander I to declare himself dictator in 1929 and change the country's name to Yugoslavia, which was retained after Alexander's assassination in 1934. Germany and the other Axis powers invaded Yugoslavia during World War II. After the war, Josip Broz Tito assumed leadership, and Yugoslavia became a Communist republic. Tito's policy of nonalignment caused the Soviet Union to break off diplomatic relations from 1948 to 1955. After Tito's death in 1980, the country was governed by a presidency rotating amongst the republics. In June 1991, the federation began to break apart as Croatia and Slovenia declared their independence, followed by Macedonia and then Bosnia and Herzegovina, leaving Serbia and Montenegro as the remaining Yugoslav republics. Continuing aggression against its neighboring former republics led to international economic sanctions and an economy in a shambles. By the end of 1995, a peace agreement was signed and war-weary civilians began to put their lives back together. The economic sanctions were lifted in 1996. Yugoslavia now comprises only the republics of Serbia and Montenegro. There is still political tension in Kosovo. ∎

ZAIRE
See CONGO, DEMOCRATIC REPUBLIC OF THE.

ZAMBIA

Official name Republic of the Zambia

PEOPLE
Population 9,448,000. **Density** 33/mi² (13/km²). **Urban** 43%. **Capital** Lusaka, 982,362. **Ethnic groups** African 99%, European 1%. **Languages** English, Tonga, Lozi, other indigenous. **Religions** Christian 50-75%, Muslim and Hindu 24-49%. **Life expectancy** 47 female, 45 male. **Literacy** 78%.

POLITICS
Government Republic. **Parties** Movement for Multiparty Democracy, others. **Suffrage** Universal, 18 and over. **Memberships** CW, OAU, UN. **Subdivisions** 9 provinces.

ECONOMY
GDP $8,900,000,000. **Per capita** $930. **Monetary unit** Kwacha. **Trade partners** Exports: Japan, Germany, U.K. Imports: South African countries, U.K., U.S. **Exports** Copper, zinc, cobalt, lead, tobacco. **Imports** Machinery, transportation equipment, food, fuel, manufactures.

LAND
Description Southern Africa, landlocked. **Area** 290,586 mi² (752,614 km²). **Highest point** Namitowa, 7,100 ft (2,164 m). **Lowest point** Along Zambezi River, 1,079 ft (329 m).

People. Virtually all Zambians are black Africans belonging to one of more than seventy Bantu-speaking ethnic groups. Besides the indigenous Bantu languages, many speak English, a reflection of decades of British influence. Although most Zambians are Christian, small minorities are Hindu, Muslim, or hold indigenous beliefs. Many Zambians are subsistence farmers in small villages; however, the mining industry has caused many people to move to urban areas, where wages are rising.

Economy and the Land. The economy is based on copper, Zambia's major export. In an attempt to diversify the economy, the government has emphasized the development of agriculture to help achieve an acceptable balance of trade. Zambia is a subtropical nation marked by high plateaus and great rivers.

History and Politics. European explorers in the 19th century discovered an established society of Bantu-speaking inhabitants. In 1888 Cecil Rhodes and the British South Africa Company obtained a mineral-rights concession from local chiefs, and Northern and Southern Rhodesia, now Zambia and Zimbabwe, came under British influence. Northern Rhodesia became a British protectorate in 1924. In 1953 Northern Rhodesia was combined with Southern Rhodesia and Nyasaland, now Malawi, to form a federation, despite African-nationalist opposition to the white-controlled minority government in Southern Rhodesia. The federation was dissolved in 1963, and Northern Rhodesia became the independent Republic of Zambia in 1964. In late 1991 the first multiparty election in decades brought a landslide victory for democratic forces, as well as a sound rejection of socialism. Zambia is now undergoing a painful conversion to capitalism. ■

ZIMBABWE

Official name Republic of Zimbabwe

PEOPLE
Population 11,510,000. **Density** 76/mi² (29/km²). **Urban** 33%. **Capital** Harare, 1,189,103. **Ethnic groups** Shona 75%, Ndebele 24%. **Languages** English, Shona, Ndebele. **Religions** Mixed Christian and Animist 50%, Christian 25%, Animist 24%. **Life expectancy** 52 female, 50 male. **Literacy** 85%.

POLITICS
Government Republic. **Parties** African National Union-Patriotic Front, others. **Suffrage** Universal, 18 and over. **Memberships** CW, OAU, UN. **Subdivisions** 8 provinces.

ECONOMY
GDP $18,100,000,000. **Per capita** $1,581. **Monetary unit** Dollar. **Trade partners** Exports: South Africa, U.K., Germany. Imports: South Africa, U.K., U.S. **Exports** Tobacco, gold, ferrochrome, manufactures, textiles. **Imports** Machinery, transportation equipment, manufactures, chemicals, fuel.

LAND
Description Southern Africa, landlocked. **Area** 150,873 mi² (390,759 km²). **Highest point** Inyangani, 8,504 ft (2,592 m). **Lowest point** Confluence of Sabi and Lundi Rivers, 531 ft (162 m).

People. The great majority of Zimbabweans are black Africans of Shona descent, with a small but economically significant minority of white Europeans. Most Zimbabweans are subsistence farmers. The influence of British colonization is seen in the official language, English, and in the influence of Christianity.

Economy and the Land. Zimbabwe's natural mineral resources have played a key role in the country's sustained economic growth. The subtropical climate supports the exportation of many agricultural products and makes large-scale cattle ranching feasible. Though primarily a landlocked country of high plateaus, transportation of goods is facilitated by an excellent system of paved roads and railways.

History and Politics. Zimbabwe was populated by Bantu groups until European exploration in the 19th century. British influence began in 1888, and eventually, the region was divided under British rule as Southern Rhodesia and Northern Rhodesia. In 1953, Southern Rhodesia, Northern Rhodesia, and Nyasaland, now Malawi, formed a federation that ended in discord after ten years; Zambia and Malawi gained their independence, and Southern Rhodesia, which remained under British control, became Rhodesia. In response to British pressure to accept black-majority rule, Rhodesian whites declared independence from the United Kingdom in 1965, which led to economic sanctions imposed by the United Nations. These sanctions and years of antigovernment violence finally forced agreement to the principle of black-majority rule. In 1980, Rhodesia became independent and changed its name to Zimbabwe. The country continues to struggle with major issues concerning property rights. Countering the trend in Africa toward multiparty democracy, President Robert Mugabe and his ZANU party maintain strict control over Zimbabwe politics. ■